The Wall Falls

*An Oral History of the
Reunification of the Two Germanies*

Cornelia Heins

The Wall Falls

An Oral History of the
Reunification of the Two Germanies

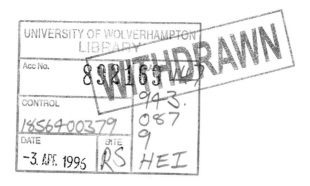
Grey Seal London

First published 1994 by *Grey Seal*
28 Burgoyne Road, London N4 1AD, England

British Library cataloguing in publication data

Heins, Cornelia
    Wall Falls: Oral History of the
    Reunification of the Two Germanies
    I. Title
    943.087

    ISBN 1-85640-037-9

The author. Born in the former East Germany, Cornelia Heins is a journalist who moved, with her family, to a village near Frankfurt before the Wall was built in 1960. She worked for Europe's largest television network, the German ZDF, as a script writer for its news and entertainment departments, before moving to Dallas where she is correspondent for the Swiss financial newspaper *Cash* and a contributing writer for several German and Swiss magazines and newspapers, including to *Neue Zürcher Zeitung, Frankfurter Allgemeine Zeitung* and *Der Spiegel*. Ms Heins conducted the interviews for this book during 1990–3.

Contents

Contents

Prologue

Thuringia

The history of Thuringia is closely tied to the history of my family. Related to the Ludowinger, the builders of the Wartburg Castle,[1] the Wettiner dominated Thuringia from the middle of the 13th century onward. The history of Thuringia was affected not just by conflicts between brothers and wars of succession waged by my ancestors, or by marriages skilfully designed to secure power, but more so by the sustaining cultural values that the Wettiner left to posterity. Under the reign of the Wettiner Balthasar, the first university in Erfurt opened in 1392. In 1409, Balthasar's nephew, Margrave Frederick of Meissen, founded the university in Leipzig and received the Electorate in 1423. Until the 15th century, the wealth of the Wettiner was evenly distributed among all male descendants of the dynasty. The even distribution of possessions produced a number of family branches whose wealth was given back to the main dynasty after their deaths. The last great division of the dynasty was between Ernst and Albert, the two sons of Frederick the Gentle. The descendants of Ernst were called the Ernestine line and the descendants of Albert became the Albertine line of the dynasty of Saxony. A large part of Thuringia was given to Ernst, who as the first-born also

---

[1] The Wartburg is the former castle of the Count of Thuringia. It is located southwest of the city of Eisenach on a rock about 1,300 feet high. The oldest part of the castle was built in 1180. The rest of the Wartburg underwent several periods of restoration. Between 1221 and 1227, Elisabeth th Holy lived at the Wartburg and in 1521, Martin Luther started his translation of the New Testament into German here, a translation which became the foundation of the newer German language. In 1817, German students by invitation of the Jenaer Student Organization (Burschenschaften) celebrated the Wartburgfest in memory of the Reformation.

received the dukedom of Saxony. Two of his sons, Frederick the Wise and Johann the Steady, governed their countries together after their father's death. Frederick the Wise was named imperial administrator, and Emperor Maximilian I made him elector and general. Because Leipzig had been given to the Albertine line owing to the division of the country, Frederick the Wise founded the university of Wittenberg in 1502. Both reigning brothers supported Martin Luther and developments that sprang from the Reformation.

In 1531 the protestant sovereigns in Schmalkalden joined to form a defensive alliance against Catholic aggression led by Emperor Charles V. Johann Friedrich the Generous and Phillip von Hessen were among those selected as leaders of the Protestant alliance. Shortly after Luther's death in 1546, the religious war broke out. Duke Moritz of Saxony, of the Albertine line, not only decided to fight on the side of the Catholic emperor, but also betrayed his cousin Johann by ambushing his cousin's troops. This maneuver brought the Electorate to the Albertine line and, of course, to the Catholic Church. Johann Friedrich the Steady stood firmly by his beliefs and spent five years in prison. His close friend, the famous painter Lucas Cranach, voluntarily spent time with him under arrest. Later, Johann Friedrich chose Weimar as his residence.

For almost two centuries the Ernestine line divided its possessions among its male offspring. In the 17th century it was decided that only the oldest would inherit the possessions and regency rights. The progenitor of the Weimar line was Wilhelm IV who built the Wilhelmsburg castle and, as Swedish general lieutenant, was the general of Gustav Adolf in Thuringia (his brother Duke Bernhard was general of the Swedish army and representative of Sweden's King Gustav Adolf). Under Wilhelm's son Carl-August, Weimar developed into a centre of classicism. Influenced by Christoph Martin Wieland, Carl-August developed a deep appreciation of literature, art, theatre and science. His close friendship with Goethe has been amply described in literature.The cultural blossoming of Weimar attracted such intellectuals as Wieland, Herder, Schiller and Falk. Owing to Carl-August's skilful politics, the dukedom of Saxony-Weimar and Eisenach received the first constitution of Germany in 1816.

The grandson of Carl-August, Grand Duke Carl-Alexander, who grew up and was tutored with the grandsons of Goethe and Herder, prepared himself for his reign by taking up the study of law at the University of Jena. Modest in character, he was more interested in cultural events than in the military. The main goal of his reign became the revival and preservation of Weimar's intellectual tradition and *bel esprit*. Among his most remarkable initiatives was the rebuilding of the Wartburg castle along the lines suggested by Goethe.

Luther's Reformation and the intellectuality of the classical Weimar, which was initiated and supported by Carl-August and his grandson Carl-Alexander, are the pillars of the history of Thuringia. What would the world be like without Luther's Reformation? What would the German classics be without Weimar? The answer is: different! The answer to the question symbolizes strongly how the concerted actions of a region, its people and a family made history.

The family

The dramatic change in value systems and the neglect of past norms of the first part of the 20th century uprooted our family totally. The traumatic experiences of Nazi Germany and the experience of expulsion from Silesia (Heinrichaus) and Thuringia, dominated my father's life until his death. He died on 14 October 1988, a year before the silent revolution in the former GDR. Maybe it was better that way, since he was spared another disappointment and humiliation, this time of the German government.

I have always been curious about the 'other' Germany. (Because my father had been a professional in the German army, he was not allowed to visit the GDR.) In 1972 I dared to make a first visit to what was then the GDR. As a British subject by birth, I felt secure travelling there. I visited Eisenach, the Wartburg castle and Weimar as well as real estate once owned by my family. In my encounters with people, their charm and their willingness to share their backgrounds were overwhelming. A thoughtful review of both these encounters and our family history made it very clear to me that this region was home (*Heimat*) to us. I decided to have my daughter baptized in the Herderkirche in Weimar in 1987. Although only a very few people had been notified of the occasion, the church was filled to the last seat. The pastor opened his sermon: 'We are very happy to baptize a member of the dynasty of Saxony-Weimar and Eisenach for the first time since 1917.'

For my wife, myself and our friends, the christening of my daughter was a moving experience. Since that date, Thuringia has become closer and closer to me. The first conversations I had after the Wall had fallen in 1989 were held in an atmosphere of mutual understanding, even though Weimar's mayor, Dr Volkmar Germer, had been a member of the Socialist Unity Party (SED), but later was one of the first to leave the party. During the revolution in 1918, his grandmother had brought our fleeing family to safety through a back door of our castle. Germer and I had many talks about the rebuilding of Weimar. The city's current mayor, Dr Klaus Büttner, is an idealistic and competent 'west import' who shares with me the goal of restoring Weimar to its former glory and cultural importance. With his help I have found much to do not only in Weimar, but also in Eisenach.

Owing to the efforts of Hans Matschke, the director of the Wartburgstiftung (Wartburg Endowment), the endowment had a head start even before the official reunification of Germany and is today one of the few success stories in the former East Germany. Meanwhile, I have a vote and share responsibilities on the board of directors of the Wartburgstiftung and am the chairman of the Wartburg Wirtschaftsbetriebe GmbH (Wartburg Economy Council).

Chances for tomorrow?

German reunification is a unique gift of history. Although the reunification has brought with it some avoidable injustices, there is almost nobody who wishes that history took some other course. Thuringia is blossoming into a thriving cultural centre. Industries and trades are growing more quickly than in other regions of the former GDR.

One of the major problems in the former GDR is that many people have tied the idea of prosperity and democracy very closely together, so that the lack of prosperity is taken as signifying a lack of democracy. The result has been a loss of trust in the current leadership and a tendency to vote for radical parties. Unfortunately, the big and dramatic burden that has been placed on the citizens of West Germany, who transferred 5 per cent of their GNP to the former GDR, has not yet been recognized.

The problem of reunification has not yet been processed intellectually. We are not only transferring money, but we also have certain expectations. We are in search of an order in which East and West Germans can recognize each other. This order can only be successful if the current central government is reduced step by step in favour of separate, small communities, and these smaller units acquire a natural understanding of the responsibilities of citizenship. Only if self-determination grows and external influences wane can we avoid not just falling into pathological dependency, but also disorder and the loss of all traditional values.

The rapid and radical nature of the changes taking place in Germany is leaving behind most of those whose education has been deficient. This part of the population, therefore, has a hard time understanding what changes are needed to secure a worthwhile future. The ignorance results in a hollow fear that can turn into aggressiveness at any time. The looming chaos can only be avoided if a group of citizens is able to find a consensus to engage selflessly in future-oriented projects in the former GDR in order to create a basis for the future. A supportive, future-oriented and common basis for all Germans has not yet been found.

Michael, Prince von Sachsen-Weimar und Eisenach
Winter 1993

Acknowledgements

This book would not have been possible without the willing participation and frankness of the fifty-two individuals who shared their experiences and views on the issues surrounding the German reunification. I owe particular thanks to my husband Ralph and my friends on both sides of the Atlantic for their continual support and encouragement during the three years it took to complete this project. Thanks also to Sabine Sherman, who spent endless hours patiently transcribing the tapes of the interviews and typing the manuscript—sometimes far into the night. Doug Benson used his keen historical understanding and emphatic red pencil to make the book far better than it would otherwise have been. The Inform team at the Minneapolis Library and the research team of the Dallas Public Library were extremely helpful and always pleasant to work with. And, last but not least, thanks to Cam Blodgett, who suggested the ideas that grew into this book during some creative and joyful hours of sailing on Minnesota's Lake Minnetonka.

Dallas, Thanksgiving, 1993

Timetable

30 April 1945. Berlin. A group of Soviet trained men arrive in the city preparing the establishment of an independent East Germany. They later are known as 'Gruppe Ulbricht'.

7 May 1945. Reims. At the headquarters of the western Allies the capitulation documents are signed by General Jodl.

5 June 1945. Berlin. The Allies meet at Potsdam and install the four-power Allied Control Council which will govern Germany according to a fifteen article declaration.

22 April 1946. East Berlin. The Socialist Party is merged under pressure with the Communist Party into the German Unity Party (SED).

18 June 1948. Berlin. The western Allies announce the currency reform.

24 June 1948. Berlin. Soviet troops cut off all access to West Berlin.

1 July 1948. London. The Six Power Conference results in the decision that a constitution should be developed for all western zones of Germany.

12 May 1949. Berlin. Western Allies and the citizens of Berlin celebrate the end of the blockade.

23 May 1949. Bonn. Founding of the Federal Republic of Germany (FRG) of which Konrad Adenauer becomes the first chancellor.

7 October 1949. East Berlin. Following the installation of the first cabinet of the Federal Republic, the People's Congress in East Berlin acknowledges the formation of a German Democratic Republic (GDR) which is headed by Walter Ulbricht.

5 March 1953. Moscow. Josef Stalin dies in Moscow.

17 June 1953. East Berlin. Construction workers initiate an uprising against the communist East German regime. Soviet tanks stop the revolt.

16 October 1954. Paris. West Germany becomes a member of NATO.

5 May 1955. Bonn. The western Allies declare the end of West Germany's occupation status.

7 October 1955. Friedland. The last German Prisoners of War return from Soviet captivity.

14 February 1956. Moscow. Nikita Khrushchev declares the end of the Stalin era.

24 October 1956. Budapest. Encouraged by the message from Moscow, Hungarian citizens start an unsuccessful uprising against Soviet presence in their country.

27 November 1958. Berlin. Khrushchev sends a note to the three western Allies demanding that West Berlin should be turned into a 'free and non-military city'. The note becomes known as the Berlin Ultimatum.

3 June 1961. Vienna. Khrushchev meets the newly elected American President John F. Kennedy.

13 August 1961. Berlin. Ulbricht gives order to built the Berlin Wall.

23 June 1963. Berlin. Kennedy visits West Berlin.

26 November 1966. Bonn. The West German Christian Democrats and the Socialists form a Grand coalition which leads to changes in the West German–East German politics.

20 August 1968. Prague. East German troops stop citizen revolts in Prague.

30 January 1970. Moscow. West German's State Secretary Egon Bahr begins talks with Moscow which eventually lead to the Moscow Treaty between the UdSSR and West Germany.

3 May 1970. East Berlin. Erich Honecker replaces Walter Ulbricht as SED leader.

12 May 1972. Bonn. After weeks of controversy, the West German Parliament accepts the German–German treaty which was initiated by Bahr and Chancellor Willy Brandt.

25 April 1974. Bonn. Günther Guillaume, a GDR spy and close advisor to chancellor Brandt is arrested for espionage.

7 September 1987. Bonn. Erich Honecker visits West Germany and despite public protest is received with all honors.

11 October 1987. Reykjavik. American President Ronald Reagan and Soviet President Mikhail Gorbachev meet in Iceland for disarmament talks.

21 August 1987. St Magarethen. Dr. Otto von Habsburg initiates a 'walk along the green border' at the Hungarian-Austrian border which led to a mass exodus of GDR refugees.

4 September 1989. Leipzig. The Nikolai-Church becomes centre for the oppositional movement in the GDR. Every Monday night thousands of protesting citizens gather at the church.

10 September 1989. East Berlin. Official oppositional parties form in the GDR, among them 'Neues Forum' and 'Demokratie Jetzt'.

6 October 1989. East Berlin. The GDR celebrates its 40th anniversary. Gorbachev is guest of honor in East Berlin.

19 October 1989. Leipzig. Kurt Masur and his 'group of six' intervene to prevent the use of force on demonstrators.

18 October 1989. East Berlin. Erich Honecker resigns. His successor becomes Egon Krenz.

27 October 1989. East Berlin. The GDR announces an amnesty for all refugees who have left the country during the last months.

4 November 1989. East Berlin. Over half a million people protest, demanding freedom of speech.

7 November 1989. East Berlin. The GDR government under Willi Stoph resigns.

8 November 1989. East Berlin. The politburo of the SED resigns. Dr Hans Modrow is regarded as one of the leaders of the reform movement within the government.

9 November 1989. Berlin. The Wall falls.

28 November 1989. Bonn. Chancellor Kohl announces a ten-point plan for a common German–German future.

6 December 1989. East Berlin. After 44 days in power, Egon Krenz resigns under public pressure.

22 December 1989. Berlin. After 28 years, the Brandenburg Gate opens. Chancellor Kohl and Hans Modrow open up the gate for pedestrian traffic.

18 March 1990. Bonn. During the first free elections in East Germany, the Christian Democrats receive a majority.

5 April 1990. East Berlin. Lothar de Maizière, head of the East German CDU, establishes government.

18 May 1990. Bonn–East Berlin. The two governments agree on a currency union.

30 August 1990. Berlin. West German Minister of Interior Wolfgang Schäuble and State Secretary Kraus sign the Unity Treaty.

2–3 October 1990. Berlin. The two Germanies celebrate their reunification.

The Cast

The following people were interviewed by the author between 1990 and 1993. The city and date at the end of each entry are the time and location of the interview.

Michael Bacher (27), a law student in Berlin, joined the Communist youth organization, FDJ, as a youngster and headed one of its divisions in East Berlin. Disillusioned, he left the organization after the Wall fell in November 1989. Berlin, May 1990.

Egon Bahr (71), 'Father of the Ostpolitik', served under Chancellor Willy Brandt, 1969–72, as State Secretary at the Bundeskanzleramt and Plenipotentiary of the Federal Government in Berlin, and was a member of the Bundestag. In 1972-4 he served as Federal Minister without Portfolio attached to the Federal Chancellor's Office. Since 1974 he has served as Director of the Institut für Friedensforschung und Sicherheitspolitik (Institute of Peace Research and Security). He is a member of the German Socialist Party (SPD). Hamburg, June 1993.

Robert W. Becker (54) has headed the American Consulate General in Leipzig since 1990, when it was reopened after 60 years. The consulate's principle goal is to re-establish ties to the eastern part of Germany. Before his assignment in Leipzig, Becker, who had studied German history, served as deputy consul in Munich, 1985–9. He is among the few foreigners who lived in an eastern city during the years after the *Wende* without shuttling back and forth between East and West. Leipzig, October 1993.

The Cast

Jens Berndt (30), a member of the Olympic swimming team, has held the world freestyle record. He fled the GDR while in the United States for a swimming contest by hiding in an airport men's room. He was adopted by the American host family with whom he stayed during his college years in the USA. Hamburg, March 1992.

Csilla, Baroness von Boeselager (50) was born Csilla Fenyes de Denjelegh in Budapest. During the war years her family took her to South America, followed by university in Connecticut, before she returned to West Germany as the wife of a nobleman. She is the founder of a charity organization and a major conduit for relief supplies for eastern Europe. She helped German refugees who came over the Hungarian border in 1987. Chancellor Kohl awarded her the *Bundesverdienstkreuz* (German Federal Medal of Honour) for her work, and in 1990 she was named woman of the year. Höllinghofen, September 1991.

Klaus Böling (61), press secretary and confidant of Chancellor Helmut Schmidt, was later editor-in-chief of Germany's largest daily newspaper *Die Bild Zeitung*. He headed the Washington office of one of Germany's largest television stations, ARD (Erstes Deutsches Fernsehen), 1969–73. Today he lives in Berlin and is a frequent contributor to the Sunday newspaper *Die Welt*. Berlin, August 1992.

Thassilo Borchart (53), a banned journalist who lost the right to express his opinions during the Honecker era, became a bricklayer. Now he operates a construction company in Berlin. The oldest of three sons, he stayed with his mother in the GDR when his brothers fled to West Germany. Berlin, November 1992.

Wolf-Rüdiger Borchart (51), a renowned West Berlin architect, left East Berlin and his two brothers and mother in 1961. His younger brother Ingo followed five years later, but his older brother Thassilo remained in the GDR. His firm won the Schinkelpreis, an important international prize for architecture, in 1983. Berlin, November 1992.

Eberhard Diepgen (51), mayor of united Berlin since December 1991, is a member of the conservative Christian Democratic Party (CDU). He has been leading the city government since December 1990, when the CDU won the city council elections by overthrowing the socialist majority. He proposed a 'grand coalition' of the CDU and the SPD (Socialist Party) to resolve the city's problems. Berlin, November 1992.

Janos Fekete (74), a Hungarian banker once described as the favourite eastern banker of western bankers, served as deputy president of the National Bank of Hungary and raised hundreds of millions of dollars in loans that helped keep afloat Hungary's distinctive and partially decentralized brand of communism. One of the designers of the reform movement in Hungary, Fekete was responsible for replacing rigid central planning with market economy techniques. He is president of Leumi Bank and the Bank of Israel in Budapest. Budapest, May 1991.

Dr Johannes Fuchs (76) grew up in Jena, where he studied medicine at the university. Later he headed the ophthalmology department of the university. After being arrested in the East he decided to leave with his family a few months before the wall was erected. Frankfurt, September 1990.

Margarethe Fuchs (63) grew up in the Soviet Occupation Zone and fled East Germany only six months before the wall was built. She witnessed the developments in the Soviet Occupation Zone as a teenager and as a young adult. After moving to West Germany in 1961, she took up studies specializing in German history. Frankfurt, September 1990.

Dr Wolfgang Gäbelein (69) was 18 when he returned from the eastern front in Pomerania. He grew up in the city of Gera, in Thuringia, where he was imprisoned by the Soviet Red Army. The Soviet Occupation Power had intended to blackmail Gäbelein into working for their intelligence office as an informer on anti-communist movements at the university and among family friends. He left the Soviet

Occupation Zone in 1948 and became a prominent finance attorney in West Germany. He served on the board of Mannesmann AG in Düsseldorf and as chairman of the board of the Federal Association of German Industry (Bundesverband der Deutschen Industrie). Düsseldorf, May 1991.

David Gill (30) is one of the co-ordinators and heads of the citizens committees responsible for dissolving the Ministry of State Security (Ministerium für Staatssicherheit, or 'Stasi') of the former GDR. Together with Joachim Gauck, Gill was appointed by the West German government to oversee the cataloguing and computerization of the Stasi archives. Gill is one of only a few outsiders who did not work for the Stasi who is familiar with its methods and structure. Berlin, September 1992.

Dr Otto von Habsburg (80), son of the last Emperor of Austria and King of Hungary, married to Regina, Princess of Saxony-Meiningen. His forebears ruled Spain, Austria and Hungary. After his father abdicated, he was not allowed to return to Austria, and he became a West German citizen. Today he heads the Pan-European Parliament in Brussels. His weekly columns appear in 21 daily newspapers in five languages, and he has written 23 books on history, politics and world affairs. The 'walk along the Austrian-Hungarian border' he initiated in the summer of 1989 triggered an exodus of East Germans to Hungary, and precipitated the crisis which culminated in the fall of the Honecker regime. Pöckingen, March 1991.

Hannelore (43), a divorced pharmacologist living in East Berlin, witnessed the uprising in Prague in 1968. The love of her life was a West German who was unable to help her to leave the GDR in the late 1960s. Berlin, January 1990.

Wolf von Holleben (43), head of programming at the Second German Television in Mainz, Europe's largest broadcasting network, has been involved in restructuring East German television. He left East Germany with his parents in the early 1950s. His family still holds property in the former GDR. Mainz, February 1991.

Johannes (20), a medical assistant in a major Leipzig hospital, participated in the Monday demonstrations very early on. He visited the West for the first time after Wall came down. Berlin, August 1992.

Donald Koblitz (41), legal adviser for the US delegation to the Two-plus-four negotiations on the reunification of Germany between March and September 1990, acted as legal adviser to the US mission in West Berlin, 1985–9. Today, he practices law in Berlin, often representing American clients. Berlin, September 1993.

Dr Walter Köcher (76), a member of a large industrialist family who manufacture knitwear, is a chemist who specializes in the production and invention of new fabrics and synthetics. He left the Soviet Occupation Zone after his family was dispossessed. Berlin, September 1993.

Lothar Loewe (66) was the first West German correspondent in 1974 to be allowed to work in East Germany for the first German television network, the Allgemeiner Rundfunk Deutschlands (ARD). Within 24 months he was expelled because of his open and aggressive journalistic style. In earlier years, he had been the network's foreign correspondent in Moscow and Washington. After 1983, he headed the SFB (Sender Freies Berlin—Broadcast Free Berlin) in West Berlin. Retired, he is working on several book projects. Berlin, August 1992.

Mario (30) left the GDR via the Hungarian border in the autumn of 1989 and worked in an automobile factory in Chemnitz, formerly called Karl-Marx-Stadt. He had not been allowed to pursue a degree in engineering because he had actively participated in his community's church, and the only job he found in his town was working for VEB IFA Kombinat Pkw, a leading state-owned East German automobile company. Mario is now retraining to work in the main Volkswagen factory in Wolfsburg. Berlin, January 1990.

Professor Kurt Masur (66), recently appointed music director of the New York Philharmonic Orchestra, worked his way up through

East Berlin's Komische Oper to the famed Leipziger Gewandhaus. Although he openly supported the reform movement in the GDR, he had been a faithful supporter of the Honecker regime. He initiated an appeal to the regime not to use force on demonstrators in autumn 1989. Chicago, February 1991.

Dr Kristina Matschat (43), born in East Germany with a Ph.D. in chemistry, had wanted to study medicine, but was assigned chemistry. She quit her job as a chemist with a government agency when she was asked to do chemical weapons research. She has been a housewife since then and was politically active throughout the autumn of 1989. She now lives in Adlershof, a suburb of East Berlin. Berlin, January 1990.

Dr Ralf Matschat (49) is a physicist at the Akademie der Wissenschaften, one of the foremost academies for research and development in the former GDR. He was not a party member, although in his position he was expected to be 'loyal'. He held his position by being 'carefully' oppositional. He also was among the hundreds of scientists who were 'secret-holders', and was therefore not allowed to have contact with the West. He visited West Germany for the first time in 1989. Berlin, January 1990.

Francis Meehan (68) was US ambassador to East Germany, 1985–8. He served as a deputy chief in the mission in Vienna, 1975–7, followed by four years in Bonn. US ambassador to Czechoslovakia and Poland, 1981–4, he now lives in Great Britain. Glasgow, March 1992.

Dr Werner Meyer-Larson (62) covers international economic affairs for *Der Spiegel* in Hamburg, having headed the *Der Spiegel* New York office in the 1980s. He is the author of seven books on political and economic matters. Hamburg, September 1993.

Wolfgang Mischnick (65), national chairman of the Liberal Party (FDP) in Germany, is one of the country's most respected politicians. He is a close associate of Hans-Dietrich Genscher, West

Germany's ex-foreign minister, who helped plan reunification. He was heavily involved in building political relationships with the Honecker regime in the 1970s and 1980s. He was born in Dresden but left the Soviet Occupation Zone for political reasons in 1946, and now lives in Kronberg near Frankfurt. Berlin, March 1991.

Walter Momper (48), mayor of West Berlin when the Wall fell, ran the West Berlin government for 20 months until his coalition with the radical environmentalists, Alternative Liste, crumbled as a result of a police raid on squatters whom the group supported. Berlin, August 1991.

Gabriele Müller (66), former head coach of the GDR figure-skating and ice-dancing Olympic team, trained Katharina Witt and her own daughter, Jutta Seifert. She had to be a loyal party member. Leipzig, March 1991.

Marisa Müller (48), widowed mother of four grown sons, works part-time in a chemical distribution plant. Although she had been a teacher of chemistry and physics, she was not allowed to teach in the GDR school system because she was not a party member. Berlin, March 1991.

Pastor Johannes Neudeck (33) had been visiting the former GDR since the mid 1980s and had developed contacts with East German pastors and congregations. He happened to visit the GDR during the October and November demonstrations in 1989. Today he organizes trips to the United States for people from East and West Germany and is the head of the CVJM (YMCA) in Kassel, Germany. Minneapolis, January 1990.

Ferdinand Nohr (64), a well-known GDR writer who used to work for one of the government-owned radio stations, left the Communist Party in the early 1980s. He and his wife were among the few privileged East Germans who were allowed to travel to western Europe. He lives in East Berlin. Berlin, January 1990.

Sergeant Cloyde Pinson (69) participated in the Allied Airlift in 1949 as an American soldier. Today he lives in Dallas, Texas. Dallas, May 1993.

Ulrike Poppe (40), one of a pacifist group who protested against women serving in the military, was arrested along with her husband and imprisoned several times in the latter half of the 1980s. The Poppes founded the dissident party Neues Forum and helped lead the peaceful revolt that toppled communism in the GDR in the fall of 1989. Berlin, February 1993.

Henning Prenzlin (37), owner of a software development firm in Cologne, started a construction and development business in Dresden after the wall came down. Three or four times a month he travels to Dresden to supervise the firm's activities. Dresden, November 1990.

Ludwig A. Rehlinger (67), as State Secretary of the Ministry of Interior, was one of the few direct contacts of Dr Wolfgang Vogel, an attorney and representative of the former GDR in charge of the exchange of political prisoners. Rehlinger, who was born in Berlin and studied law at the Humboldt University, the Free University at Berlin, and in Innsbruck, arranged exchanges of prisoners for commodities and later for German marks between the early 1960s and 1980s. A member of the Christian Democratic Party (CDU), he serves as Senator of Justice in Berlin today. Bonn, September 1993.

Waltraut Rothenbächer (73) was born in Transylvania and moved to the GDR as a young girl. Her husband was a prisoner-of-war and died soon after his release, leaving her to raise their four children. Her son Wulf was held prisoner for over a year, accused of 'a negative attitude towards the German Democratic Republic and the attempt to escape the people's republic'. She now lives in West Germany. Diez, September 1990.

Dr Wulf Rothenbächer (48) was a political prisoner in the GDR for over a year. He and his future wife were captured when attempting to escape East Germany via the Romanian border. During most of

his imprisonment he was isolated in a dark cell. Through his mother's efforts, he was traded to West Germany for $75,000, as were
an estimated 300,000 other political prisoners. Today he is a successful ear, nose and throat specialist in Germany. He is co-founder
of a human rights organization that has documented the GDR's
harsh treatment of political prisoners and has brought the merciless
political persecution of Germans in the GDR to public attention.
Diez, September 1990.

Michael, Prince von Sachsen-Weimar und Eisenach (43) is the
grandson of the last King of Saxony. The family of the duchy of
Saxony Weimar owned and governed the region from 940 to 1918.
In 1948, all their property, including personal belongings, was expropriated by the Soviet Occupation Power. Today, the Prince works
for Deutsche Bank, heading up the branch office in Mannheim.
When the Wall came down, he was able to reclaim part of the lost
properties, among them the 'Wartburg'. He has since been heavily
involved in the reconstruction of the city of Weimar, capital of German romanticism. Mannheim, February 1991 and September 1993.

Dr Wolfgang Schäuble (50) served as Minister with Special Re-
sponsibility and Head of the Chancellery, 1984–9, under Chancellor
Helmut Kohl. During this period of reunification, as Minister of the
Interior he represented West Germany in talks with East Germany.
Now leader of the Conservative Christian Democratic Party, he was
shot and wounded by a political fanatic while campaigning in the
1991 elections. Since then he has been confined to a wheelchair.
Bonn, September 1993.

Wolf Schöde (47), a representative of the Treuhand, was the assistant to the head of the agency, Detlev Karsten Rohwedder, when he
was fatally shot by the Stasi on 2 April 1991. The Treuhand has the
task of privatizing the 8,000 businesses inherited from the now de-
funct East German Communist government. Berlin, March 1991.

Pastor Friedrich Schorlemmer (46), a theologian and spokesman
for the Democratic Awakening, was long known to the East German

regime as the 'enfant terrible'. The well-connected pastor of the All Saints Church was among the few members of the Protestant clergy openly to oppose the regime and the military consequences of the Cold War's armament race. As a member of the dissident peace movement in the GDR in the mid-1980s, he announced to his congregation, 'we will bring about change without violence'. With other church leaders, he organized peaceful demonstrations in Leipzig and Wittenberg, including a 1983 protest demonstration in Wittenberg's main city square for the 500th anniversary of Martin Luther's birth. Halle, March 1992.

Jorge Seidel (33), member of the Stasi and agent for Markus Wolf, was involved in anti-CIA counterespionage for the GDR. Co-founder of the Insider Committee for Re-examination, he admits his own excesses and is willing to meet ex-targets. He believes he is as much a victim of the system as his targets and is still convinced that he was on the right side of the Berlin Wall. Berlin, September 1993.

Ota Sik (73), an ex-communist leader of Czechoslovakia and developer of the Sik economic theory, a partially market-driven form of communism, was Deputy Prime Minister in 1968 and member of the Economy Council, 1968–9. Deprived of his Czech citizenship, he was granted political asylum by Switzerland, in 1983 became a citizen and now teaches at the University of St Gallen. St Gallen, May 1991.

Wolf-Jürgen Staab (60) served as a West German representative at the permanent mission in East Germany, 1980–9. As Secretary of the Department of Inner German Relations, he administered refugee issues. Before that he was a member of the team responsible for the exchange of political prisoners. Bonn, May 1991.

Robert Vogel (73), a major developer and businessman in Hamburg, is the leader of Hamburg's Liberal Party (FDP) which, in coalition with the CDU, designed the reunification agreement. He is personally involved in the rebuilding of the GDR, and was a prisoner of war in Russia during World War II. Hamburg, February 1991.

Christian, Count von Wedel (43), owner of a Frankfurt advertising company, first visited the GDR in November 1989. His family originally came from a small GDR village where his mother still owns a castle. He and a GDR partner opened a store selling stereo equipment in the former GDR. Frankfurt, November 1991.

Caspar W. Weinberger (75) served as Secretary of Defence in the Reagan Administration and was one of the key aids to push the Strategic Defence Initiative. He had earlier served as Budget Director and Secretary of Health under President Nixon. His zeal to cut the budget earned him the nickname 'Cap the Knife'. Today he is a consultant with the New York law firm Roger & Wells. Washington, April 1991.

Mark Whitehead (55) is Chairman and Chief Executive Officer of the international law firm of Popham Haik. He is active in international environmental law and is a frequent participant in national and international seminars on product liability and environmental law both in the United States and Europe. Minneapolis, August 1993.

Uwe Wunderlich (39) is a former director of a Kombinat, a people-owned collective with 3,000 employees. Wunderlich was a member of the SED and is now working in Dresden as a representative for a major law firm based in Stuttgart. Dresden, November 1990.

Harald and Elke Zimmer (51 and 48), who own a wood ternary outside Berlin, were both part of a GDR opposition group. They were among thousands of GDR citizens who stormed the Stasi headquarters. Berlin, January 1990.

Abbreviations

CDU	Christliche Demokratische Union (Christian Democratic Union)
CSU	Christliche Soziale Union (Christian Social Union)
COMECO	Council for Mutual Economic Assistance
DKP	Kommunistische Partei Deutschlands (German Communist Party)
EDC	European Defense Community
FDP	Freie Demokratische Partei (Free Democratic Party)
FDJ	Freie Deutsche Jugend (Free German Youth)
LDP	Liberale Deutsche Partei (Liberal Democratic Party)
NATO	North Atlantic Treaty Organization
NDPD	National Demokratische Partei Deutschlands (National Democratic Party)
SALT	Strategic Arms Limitation Treaty
SED	Sozialistische Einheitspartei Deutschlands (Socialist Unity Party)
SPD	Sozialdemokratische Partei Deutschlands (Social Democratic Party)
VEB	Volkseigene Betriebe (People's Plants)
VOPOS	Volkspolizei (People's Police)

Part One

Ruins 1945–1949

In war there is no substitute for victory.
Douglas MacArthur

Chapter One

Returning Home and the Allied Forces

On Capitulation Day, in early May 1945, the German Reich came to an end. It had existed for seventy-four years, long enough for most Germans to regard their country's unification as irreversible. But the developments that began to unfold that spring proved otherwise.

The idea of a united Germany had been born at the Hambacherfest in 1832,[1] when Germany was still splintered into 39 separate kingdoms and duchies. Almost forty years later, in 1871, the Reich became a reality, ending centuries of German political fragmentation. By then, in 1871, the kingdom of Prussia, led by Prime Minister Otto von Bismarck, had defeated Austria and France, eliminating a historical threat to Prussian hegemony, and had succeeded in bringing the smaller German states into a new unity.

Bismarck wanted a 'German Reich' headed by the emperor. Prussia's King Wilhelm I rejected Bismarck's suggestions initially, fearing that his image as king of Prussia might suffer. But his nephew, King Ludwig II of Bavaria, finally convinced him that Germany needed a federal monarchy, under an emperor from the Prussian ruling house of Hohenzollern. Under Bismarck, who served as chancellor until 1890, the new Germany displayed great vitality, and its rapid industrialization put the country at the forefront of European economic development. What the patriots of Hambacherfest had only dreamed of had become reality—not through the influence and willpower of the German people, but through the political strength and wisdom of Bismarck, whom Friedrich Engels once called 'the Prussian revolutionary'.[2]

Bismarck's national state, the Second Reich, lasted forty-eight years, until the November revolution of 1919. Hitler's Third Reich, which he had proclaimed would last for 1,000 years, turned into twelve years of nightmarish horror. Wartime atrocities—including the murder of

---

[1] The Hambacherfest was celebrated as a democratic movement in the south of Germany during which speakers demanded the formation of a German republic, the country's unity and a confederate, republican Europe.

[2] Karl Marx, *Revolution and Counter-revolution*, London, 1896.

3

millions of people in German concentration camps and the banishment of millions from Pomerania, East Prussia and Silesia—became associated with the word 'Reich', a vocabulary that horrifies Germans to this day.

The twelve years of Hitler's tyrannical dictatorship ruthlessly crushed the country's democratic organizations and drove their leaders into exile or subjected them to imprisonment. Universities, the arts, the media and other institutions and professions which were found to be 'racially impure' were systematically 'cleansed' of unwanted elements. In peril of persecution, thousands of Germany's most talented people fled abroad.

Morally, the country was bankrupt in 1945. Not only had the Nazi regime inflicted a repressive dictatorship on Germany, but it also had unleashed a brutal war of conquest that resulted in the death of 40 million people in Europe. The Nazis mass-murdered 6 million men, women and children whose only offence was their Jewish ancestry. Millions of others, such as gypsies and mentally retarded children, were classified as subhumans unfit to share the earth with a 'German master race' and were executed or worked to death. Not surprisingly, the end of the Second World War found the victors, to whom the capitulation documents transferred sovereign authority, in possession of a devastated and disrupted country.

Whereas the Reich had escaped physical damage in the First World War, which was fought almost exclusively on foreign soil, the second great conflict had brought home all the horror of modern mechanized warfare. An estimated 5.5 million Germans—in addition to those murdered in the concentration camps—had died during the war either as civilians or in the military. One-quarter of the country's housing lay destroyed or damaged beyond use, leaving thousands homeless. A disrupted and understaffed health care system struggled to cope with diseases whose incidence frequently reached epidemic proportions. What was left of the German economy was debilitated, with thousands of factories, warehouses and businesses damaged and non-functioning. The most pressing problem of all, however, was a dire food crisis that reduced the average German's diet to a level dangerously close to malnutrition. Food had become increasingly scarce as fighting surged into the agricultural regions of eastern Germany and eastern Europe, where most of Germany's grain came from.

Even before Germany's capitulation, a European Advisory Commission was planning for temporary occupation of a Germany reduced to its 1937 borders. Using these boundaries, the advisory council divided the country into four occupation zones: The Soviet Union was assigned the eastern part; Britain, the northeast; the United States, the south, with an additional enclave around the northern port city of Bremen to permit access by sea for American troops; and France was given control of the

Rhineland. Berlin was to be occupied jointly by the Allied Forces, with each being accorded a sector of the city. An Allied Control Council in Berlin was to act on behalf of the victors to exercise joint authority over Germany. Before the occupation began, these plans underwent several modifications. At Yalta, Franklin D. Roosevelt and Winston Churchill secured Soviet leader Josef Stalin's approval for creation of a French occupation zone and a French sector in Berlin. Stalin himself acted independently and assigned parts of the British occupation zone to the USSR. The occupying powers agreed that Germany should be subject to 'denazification, demilitarization, democratization and decentralization'.[3] The Potsdam conferees also agreed that the living standard of Germany should be well below that of its European neighbours. War reparations were to be extracted in the form of machines and other industrial goods rather than in monetary payments. Since the greatest concentration of heavy industry lay in the western zones of the occupation, a portion of their reparations were to be turned over to the Soviets. As for German political life, the Allies allowed the revival of democratic parties and trade unions on the local level, staffed by non-Nazis.

Germany's military defeat and unconditional surrender had also resulted in the expulsion of millions of 'Volksdeutsche' (ethnic Germans) from their ancestral homes in East Prussia and the territories east of the Oder–Neisse line that came to demarcate Poland's western frontier. In 1939, the territories that would comprise postwar Germany had a population of 59 million. In 1946, 64 million people inhabited the same area, despite the heavy wartime losses and the absence of millions of German soldiers held as prisoners of war. The additional Germans from the eastern exodus compounded the problems of food and housing, particularly in the larger cities. Daunted by Germany's immediate past, struggling with ruins, hunger, missing family members and a lost war, most Germans hoped to be able to erase the past from their minds and to achieve a new start for themselves and their country.

Wolfgang Gäbelein

I can still hear the words of my brother, who was eight years older than I, when he returned in 1942 from the Russian front near Moscow. He had walked for days and weeks to return to our German hometown of Gera, in Thuringia, and had arrived totally exhausted. 'Little one', he said, 'what is going on right now is crazy. Hitler has

---

[3] Berlin Declaration of the Allies, in Döllinger, *Die Bundesrepublik.*

made the world a madhouse. I know that after I return to the front in a few days, I won't come home again.' Unfortunately, he was right. He died just a few weeks later, in January 1943. Shortly before departing, he had told me to avoid joining the German Infantry, as the average soldier could not expect to survive more than 43 to 44 weeks. I was 16 at that time and had promised myself to take my brother's advice to heart. But I knew I couldn't escape the authorities, and the daily obituaries of older classmates in the newspapers reminded me of what was awaiting me at the front. I was drafted when I was just 17, but fortunately into an artillery brigade.

By the time I was 18 and coming home from the eastern front, I had seen a different world. Being the younger of two boys, I had not been handled with kid gloves, but all the sports contests, all the fights with other boys in school and on the streets were nothing compared with what I had experienced briefly during the war.

I remember two other youngsters like me in the brigade, one of whom had a stamp in his Wehrpass (military passport) stating: 'No war activities at the eastern front'. I asked him one evening, 'Well, how did you do that? I don't want to meet an Ivan and would like to have a restriction like that in my papers.' He politely answered, 'I'm a Communist'. 'Are you crazy—a Communist?' I countered. 'We want to have a pluralistic democracy when all of this Hitler madness is over, not another dictatorship.'

That is how most of the German soldiers I met thought. We just wanted to end the war and the Third Reich. It was also pretty clear, at least to us younger ones, that in case we were asked to fight on the western front, we would try to fall into American hands to avoid the Red Army. Such hopes were shattered, however, when we received orders to move into Pomerania. On 16 January, the Russian troops broke through the Weichselbogen, the German corridor to Poland, over which the war had started in the first place.[4]

With 29 other men, I received orders to take over an old farm estate and await the arrival of the Soviet troops. This was almost an order to get killed. All of Pomerania around us was already in flames. Here we were, 29 men waiting for the Red Army to come from the east. One of the soldiers had removed an antique piano from the estate, and placed it in a glade. While the rest of us were

---

[4] At the outbreak of the war, in September 1939, Hitler had intended to widen this corridor to Poland in order to have free passage to Moscow at all times.

securing our positions and now and then firing in the direction in which we assumed the Soviets to be lying, he played Beethoven and Bach all through the night. He had told us that, if he had to be killed, he wanted it to be while doing something civilized. He was almost delirious and was not about to be stopped. Fortunately, the Red Army never came close enough to shoot him that night.

Later, thousands of refugees started to come our way. The Red Army pushed the German lines farther and farther back. On the radio we heard the official military reports, which still spoke of 'the German victory on the eastern front'. We knew better.

On another occasion, our small group of ten artillery men was sent out again 'to kill the Ivans'. That was the official order. We lay in a muddy forest for hours until it grew dark. We were spread out over several hundred yards. Then we heard them come closer. Somebody shot, and there was an exchange of fire. Because it was nighttime, I couldn't see a thing, and I didn't realize that my friend and neighbour had been badly wounded. We began retreating, and my arm was grazed by a bullet. I felt dizzy but pulled myself together. Finally, there was the official signal to pull back. Almost everybody in our troop was wounded but no one was killed. We scrambled out of the forest. The sky was aflame; Pomerania was burning. Refugees were coming towards us from all directions.

Some time later, we sighted an empty bus. The only driver around was a Pole who insisted on waiting for the German commander who had paid the Pole to bring the commander to the eastern front. Some in our group became impatient, and before long two of us 'persuaded' the Pole to take us instead. Our method of persuasion was simple; we held our guns as if to shoot the tyres of his vehicle. Nothing else was said, and he took us to the nearest railroad station serving trains going to Berlin. No trains were running regularly, however.

After hours of waiting around the overcrowded platform, we saw in the distance a small train coming in. Those waiting were mainly mothers with crying babies, and a lot of old women and men. We were the only soldiers around. When the train finally stopped, everybody rushed toward the cars. We were all pressed against one another. I didn't even have to move my feet; I was just dragged along with the crowd. Somehow we all made it into the train, which took us slowly but safely to the outskirts of Berlin. There, under the towering Siegessäule, the symbol of the German victory over the French in 1871, we split up.

My friend Hans Leibkutsch and I set out on a hike of several days to Gera, which was nearly 200 miles away. It then dawned on us that we didn't have any official papers to document our release from military service. Upon our arrival home, my father, who had been the district judge for almost two decades, arranged for us to see the local doctor. My bullet wound was enough to convince him that I was unable to return to the front. At that time, everything in Germany was in such a disastrous state that nobody cared or could afford to care about the chain of command and bureaucracy. On the doctor's say-so I was officially discharged from the army and, so I thought, free to do whatever I wanted to do.

During this same time, in February 1945, we heard on the radio that the American President Roosevelt and British Prime Minister Churchill had secured Soviet leader Stalin's approval for the creation of a French occupation zone in the southwest of Germany and a French sector in Berlin, areas that were originally earmarked for occupation by the UK and the USA. At Yalta, it had also been decided that Germany was to be divided into four occupation zones.

The Soviets, by that time, had advanced well into the eastern parts of Pomerania and Silesia. Word had already spread that the Soviets were not planning to treat these eastern parts of the 'Old Reich' as occupied territories, but rather as lands to be 'administered by the governments of the USSR and Poland'. The western powers had already agreed in principal to some sort of eventual territorial compensation in the east at Germany's expense, but the Soviets presented their wartime allies with a major *fait accompli* by carrying out this massive transfer strictly on their own. A large part of German territory was handed over to Poland, and the East Prussian city of Königsberg was renamed Kaliningrad in honour of the nominal Soviet head of state. Because the Soviets and the Poles expelled almost all Germans from the areas placed under their administration, their action amounted to a de facto severance from Germany of all territories to the east of a line that ran along the Oder and Neisse rivers, including large areas that had been inhabited predominantly by Germans for centuries. In this manner, nearly a quarter of the 'Old Reich's' pre-1938 territory ceased to be part of the country. At the time, American and British officials took the position that such measures were merely provisional, but these demarcation lines soon became a permanent feature of the political geography.

It was a strange time to be 19 years old. Over 17 million refugees from Prussia, Silesia, territories of the USSR, and Poland came pouring into Germany. For over two years, women and children from the former eastern parts of Germany were commonplace everywhere in Germany. During the first three months after the war ended, 1.3 million refugees came to Berlin alone. Crime, poverty and the effects of disease increased dramatically. Most of the exiled refugees didn't speak German or spoke it with a strong accent. They had come with only the possessions they could carry on their backs to a part of the country that was, for the most part, destroyed, and they could only share in what little the Germans in the occupied zones had at the time. Food rationing made hunger an everyday occurrence.

At the same time, millions of German soldiers were prisoners of war. They were lucky if they had been able to surrender to the Anglo-Saxons or the French. Those who had fallen into the hands of the Red Army either died or were imprisoned, destined not to see their homes and families again for years, some as late as 1956.

Not immediately, but within a few months after the Allied Forces had occupied Germany, the question of guilt was a common theme among families and friends. With the condemnation of Hitler, questions arose about the German bourgeoisie, their involvement in bringing Hitler to power, and the role of Prussian–German militarism in the war. Another concern was the flood of returning soldiers, many of whom were crippled, sick and emaciated from prisoner-of-war camps. Hitler's lofty and nationalistic vocabulary was suddenly replaced with temperance, reverence and silence.

Of course, we were happy to see American soldiers marching into our city. When the first GIs were announced, I hastily went to the military hospital. My arm had almost healed, but I knew that the occupying powers would treat with more respect those German soldiers registered at a military hospital than those roaming the streets. We were amazed when we saw the first American soldiers—tired, but clean and young—coming into our city.

During the first days, contact with the GIs was rare and very official. They inspected the military hospital, took over city government, and interviewed people like the mayor and judges. Although I was officially a prisoner of war of the American troops, I was allowed to go home every night; I had to report again in the morning, however, to the commanding officer at the military hospital.

A week or so after the arrival of the Americans, each side was becoming more and more curious about the other. The Americans and the Germans both wanted to know more about the people they were dealing with. On one of my evening walks home, I approached a GI who appeared to be about my age. He was one of many guarding the military hospital. I offered him a cigarette, and he in turn offered me a marvellous-tasting piece of chocolate. It was only 15 minutes before curfew, but we nevertheless started talking as much as my limited English would allow. I remember him saying at the end of our chat something like, 'That's almost unfair; we won the war, but you get to go home to sleep in your own bed, while I have to stand here keeping an eye on you guys. I don't know who is better off, you or I.'

During the first spring days, before the surrender on 7 May 1945, the city commander asked me to meet him. He had spoken to many German soldiers and had interrogated them about their political past and their activities. He had heard about me because of my sports activities in the German National team, in which I had been the champion in the javelin throw before the war started. I went over to the city hall and was taken to his office, where he smilingly offered me a cigarette. First he just asked me about my records in the javelin throw and when I had practised last. Soon, however, he turned to the hard-core question of whether I was part of a right-wing group called the Werewolves, an organization that was trying to undermine the efforts of the occupying powers. I told him about my military past and ensured him that I was very happy that the war had ended and that the Americans, and not the Soviets, were occupying our city. I stressed my hope that they would stay with us as long as the political situation in Germany was unstable. He replied, 'Listen, boy, what we have conquered with our blood we are not going to give away until we know that democracy is installed'. However, as history shows, the American troops moved out of the eastern parts of Saxony, Thuringia and Bohemia in June 1945 and turned over these territories to the Red Army. We later learned that the Soviets had already earmarked those territories for occupation at the Yalta conference, but American troops, who had been moving faster, had arrived unexpectedly early, via Bavaria, into these eastern parts of Germany.

Margarethe Fuchs

I turned 16 several days after Capitulation Day in 1945. We were all happy that the shooting and bombing had stopped, for we young people had waited so long for a chance to lead a normal life. Days before the capitulation, life had almost stopped in the eastern parts of Germany as the bombing got heavier and heavier. It was a beautiful spring, and the blue skies made it easy to spot approaching fighter planes; the streets usually were empty within minutes.

The day the Americans marched into Glauchau, a village close to Weimar, a special train had stopped at our station with food supplies. I had been sent by the family to get what I could carry home. Then somebody shouted, 'They are coming, the Americans are coming'. There were mixed feelings among the population. Most were glad that the American troops were marching in instead of the Red Army. I didn't really know what to think, except that I was curious.

Just after I arrived back home with all the supplies I could get, a Jeep stopped in front of our house. We were only three women at home: my grandmother, my aunt Ann and me. We were frightened when three tall GIs and one officer rang the door bell. I was sent to open the door. My aunt, who had lived for 11 years in Australia between the wars, was standing behind me. In fluent English she asked what the four men wanted. As we soon found out, they wanted my aunt to help them to communicate with the people and to translate some documents. The funny thing was that one of the soldiers had greeted us by slowly moving his right arm up to make a broken 'Heil Hitler'. That was the first time I heard an American saying that particular greeting. He probably thought that was very friendly and German. I started to giggle until my grandmother jabbed me in the ribs so the attention of the three soldiers wouldn't fall on me.

From that day on, for roughly two months, my aunt was picked up every morning around eight o'clock by the same American Jeep with the same driver and brought to City Hall, where she assisted the American commander. A dusk-to-dawn curfew was imposed, and the city's power was shut off for several hours a day. Sometimes we had to go to the nearby river to get water. But life was not unpleasant; the farmers around us had started to harvest, and everybody had little gardens they had planted during the war which were now producing strawberries, tomatoes and other fruits and vegetables. My school had not yet started again and I was helping in a nearby military hospital as an assistant nurse. It wasn't a terribly interesting job, but at least it was a helpful one.

What I remember most from that time was the devaluation of the old Reichsmark. The more than 300 billion Reichsmarks that had been printed and circulated under the Hitler regime were essentially worthless compared to the prices charged for goods available in stores. The few things that could be traded were traded on the black market. After the war, Germany was a country with two currencies: the old Reichsmark, in which salaries and taxes were paid, and, starting in August 1946, there was Allied money, which could not be converted into Reichsmarks. The most common form of payment was cigarettes. A cigarette was traded at a value of 10 Marks. Almost anything was available to you if you had a package or more of cigarettes. All of a sudden money was worth nothing. The cost of a loaf of bread was around 30 to 35 Marks or three cigarettes (roughly $20 to $25); a pound of coffee with a price tag of 500 Marks ($300) was unaffordable unless one had a good source of tobacco.

One evening in June 1945, I came home when my aunt had just returned from working for the American commander. She looked very pale and troubled. She said, 'I really shouldn't say anything, but we have to make a decision. The Americans are leaving over the weekend, and on Monday the Red Army is taking over the whole area.' Everybody was silent. Hopes had been so high that with the Americans present, this part of Germany would quickly develop into a free, democratic and functioning country again. My aunt was ready to leave very quickly and had made arrangements for transportation. The American commander had offered to send a car to take us to the next larger city where trains were running to the western occupation zones. Aunt Ann even had the papers that ensured our safe passage from zone to zone, but my grandmother refused to leave the house, furniture and everything else behind. She said, 'We are not giving up and leaving everything for those Soviet scoundrels'.

Thassilo Borchart

My father was a pilot in the war, serving in Finland and Norway. One day in March 1945, just eight weeks before the end of the war, we received notice that my father had died in a fighter attack over Stettin. I was just 6 years old.

Towards the end of the war, the stream of refugees pouring into Berlin from East Prussia, areas which now belong to Poland, was astonishing to watch. Sometimes, my friends and I would hand them apples or bread that my grandmother had just baked that day. For us children, it seemed adventurous and exciting, watching these thousands of strangers, who had obviously been walking for weeks, pulling carts with the remnants of their belongings. But the front drew ever nearer, until finally, we too had to leave.

My mother had arranged for us to leave by bus. She had known the driver for some time, and she trusted him. As we were stowing our belongings aboard the bus, he received orders to clear his vehicle for the transport of soldiers. We unloaded everything in a hurry, and for a day or so, my mother tried to find another way for us to leave Berlin as soon as possible. She had heard that a train with sleeper cars was leaving the city from a little station just outside Berlin. It was December and very cold. My mother, grandmother, two brothers and I bundled up and found our way to the train; parts of Berlin were already smouldering.

The train was packed with all sorts of people. My mother managed to find two seats. All of a sudden, the train, which had been moving along rather rapidly, appeared to slow down. A woman screamed that our cars had been uncoupled. We started to roll backwards. My mother opened one of the doors and was about to push us all from the moving train into the snow when someone pulled the emergency brake.

The train sat on the tracks for almost a day until we could be towed to the next station, still on the outskirts of Berlin. My mother finally decided that we would hide at our Müggelsee summer house.[5] Being a totally different environment, the house was paradise for us children. There was a big lake in front of the house and a forest where we played hide-and-seek. Hide-and-seek became part of our daily routine—whenever the sirens sounded to warn of approaching bombers. Every night my grandmother reminded us to lay out our shirts, sweaters, socks and shoes so we could dress quickly in case of an air raid. Some nights, we got up three or four times to go and hide

---

[5] Müggelsee, a lake southeast of Berlin, was a popular location for vacation homes.

under a nearby bridge. On the horizon, we could see Berlin after an air attack, lit up like a birthday cake.

When we received news that the Russians were just a few miles away from our summer home, my mother immediately began stitching a white flag out of bed sheets. One night, we heard several shots from a neighbour's house. My mother and grandmother stayed calm and shoved us children inside the house. Soon we saw flames licking the sky; a neighbour had shot his wife and children, set the house on fire, and then shot himself. The Russians arrived at our house the next day.

Chapter Two

The Soviet Occupation Zone

Most Germans assumed that, as happened after other wars, the issues the war had raised would be resolved in a peace treaty. The increasing differences among the Allies made such a solution impossible, however, and a peace treaty was never signed.

As soon as the occupying powers turned to the task of governing their respective parts of Germany, disagreements arose—particularly over reparations. The Soviets, whose country had been devastated during the years of fierce fighting, felt that they were entitled to as much German industrial equipment as they could seize. Entire factories were dismantled and shipped to the Soviet Union, along with motor vehicles, rails, and trains. It has been estimated that one-quarter of the Soviet zone's entire productive capacity was removed in this fashion. The western powers, however, soon recognized that seizing all of Germany's industrial potential would extract a price: the occupying powers—and their taxpayers—would have to bear more of the cost of feeding the German citizens. The problem was aggravated when the Soviets failed to comply with the agreement to provide western zones with food in compensation for some of the German equipment shipped to Moscow.

One of the earliest and sorest points of disagreement between the USSR and the Anglo-Saxon Allies involved the Soviet practice of printing large quantities of German banknotes, which they used to pay for the equipment they took, thereby accelerating inflation in all the occupation zones.

In 1946, after all efforts to resolve the reparation problem had failed, American General Lucius D. Clay ordered an end to the dismantling in his zone. The British and the French soon followed his example. All three western Allies began to foster Germany's industrial recovery in order to enable Germans to pay for food. The Soviets, on their part, accused the western powers of violating the Potsdam Agreement and used their veto power in the Allied Control Council to block joint actions in support of German economic development. This chilling of the relationship between the Soviets and the other Allies instigated the onset of the Cold War and provided a chance for the East German puppet regime to gain power, in violation of the Allied Forces' agreements to permit the establishment of independent governments based on free elections. In line with communist ideology, the Soviet zone was socialized and radical agrarian reforms were put into effect, eliminating the economic foundation of the Prussian gentry.

The increasing divisions between the once Allied Forces became most apparent at the London Conference in May 1948. To deal with the economic problems that a still-prostrate Germany posed for much of Europe, Britain, the USA, France and the Benelux countries (Belgium, the Netherlands and Luxembourg), the Conference decided to extend the US-sponsored Marshall Plan for economic recovery to all western occupation zones. The battle lines of the Cold War hardened when the Soviets refused to allow their satellites or their zone to participate in the plan.

Wolfgang Gäbelein

In the two months that the American GIs had been in our city, the German citizens had alrcady started hoping for a great new beginning to their lives. Economic and industrial groups had been formed to revitalize the area. People were busy cleaning up the ruins left by the bombing and had started to build houses again. Everybody, with the exception of a few communists, was devastated when the Americans departed and left the area to the Red Army. We had heard about the rapes committed by Red Army soldiers, their brutality and their primitive ways. Some of the stories were unfounded but most of the tales, unfortunately, were true.

When the Red Army marched into Gera, the picture was quite different from what we had seen when the GIs had marched in several weeks earlier. Most of the Red Army soldiers were poorly dressed for the occasion; some didn't even have shoes. Bicycles, cars and anything moving was immediately confiscated or torn apart. Life suddenly became very quiet again in our city.

I had already enrolled in a course to prepare myself for the university when news reached me in the classroom that six members of my basketball team, which I had organized after my return from the front, had disappeared. They had been imprisoned by the Red Army under a false charge of espionage for 'fascist elements in German society'. This, of course, was bogus. The boys the Soviets had thrown into prison were all between 19 and 24 and had never had anything to do with fascism. They had merely served as very young soldiers in the war, and nothing more. Most of us had simply viewed it as our duty to follow the orders of our military commanders.

That same evening on 14 December 1945, a group of Red Army officers forced their way into our house, their Kalashnikovs at the ready. They forced my father and me from the dinner table, pushed us against a wall, and searched us as we held our hands over our heads. My father, who was a 65-year-old retired judge at the time, spoke some Russian and tried to communicate with them, but they ignored him and proceeded through the house, searching it inch by inch. We didn't know why. My frightened mother was left behind while my father and I were taken, handcuffed, to the city hall. On the way there, we had to pass through a dark tunnel underneath the train station. Ever since we had left the house, I was trying to figure out how to use my knowledge of the city to escape. I was tempted to try to escape while we were in the tunnel, because I knew of a side street that branched off, one that only locals were aware of. But I quickly abandoned the idea for fear of leaving my father behind.

When we reached the city hall, we were thrown into separate cells. One of the soldiers searched me again and found a picture of my fiancée. He confiscated it and tried to make me write down her address. The results of my refusal were a very uneven fist fight and a heavy blow to my stomach with the butt of his Kalishnikov. He also took my belt and my shoe laces. This was to ensure that no prisoner would hang himself in his cell. Some hours later, not having seen my father yet, I was guided upstairs to meet a Georgian lieutenant called Motvow, who was accompanied by a very pretty Russian translator whose name was Dianushka. The interrogation began with his asking me several questions about my 'fascist past'. I didn't answer. Then he continued by asking, 'Do you know where you are sitting now?'

I said, 'Yes, I'm sitting in the district court house of Gera, and you are sitting on the chair that my father used to occupy when he was the judge'.

He started to scream at me, 'Do you know whom you are talking to?'

'Yes', I said, 'the Soviet-style Gestapo'.

His face turned red, and he gasped for air. Dianushka squirmed nervously on her chair, but nothing happened. The interrogation continued, but in a milder tone. The lieutenant suggested that I had been working with a ring of organized spies to undermine the Soviet troops. He wanted names, but I couldn't give him any. During six weeks in prison under Red Army supervision, I was asked the same questions daily, again and again, and then thrown back into the cold cell.

I had barely enough food; it tasted horrible, but at least it was something to chew on. The others from my basketball team, who had been arrested a short time before me, were in the same prison. My father, being an old and frail man, had been released after only 24 hours in custody. We prisoners seldom saw one another, but we had developed a communication system by tapping out Morse code on the heating pipes, which ran through most of the building.

Six weeks in prison doesn't sound too long, but you have to keep your mind working, or you go mad. I made up law cases in which I was the defendant, or I envisioned a date with my fiancée, imagining where I would take her the first time we saw each other again. I also tried regularly to do push-ups to stay fit, which I thought would prove to be helpful.

One night I was awakened by two guards, who pulled me out of bed. I barely had time to slip into some clogs that my mother had been able to bring to me. I could sense that nothing good awaited me. The guards pulled me into an empty room and started to beat me.

When I fell to the floor, my nose and mouth bleeding, I had little strength left, but I knew that if I didn't fight back, I would become their regular evening entertainment for the rest of my stay. I slowly stood up, grasped my wooden shoes, and quickly began to beat the guards on the ears or wherever I could hit them. After the fight, all three of us were lying on the floor. The next morning during my daily interrogation, Motvow grinned and asked how I felt 'after so unfortunately running into the prison cell door'.

Why I was imprisoned was never explained. But one morning, several weeks after Christmas, I was read my sentence. I was ordered to serve 15 years because I had been found guilty of being a 'fascist militarist', but was told that, if I would sign certain papers, they could let me go within 24 hours. I briefly looked the papers over but refused to sign them. The Georgian lieutenant pulled his chair closer, leaned over and told me not to be foolish and to mark those passages I couldn't agree with. He told me that he would try to rephrase the disagreeable passages as much as possible. The papers mainly obligated me to do some 'snooping around' among my father's circle of friends and among some close friends of mine. They also stated that I was being released only because of the Red Army's decision that I was a 'dutiful servant to the Soviet occupation power'.

I signed, and that same February day I walked home, wrapped in little more than a dirty blanket. Within minutes of arriving home, I told my parents that I wanted to leave immediately for one of the western Allied occupation zones. I was ready to take any train that would carry me west. I remember my father's sad eyes. They had never looked at me so emotionally, yet they seemed empty.

He said, 'Wolfgang, they visited me yesterday and told me that if you leave Soviet territory, I'll go to prison'.

'Well, easy enough, we'll all go to one of the Western occupation zones,' I answered.

'I'm ill,' he quickly replied, looking away. 'I just had a heart attack.' I hadn't known.

So I remained and made plans to study law in Jena, which not only was the closest city with a good law school but also had one of the oldest universities in Germany, founded in 1558. My chances of being admitted were slim, since the Soviet occupation powers had ruled that only children of farmers and workers were allowed to study at the university. During the application process, however, I stressed that I had signed papers with Lieutenant Motvow and that, if officials had any questions about my status, they should check with him. This time, I made the system work for me. Except for a young blind man who had been wounded during the war, I was the only 'non-proletarian' student in my first law lectures at the university in Jena in 1946. In September of the same year, the British and American zone commanders signed an agreement to operate their zones jointly. US foreign minister James Byrnes had announced on the radio in Stuttgart that the jointly operated zone was to be administered through Frankfurt on Main and represented the first step in strengthening the economic development of all of Germany. With this step, our hopes rose in the east that this constructive policy would also have some positive result for our area. It didn't.

It was already apparent at that time that the foundation of postwar life in our occupied territory was quite different from that of the western parts in the country. All the changes made by the Soviets were in line with communist ideology. Much of the eastern zone's industry was socialized. The major agrarian reform imposed on farmers and the Prussian gentry redistributed large amounts of land among socialists and communists. All rural estates that had served for centuries, particularly in Thuringia, as the agrarian foundation of well-known families of the Prussian and Thuringian gentry were eliminated within months. Most of the dispossessed gentry fled to other Allied occupation zones and started new lives there.

Every three weeks, like clockwork, I was asked to show up at the same building in which I had been held prisoner to report on the people I was studying with, on the behaviour of teaching professors, or on people I had simply met on the train. The Soviets were looking for people who were actively trying to undermine the communist policies they had installed. I couldn't, and wouldn't, tell them anything that was of interest to them. They were amazingly well-informed as to whom I had contact with, and even when and where I had met friends for a glass of beer. It was frightening. I was being watched exactly as they wanted me to watch other people for them. It was as if somebody were following me like a shadow, step by step. Sometimes they got rough with me because I hadn't given them names of groups and people who were working against the 'Socialistic Revolution', as the Soviet authorities called the communism imposed on the territory.

Two years later, my father died. As soon as he was buried, I left the east and continued my studies in the west. The Red Army interrogated my mother several times about my whereabouts, but she never suffered any harm. I was again approached by the Soviets after I had been living in Frankfurt for sometime—I believe it was in the early 1950s. An older student joined me in a crowded café, obviously trying to recruit me for some 'dirty work'. He never explicitly asked me to work for the KGB, but he mentioned Motvow's name, my imprisonment and some well-paid work. I just got up from the table, told him to go to hell, and threatened to call the police.

I was hardly the only one who had been trapped in the net of the Soviet occupation power. As early as 1945, the Soviets had slowly begun to build up a surveillance network within their territories. The political puppets of the Soviets, such as Ulbricht and Honecker, fine-tuned this network over the years with extreme Prussian/German precision. Many of the people who were later involved in the East German system had already served dutifully under the Nazi regime and continued their 'duties' after 1945 with the Soviets. The regimes had changed, as had their political colouring, from brown to red, but their methods and their mind-sets were the same.

Without my prison experience and the attempted blackmail by the Red Army, I would probably have stayed in East Germany somewhat longer. I believed—as did most people—that one day in the near future the Red Army would leave and, as the other occupying powers did in 1949, give the territory back to the Germans. To me, looking back today, that hope seems politically naive. The people who stayed behind had to pay dearly.

Wolfgang Mischnick

I had been a soldier until the end of the Second World War when, owing to an injury, I had been lucky enough to be allowed to sign my own dismissal papers. After I had returned to my home town of Dresden, I was looking for work, like all the other men who had made it back. I found Dresden, which was now part of the Soviet occupation zone, totally destroyed. Upon my return from the war front, I had toyed with the idea of getting an advanced degree, but, as I quickly learned, that was not an option for me. As a former reserve officer, I was not allowed to start any studies in 1945.

Together with my father I started to work in the ruins of Dresden, removing dirt, hammering stones into shape and slowly rebuilding what the rubble covered. On one of my trips to a construction site I discovered a hand-painted sign that said, 'Headquarters of the Liberal Democratic Party'. My curiosity made me step into a little room that was filled with young German people. Their discussions were focused on how to rebuild the city and how to come to terms with the Soviet occupation power. After I joined the liberal party on 6 August 1945, I almost immediately got on the elector list for the first election, to be held in 1946. Soviet officials took me off the list, however, using the sleazy argument that I had been a member of the Hitler Jugend as a young boy. All the communists stayed on the list. A short while later, a Soviet official came to our home and informed me that I was not to write or speak publicly. Friends inside the party warned me not to argue and—even better—I should leave the Russian occupation zone. So much for my personal history.

Politically I believed in 1945 that it would be possible to re-establish a democratic system in the Soviet occupation zone. The older and wiser Ernest Meier, one of the founding fathers of the Liberal Party of Germany, had always disagreed with me on that subject. But the mere existence of four political parties left me with the impression, at least in the beginning, that all the occupation powers intended to put a democracy together. The four parties were the Christian Democratic Party (CDU), formerly active with the moderate parties of the Weimar Republic, including the Catholic Centre Party; the Liberal Democratic Party (LDP), which had its heritage in liberal German politics; the Socialist Party (SPD); and the Communist Party (KPD).

Initially, the Communist Party denied any intention of promoting Soviet-style communism. But the plundering and raping committed by soldiers of the Red Army when they arrived in German cities worked to the Soviets' disadvantage with the population. As members of the KPD became more and more aware that they lacked popularity among the people, they pressed for a merger of the KPD and the Socialist Party, the result of which would be named the Socialist Unity Party (SED). Then the communists immediately gained a majority within the SED and completely overshadowed the non-Marxist members. The young members of these non-Marxist parties tried very hard to work against the SED, but without much success. The youths in the LPD formed the strongest opposition to communism, particularly when the SED tried to recruit young people for the Communist Young People's Organization. The organization, called the Freie Deutsche Jugend (FDJ or Free German Youth) later introduced a political ceremony to replace the Catholic first holy communion and the Protestant confirmation. Democrats and churches were outraged. Nevertheless, individuals who failed to participate in the FDJ and the ceremony usually were banned from higher education. This remained true right up until the Wall fell in 1989.

The results of the first local elections in the Soviet occupation zone in 1946 showed a dubious majority for the SED. The Soviets in many cases had delayed the certification of non-Marxist parties such as the CDU and LPD, which therefore were not even represented on the ballot. A month later, during the provincial elections, the SED fell short of a majority, since other parties were more fully represented. The election loss came despite the fact that the Soviets had made it difficult for parties other than the SED to set up posters, place ads in newspapers or distribute brochures. As the first postwar election of a city-wide assembly would prove, the SED did not have the slightest chance of getting a majority if it had to compete fairly.

Because the four-power rule had been applied and the elections were observed by officials of all four occupying powers, the members of the SPD who had opposed the merger with the Communist Party won by a wide margin. Stung by the defeat, the SED didn't seek another democratic election contest thereafter. For no longer than a year, the LPD—which called itself the FDP in the western occupation zones—became active in all four occupied territories of Germany, despite the problems that were already becoming apparent in the Soviet zone.

Every day, those in the FDP who were still active in the eastern territory had to face the political restrictions imposed by the leadership in the Soviet occupation zone. I can think of one example: in 1946 I had designed an election poster showing a capital 'D' in the middle, standing for democracy. The D was held by four hands representing the four occupation zones. The background of the poster was covered by a rising sun. The message was clear: my party supported democracy in all four sectors. A Soviet officer had to give his permission before we could print the poster. He stared at it for awhile and then gave it back to me with a cynical grin saying, 'The D stands for Deutschland [Germany], and a nation called by this name does not exist anymore and won't exist again. This poster cannot be printed.' The political repression and the lack of freedom in the Soviet zone increased monthly. Politically active people who opposed the policies of the Soviet occupation power were insulted, and their lives and their families' lives were made difficult by requiring them to report to a Soviet officer daily. Others just disappeared for days; they ended up in a political prison camp for 're-education'. It was part of everyday life that communist-led mobs repeatedly disturbed our political meetings and physically menaced us.

As I didn't have a family except for my father, who wanted to stay in Dresden, I decided in 1948 to leave the city and move to

Frankfurt and the American occupation zone, where the democratic reconstruction of Germany had proceeded and prospered. Soon, I headed the national youth organization of the FDP in the western occupation zones. I tried to resurrect contacts in the east, particularly with friends who I knew were not active in the SED and were looking for political alternatives. Many others in the party considered various ways to hold Germany together, but the emergence of a Bizonia seemed to be a fact.[1] It became clearer and clearer every day that post-war circumstances had produced two Germanies with two very different sets of political and social goals.

The proposal of the London Conference in 1948, which called for the formation of a West German government, had laid the groundwork for a consolidation of the western zones. Part of the proposal was to introduce a new monetary system to revive the economy, to stabilize social conditions and, most important, to relieve the financial burdens the occupation had imposed on the victors. The Soviets strongly opposed the introduction of a new western currency, and the divided city of Berlin became the focal point of the disagreement. That was the beginning of the Berlin Blockade.

Originally the proposal of the London Conference was not received very well by most German politicians in the western occupation zones, since it reflected the inability of the four Allies to resolve their differences and deal with Germany as a whole. But misgivings about the possible consequences of forming a government in the west soon gave way to fears of Soviet expansionism. Finally, the three western governments asked the West Germans to convene a constituent assembly to draft a constitution for a new government and submit it to the population for ratification. The new government would operate within the confines of the occupation statute that closely regulated authority and power.

I remember that negotiations between the occupation powers and German politicians were delicate and slow. It was finally agreed that the new government should be a provisional arrangement that could cease to exist as soon as the country as a whole could determine its destiny. A parliamentary council designed a Basic Law. By the end of May 1949, the council had worked out a text comprising suggestions from German delegates and the general policies of the

---

[1] On September 5, 1946, the Americans and British signed a treaty that combined their zones to the Bizone.

occupation powers. The Basic Law carried within it an acceptance of the Occupation Statute that described the control of the Americans, British and French over foreign relations, foreign trade, industrial production, reparations, research and all areas related to the military. The Basic Law also declared Berlin to be part of West Germany or, more correctly, the Federal Republic (FDR), but the provisions were only applied to the western sectors of the old German capital.

In contrast to the manipulated electoral process in the east, voters in the first election for the West Deutsche Bundestag chose from an array of parties. The CDU and its Bavarian sister-party, the CSU, received the majority and formed a coalition with my party. Theodor Heuss became the federal president, and 73-year-old Konrad Adenauer was elected chancellor by a margin of one vote—his own. Heuss, the man who headed the Board of the FDP, became the first elected president of West Germany at the same time.

While the Basic Law was designed in Bonn by the Parliamentary Council, government in the eastern occupation zone developed quite differently. The USSR increasingly demanded political conformity. A Soviet-style 'democratic centralism' prevailed, in which all authority flowed downward from the leadership. The principle of equal representation of socialists and communists with the SED was abandoned. Many former SPD and KPD members were declared to be disloyal to the system, purged from the SED and in some cases sent to prison after being accused of spying. The Politburo, which was elected by the Central Committee, a body of several hundred party members, developed into a small inner circle of decision-makers and power brokers. The decisive figure within the SED and the Politburo became Walter Ulbricht. He had joined the KPD during the Weimar Republic shortly after its formation in 1918. After having been exiled in the Soviet Union during the Third Reich, he returned to Berlin in 1945 to oversee the re-establishment of the party in Germany. His position as general secretary of the SED would make him the key figure of the new regime for the next 22 years.

The pledge of the SED to follow the path of a 'distinctively German socialism' was abandoned. The new goal became the construction of a 'people's democracy' similar to those of the regimes in other Eastern Bloc countries. Repressive measures were applied throughout the Soviet occupation zone. Those who held any economic or social position of importance—such as teachers, judges and administrators—had to pass ideological scrutiny. All media were restricted by a tight system of censorship. The regime developed a political police apparatus that kept almost everyone under close surveillance. Dissent and behaviour construed as disloyal were immediately punished by denying the guilty parties access to education, putting their careers on hold, dismissing them from their jobs or, in the worst cases, imprisoning them. Politicians who had kept in touch with their colleagues in the west were anathema in the eyes of the SED. An estimated 200,000 members of the former democratic SPD were purged from the party. And from 1948 to 1950, over 5,000 people landed in prisons or in Soviet labour camps; an estimated 400 people died while incarcerated. In practice, the government of the GDR quickly became an extension of the Communist Party and Politburo in the Soviet Union.

Margarethe Fuchs

Our dream was destroyed when the first Red Army soldiers came to our village. The Soviets immediately replaced the mayors and every official they could with people from outside, mostly communists. Even the policemen were replaced. Within a couple of weeks a wave of arrests swept through our town. Two classmates of mine who had refused to take up Russian in school were missing for over six weeks thereafter. One was sent to Buchenwald. The Red Army had reopened Hitler's concentration camps and used them as prisons, either to lock people away for good or, as in the case of my classmate, to intimidate them.

Many family members of the German gentry were locked away during that time. In their absence, it was easy to seize their land and estates, divide them up into many small farms, and then transform them into state-owned property. All the industries seized during the Soviet occupation became 'Volkseigene Betriebe' (people's organizations—VEB) and were operated first by Soviet officials and later, after they had successfully installed a German Communist Party, by the SED.

The economy was socialized step by step. Special occupation decrees resulted in the wholesale take-over of certain categories of enterprises, such as banks, energy-producing utilities, pharmacies, and motion picture theatres. Other industrial plants were seized and exploited solely for the Soviet Union, which only later relinquished them to the GDR, for the most part years after the East German state's formation in 1949.

The Red Army brought with it to the eastern parts of Germany a political terror system, a continuation of Hitler's regime. That and the planned economy were instruments certain to kill any creativity or self-initiative of any kind. Politically, what was happening in the east produced a strong anti-communist sentiment in the western part of the country. Many people tried to stay objective and reminded radical anti-communists of the atrocities German troops inflicted on Russian citizens during their march into Soviet territory; 3.5 million Russians had died during the war years. But it seemed at the time as though the Germans in the eastern zone were the ones who had to atone for those transgressions.

Thassilo Borchart

People were terrified of the Russian soldiers. Everyone swapped stories about their brutality. Women without men in the household, like my mother, hid in their cellars when the Russian troops advanced on a village. During the night, Russian songs could be heard floating through their encampments. The women knew that this meant the soldiers were drinking and probably hoping to drag a woman off into the woods to rape her.

At the beginning of May 1945, a bus load of Russian soldiers stopped in front of our house; they asked where we'd hidden our car. We had buried the vehicle months before, but I don't know how the Russian soldiers could have known this. They dug the wheel-less car out of the mud and loaded it onto a transporter. My grandmother said that one friendly soldier, who spoke some German, had written out a receipt for her in Russian. I had it translated later. It said, 'This German car has to be transported to Moscow for inspection, 1945'. They took our car, but left us alone. Thank God!

We were lucky enough to live by a lake in the country. We were able to live on chickens, goats and fish. Once, when my younger brother and I were fishing, we heard Russian soldiers approaching.

We hid ourselves and our catch in the bushes, until one of the soldiers reached into his pocket and pulled out a hand grenade. I grabbed my little brother's hand and we ran home as fast as we could go. The food shortage in Berlin was most extreme in the Soviet occupation zone. The Russians had failed to keep the promise they made at the Potsdam Conference to supply East Berlin with food as compensation for German industrial equipment shipped to Moscow. The Russians printed large numbers of German banknotes for purchasing goods in the western zones. While the Allies tried to help the country recover, so that Germany could pay for imported food, the Soviets blocked those actions.

Chapter Three

The Berlin Blockade

In addition to extending the Marshall Plan, the western Allies introduced a new monetary system in Germany to stop inflation and guarantee the kind of economic revival needed to stabilize social conditions. The Soviet response was the Berlin blockade of 1948. Surrounded by territory occupied by the Red Army and a hundred miles from any western occupation zone, West Berlin's feeder highways, railroads and canals were sealed. The plan was to hold West Berlin hostage until the Allies abandoned the attempt to form a consolidated government and economy in western Germany. Khrushchev himself summarized his goal: 'Berlin will fall into our hands like a ripe apple'.[1] Stalin had predicted in a newspaper article that the west would make western Germany its own, and the Soviets would turn eastern Germany into its own state, a self-fulfilling prophecy.

The 1945 agreements of Potsdam, in which the Allies had agreed to govern Germany as a single entity according to common policies, were soon circumvented. What the western Allies had forgotten at Potsdam was that it would mean the intrusion of Marxist doctrines into the eastern territories. Almost at once, the Soviets began to strike at the socio-economic roots of Germany through extensive land reform, nationalization of banking and heavy industry, and the expropriation of the holdings not only of leading Nazis but also of common citizens. Behind the social and economic changes were the dynamics of full-blown communism. The imposition of the Soviet system on eastern Germany was bound up with the diplomacy of conflict and competition between east and west.

With the founding of the Socialist Unity Party, the forced merger of the German communists and socialists, the Soviets had not only openly supported German communism, but also brought about the eventual emergence of a 'People's Democracy', which was to remain independent of the other occupation zones. The obviously anti-democratic behaviour of the Soviets not only inaugurated broader co-operation between the western Allies, which in the end made the creation of the Federal Republic possible, but also brought about a change of atmosphere among the other

---

[1] Rolf Steininger, *Germany after 1945*, 1967, pp. 107–13.

occupying powers. Rather suddenly, just a year after the end of World War II, Germany had developed into the focal point of the Cold War.

The role adopted by the commanders in the American and British occupied territories was quite different. As early as July 1946, the Anglo-Saxons realized that the formation of a jointly administered zone (Bizonia) would help bring Germany back to self-reliance. American Commander and Military Governor General Lucius D. Clay, and his British counterpart Sir Brian Hubert Robertson, began work on forming a Bizonia, in which the British and Americans together would orchestrate the economy, finance, food supply, health care and the traffic and mail systems within their territories. At the same time, the Soviets were hoping that the Americans would move out of other parts of Germany, such as Stuttgart, which the Red Army would then annex.[2]

The Bizonia not only created a new economic configuration, but it also had political consequences. Following the American model of single states, each headed by a governor or a minister president, the Bizonia operated through a set of administrative offices situated in Frankfurt. The zones' activities were co-ordinated by an Executive Council, which consisted of a number of democratically elected representatives. The Executive Council's policies, in turn, were subject to review by an Economic Council. Political parties, such as the SPD (Socialist Party) and the CDU/CSU (Christian Democrats, Conservatives, and the like) were represented in proportion to their political strength. The goal of the Bizonia was that it should be a self-sufficient system by 1949.

A less favourable feature of the Bizonia was that, with its creation, there was also brought into existence a formal policy of partition that threatened Germany's unity. That fear soon proved to be justified when, in February 1948, the Anglo-Saxons decided that the process of defining a future for Germany could no longer be halted by ideological differences between the eastern and western powers. Meetings of the Council of Foreign Ministers of all the occupying powers had failed to arrive at a peace settlement. Economic and living conditions, despite the Bizonia, had further deteriorated. Public transportation was not functioning, food was difficult to obtain in the largest cities, and daily food rations were cut from roughly 1,500 calories to 700–800 calories.

The Americans, the British, the French and representatives from the Benelux countries met in London for two sessions, first in April, and then again in June 1948. During the London Conference, the United States offered a generous recovery plan that would benefit war-damaged Germany: the European Recovery Plan, better known as the Marshall Plan. The Marshall Plan was motivated not only by humanitarian reasons, but

[2] See also Knapp and Kuhn, *Die Deutsche Einheit*, p. 58.

surely also by Harry Truman's politics of containment. Truman wanted to ensure that the Red Army would be limited to occupying the territories the Soviets controlled at that time. Altogether, the USA made $5.3 billion available in 1947–8 for the recovery of Europe. While the British prime minister said he would 'grab the Marshall proposal with both hands', Yugoslavia, Bulgaria and Poland—countries that initially wanted to accept the generous gesture—declined under pressure from the Soviet Union. Soviet Foreign Minister Skriabin Molotov referred to the countries that accepted the Marshall Plan as 'bloodhounds hunting for dollars'.

Earlier that year, in March, the Soviets had already made headlines when the Russian Marshal Vassily Danilovich Sokolovsky and his whole delegation abruptly left a meeting of the Control Council in Berlin. Part of the Marshall Plan, and a step towards consolidation of the western zones, was currency reform in those zones. The old Reichsmark had suffered from severe inflation and had finally become worthless because the Hitler regime, and later the Soviets, had continued to print large numbers of bills with no economic backing. The black market had obviously flourished then, and almost anything could be got in exchange for cigarettes.

With the currency reform, even cigarettes lost their value overnight. At 21 June 1948, all debts of the old German Reich were nullified. All private debts as well as bank accounts and other cash valuations were devalued at 10 Reichsmarks to 1 Deutsche Mark (DM). Everybody got a first 'Kopfquote' of 40 DM and a second payment of 20 DM eight weeks later. Thereafter, 100 Reichsmarks were devalued to the equivalent of 6.50 DM. The currency reform had been handled by the western occupying powers as a secret mission. The Americans, it was learned later, had brought a large number of crates into Germany, labelled 'Bird Dog'.[3] The first German money had been printed in the United States. In other words, together with the Marshall Plan, the currency reform made the Wirtschaftswunder (economic miracle) possible.

Suddenly, within weeks, the shops were filled with goods again, the likes of which people had almost forgotten: soap, salt, butter, textiles and even shoes. Supported by the Allies, the German politician and later Minister of Finance Ludwig Erhard abolished nearly all ration cards.[4]

The currency reform was a leap into the western economic system that was not without some risk, but it was probably the only reasonable alternative. Few of its supporters had any extensive knowledge of the supply

---

[3] The western Allies and some German economists prepared the currency reform in an American garrison in Kassel. German money was to be printed in the United States and later secretly brought to the western zones of Germany. See *The Great Republic*, vol. II, Lexington, MA, 1977, p.1187.

[4] Housing, steel, sugar and fertilizer were still rationed or controlled until 1950.

of raw materials, the value of goods or even the value of Reichsmarks in circulation before and after the reform.

Because the currency reform was in effect only in the three western occupied territories, and because the Soviets had prohibited the use of the Deutsche Mark in their zone, Marshal Sokolovsky announced a currency reform within his territory because he feared that his zone would be overwhelmed by a wave of old Reichsmarks of no value.

During this time, the Soviets began to control all traffic going into and out of Berlin, including the trucks of their 'Allies'. General Lucius D. Clay made it clear in a radio broadcast that the Americans would not give up Berlin. He said, 'If we want to defend Europe from being taken over by communism, we have to be strong. We can take any pressure and humiliation in Berlin short of war.'[5]

The Soviet attempt to prevent the political consolidation of western Germany by blockading Berlin ended in accelerating it. The success of the Berlin Airlift, in which the western Allies provided 2 million West Berlin civilians with food, fuel and clothing by air, not only increased co-operation among the Allies but also brought the western Allies and the Germans closer together. The airlift became a symbol of the German struggle for freedom against the Soviets. And the Americans, British and French found themselves working side-by-side with the Germans.

The Berlin blockade, during which 900 twin-engined aeroplanes landed and took off from Berlin's Tempelhof Airport every day, became a legend. Once again, Berlin had been the focal point of world politics, but what had changed were the adversaries.

The Berlin crisis showed how closely danger and chance flowed together: the danger of a third world war and the chance for a new-found trust between German citizens and western Allies. Especially impressive was the rejection by West Berliners of supplies offered by the East Berlin regime to bribe them to reject the western help. By the time the Soviets lifted the blockade on 12 May 1949, the war years' resentments had rapidly started to disappear and had given way to recognition of common political and economic interests, shared values and respect between the western Allies and the Germans.

Walter Köcher

In the summer of 1945, in one of the MGM cinemas in Berlin, the American weekly news had the headline, 'We won't yield to Soviet

---

[5] Clay, *Entscheidungen in Deutschland*, p. 401.

customs control'. The atmosphere in Berlin was tense. I visited Berlin from the Soviet occupation zone several times to meet with friends who had left the east to live in West Berlin, and the increasing harshness of the Soviet controls soon became apparent. Then something happened that many had feared: there was an air collision between a Soviet MIG and a British Viking transporter in the airspace over Berlin. Fourteen passengers died, among them two Americans. It was never determined whether or not the Russians had planned this collision to incite anger among the westerners and to test the tenacity of their will to control Berlin.

About the same time, there were rumours that General Clay was planning to send a trainload of supplies, accompanied by American soldiers to Berlin, through the Soviet occupation zone. We all knew that this would mean war. The political and psychological importance of Berlin has always been fascinating and, during that time, grew to be the focal point of world politics.

The psychological warfare continued when, shortly after the west had introduced its currency reform, the Soviets announced a currency reform for their own territories. It was poorly organized; the money did not reach the hands of the citizens living in the eastern part of the zone until four to six weeks after the announcement. The so-called 'Ostmark' (Eastmark) consisted merely of old Reichsmark notes on which coupons had been superimposed. We disparagingly called them 'wallpaper marks'.

The Allies had long feared that the introduction of any currency reform in Berlin would be disruptive, and therefore they had introduced the new money only in their areas outside Berlin proper. The Soviets proceeded to proclaim that their new Ostmark was valid throughout all sectors of Berlin. Only then did the western Allies introduce the Deutsche Mark to Berlin also. The Deutsche Mark notes for Berlin distributed by the western Allies were marked with a big 'B'. Occupied Germany now had three different currencies. Within the eastern occupied zone, possession of the western currency was forbidden, and violators were punished with prison and a hefty fine.

During the night of the 23–4 June 1948, Stalin made his position clear. All the lights in West Berlin went out when the Soviets cut off an electric plant that supplied West Berlin. On the 24th, Soviet troops cut off all road, canal and train connections to Berlin, thus beginning the blockade. The official argument from the Soviets was that there were 'technical problems', but the real reason was that the Soviets feared losing political control over parts of Berlin and wanted to prevent the formation of a democratic West Germany.

In the euphoria of victory over Hitler's regime, the western Allies had neglected to secure from the Soviets the right to use Soviet-controlled territory to gain access to Berlin. The only access to the old capital was by air. General Clay declared on the 24th, 'We have a right to stay in Berlin and we are going to make every effort to maintain that right'. British Foreign Minister Ernest Bevin said succinctly, 'We must stay'. Operation Vittles, the air lift, was to go into the history books as the largest air transport operation ever.

The planes, at first without radar, flew in supplies to the cut-off city every 30 seconds. The Americans and British turned into victory what everybody had thought would be a certain defeat of democracy. Through a harsh winter, Berlin was kept alive with coal, food and clothing. Most important to the people was that they were not abandoned, which had a tremendous psychological effect on the co-operation between the German citizens and the Anglo-Saxons and on the general confidence of the German people. The Allies, originally the adversaries, had become the protectors of Germany. Although the Soviets offered West Berlin citizens the opportunity to buy supplies in the eastern sector, fewer than 2 per cent of the population accepted. About a year later, Philip Jessup, representing the American side, and Jakov Malik, for the Soviet side, met in New York at the United Nations to announce the end of the blockade. I remember the American Radio Broadcast Channel RIAS (Radio in the American Sector) announced, 'At 8:00 p.m. on 12 May 1949, the Berlin blockade will be lifted'. People lined the streets to greet the western vehicles, mostly Jeeps, which had reached Berlin for the first time since the blockade had begun. The west had shown the Soviets their strength, but it would not be the last time that Berlin would be the focal point of east-west conflict.

Sergeant Cloyde Pinson

After returning from the war in North Africa and Italy as a member of the infantry, I was stationed in New Orleans. I was on recruiting duty for two years, on what they called DEML (detached enlisted men's list), in other words, never-never land. I wasn't really a member of the army or of the air force, but I was recruiting for everybody. When I was transferred at the end of 1947 to an air force base in Austin, Texas, I didn't know that I would soon be part of the Berlin Airlift or, as we were to call it, 'Operation Vittles'. Within days of my arrival in Texas, I became a member of the air force and was promoted to Sergeant-major when I was just 23. Three years after the war had ended, I found myself again on a boat to Europe. I had mixed feelings about the venture, like most of us on the ship.

Altogether, I believe, hundreds of Americans were involved in the Berlin Airlift. We knew that the planned introduction of the Marshall Plan for all four zones had failed. When this plan for the economic recovery of Europe had been announced, the Soviets had shown no interest, just as they had shown no interest in introducing a new monetary system. Nevertheless, the western occupying powers authorized issuance of new money. In response, the Soviets walked out of an Allied Control Council meeting in Berlin. I remember the headline saying, 'Soviets Protesting the London Conference'. They claimed the westerners had violated the Potsdam Agreement by undertaking far-reaching decisions on Germany without their participation. In June 1948, the Soviets objected strenuously to the introduction of the new western currency in the western sectors in Berlin. That was the beginning of the Berlin blockade. Around the same time, the first supply barge, which was part of the Marshall Plan, left the Texas harbour of Galveston to sail to Bordeaux. For good reasons, the Marshall Plan and the Berlin blockade had almost coincided.

The Soviets imposed a blockade on Berlin, a city surrounded by territory occupied by the Red Army and situated more than a hundred miles from the nearest western-occupied territory. The Soviets sealed off all highways, train connections and water canals to Berlin, which that city relied on for the delivery of food, fuel and coal, finished products and practically everything else.

The newspapers were full of discussion about what the Soviets were up to. In their communications with the western powers, the Soviets had openly claimed that the American, British and French sectors of the former German capital lay in their zone. The Soviet Marshal Vassily Danilovich Sokolovsky had designated himself as the military governor of all of Berlin.

We learned from one of our commanders during our week-long

boat trip to Europe that the western Allies had neglected to reach a written agreement with the Russians guaranteeing the westerners the use of rail lines, highways and canals between West Berlin and their occupation zones. The only way to reach Berlin was by air, and I was obviously going to be part of the mission.

The atmosphere on the boat was one of ambivalence. On the one hand, we were optimistic that our efforts would help the more than 2 million people of West Berlin to survive the blockade; on the other, we were pessimistic about the meaning of the sudden change in world politics. The concept of 'allies' had changed quickly. Within slightly less than 24 months, it seemed, it was the Soviets who were the 'adversaries', and no longer the Germans. Some even voiced the fear of the outbreak of a third world war over the Berlin blockade. In fact, some American and British officials had already advocated challenging the Red Army by sending a supply column, accompanied by tanks, along one of the Autobahns that linked Berlin to the western occupation zones. We all feared that a decision in that direction, as a test of will, could trigger another war. The Cold War would then have turned into a shooting match, which I definitely did not want to be a part of.

In September 1948, my troop arrived in Bremerhaven, well informed about what was going on in Berlin. At the port, there was nobody to meet us. I remember a row of sailors and soldiers hanging on the rail that afternoon, anxiously wondering what was awaiting us. Later in the afternoon, we received the order to board a troop train. During the night, we arrived at the British air force station on the outskirts of Bremerhaven. The unusual thing about the base was that it was as light as day and very busy. Planes were taking off every 30 seconds, soldiers were loading trucks, the maintenance shops were a beehive of activity, and the mess halls and clubs were open. The base was functioning just as if it were daytime. Operation Vittles was a 24-hour operation. Most of the loads were coal and food. Included in the cargo were Hershey chocolate bars, and milk powder for the babies. The commanding officer stood in the control tower with his stop watch, checking the timing of the planes.

They were old four-engine aeroplanes that had been used during the war. The pilots had to be superbly trained, because they had only three narrow air corridors to fly through to get to Berlin. The pilots had to be very careful to stay within the corridors; otherwise the

Russian fighters would have had an excuse to attack. Usually the planes came in from all corridors. They came in at a specified altitude and worked themselves into a landing pattern over Berlin's Tempelhof Airport, descending within its limits. If they strayed from the landing pattern, they could not get back in it, but had to take the next corridor out, get in line again and land, take off again and come back. To most, it seemed an impossible task to meet all the needs of more than 2 million people by airlift. But except for water, Berlin was supplied with everything by the airlift. Several times, I accompanied pilots on flights to Berlin. We dropped mostly clothes and other necessities, often by parachute onto fields cleared for that purpose. Sometimes, however, we had to land. It all depended on the cargo and on the flight pattern the pilots managed to come in on.

A high cost was paid for the airlift. I believe over 30 American, 40 British, and five German crew members lost their lives in air crashes. In the spring of 1949, almost a year after the time that the lights had gone out in Berlin, and after a severe winter, the Soviets lifted their blockade and restored land access to Berlin.

Thassilo Borchart

I remember vividly those twin-engined American planes dropping supplies, while hundreds of Germans applauded and waved, hardly able to believe that those same planes had been the enemy just four years earlier. We called them 'Rosinenbomber' (raisin bombers). At the time of the blockade I was 10 years old. I asked my mother why all the American potatoes were so uniformly round and big. I had never seen big potatoes like that before, nor had I ever seen or tasted powdered milk.

From 1945 to 1949 we knew that the Allies and the Soviet Union could not be reconciled. More than any other event, the Berlin blockade proved President Truman's worst fears of Soviet aggression. Overnight the Soviets had sealed off not only the transportation to and from Berlin but also 19 waterworks, cutting the city off from the outside world. General Lucius Clay became Berlin's hero.

Just a few days after the Soviets had implemented their blockade, a number of communist demonstrators pushed their way into the Allied Forces Administration, which was located in the eastern part of the city. Within days, the council was moved to the western part. During that time in Berlin, there were few jokes, for everybody knew the situation was far too serious. But I still have one pamphlet that was distributed throughout the western part of the city:

> When entering the border area between the east and west it is forbidden to inhale air to prevent any western air from going to the east and any eastern air from going to the west. The administration also has undertaken acts to prevent west winds from entering the east and vice versa. The Easter bunny will still work in the western territories of Berlin this year. Next year the bunny will be renamed 'Wester bunny'.

Unfortunately, the situation in Berlin was anything but a joke. Without any help from the west, the citizens of West Berlin would have had to rely on eastern help, and that was exactly what Moscow was waiting for so it could annex the rest of the city. Eight weeks after the blockade began, the Mayor of Berlin, Professor Ernst Reuter, gave a speech to a large group of people demonstrating against the blockade, among whom was my mother. Part of his speech became so famous that many Berliners memorized it. My mother made us remember the following: 'People of the world, people of America, England, France, look at this city! You may not and cannot abandon it or its citizens. Giving up Berlin would mean giving up a world, giving up values, giving up yourself.'

During that demonstration, an angry group of people tried to tear down from the Brandenburg Gate the red flag that had been flying over it since the Soviets had come to Berlin in 1945. One boy was killed. What followed was the step-by-step division of Germany. The westerners had no other choice but to follow their determination to at least secure democracy within their territories. Beginning in the west, then in the east, two new Germanies were produced. At the time, they seemed mere improvisations, but they proved to be durable.

Chapter Four

Comrades and Stalinism

Walter Ulbricht symbolizes the triumph and tragedy of a veteran Stalinist subaltern who had been Moscow's key functionary since April 1945, weeks before Germany's capitulation. He was the first and most influential dictator of East Germany for 22 consecutive years following the early post-war years, and left an indelible imprint on the country.

In the end, he was replaced by the same brutal methods he had used on his adversaries. As head of the SED and as party general secretary, he functioned as the satrap of Stalin. Under Ulbricht's administration from 1949 to 1971, party purges became excessive, resulting in the expulsion of 150,000 rank-and-file members on grounds of various ideological failings, especially 'social democratism'. The purge also reached into the SED top echelons, where individual communist leaders fell victim to 're-velations of Stalin's show trials'. Even today, it is not known how many people disappeared in prisons or Soviet camps because of political disagreements in the initial post-war years between 1945 and 1949. Ulbricht's biographer, Carola Stern, called him a 'boring man who made millions of lives miserable'.

Born in Saxony, Germany in 1893 as the son of a tailor, Ulbricht grew up in a workers' milieu and joined the SPD (Socialist Party) when he was 19. He was one of the first members to join the German Communist Party (KPD) after it was initially formed in 1918. Ulbricht rose in the KPD ranks as a full-time functionary and sat in the Reichstag of the Weimar Republic as a party deputy from 1928 to 1933. Subservient to the Soviet Union and a simplistic interpreter of Marx and Engels's ideology, he looked for close contacts among the Soviet party's *apparatchik*. Thus, his exile to the Soviet Union during the Third Reich seemed logical.

Ulbricht returned to Berlin well trained eight weeks before the German capitulation, with the task of overseeing re-establishment of the Communist Party in Germany and 'domestic Sovietization'.

As early as 1946, Ulbricht and his top SED functionaries were speaking openly about the transitory character of the Soviet zone's antifascist democratic order. During the following years, Ulbricht proclaimed the idea more insistently and coupled it with an assertion of the SED's claim to play the leading role during the 'transition'. Such claims obviously enjoyed the Soviet occupation authorities' full endorsement.

Among a group of trained Soviet men who had been flown into Berlin from Moscow in the spring of 1945 and who were known as 'Gruppe Ulbricht', were Wolfgang Leonard, Wilhelm Pieck, Peter Florin and Anton Ackermann. Ulbricht's order for them was 'It has to look democratic, but we have to control the situation'.[1] Eight weeks after their arrival, the German Communist Party was founded with the support of the Soviet occupation powers. The Gruppe Ulbricht broke up, and Ulbricht and Pieck took leading roles in the new party, which worked towards a union of the KPD with the SPD. A year later, against heavy protest from German socialists, the SPD was forced to join the KPD.

German socialist Otto Grothewohl surrendered to the power of the Soviet occupation authorities and was publicly asked to shake hands with communist Wilhelm Pieck. This symbolic handshake later became the emblem of the new SED party. Two 'bourgeois' parties, the CDU (Christian Democrats) and LPD (Liberal Party of Germany), were reduced to complete political impotence. While both parties continued their separate organizational existence, neither enjoyed a shred of political independence. Their existence was a camouflage for the one-party system that really started to exist in the Soviet occupation zone. More importantly, they developed into a kind of transmission belt to sectors of the population relatively inaccessible to direct penetration by the SED.

The wave of imprisonment of non-communist politicians and protesters increased to a point where many citizens could see no alternative to leaving the Soviet occupation zone in order to preserve their freedom. Many others still believed at that time that the Soviet occupation zone and Soviet authority were just provisional.

Systematically, between 1945 and 1949, the SED was transformed into a 'party of new type', a Leninist party.[2] Centralized zonal administrative structures were developed to secure communist control. Foremost was the German Economic Commission (DWK), established in 1947 for the co-ordination of economic planning. The DKW was staffed solely with communists, thus bringing the SED into control of a quasi-governmental apparatus covering the entire Soviet occupation zone long before the formal establishment of the German Democratic Republic.

The delay in proclaiming a separate East Germany was intended by the Soviets to make the formation of the GDR look like an inevitable reaction to the establishment of the Federal Republic by West German

---

[1] Leonard, Das kurze Leben der DDR, p. 11.
[2] Ibid, p. 377.

'separatists' and Anglo Saxon 'imperialists'. Stalin and the German group led by Ulbricht also wanted to present themselves as fighters for Germany's national unity. To accomplish those ends, a Volkskongress (People's Congress) was established by the Soviet occupation zone in December 1947. The Congress simultaneously beat the drums for national unity—Soviet style—and prepared the way for the formation of a separate communist state in East Germany.

Starting in the spring of 1948, the People's Congress furnished the necessary constitutional groundwork and provided a pseudo-parliamentary façade for what was to follow. By May 1949, all that remained was for the Volksrat (People's Council), an offspring of the parent People's Congress, to transform itself into the Volkskammer, a provisional East German legislature. This occurred on 7 October 1949, the day the establishment of the German Democratic Republic was officially proclaimed. The German people living in the Soviet occupation zone were as overwhelmed by the events as the western Allies were: although by 1949 over a million people had left the Soviet occupation zone to start new lives in the western zones, the rest, 17 million people, stayed behind in the hope and belief that Germany would soon reunite under a democratic leadership.

West Germany's Chancellor Konrad Adenauer officially protested against the formation of East Germany as a distinct nation, declaring that, 'The Soviet occupation power does not give the German people the right to freedom. What is happening over there now is not the will of the citizens, nor is it legitimate. For that reason, until the reunification of Germany, the FDR is the only legitimate government of the German people.' East Germany would not overcome its status as an international pariah for well over two decades, during which only the Soviet Union and a few other communist-ruled countries gave the separate state diplomatic recognition.

Margarethe Fuchs

I have very often asked myself whether the developments in the Soviet-occupied territory during the years 1945 to 1949 had been planned by the Soviet leaders, or whether they were merely a reaction to the West German constitution in 1949 and the behaviour of the western Allies. The truth probably lies somewhere in between.

Looking back further to 1944, the Soviets' clear priority then was to work together with the western Allies to destroy German fascism, to secure Russian-occupied territory in eastern Europe with legit-imate peace agreements, and to gain 10 million DM in reparation money. They also wanted to continue as one of the four powers con-trolling the mineral-rich Ruhrgebiet in the western part of Germany. An additional goal was to make the Communist Party a contender for a majority role in Germany.

The Soviets' hopes for that last goal were dashed when, during the elections in 1945 in Austria and Hungary, it became obvious that the Communist Party would never be anything more than a minority player in free elections. That fact was proved again during the first and only free election held in the Soviet zone in September 1946, when the SED competed with non-communist parties and fell short of the majority. Thereafter, the SED avoided contested elections.

Within the first months of their occupation, the Soviets' priorities changed; working together with the other Allies became less import-ant than securing Soviet-occupied territory in eastern Europe and Germany. In 1945, Soviet leaders followed a zigzag political course that I believe intentionally left Germans and the leaders of the other occupation powers in the dark about the Soviets' intentions.

I believe the formation of the GDR was not a result of or reaction to the formation of the Federal German Republic, as many have said. The West German establishment just affected the form and timing of the separation. It is common knowledge that the GDR was built with the help of communists who had fled from Germany to the Soviet Union during the war and who returned to the occupied zones as early as 1945. Some came back as civilians, others as soldiers of the Red Army or commanders of Soviet prison camps.

In the Soviet zone the constellation of competing democratic parties soon gave way to arrangements designed to produce political results desired by the Red Army. By permitting political activity in their zone with the condition that all parties join together in an 'anti-fascist bloc', the Soviets forced all other parties into a permanent coalition with the KPD. Since the bloc determined the ground rules for political activity in the Soviet zone, it placed tight limits on the other parties' independence and effectively excluded an anticommun-ist alliance.

Alarmed at the signs that the KPD lacked popularity, the German communists also pressed for a merger with the larger Social Demo-cratic Party. Many true socialist leaders had been put in jail prior to the merger for voicing their concern about the KPD's subservience to Stalin's totalitarian regime and the German communist leaders' reliance on Lenin's methods. The SPD, led by Grothewohl, finally agreed to the merger in April 1946. The Socialist Unity Party (SED) was formed. The new party completely overshadowed the non-Marxist parties of the Soviet zone.

In his first speech as a member of the new SED party, Grothewohl stressed that the SED would bring security to the eastern zone which would make the presence of the bayonets of the Red Army unnecessary. That was obviously a lie. Soldiers of the Red Army were stationed between the Oder and Neisse rivers until 1992. Many of the original founders of the SED disappeared over time, having fled to the west or having been denounced as 'enemies of the party'. Of the official 14 members of the first Central Committee, only three were still active in 1948: Walter Ulbricht, Otto Grothewohl and Wilhelm Pieck.

Thassilo Borchart

In the autumn of 1949, two German states existed, each mirroring the political system it represented. Stalin had called the founding of the GDR a 'turning point in Europe's history'. But it really was a defeat for the Soviets, who had hoped to expand Stalinism beyond their current territory and into Central Europe. It was also a defeat for the Allies and the German wish for a unified Germany. East Germany—the GDR—included Mecklenburg, Saxony, Brandenburg and Saxony-Anhalt. East Prussia, Pomerania and East Brandenburg, as well as Silesia, states that had earlier belonged to Germany, had gone to Poland and the Soviet Union. For the division of Germany the old principle confirmed itself again, *Cuius regio eius ideologia*: the ruler and the ruling system go hand in hand.

The options, other than a divided Germany, were few. I strongly believe that had Germany not been divided at that time, the Soviet Union would have used military power to expand its territory, or others—with the assistance of the communists—would have made an undivided country ungovernable by churning up the administration and raising cost of living. But the Allies and the German representatives quite correctly feared the worst from Stalin's plans.

To some degree, the division of Germany probably also resulted from the German political representatives' lack of commitment to keeping the country together. Looking back, they belittled the significance of the division of Germany at that time by characterizing it as only provisional.

In 1945 Ulbricht was the man of the hour. He used typically dictatorial methods to reach his goals. In the beginning, for example, he employed tactics such as smuggling KPD members into democratically oriented parties such as the CDU and SPD. Those party spies in the long run made possible the degradation of other parties into mere extensions of the KPD. The Soviet occupation authorities, of course, worked hand in hand with those methods. In the early spring of 1946, for example, Heinrich Hoffmann, who was a socialist candidate in Thuringia, and a colleague of his, Otto Buchwitz, were the first to officially advocate a political union between the KPD and SPD. This was unheard of previously and nobody really knew within the Socialist Party who had given them the right to make such public statements. Both, as we learned later, were tools of the KPD who had been implanted into the SPD. Initially, however, the Communist Party denied any intention of imposing a Soviet-style regime and promised to work towards the creation of a parliamentary democracy.

The KPD had promised that there would be a democratic vote about the possible merger between the Communist Party and the SPD. Nevertheless, the Soviet occupation authorities forbade such a vote. It never took place. The vote took place only in the western parts of Berlin, where 2,937 of 32,447 SPD members voted for the immediate union of the KPD and SPD, while 5,559 were against it. The majority of the socialists voted for a working liaison but raised their voices against a firm and immediate unity. Many of those who voted for a loose working relationship with the KPD saw in their close ties to the communists a safeguard against repetition of the calamitous period between 1933 and 1945. However, the truly socialist-oriented politicians never intended to effect a complete unity.

Soon after the SED was formed, the Soviets announced the first local elections in their zone. The SED was competing for votes with the CDU and the LPD. The SED attained a majority, but that apparent show of strength stemmed from the absence of non-Marxist parties on the ballot. The Soviet occupation powers had conveniently delayed the certification of non-Marxist political organizations, which therefore were not represented. There was a protest, and the election was repeated a month later. By then the SED was confident it would win, but in reality it fell short of attaining majorities in the Soviet zone. These were the last free elections in the Soviet zone, and the SED avoided any further contested elections.

The promise that an equal number of socialists and communists would be represented in the party was broken within months. The actual ratio was seven communists for every two socialists. These developments within the party resulted not only in the oppression of socialist opinions but also in a purge along party lines. One case that comes to mind is the kidnapping of Robert Bialek, who was abducted toward the end of the 1950s. A young socialist in 1946, he was given the task of building a communist youth organization, Freie Deutsche Jugend (FDJ)—ironically meaning Free German Youth. However, disheartened by undemocratic developments in the SED, he voiced his anger and disagreement with the official party line in several radio broadcasts. I think he worked with RIAS (Radio in the American Sector). He protested about the fake elections, the abolition of workers' rights, the contradictions between Marxist theories and SED reality. Bialek fled to the west as early as 1948. Years later, I believe in 1956, Bialek was still an active protester against the then well-established SED regime when he was abducted from his house in West Berlin and chloroformed. What happened to him afterwards, I don't know. Bialek is just one among hundreds of victims of Ulbricht's Leninist methods.

What had at first looked like a bad dream that would resolve itself during the years after the war was to become a permanent nightmare. Eastern Europe—including the Soviet occupation zone in Germany—was to be patterned after the Soviet system politically, economically, ideologically and militarily.

Part Two

A Land Divided 1949–1961

Man only can enslave man.
Simone Weil

Chapter Five

The Stasi and Its Apparatus

Every Tuesday afternoon two old men met in the conference room of the dark, grey Central Committee building in East Berlin at the Werderscher Markt. Protected by a tightly woven net of security, the two men, Erich Mielke, the 85-year-old head of the secret police (Stasi), who was a four-star general and the recipient of more than 250 decorations, and Erich Honecker, the 81-year-old leader of the GDR, conferred about the state of East German security. For years Mielke's report to Honecker was more or less the same week after week. 'Everything is under the control of the Stasi.' Mielke vigorously established the GDR's secret police in 1957 and quickly developed it into a ubiquitous army of spies and denunciators. Undercover agents spied on close relatives and surreptitiously poisoned relationships between families and friends, carrying out 'operative orders to split, paralyse and isolate negative enemy elements working against the interests of the GDR'.[1] The 'enemy elements'—critics of communism and other free thinkers—caught in the Stasi's web were trailed, punished and/or indoctrinated outside the bounds of any legal systems or standards. Individual freedom for the pursuit of happiness simply did not exist within the GDR. Citizens had to accept the fact that anything they said or did—even the expression of emotion—was probably being watched, recorded and subjected to political scrutiny. Almost 6 million individuals' dossiers were found in the Stasi archives, one for every two adults in the GDR. The dossiers occupy 125 miles of shelves. The Stasi created a state within a state and produced 'adapted' citizens who were obedient and hypocritical. The regime turned hundreds of thousands of people into denunciators; many young people became opportunists. Critics of the regime and the system were declared criminals. Those who were trapped in the arms of the Stasi often had no chance of survival other than to become adapted party members.

Fear was the system's most powerful tool. Files retrieved from the Stasi headquarters—i. e., those that were not stolen or hastily transported to the Soviet Union—paint a horrifying picture of the realities of the

---

[1] Gill and Schröter, *Das Ministerium für Staatssicherheit*, p. 28.

GDR's socialist political system. According to a recent account, the Stasi employed 100,000 full-time agents and used some 300,000 so-called 'informal informers' (Informelle Mitarbeiter). East Germany had the highest per capita rate of spies, tapped telephones and bugged living rooms and bedrooms in the world. Indeed, before the Stasi documents came to light, even the harshest critics of the GDR system had refused to believe the true extent of the spying.

In addition to its legions of agents and informers, the Stasi had a weapon supply worthy of a military armoury: 124,593 pistols, 76,592 automatic hand guns, 3,611 rifles and 766 machine guns. The Stasi also owned 2,037 buildings; some of them were apartments, others were income-producing land holdings. This Moloch was supported with 3.6 billion Deutsche Marks annually from the GDR domestic budget; in short, the system was supported by its own victims.

In the last resort the Stasi controlled virtually everything and everyone. No important party decision was made without Stasi approval. Because decisions might later be questioned and have to be defended, every detail, no matter how small, became important. Anti-regime graffiti found in subways or on walls were photographed and filed. Every street rumour was registered by agents and circulated throughout the upper levels of the secret bureaucracy. If somebody was to join the army, or was chosen by the politburo to head a district, or was applying for an entry exam for a college or university, everything and anything that could be known about the person had to be checked and approved by the Stasi. A negative report could be disastrous. For example, many free-thinking economists and scientists were not allowed to work at their professions because the Stasi decided they harboured 'dubious attitudes towards the party'. Children were denied access to appropriate schools and universities because of their parents' 'unacceptable political conduct'. Teachers even filled out forms on children—some as young as 9 years old—who expressed views critical of the state or favourable to the west. Even after he had been gone for 20 years, making a critical comment about Walter Ulbricht could lead to the denial of a travel pass.

Informers used a 101-point check-list to compile facts about their victims. The resulting report included information about a person's attitude towards work, about his or her friends and lovers, and any contacts with authorities. It described the subject's apartment, hobbies, traits and language skills, and detailed his or her favourite foods and sexual behaviour and numerous other aspects of personal life. Such information was at times obtained legally through informal conversations with a subject's friends and acquaintances, but most often through illegal means, such as break-ins, which usually were meticulously planned. The subject of the investigation received an official order to visit a doctor or a high-ranking party member, during which time agents scheduled the break-in. At the beginning of the illegal entry, agents took pictures of the quarters with a polaroid camera, which enabled them to replace books, diaries and picture frames in exactly their original locations at the end of their search. The agents were looking for such items as western European newspapers, anti-government political leaflets, letters containing criticism of the government, and anything that might hint at a planned escape. If questionable material was found, the victim was detained within days or even hours. During the 1950s and 1960s, dissidents often vanished to the Soviet Union where they were imprisoned for years in dark cells or executed. In later years, opponents of the socialist ideology were put into mental hospitals and brainwashed. [2]

The heart and brain of the Stasi was Department XX, which was solely responsible for detecting citizens who opposed the government. The arm of Department XX reached far beyond the boundaries of the GDR into other Warsaw pact states such as Czechoslovakia and Yugoslavia.

Informers were everywhere and could be anybody—waiters, doctors, priests, soldiers, housewives, neighbours or friends. Informers were even placed in the prisons. The incentive offered to the thousands of agents and informal informers was small in comparison to what could be expected from them: informers were paid a regular salary of $75 per week and had the privilege of owning a car and going shopping in the so-called 'Leiterläden', which offered western gourmet foods for western currency. The hundreds of Stasi officers received both special training and special privileges at a university that only few people knew about and that collectively constituted a forbidden city with its own barbers, grocers and sports facilities. Other privileges for high-ranking agents included travel to the west and ownership of houses, as well as access to otherwise unaffordable recreation such as horseback riding.

The growth of the Stasi's control apparatus increased in direct proportion to the SED regime's fear of losing control over the population. The Stasi operation grew rapidly, from 50,000 informers and agents in the 1970s to almost 100,000 full-time agents by the end of 1989. The main reason for that tremendous increase was the SED's fear of not being able to maintain the status quo, because information sources from the west, such as television and radio, were challenging the state-prescribed 'truth'. Willy Brandt's *Ostpolitik* made the border more transparent, at least for retired people over the age of 65. As the Stasi grew, competition was encouraged between agents, each of whom had to supervise up to 35 informers. Agents scheduled from 50 to 60 meetings per month with their

[2] International Society for Human Rights, *Menschenrechte in der Welt*, pp. 29–54.

informers. The goal was the perfection of an espionage network that ultimately would cover each and every citizen in the GDR.

The Stasi's criminal conduct did not stop at its country's borders. Today it is known that the Stasi was involved in several murder cases in West Germany as well as the largest postal robbery, and several abductions that took place there.

Markus Wolf, the former head of East Germany's spy service, employed the most notorious agent, Günter Guillaume, who spied for years in the chancellory and his unmasking led to Willy Brandt's resignation in 1974. Another affair which was tied to the Stasi after opening up their files was the Kissling affair which almost toppled the government in 1984. Manfred Woerner, West German secretary of defence, sacked army general Guenther Kissling after reports from the Militärischer Abwehrdienst (Military Counter Intelligence) that he was secretly homosexual and therefore a potential security risk. Kissling was cleared and Woerner offered his resignation. A victory for the Stasi who was behind the affair was only avoided because Chancellor Kohl did not accept the resignation. These affairs and others show how riddled Bonn's spy network was with moles from the east trying to embarrass the West German government.

Two discoveries came as a surprise even to West German intelligence agents. One was the discovery of documents that laid out plans for the establishment of concentration camps throughout East Germany. The documents list in detail 'specific and operative preventive measures to seize, hold, isolate' and under certain conditions also 'liquidate' up to one hundred thousand persons with a 'hostile negative basic attitude' (*feindlich negative Grundeinstellung*). A 1986 list of potential East German concentration camp inmates included 'reactionary church members', 'applicants for exit visas', 'co-signers of petitions', and 'decadent youth'. The other surprise involved spectacular charges against the Stasi related to its reported support of the Red Army Faction. The Stasi was charged with training Red Army Faction members to use the antitank grenades they fired in a failed attempt to kill General Frederick Kroesen, commander of the American forces in Europe, in 1981. The Stasi is also believed to have trained Red Army fighters who bombed the American air base at Ramstein around the same time. Just months after the Wall fell, it was learned that over a dozen members of the Red Army Faction over the past 15 years—among them Susanne Albrecht who was involved in killing her godfather, Jürgen Ponto, the head of Dresdner Bank—had found hideouts in the GDR when Interpol and the West German police were looking for them.[3]

---

[3] International Society for Human Rights, *Der Stasi Staat*, pp. 48–58.

Mielke, the man who together with Honecker built, and until the end ran, the communist bloc's most pervasive internal security network, was widely seen as being responsible for the mixture of blackmail and fear that controlled East German society. Even now, several years after the fall of the Wall, new knowledge of Stasi methods and secret members of the organization pops up. It may take years to examine the millions of files and expose their dark secrets. There have been calls to 'draw a line under the past' and even to burn the entire Stasi archive in the name of 'national reconciliation'. Others, like Protestant clergymen Joachim Gauck and David Gill, both former Stasi victims and in charge of opening up the Stasi files, insist that there can be *no* 'national reconciliation, except in truth' and that they 'will spare no effort to expose all of the truth, even when it is unpleasant'. [4]

Beyond the question of guilt and responsibility, both East and West Germans have wondered whether the great diarist of the Weimar period, Harry Kessler, was at least partially right when he complained, 'Such petty principles of which there were more than two dozen in Germany before the First World War, among them servility and obsequiousness, spread like a pestilence. It is because of these petty principles that Germany is the most cultured and the most spineless European nation.' [5]

Johannes Fuchs

It was the summer of 1960. As usual, I left my house in Jena in the early morning to get ready for surgery. I was a little early on this particular morning and had a chance to chat with the head operating nurse, who during the conversation pointed out two guys in the waiting room for outpatients. 'They have been asking for you,' she said. 'One of them speaks Russian.' I ignored them, slipped into my robe, talked briefly to my assistant and went into surgery.

At the end of the procedure, when everybody else had left the operating room, my nurse whispered without looking at me, 'Do you know that your friend left tonight?' She mentioned the name of my closest friend; we had gone to high school together, studied medicine together and now worked at the same university. He headed the department of internal medicine, and I was the head of the ophthalmology department. We were godfathers to one another's children, and we had spent many nights discussing politics together since the

[4] Gill and Schröter, *Das Minsterium für Staatssicherheit*, p. 13.
[5] Harry Kessler, *Tagebücher 1919–1937*, Paris, 1962.

unsuccessful uprising against the SED in 1956. Yet, he had never mentioned any plans to leave. For a moment I was in shock. I had seen him, his wife and his three little children just the previous night.

There were reports about people who had tried to cross over the 'green border' and had been shot at or caught and thrown into prison. It was common knowledge that refugees who were caught at the border, which was harshly controlled, would end up in prison for 'attempting to leave the Soviet occupation zone'. Children travelling along would be separated and sent to different orphanages. A few other friends and many colleagues had successfully made it into West Berlin and the western zone, and I was desperately hoping this friend and his family had made it too.

It was the rule not to tell even relatives about plans if you were intending to leave, because anybody who knew would be charged with collaboration in a potential interrogation. Even knowing about somebody's plans to escape was an offence.

I left the operating room and was startled by the two guys from the waiting room, who came charging towards me. They didn't introduce themselves, but with all my other patients listening, just asked, 'Do you know where your friend the professor is?'

'Of course,' I replied, playing dumb. 'He is doing the same thing I intend to do now; he's taking care of his patients.'

'He is not; he left!,' one guy in a dark suit said.

'Well, then you know more than I do. I was planing to have a beer with him tonight,' I abruptly countered.

'You have to come with us,' they said.

A murmur went through the room. The waiting patients started to whisper. My guardian angel was a comrade who was sitting on a bench holding his handkerchief over a bad eye injury. He said: 'Let the doctor take care of me first.' They looked at him and nodded their heads in respect, since he was obviously higher-ranking than they were. I walked into my examining room and had the comrade with the urgent eye injury called in first. He was a nice guy, apart from being a self-proclaimed communist.

'Doctor,' he said, 'I like you, but did you know anything about the professor's intent?

'No,' I answered.

'You aren't leaving as well, are you?' he enquired.

I said I wasn't—and said it firmly, which wasn't too easy. 'Keep those guys away from me. I 'm busy today, as you can see,' I added as I put a bandage over his left eye. 'I don't have time for your interrogation games.'

'Sure,' he replied. 'Thanks for taking me in first.' He smiled and left.

In the evening as I walked back home from the clinic, two shadows followed me but didn't approach me. They followed me for the rest of the week, in the morning and the evening, every day. Our two dogs, two little dachshunds, were usually waiting for me in the yard when I got home. At the end of one day one of the dogs got out through the gate and ran barking down the street chasing the men who were following me. The next morning I found the dog lying dead in the front yard—he had been poisoned.

That my best friend had left made me seriously consider taking the same step. But somehow I still could not imagine that the area where I had grown up, studied and taught at the university, and where my children had been born, would be governed by a communist regime for a long time. I also didn't want to give up on the idea that by working together with others who were yearning for democratic government, I could help to change the political situation for the better.

Apart from the moral obligation to stay and try to change things, and the roots that obviously kept me in Jena, I knew that starting from scratch in the west at the age of 42 wouldn't be easy either. If we were to go, we would have to leave everything behind: house, art, belongings that had been in the family for a long time, everything except maybe a few very personal items that would fit in a trouser pocket. The system had not yet become so unbearable for me that I was ready to give up everything that I had worked so hard for since the end of the war. After the children had gone to bed, I had endless discussions, sometimes even quarrels about our future with my wife, who was more inclined to leave. She insisted that even the children were suffering in one way or another from the regime. The oldest children, then between 10 and 14 years old, had already had to learn the 'International', the communist anthem. They had to wear red scarves around their necks, also a communist symbol, when they went to school. The schools made a systematic effort to distance children from their 'capitalistic' parents who had a higher education and turn the children into 'workers of the proletarian state'. Yet, I told my wife over and over again, that I could use my contacts at the university and my opportunities to lecture there to turn the political situation in a different direction. And I did, to a certain degree.

There were very close ties among the people in the eastern sector who opposed the SED regime. By 1960 we routinely helped one another even if we weren't personally acquainted. For example, I remember a patient who was brought to me in handcuffs by two Stasi members. I asked them to undo the handcuffs, insisting that I wouldn't treat a patient whose hands and feet were tied. I also asked the two to wait outside. While I removed a small splinter from the man's eye, I asked him why he was being held by the secret police. He answered, 'I told a nasty joke about Ulbricht, and the wrong people were listening.' I offered him the back door to flee. 'No, Doctor,' he said. 'That's very nice of you, but I would have to punch you unconscious so they wouldn't wonder if you were my accomplice.' 'Anyway, I think they will let me go within the next week or so,' he added.

Among my assistants was a young doctor who had been with me for only a short time. He seemed very nice. Within a few weeks after he started, he gave me subtle hints that he was ready to leave the Soviet zone: he made remarks about how other people had left or mentioned how much easier certain things would be in the west. At that time, I had decided that eventually I would also leave with my whole family, but I hadn't yet set an actual date. I was still hesitating, probably still hoping for political change. The young assistant became more and more assertive every day, until finally he asked me openly if I could help him to get to West Berlin. Looking back, I should have noticed that this was an unusual request, but at the time it didn't rub me the wrong way. He asked me if I could bring some of his personal things, such as documents and his birth certificate, to a certain meeting point. His request made sense, because getting caught with his own personal papers would have been viewed by the Stasi as a sure sign that he was attempting to leave the eastern zone. I on the other hand, being his supervisor, could say that I wanted to start a file at home on my assistants or that I just wanted to review the papers.

Fortunately, my wife had an inkling that something was wrong. She couldn't put her finger on it, since she liked the young man and thought he seemed trustworthy. Anyway, my wife and I discussed what we would both say in the event that somebody should stop me and question me. Our story was that I was planning a congress meeting and reviewing personal documents of assistants to put together a programme and curriculum vitae for it.

The date and time were set for the meeting with my assistant. I got in my car with all his papers under my arm. We were supposed to meet in a very quiet side street close to Berlin, which was a good two-hour drive away. He was waiting for me when I got there. It had started to get dark and there was nobody else, no car, nothing around. We briefly greeted each other and I was handing him the papers when suddenly two men sprang out of the bushes with pistols in their hands shouting, 'What are you doing there?' They handcuffed both of us and made us walk a good way into the forest to where their car was parked. We were brought to Königswuster-hausen, where the Stasi had a central interrogation building I had heard of. We were put into separate cells. It began to dawn on me that the whole thing had been a set-up. For two days I answered the same questions over and over again.

I insisted on my congress story. Later, I learned that my wife had been interrogated at home at the same time. They could have found a reason to arrest me and put me in prison, but since doctors had become scarce in the GDR, I presumed they would let me go.

Within a couple of days, my wife and I, our newborn baby and our two older children left during a stormy night. It was raining cats and dogs. We had told our older children that we were going to see their grandfather in West Berlin just for the weekend. At that time, Christmas 1960, it was still possible to get to West Berlin, but usually only with a permit and without the whole family. We had locked the house and had taken just a few personal belongings and valuables with us. It was a very strange feeling knowing that this would be the last time that we would close the front door, leaving everything behind. It took us a good two hours to get to the border. We saw the bright lights of the border guardhouse at Glienecke Bridge from afar. We were all very tense. My nine-year-old son Michael just asked one more time, if we were really going to see grandfather. I knew that he felt I hadn't told him the truth.

The thing that worried me the most was that we had to split up the family, because crossing the border as a whole family would have been suspicious. I had heard of families who had been caught, the parents ending up in prison and the children in various orphanages. Nevertheless, we had to take the risk. I sent my wife, my oldest daughter and the newborn baby first. Michael and I stayed in the car waiting and watching. We saw the little group walking off in the rain and than they were gone. After a while, we saw a car coming from the other side and illuminated by its headlights we saw my wife and the kids crossing the bridge. They were safely in the west already.

We waited another 20 to 25 minutes. Then I took my son by the hand, locked the car and started walking. Just seconds later, a Volkspolizist (member of the People's Police) approached us. He was soaking wet just like us. Before he could even say anything, I said, 'Is it okay to park the car here for 24 hours? Can you have an eye on it while we are gone? We'll be back tomorrow.' He just nodded and walked on. The border guard didn't even look at us, just waved us through. We were walking towards freedom.

In the west we boarded an airplane from Tempelhof to Bayreuth (Bavaria), where we stayed with friends who had earlier settled at the university clinic in Bayreuth until I found an opportunity to open my own practice.

We literally had left behind everything, but mainly the taste of a very bitter medicine and the question, why didn't we leave earlier?

Ulrike Poppe

I had not been allowed to study psychology as I was not organized in the FDJ. After I finished high school, I spent some time working in children's homes, taught disabled children or helped out in clinics for addicts. All those occupations were considered below status as in the former GDR everything that wasn't perfect didn't fit into the picture of real existing socialism. In other words, addicts or disabled people were not talked about and definitely should not be part of public knowledge. Strangely enough, although I was kind of an outcast because of my interests in the needy, I was still approached by the Stasi with the request to work for them. One morning, I received a note that an anonymous charge had been brought against my professional conduct. I was requested to come to a certain police station upon receiving the note. When I arrived at the police station, I had to wait for a while in an almost empty room until two men arrived, and without saying much, showed me their identification, which said, 'State security'. Although I was in my twenties, I wasn't stupid enough not to know who they were. A brief, professional interrogation began. They asked me about my work, some friends and co-workers. After an hour or so, they said, 'We are working for the Stasi and KGB and have found evidence that the West German intelligence service has information on you and some of your friends. For your own protection, we have to know why.' I hadn't a clue. They pressured me to have dinner with them the following night in a well-known hotel in Berlin. When I asked why I should have dinner with them, one just answered, 'Don't ask questions, just tell what you like to eat and drink and we'll make sure you have a good time.' Looking back today, it was most degrading to be taken for somebody that could be lured into working for the Stasi just because one is offered a decent meal at an elegant place. Several times throughout the interrogation, I was told and warned not to tell anybody about our meeting or that I knew that they would be with the Stasi and working for the KGB. My head was hammering to think of a way to get out of the dinner 'invitation' and unconsciously I asked for a contact telephone number which they willingly volunteered. After reassuring them that I would see them the next evening, they let me go.

Late the next afternoon, I left a message that I was sick and couldn't make it. Since they had approached me, I had spent the entire time telling everybody about the meeting, giving detailed descriptions of the men and saying that they had invited me to dinner. I hoped that my gossiping would protect me from further contacts. And it worked. Within days, the charges were dropped; I didn't hear from them again. My talking made me an unsuitable informer.

Around the same time, I met some people who were part of a literature group which had access to forbidden books. Maybe as a reaction to this brief intermezzo with the Stasi, I became politically more interested. Via this literature group, we formed some years later a group of people that publicly opposed women's mandatory service in the Army. In 1979 the GDR wanted to pass a law that women should serve in the Army and in case of war should be ready to serve. Together with Bärbel Bohley, a painter and illustrator, I collected a list of signatures of women who objected to the law. It was surprising how quickly we had several hundred signatures together even though everybody who volunteered assistance knew that potential interrogations or even arrests could follow. I think we could have easily collected several thousand signatures, but we didn't intend to create a power struggle between the women and the regime. We send the letter to Honecker requesting that women should be given the option to refuse to serve.

The western press had covered our actions and within months we had contacts with other peace movements around the world. We couldn't travel, but they came to us. Obviously, by that time I had a shadow following me everywhere I went. My husband, a physicist, lost his job without explanation. The only work they allowed him to get was as a stoker. From time to time when I was alone at home I got visits from the Stasi. One morning around six o'clock the door bell rang. A voice yelled, 'Open the door immediately.' I knew it was the Stasi and answered that I had to put some clothes on first. Impatiently, they kicked in the door. Two men, accompanied by a woman under whose supervision I got dressed, started to ask me all kinds of questions, such as, where was my husband and with whom had I dined the night before.

Finally, they said that I had to come along. I just said, 'I cannot leave the apartment with a kicked-in door. Things will get stolen.' I firmly said, 'I'm not leaving until the door is repaired to a point that I can lock this place'. Surprisingly enough, both men actually knelt down in an attempt to repair the door. The woman was looking out the window. My neighbour had heard all the noise and curiously was watching with curiosity through her slightly opened door what was going on in our apartment. She quickly took the door chain off and pulled me inside her apartment. She was an older woman and still today I see her somewhat frightened, but proud face in front of me. In the GDR, human gestures like that were very uncommon among people who just knew each other from passing. But here and there one met somebody whose anger and fear were surpassed by the wish to do something, anything which could hurt the system. Of course, within seconds the two men beat on her door and screamed, 'We'll take you both, if you don't open up.' There was no way to escape, so we calmly opened the door and I left with them for some hours of interrogations which usually took the same course every time. I already knew the questions and they knew already what I would answer. It was a game, psychological warfare to frustrate us to get us to a point where we should give up. And I have to say, I sometimes was thinking about giving up, particularly when my two children were at home with me when the Stasi came. Several times I feared when they took me that upon my return they would have taken the children to a foster home, but fortunately they never did.

In the course of events surrounding the action against women's mandatory service in the military, we had heard that a group of women in West Berlin was planning a silent demonstration. All women were supposed to wear black to symbolize their sadness about the law. The demonstration was a support action stressing the importance of the open letter which we had sent to Honecker. I rounded up some friends and organized a parallel demonstration starting at a postal office on Alexanderplatz. I remember very well that when I left the house on the morning of the demonstration, two men were standing at the street corner smoking. My husband had offered to accompany me on his bike to the demonstration. All what was going through my head at the moment was, 'Here they are again to get me'. The street was going downhill at that point. I swung on my bike and pushed the pedals as strongly as I could. The Stasi who had not expected me yet, ran back to a car parked across the street. Traffic was heavy. I had a head start and I could slip away. Rather exhausted, I arrived at Alexanderplatz where the demonstration was already underway. We were scared to a certain point as demonstrations were not allowed in the GDR, but on the other hand we were hoping that the eyes of the western media would protect us. We were all very attentive if somebody was approaching us or a number of cars were coming towards us. After just a little while, I spotted the same men that had waited in front of the apartment for me. With forceful strides they were coming towards our group. One pointed at me from the distance. Quickly, all the women formed a dense circle and started screaming. We drew so much attention towards ourselves that many pedestrians stopped and wondered what was going on; as a result, the men became confused about their procedure. Nothing happened. When we felt safe, the group dispersed, but a few of us went to a small coffee house nearby. When we got there I noticed Superintendent Grusche from the Protestant Church sitting at a neighbouring table. As soon as we had ordered some hot drinks, the Stasi came into the little place and charged towards me. Grusche, who had heard about the demonstration and knew me from church activities must have felt what was about to happen. He pulled his chair up to me, put one arm around me and guided me out of the place. He was a well-known figure and had good contacts through his church channels. Once again I had been lucky. The two bullies stood there again not being sure about what to do.

The little demonstration in Berlin's Alexanderplatz which took place in 1982 somehow was the beginning of the dissident and peace movement. We met regularly with other peace groups from other countries, usually under the protective umbrella of church activities. On one of these occasions, Bärbel Bohley and I met with Barbara Einhorn, a New Zealander and a representative of the British peace movement. Einhorn had visited us at our apartment and we mainly discussed how to put together a document on the peace movement in the GDR which should be published in several languages. After dinner, Einhorn left the apartment with the intention of visiting some relatives living in East Berlin. The following morning we heard that she had been arrested. The West German press reported during the next days that Einhorn had been interrogated for four days and then under pressure from western governments was allowed to go to West Germany. The same day that Einhorn was free to leave for the West, Bärbel Bohley and I were arrested.

I had just picked up my children Johanna and Jonas from nursery school when several Stasis approached me on our way home. They simply said, 'You have to come along'. I politely asked if I could bring the children home first. I was hoping to bring them to a safe place and that my husband would be home, so he would know my whereabouts. The Stasis agreed since the apartment was just a few blocks away. Coming home there were about ten people present in our apartment searching through documents, books and personal belongings. I knew that moment that this arrest would be different from the previous ones. This is going to be the real thing, I thought. I was brought to Schönhaus, which was known as one of the Stasi headquarters for interrogations for political opponents and dissidents. I was told that I had been arrested under paragraph 99, a law that enforced prison terms between two and twelve years for treason. The exact text says, 'The exchange of GDR secrets or the exchange of information harming the GDR with foreign powers, their representatives or their secret service can and will be punished with prison terms of two to 12 years.' A series of interrogations lasting up to 80 hours followed. The interrogators shifted every five to six hours.

Some offered me cigarettes, some yelled at me, some became violent. After 80 hours of questions and answers, I was allowed to sleep for two to two and a half hours. This rhythm continued for four days. I was totally exhausted but still believed they would let me go again. I hadn't done anything. After several days, I was introduced to a judge who again read to me paragraph 99. It was shortly before Christmas and in the fourth week in prison I thought that next week is Christmas, I'm going to be free and spend it with the children. Christmas passed, the New Year passed. By the beginning of the year my optimism changed and I was sure that a trial was soon awaiting me with a prison term of several years. I had briefly seen my husband on 21 December. He suggested that we should apply for a travel permit and officially leave the GDR. At that time, I still disagreed. We had work to do here and I didn't want to leave for West Germany. When I became sure in January that a prison term was awaiting me, I changed my mind for the sake of the children and I'm sure they would have let us go with joy. That was a major difference between East Germany and the rest of communist Eastern Europe. Most dissidents in Eastern Europe spent years in prison, but in East Germany people were let go for hard currencies.

Then on 24 January, Bärbel Bohley and I were set free. The protestant church in West Germany and peace movements around the world had put so much pressure on the regime that they let us go. I volunteered a statement for the sake of the family saying that I would not be an enemy of the GDR, but I would work to improve its system in certain areas where it was bound to fail.

David Gill

The Ministerium für Staatssicherheit (Ministry for State Security—MfS) was established in 1957 under Erich Mielke, although its tradition goes back to the 'cheka'—the brutal Bolshevik secret police organization that spread terror in the early years after the Russian revolution. The MfS was absolutely subordinate to the SED party. The relationship between the Stasi and the SED is best described by the metaphor 'shield and sword of the party'. Important political decisions of the MfS were not made within the organization, but came as orders directly from the politburo or the Central Committee.

According to a 1950 law, the MfS was an espionage organization using secret service methods to guarantee both the domestic and the foreign security interests of the GDR. Altogether, the MfS had seven main tasks. First, it was to undermine and combat plans and activities of foreign countries that were not in the interest of the GDR or its allies, particularly embargoes aimed at 'young national states' or communist 'freedom movements'. Second, the MfS was to report on all anti-regime movements within and outside the country and effectively work against them. In addition, the MfS was to start secretly documenting citizens and their political attitudes. Third, the MfS was supposed to infiltrate 'illegal organizations' working against the interests of the GDR. The fourth task was to prevent any mass demonstrations opposing the regime. Its fifth task was to start a counter-espionage organization to prevent foreign spies from entering the country. The sixth task was to infiltrate the postal and telephone systems as well as the country's transportation system. Finally, the organization was supposed to prevent 'crimes against GDR boundaries', meaning it had to stop citizens from fleeing the GDR.[6]

While the MfS remained responsible for all these tasks, from time to time the organization might emphasize one task more than another. For example, after the transit agreement with West Germany was signed in 1972, the MfS greatly intensified its enforcement of border controls to prevent any mass exodus from the east.

Over the years, the MfS developed into an agency whose main jobs were to destroy opposition movements within the country and to prevent a mass exodus. As its tasks became more difficult, the organization grew. The combination of the party's absolute power and its misjudgement of the political and socio-economic situation led to rising discontent among the citizens and to a dramatic increase in the number of people working for the MfS. The gap between reality and party doctrine grew over the years, as did the gap between what citizens knew and what the party told them. The MfS was, therefore, necessary to maintain the status quo and keep power in the hands of the few who didn't want to see the gap and didn't want to give up their control.

The main department in the fight against 'other-thinking citizens' was Department XX. Its thesis was that 'Everybody is potentially a

[6] The so-called 'Republikflucht'—leaving the country illegally according to Article 213 of the GDR criminal law was punishable with prison terms of two to five years.

security threat and, therefore, the MfS has to know everything. Security comes before law.' Department XX was responsible for fighting 'political–ideological subversion' as well as political subcultural movements. They infiltrated church groups, sports clubs, hospitals and music groups. At neighbourhood meetings, even state-organized functions, hundreds of obvious secret service agents were present. When soccer teams from the west visited Czechoslovakia and hundreds of GDR citizens travelled to Prague to watch the games, a like number of Department XX spies travelled along with them and made lists on who had waved the West German flag or had hummed along when the West German anthem was played.

Stasi members were not allowed to speak about their work at home, to their wives, parents or children. They had to invent a job and a fictitious existence. Most lived like schizophrenics, without a real life and with no close friends. On being accepted, every MfS member had to swear in writing that he would obey any order and that he would report on anybody—even on his closest relatives.

Another important organization within the Stasi was Department XXii, in charge of 'terror prevention'. This department provided a hiding place and a new existence in East Germany for members of the Red Army Faction which was responsible for murdering and bombing western European politicians and military personnel. Department XXii also trained the terrorists in the use of certain weapons and supplied them with fake passports and other papers to get them re-established in West Germany during the 1980s. Some terrorists were also trained by the KGB in the Soviet Union.

The KGB had a great influence on the MfS from the very beginning. From the time East Germany was established in 1949, leading MfS members were trained in the Soviet Union and were periodically sent back for retraining. The MfS and the KGB were directly connected by computer. All information obtained by the MfS was also sent to a central computer system in Moscow, which transferred information on foreign spies as well as on West and East German relatives who remained in contact, Zionist groups in Germany, diplomats, and media correspondents. The MfS had contact with the secret services of all other communist satellite states but Romania. Links with Romania were cut off as early as 1956 because it was feared that Romania had co-operating partners in the West. Nations such as Angola, Zambia, Tanzania, Vietnam, North Korea, Cuba,

Nicaragua, Ethiopia, Mozambique and South Yemen had people who were in weekly contact with the MfS, who assisted in putting together national secret services in those countries.

The members of the MfS who worked as foreign spies were the elite of the Stasi, but they were often hated because of the privileges of living abroad. The success of the GDR's foreign espionage is tightly linked to Markus Wolf, who headed the department for years. Wolf was responsible for infiltrating democratic movements in West Germany. From Stasi files we have learned that Wolf usually looked for worldly, well-educated people with language skills. Once he had his eye on a 'candidate', he ordered another department to dig up some dirt on the person; then the victim could be psychologically pressured into joining Wolf's espionage team. Wolf's operations were mainly in West Germany, the USA and other NATO countries.

The main focus of Wolf's organization was economic, political and military counterespionage against western agencies. But there was also a strong concentration on industrial espionage, resulting from the permanent lack of hard currencies in the GDR and the technological underperformance of the country. For example, a megabite chip that purportedly was developed at the Carl-Zeiss Laboratory had actually been stolen from the west.

The Stasi rewarded docility with certain privileges, while disobedience was met with harsh sanctions and punishments. The average salary of a Stasi member was about 2,000 DM ($1,500) per month and was much higher than any other paid job in the country. The better the information and the more diligent the performance, the more extras were paid—such as a 'company' car which was usually a Polish-made Lada. Every general drove a French Citroën. Vacations were usually organized in MfS holiday homes in Bulgaria or on the Crimea in the Soviet Union.

High-ranking party members and MfS members lived in a special area that was off-limits to outsiders. This so-called 'inner circle' consisted of 20 to 40 people living in Wandlitz, a suburb of East Berlin. Originally, the houses in Wandlitz were taken care of by housekeepers and workers from Berlin, but soon they started to talk and were replaced by 'honest' Stasi members. I believe up to 700 people worked there daily taking care of 25 houses. Chauffeurs, gardeners, even the sales people in the western-style stores in the enclosed area were Stasi-trained and bound to their oaths of obedience.

Like high-ranking party bosses, MfS members could buy western products for discounted prices in certain stores in larger cities. Many of the stores were filled with western goods. How the western goods came into those stores was always a mystery to me until I read reports at the Stasi headquarters. The East German government and the Stasi had organized what is known to have been the biggest postal crime in German history. Starting in 1984, many packages that were sent from West German relatives to the east, and other packages routed through the GDR by mistake, were confiscated by the Stasi at the customs office. The packages were then transferred to Freibrink, near Berlin, were they were x-rayed and opened. The contents were recorded and then sorted by item and product groups. The empty cartons were recycled into toilet paper which was known for its roughness throughout the east. During the Christmas and Easter seasons truckloads of packages from West Germany were delivered twice a week to Freibrink. In an attempt to cover up the criminal action and to prevent questions from western authorities, 5 per cent of the packages were returned after they had been x-rayed and found to be of little value. The hands of the postal ministry in West Germany were tied, since they could not prove misconduct.

One thing was clear: Stasi members had to be present in West German postal stations to misroute packages. About 20 to 25 per cent of all packages sent from west to east never made it to their recipients. I had a chance to wander through the shelves where the goods were stored; literally everything that we couldn't get in the east, but was available in the west, was there: TVs, video cameras, stamp collections, surfboards, Italian shoes and textiles, jewellery and even western money. All the goods were usually transferred to the 'Department of Commercial Co-ordination' (KoKo), operated by the foreign currency smuggler Alexander Schalck-Golodkowski. He took certain items that couldn't be sold in the GDR and resold them to West Germany. I know from one report that a whole load of monopoly games ended up in his hands, but the party decided that this 'imperialistic game' was not good for GDR children. Schalck-Golodkowski resold the games in the west for hard currency. Pharmaceuticals for aging party members came mainly from thefts. Only the lower-ranking Stasi members came out empty-handed.

Schalck-Golodkowski was one of the most powerful men in the GDR because he helped to sustain its economy by acquiring hard currency. He was called 'Big Alex', not only because of his six-foot height, but also because of his power: he controlled more than half of the currency flowing into the country, usually illegally. A Honecker favourite, he worked closely with the Stasi to build KoKo into the largest East German trading firm. He not only dealt in weapons which were transferred to Third World countries, but also put together lists of products to be obtained from the west in exchange for political prisoners. He established a number of companies in West Germany whose revenues financed the Communist Party there as well as communist movements in Africa and South America.

KoKo was a tool used by the Stasi to get hard currency into the country and to secure a luxurious lifestyle for Stasi and party members. As Koko's top official, Schalck-Golodkowski was one of the highest-ranking Stasi members and was decorated with both the Karl Marx Medal and the 'Big Star of Friendship'. When he left the GDR in December 1989, he received a safe haven in West Germany for some information that was never made public. Today he is working as a business consultant in Bavaria and living somewhere on Lake Starnberg.

Schalck-Golodkowski helped to set up what was called a 'technology transfer', but was really industrial espionage. Stasi agents who infiltrated West German engineers' offices snooped around for years and came back with plans for everything from computers to production plants. These plans were then sold to other communist countries or used within the GDR. He also organized the production of counterfeit products such as western perfumes, brandies and tobaccos.

To break embargoes secretly, coal was brought in from South Africa via his trading companies, which had branches in over 36 countries. Of course the GDR had protested officially against apartheid. Vegetables came from Taiwan and oil from Iran. Deals with western business people were usually done in one hotel, The Grand Hotel in East Berlin. This hotel was under specific surveillance of the Stasi, mainly to acquire material with which to blackmail western business people into supporting the system. TV cameras kept an eye on lobbies and on certain rooms, 25 to 30 of which were specifically set up with video cameras and bugs. There business was done regularly with the so-called 'class enemy'. Schalck-Golodkowski was the financial backbone of the party and the Stasi.

Chapter Six

Communist Reforms and a Missed Opportunity

The East German constitution of 1949 had guaranteed democratic rights, which from the very beginning were not only disregarded by the East German leaders but also intentionally violated. On paper, but only on paper, the GDR's constitution resembled the Basic Law of the Federal Republic. Ulbricht, Grotewohl and the comrades who wrote the document promised fundamental rights such as freedom of assembly, freedom of the press, freedom of speech, religious freedom, the right to emigrate and to participate in 'general, democratic elections'. In fact, the first democratic elections were not held until 41 years later on 18 March 1990, after the Wall had fallen. 'All power', so the constitution said in 1949, 'comes from the people'. In reality, the SED established a one-party dictatorship. The GDR adopted the colours of West Germany's flag for its own national flag—black, red, and gold stripes—but added the hammer and compass surrounded by a wreath of grain.

The two men who started to guide the two Germanies in 1949 could not have been more different in mentality. The western side was governed by the elderly Catholic and anti-communist Konrad Adenauer; on the eastern side was the Saxonian Walter Ulbricht, an admirer of Stalin and follower of his ideology even after the Soviet dictator's death. Reunification was not a primary concern for Adenauer; if an option at all, it was conceivable as the annexation of the total eastern zone. Ulbricht, on the other hand, could consider reunification only if all of Germany, including the western parts, were to be governed as a Soviet-style people's republic.

Ulbricht had announced publicly to his comrades that, 'To imprint the Soviet system on Germany would be difficult now, as the current political situation does not lend itself to such steps'. Instead, he added, 'We have to finish what was started in 1948 when the bourgeois-democratic movement became a parliamentary democratic republic'.[1] The communists in the Communist Party of Germany (KPD) were disappointed and confused; with the Red Army behind them, they had been ready to turn the eastern zone into a truly proletarian dictatorship. During a conference of

---

[1] Leonard, *Das kurze Leben der DDR*, p. 16.

the KPD, Ulbricht was asked in dismay how his programmes would differ from those of any other democratic parties. He replied, 'Wait and see, comrades.' They did not have to wait long.

Faster than anyone had imagined possible, the rulers of the Soviet zone, despite all their promises, changed the political, economic and social structures there. Over 7,000 owners of farms larger than 250 acres were expropriated from their land without compensation. Over 850,000 poor farmers, party members and refugees thus gained title to lands varying in size from 12 to 25 acres—parcels that usually were not big enough to farm economically. Parallel to the expropriation, which Ulbricht called 'land reform', the process of socializing other areas of the economy continued. Industries were seized and turned into 'people's plants' operated mostly by inept party members. In many cases, knowledgeable ex-owners were later asked to stay on as employees. In particular, private banks, energy-producing utilities and pharmacies were taken over by the regime. In less than three years, three-quarters of East German workers were employed by state-owned, state-run enterprises.

In October 1949 the Soviet occupation administration ordered a takeover of all German state property and property owned by the National Socialist German Workers' Party (NSDAP) and its organization. Additionally, all people who were on 'special lists or have been selected in any other way' were to have their property expropriated. These lists and selection process were never explained and gave the Soviet administration a licence for piracy. Some 129 large corporations, among them Europe's largest chemical company, Leuna, were put into a 'Soviet joint-stock company' whose assets were transferred to the Soviet Union. Until 1953 the USSR exacted heavy reparations payments, usually in the form of industrial dismantling. Whole industrial facilities that had survived the war were carried on trains and barges to the Soviet Union. Roughly 40 per cent of the pre-war industrial potential of the eastern zone ended up in the Soviet Union. One-quarter of the zone's ongoing production also ended up in Soviet hands. The remaining economy, like the economy of the USSR, was operated through central planning and administration. As in the Soviet Union, the system proved incapable of adjusting production to consumer demand or taste. Providing basic necessities such as food, housing and medicine was to become a chronic problem for the economy.

Meanwhile, on the other side of the Iron Curtain, Adenauer had established closer ties with the western Allies and, helped by the Marshall Plan, the economy in the west was thriving. For the man from the Rhine River valley, the most pressing task was not a reunification of the country, but the removal of restrictions imposed by the western Allies. For the Anglo-Saxon-oriented Adenauer, the only hope for eventual reunification lay in creating in West Germany an independent bastion of freedom and prosperity. The West German chancellor strove to win sovereign rights for the new West German government as rapidly as possible. The agreement with the western Allies (Deutschlandvertrag), which was signed in 1952, restricted the latter's authority and made the boundaries of Germany dependent on a peace treaty to be formulated at a later time. After ratification by all four occupation powers, the agreement replaced the occupation status and marked the beginning of West Germany's integration into the European Defence Community (Europäische Verteidigungsgemeinschaft—EVG).

Following the outbreak of the Korean War, the US government determined that the western policy of containment of the Soviet Union now also required a German military. In the midst of these developments, Josef Stalin unveiled an unexpected plan. In the 'Stalin note' of 10 March 1952, he offered to reunite Germany, via a peace treaty and free elections. Moscow's price: military neutralization of Germany with only a limited armed force. Historians still debate whether Stalin's programme, vehemently opposed by Adenauer and his conservative party, was a missed opportunity to reunite Germany or part of a scheme by Stalin to get all of Germany under his rule. Stalin, whose well-known capriciousness was demonstrated in the German–Soviet pact of 1939, never revealed publicly what he intended.

As a result of the note, Adenauer, more fervently than ever, assigned the highest political priority to restoring the 'moral, social and political values of western civilization' in at least the part of Germany he governed—even if doing so meant a potentially lengthy period of division of the country. The SED on the other hand, decided to reinforce 'the construction of socialism', meaning the rapid development of basic industries at the expense of producing consumer goods and improving the standard of living. The process of collectivization was further enforced, and it even absorbed independent tradespeople into co-operatives. [2]

Ulbricht also started an open remilitarization, which actually had begun earlier under cover of the formation of the people's police in barracks. Thus began a reign of terror against the entire population.

The 'construction of socialism' accelerated a large-scale flight to the west by some of the most productive sectors of East German society. Although the border between east and west had been sealed off in the spring of 1952, escape was still possible via Berlin. Between 1949 and 1953 more than a million had left the east zone. In March 1953 alone, 60,000 people left. By the end of 1953 a total of 2 per cent of the population had left and registered as refugees in the west.

[2] Adenauer, *Erinnerungen.*

Michael, Prinz von Sachsen-Weimar und Eisenach

Within three years after the Red Army arrived, Thuringia was put under the jurisdiction of the SED. Almost immediately—as early as 1948—the step-by-step introduction of the so-called 'agrarian reform' began. All those who owned more than 250 acres of land had to leave the property and were expelled from their homes. It hit all property owners hard, particularly our family.

Most of the family were anything but followers of Hitler. My father, for example, was even dismissed as a soldier with the remark in his papers that he was 'untrustworthy'. When the Red Army marched into Thuringia, Stalin's economic and social ideology was spread quickly. For our family, that meant seizure of everything: land, houses, castles and personal belongings. The slogan that gave justified confiscation of the land holdings of the gentry, at least in the mind of the communists, was 'Junkerland in Bauernhand' (gentryland to farmers).

My parents left the Soviet occupation zone as soon as they heard that the family's property and the process of expropriation had been discussed in the Soviet-installed parliament in Thuringia. Only the management stayed behind, remaining more or less intact until 1948. My parents and the whole family were pronounced 'enemies of the GDR and its population'. Security reasons, and I think even more so emotions, made the decision not to return an easy one. Visiting the GDR was a topic never even discussed in our family until the early 1970s, when travelling conditions were eased.

Many people who didn't have as high a profile as my parents stayed in the Soviet zone for a long while, believing that the Red Army would not and could not stay forever. Well, it was not forever, but it lasted over 40 years.

Wolfgang Gäbelein

It is now fairly well-established that immediately before the June uprising in 1953, Moscow was prepared to let Ulbricht go as a kind of scapegoat for the economic disaster resulting from Stalin's policies in East Germany—policies that Ulbricht had so tediously followed. Stalin, had he not died, probably would have approved of

Ulbricht's political movements, but his followers in the Kremlin were of a different mind. The pictures of Stalin's funeral in *Neues Deutschland* showed the body of the so-called 'Red Czar' surrounded by his rivals and potential successors, among them Lavrenti Beria, Georgi Malenkov, Nickolai Bulganin and Nikita Khrushchev. It seemed to us that after Josef Stalin's death, the Kremlin was planning a new course, but *which* course was not clear. We were hoping for a course of enlightenment, a course recognizing that Germany could not be a satellite of a communist Soviet Union.

The Soviet control commission was dissolved and the moderate Vladimir Semionov was given the position of high commissioner. That, of course, raised East Germans' hopes that eventually the Soviets would let go of their part of Germany as the western Allies had done. The chief of the Soviet secret police, Beria, is said to have suggested letting the GDR and Ulbricht fall in order to gain some concessions from the west.

After the uprising in 1953, however, Moscow was no longer willing to tinker with the top leadership of the SED. Ulbricht was even allowed to move against his inner party enemies, members who had contact with Beria. Consequently, the latter was arrested himself and executed in late 1953. Political recriminations aside, the uprising marked the strengthening of Ulbricht's position, but also vividly exposed the total bankruptcy of the East German communist experiment. The intervention of the Soviet Union during the 1953 uprising in East Germany, as well as Beria's death, buried all remaining hope and speculation that the Kremlin might give up the SED regime for a reunited Germany.

When the Korean War broke out, I believe I was not the only one who wondered whether East Germans might one day be asked to use their weapons against West Germans. A brothers' war seemed potentially likely. The issue became even more prominent when French Minister President René Pleven announced his plans to form a European army in which West Germany would play a part. The suggestion was in keeping with Adenauer's desire to create a bastion of anti-communism in West Germany.

But most people in West Germany were confused about the question of militarization. The war had ended only five years earlier, and the country was still in a shambles; hardly anybody was ready to pursue discussions about weapons and armouries. The West German socialists, under the leadership of Kurt Schumacher, even voted publicly against arming West Germany because a *Wieder-aufrüstung*—rearmament—would definitely prevent any potential reunification between the east zone and West Germany.

The fact that Adenauer was on good speaking terms with the western Allies, and that he agreed that the policy of western containment of the Soviet Union in Europe required a German military contribution, made Ulbricht and his comrades highly nervous. Perhaps as a result, at the end of 1950 Grotewohl suggested forming an East and West German provisional government and holding free elections. Even the West German socialists such as Schumacher were deeply concerned about the proposal and claimed it was a 'cheating contest' designed to get all of Germany under communist rule. Indeed, when Adenauer suggested that free elections should be performed under the supervision of the UN, the east, not surprisingly, declined.

Adenauer signed the German treaty with the western Allies. This treaty made West Germany the only officially recognized government of Germany. The East German rulers were stamped as pariahs. Soon after, an additional agreement made West Germany a part of the European Defence Community. Just before the agreements were to be signed, Stalin went on the diplomatic defensive. In a series of notes in spring 1952, he offered to facilitate the reunification of Germany under one condition: military neutralization of the country. Adenauer publicly called Stalin's suggestion, rightly I believe, 'just another piece of paper', the intent of which was to undermine the political, economic and military strengthening of West Germany. The so-called Stalin notes were the bait for a dangerous trap. Some people still believe that Stalin's offer was a 'missed opportunity' for an early reunification. The only reunification Stalin had in mind was one that would exist under the symbol of the sickle and hammer. Anybody believing anything else is a dreamer. Ulbricht himself said some years later, 'A reunification will only be possible under the red flag of communism.' That was the tone set for the next decades.

Walter Köcher

For generations our family owned a company that produced knitted and woven goods. All of Thuringia was well known for that kind of textile manufacturing. Obviously, during the war, production had been very limited, but my father was eager to make a new beginning, particularly since the plant had not been harmed by any bombs. He was enthusiastic about a set of new designs and had also played with ideas on how to more effectively use the weaving equipment. He had also talked to the US administration, which had been in Thuringia for a few months following the end of the war, about organizing supplies for the plant.

Within weeks after the American troops were replaced by the Red Army, however, we received a formal letter from the new commissioner stating that, as of the 15th of that month, the plant would enter into the 'people's ownership'. Somehow we all had known something like that would happen under Soviet rule but we had hoped they would start with the larger and more important industries, such as metal-producing plants. For a day or so my father simply ignored the letter, and there was really nothing anybody could have done. We knew of friends who tried to talk the Soviet administration out of expropriating certain property and industrial complexes. They were usually the first to lose their property and were treated more harshly than if they had just kept quiet.

Within a few days a group of Soviets and a translator appeared at the production plant during working hours and handed my father a copy of the letter. No explanation was given. Somehow my father got along with one of the guys and, miraculously, he arranged for the family to keep a small percentage of the plant in our name, the rest going into Soviet ownership. We worked at the business for another four years, until it was totally taken over by the Soviets. After that, I left the eastern zone in 1950. I no longer had any reason to stay on in what I had considered my homeland, nor did I want to waste my time and effort working for a regime that would always suppress owners and entrepreneurs.

Margarethe Fuchs

I had just got married in 1949, and I definitely didn't think that the economic conditions as they presented themselves at the time would continue to exist for long. Families of friends had been dispossessed, and many friends had gone to the west or at least to West Berlin, where they were looking for better economic conditions and a new start. Most of the people who left as early as 1950 and 1951 were German gentry who had lost their land holdings and who feared for their lives. Manufacturers, traders and professionals typically left later in the 1950s, when the Soviets tightened their economic control in the eastern zone.

I was not the only one who interpreted the October 1950 events in Berlin as positive. The three democratic parties of West Berlin had asked the citizens of East Berlin to send food coupons to the mayor of the western zone—anonymously, no stamp required for delivery —if they could answer the following questions positively:

1. Do you want to have free, democratic elections at the same time the west is having its election?
2. Do you want to end the terror of the Red Army in the eastern zone?
3. Should Berlin be a free and united city?

At that time food coupons were probably the most sacred of one's possessions. Without them you were unable to get any food unless you had good connections in the black market, which was expensive. Nevertheless, over 400,000 people sent in coupons, along with many who just sent in letters of agreement.

I thought at the time that these voices cannot be ignored; the west has to do something. But nothing happened. Within two weeks, in October 1950, the SED ordered East German citizens to show up for elections. They had put together a list, but it didn't matter who or what you voted for—it all ended up the same. The participation, typical for a rigged election, was over 95 per cent. The next day the party organ *Neues Deutschland* wrote something like, 'The masses of the population of the GDR have learned that peace means to love the Soviet Union, and to love Stalin.'

We should have left right then, as so many others did. Between 1950 and 1954 as many as 1.2 million people had left the Soviet oc-cupation zone. The saying, 'Let your feet do the talking', was taken quite literally. But at times, there were shimmers of hope that things would change. All easterners with deep roots in the eastern zone wanted to believe that the West German government under Adenauer had enough influence in international political circles to put an end to the communist regime in the east. We also thought, we survived the war, so why leave now? The large amount of collectivization in the east spoke for itself, as did the daily accumulation of harassments and humiliations that I called the 'terror of small steps'. Many people couldn't decide, during those first post-war years, whether leaving home would be the right decision. Their hearts were in conflict with their heads.

From the first steps toward collectivization in the east in 1949 to the end of 1950, over 5,000 companies were seized and turned into 'people-owned plants' (*Volkseigene Betriebe*—VEB). Food and consumer goods were still rationed, and their quality was very low. Because of the tremendous reparations paid to the Soviet Union, Germans in the east had to carry about 18 times the tax burden of people living in the west. The economic results were disastrous. At the Second SED Party Conference in 1952, Ulbricht announced the 'construction of socialism', meaning the strengthening of state power as well as the collectivization and liquidation of any remaining private property and holdings in industry and commerce. He also announced a 'sharpened class struggle', which translated into a reign of terror against anyone who did not support his ideology.

The terror of small steps was present daily everywhere. Little things such as listening to RIAS (Radio in the American Sector) or the BBC were punished with prison terms. Even among good friends, it was an unwritten rule not to pay a surprise visits during the times BBC or RIAS was broadcasting the evening news, so you could listen in peace and without fearing that when the door bell rang, the People's Police were at the door. I remember that we heard of Stalin's death through BBC two or three days before it was announced officially in the east. I went shopping one day with my 3-year-old son and a sales lady in the store said, 'Have you read this morning's newspaper? Stalin is dead. I wonder what that will mean for us?' My son just looked at me curiously and said, 'But Mommy, we've heard this already three days ago.' I quickly left the store. Fortunately, nobody was present at the store who was with the party or the People's Police.

We all knew that elections had been rigged and that the economy under Stalin would be a disaster, but there were other little things that started to creep up day by day. Streets named after German poets such as Schiller and Goethe were changed to 'Stalinstreet' or 'Red Army Place'. These were small things, but they were all part of the overall game plan of the regime. After a while, just the presence of two Soviet soldiers or People's Police made you change the side of the street you were walking on. You could feel from talking to people whom you trusted that everybody was very angry inside, and that it would only be a matter of time and opportunity before the volcano would erupt.

The time seemed right after Stalin's death in 1953. Ulbricht's regime simply didn't have the experience or the money to achieve investment in heavy industry and all the other mammoth administrative projects that he had envisioned for his Stalinist programme. He was forced to make an almost fateful decision, namely to 'construct socialism' on the backs of the industrial workers. His party deliberately depressed the workers' wages through steep increases in official quotas. The quotas were used as an excuse to protest Ulbricht's plan; in reality, this was the first open protest against the regime. In East Berlin, construction workers doing work in front of a party-owned building started at around eight o'clock in the morning to march towards Leipzigerstrasse in East Berlin, where most of the party buildings were. Within half an hour the news spread round the city and the whole eastern zone, and the protest of a few workers developed into a zone-wide revolt against the communist regime. From Magdeburg to Frankfurt-on-Oder and from Rostock to Zwickau people voiced their anger against the party. In Berlin state buildings were burned. As I recall, a high-rise in which the People's Police (*Volkspolizei*) had their headquarters was demolished. Workers, professionals, housewives, almost everybody who wasn't for Ulbricht and what he represented were to be found on the street.

My husband, who was an assistant professor at the medical school of the university of Jena (a major city south of Berlin) at the time, asked me to come to the university. Except for surgery, everything had come to a standstill at his department. Patients, students, nurses all were talking, taking down the pictures of Ulbricht and Stalin that they had been forced to hang throughout the hospital. I remember going around from room to room with the head nurse carrying a basket of wooden crosses that we had found somewhere in the basement and replacing the pictures with the crosses. Patients started to burn and break the pictures. What we did almost sounds silly today, but I suppose it was a symbolic gesture. We simply didn't want to have a brown regime followed by a red regime. My husband talked to a large group of students about what should be done to spread the news further around the country and about what could be done if the People's Police came to the university to arrest revolters. Quickly, leaflets and small newsletters were typed up with news of happenings in Berlin and, more importantly, with demands for free democratic elections. The red flag was pulled down from all official buildings. Around the university people were shouting, 'End to Stalinism! End to Ulbricht!' Everybody was very excited about the prospect that the Ulbricht regime could fall. Somebody was constantly sitting at the radio changing from one western station to another to learn more about what was going on in Berlin. We were also hoping for some announcement from the west or help to support the revolt.

No declaration came. Not from Adenauer, not from any western ally. The revolt was not even encouraged verbally by the west via radio. Just two hours after it started, we heard on the radio that the uprising had been stopped. Red Army tanks were rolling into the streets of Berlin, firing at demonstrators. Ulbricht had called in the Red Army to help along with the People's Police. Everybody today has seen the picture of a young man throwing stones at the first Russian T-34 tank that rolled into East Berlin. It's an unforgettable picture.

Martial law was imposed and Russian soldiers patrolled the streets throughout the zone after nine o'clock in the evening. The joy had changed back into anger, but also into fear of retaliation. As we heard the next day, in Jena, a 'Vopo', as the People's Police was called, had been thrown out of a window by angry protesters. The mayor of Leipzig had been forced to walk with the protesters with a Swiss cow bell around his neck along with a sign saying, 'I'm a communist swine'. The Soviets had protected a communist regime from its own people.

I remember vividly that, the next morning, the party-owned newspaper reported that paid criminals from West Berlin had intruded into the eastern zone and had started the revolt against the eastern population. It also stated that most of the people killed or imprisoned were from West Berlin. Everybody knew those were lies. Hours after the end of the revolt, 92 protesters were shot by sentence of the martial law. Nineteen demonstrators and four members of the People's Police had been killed during the protest. Another 52 members of the

People's Police were shot because they ignored orders to shoot their fellow Germans. Within a few months, out of 5,000 people imprisoned during those few hours of revolt, 106 received death sentences and over 1,000 protesters were given year-long prison sentences.

Adenauer and the West German Bundestag declared 17 June a national holiday thereafter and called it the 'day of German unity'. It was a holiday in the west until the Wall fell in 1989.

Chapter Seven

The Wall Rises

The uprising of June 1953 had a dramatic impact on the GDR regime: it effectively exposed as a lie the propagated image of the SED as a 'workers' and farmers' party.' Within a few months Ulbricht tried to repair the damage by proposing a 'new course' that suggested a new more consumer-oriented economic orientation. Following this course, the regime raised pensions for retired people in the eastern zone to 75 DM a month ($55) and spent 30 million DM on improving sanitary equipment in 'people-owned' plants. Likewise, the Soviet Union was willing to do its part to restore peace in East Germany. The Kremlin reduced the GDR's reparation payments from 1.95 billion DM in 1953 to 1.6 billion in 1954. The USSR also gave back a number of East German plants that had been taken over by the Soviets.[1]

Although economic conditions improved in the eastern zone, the exodus of refugees continued. Young people and professionals in particular turned their backs on their homes and fled to the west via the 'green border' in Berlin. Ulbricht himself began to tighten the reins within the party, first by eliminating his most prominent opponents, such as party leaders Wilhelm Zaisser and Anton Ackermann. A purge at all levels of the party soon followed. Motivated by both ideological and economic considerations, Ulbricht clung to the idea of a reunited Germany under his leadership. The past had proved that the eastern part of Germany could by itself create a functioning and stable economy without placing enormous burdens on its citizens. Furthermore, he hoped that his constant advocacy of a reunited Germany would make the west appear to be the spoilsport preventing reunification. The west, on the other hand, had valid reasons for rejecting Ulbricht's reunification proposals as mere propaganda, including the unacceptable totalitarian structures of the illegally established GDR state, the ideological subjugation of all people living in the eastern zone, and the GDR's slave-like dependence on Moscow.

---

[1] Knapp and Kuhn, Die Deutsche Einheit, p. 148.

From 1952 until the Wall was built on 13 August 1961, each side continued to propose plans and models for reunification patterned after its own thinking on how best to solve the internal German situation. The proposals usually disappeared as quickly as they had appeared. All papers and proposals—from British Foreign Minister Anthony Eden's plan involving free elections, a national assembly, a new German constitution and a peace treaty to Ulbricht's suggestion of a loose confederation between the two states—amounted to little more than games planned around a table without taking any political realities into consideration. Consequently, none of the plans ever had any real potential for success. French National Assembly President Jacques Chaban-Delmas summarized the situation in the late 1950s: 'The Soviets never wanted a reunification. The conferences on this topic were never more than diplomatic games. No serious politician really believed in the reunification of Germany at that time.' [2]

Both Germanies sought military alignments during the mid-1950s. While US Foreign Minister John Foster Dulles and Britain's Sir Anthony Eden tried to resurrect the EVG[3] agreement, which had failed to pass the French National Assembly in 1954, and prepared West Germany's entry into NATO, the GDR was invited to join the Warsaw Treaty Organization. Thus the two states became members of hostile military camps, and the GDR, with the formal establishment of East German armed forces, became a full-fledged member of the Soviet bloc alliance system. The process helped deepen the division between East and West Germany.

In autumn 1955 Adenauer and Khrushchev shook hands in Moscow for the media signifying Bonn's diplomatic recognition of Moscow. As a corresponding gesture of good will, Moscow promised to send home to West Germany over 10,000 prisoners of war who had been held captive in western Russia since the end of World War II. The war finally ended for those soldiers—ten years after Hitler's Reich had faltered.

Khrushchev's anti-Stalin campaign and Ulbricht's immediate attempt to disassociate himself from the late Soviet leader produced a response that quickly threatened to get out of hand. Once again opponents of Ulbricht's regime clamoured for greater freedom, this time encouraged by economists in the GDR who dared to criticize the practices of Stalinist central planning. Free speech was quickly curtailed and some prominent intellectuals were tried and imprisoned.

---

[2] Ibid, p. 178.
[3] Europäische Verteidigungsgemeinschaft (European Defense Community).

Socialist realism started to prevail in the arts and culture of the GDR.' Cosmopolitanism, bourgeois objectivism and American cultural barbarism' were officially forbidden. Only writers and artists whose work reflected the party line were allowed to be part of the culture. The arts, music and literature were to be brought much closer to the masses and, therefore, 'needed the infusion of positive socialist content.' The best-known example of the attempt of the 'cultural revolution' to get workers to contribute to the arts was the slogan, 'Grab a pen, comrade. Our socialist national culture needs you.' In the schools, children had to learn Russian and were prepared for 'ideological rearmament'. The insistence on ideological conformity did not stop at the doorsteps of the church. Communion and confirmation were replaced by the so-called 'Jugendweihe' (consecration of young people), a pseudo-religious ceremony during which children from ages 12 to 14 were asked to make a firm commitment to socialism, the GDR and the GDR's friendship with the Soviet Union.[4]

Economically, Ulbricht set about trying to fashion a *modus vivendi* between the regime and the East German population by the end of the 1950s. The 'ökonomische Hauptaufgabe'—the economic main task, a phrase used equally by Ulbricht and Honecker—involved a modest improvement in the standard of living and greater availability of foods and consumer goods. At the Fifth SED Party Congress in July 1958, Ulbricht promised that the GDR would 'catch up with and overtake' West Germany economically by 1961. Presumably, this was to be accomplished via a new seven-year plan that would bring about the 'final victory of socialism'.[5]

The classless society in the GDR had developed into a two-class system divided into those who were for and those who were against the party. The nucleus of the party, roughly 2,000 functionaries, controlled cities and communities. Over 150,000 workers and employees worked voluntarily for mass organizations of the party. By the end of the 1950s, the party apparatus itself employed over 320,000 bureaucrats. It included heads of the people's plants as well as judges, teachers and, of course, the Stasi (secret police). They all were 'insiders', with rights to judge and to 'educate' the masses.

These developments were accompanied by a latent crisis that erupted anew in November 1958 when Khrushchev issued an ultimatum to the

---

[4] *Wörterbuch zur sozialistischen Jugendpolitik*, Akadamie der Wissenschaften, 1974 (Official Guidelines for the GDR Youth).
[5] Leonard, *Das kurze Leben der DDR*, p. 115.

west demanding a change in the status of West Berlin. He demanded that West Berlin become a 'free and non-militarized city' that should be overseen by all four Allies and the UN, otherwise he would sign a peace treaty with the GDR and give it responsibility for West Berlin. He also claimed that West Berlin was GDR territory; West Germans, he suggested, would have to deal with the GDR about access to the city. Once again, conflict, if not outright war, was looming over Berlin.

The west did not react, interpreting the ultimatum as a mere bluff to force the west to recognize the GDR diplomatically. The Soviets did not take any action against Berlin. Instead, the crisis flared and subsided at the verbal level over the next three years.

If nothing else, the Berlin crisis worked against the Ulbricht regime. The number of refugees increased dramatically after the Soviet threats. Over 250,000 left the eastern zone in 1960 alone, and the monthly number of refugees rose even higher during the first months in 1961. The mass exodus put added pressure on both Khrushchev and Ulbricht to solve the Berlin question.

Almost simultaneously, on the international political scene, US President Dwight D. Eisenhower and the Soviet leader in response to world pressure had a series of meetings staged as a symbol of hope for a new era of 'peaceful coexistence.' The Americans spoke optimistically of a 'new spirit of Geneva', referring to a meeting between the powers in 1955, which was followed by a 1959 meeting at Camp David, Maryland; but the two following rendezvous were disastrous. Just before the 1960 meeting in Paris, an American spy plane had been shot down inside Russia and the Soviets displayed its pilot, Gary Powers, to the world as proof of American hostility. Mutual distrust ruined any possibility for an effective conference. The Powers case became a milestone in the Cold War and launched a series of crises that continued beyond the Eisenhower administration through the first year of the Kennedy presidency.

The tone of the relationship between the superpowers did not change when newly elected President John F. Kennedy and Khrushchev met for the first time in Berlin. Again the Soviet leader threatened to put together a separate peace treaty with the GDR. Kennedy countered in broadcast speech to the American people on 25 July 1961: 'West Berlin—lying exposed 110 miles inside East Germany, surrounded by Soviet troops and close to Soviet supply lines—has many roles. It is more than a showcase of liberty, a symbol, an island of freedom in a communist sea. It is even more than a link to the Free World, a beacon of hope behind the Iron

Curtain, an escape hatch for refugees. West Berlin is all of that. But above all it has now become—as never before—the great testing place of western courage and will, a focal point where our solemn commitments, stretching back over the years since 1945, and Soviet ambitions now meet in basic confrontation.' [6]

Khrushchev now knew he would not get the solution he had hoped for in Berlin, so he pursued a compromise. First the SED regime started campaigning against people crossing the border officially. There followed a deadly incident that occurred late in July 1961: A young woman bled to death during a miscarriage because an East German hospital refused to admit her. The reason: her husband worked in the western part of the city. The party organ *Neues Deutschland* had only one comment: 'Know where you belong.' Then, on 13 August 1961, Germany was thrown back into the stone age. 'Action X' was given a green light by Moscow and the SED. A wall was built through Berlin; houses were split and sealed off in the middle with barbed wire. Under the guns of the People's Police, workmen were forced to build a fortification around and across the city. The Berlin Wall soon would cut off any access between the eastern and western parts of Germany.

Francis Meehan

The Soviets were aware in 1960 and 1961 that the Americans were wary of the problems any US policy-maker would face if the Soviets and the GDR closed the border to the west. Americans vigorously debated the possible responses: 'Do we move tanks to Berlin? Do we bring the Seventh Army up to the Czechoslovakian border? Do we put the Strategic Air Command on alert?' Any of these actions—or even proposing them openly—could risk a war. The Europeans, on the other hand, were terrified by the thought that a third world war might break out. The Germans in particular were concerned, since war doubtless would have meant the destruction of both Germanies.

For the Americans, it was difficult to come up with suitable counter-measures. On the German side, there was a tendency to accuse the US of standing by idly and letting the Soviets and the GDR have their way in building the Wall. But in my opinion, the US had

[6] US Government Printing Office, *Public Papers of the President*, 'Radio and Television Report to the American People on Berlin Crisis, July 25, 1961'. Washington, DC, 1962.

no good options at the time. By August 1961, the Soviets were well aware of the difficulties Americans were facing. Months before the Wall went up, I took part in a task force whose purpose was to discuss what options the US might have if the GDR and the Soviets decided to put up a border. No clear decision was ever made on what the reaction should be.

Egon Bahr

From the moment Khrushchev issued his ultimatum, the East German population feared that something dramatic was about to happen in Berlin. The flight of refugees had escalated. I believe 20,000 people had left the eastern zone in June 1961 alone. Then, restrictive measures were taken against the border crossers who lived in the east but came to the west for work or visits; however, those restrictions only increased the number of people fleeing. Ulbricht was determined to end the haemorrhage of people and concluded that the only way to stop the exodus was to close the border. When the members of the Warsaw Pact met on 4 August in Moscow, they voted to support the construction of the Wall. On 13 August Kennedy, de Gaulle and Macmillan were all on vacation and it took over 48 hours for the west to even react and to protest formally. Surprised or not, the west treated the Wall as an end to the Berlin crisis, not as the beginning of a new crisis. The western Allies could have reacted differently; they could have insisted on their right to use roads to get into the eastern sector. But that probably would have triggered a direct confrontation between the Americans and the Soviets. Instead, the allies quietly issued formal demands to reopen the border and even seemed to congratulate themselves that at least West Berlin was safe.

I strongly believe, as I said in 1961, that Kennedy's formulation of three essential rights in May of that year amounted to an open invitation to seal off East Germany from the west. Kennedy had warned the Soviets that the USA would fight first for the right to freedom of the people in West Berlin; second, for the Allies' right to have troops in the western part of the city; and third, for the right of access to West Berlin by all Allies via roads, water and air. In the early summer of 1961, he stressed these points again in an address to the US, but again limited application of these rights to the western part of the city. This was exactly the encouragement that Moscow needed to erect the Wall. For the communists it was almost an open invitation to do what they wanted with the eastern sector.

I nevertheless have to admit that I was surprised when I heard the news about the Wall. I had thought at the time that a well-patrolled border between the eastern and western sectors and an additional border between the eastern sector and the GDR would probably act as a double filter system to stop the refugees. I heard about the Wall just after I had gone to bed in Nuremberg after returning home from a campaign event. At the time Willy Brandt was in a train in Göttingen where he, too, was campaigning. Mr Spangenberger, the head of the Senate, called me and gave me the bitter news. He told me I had to come back to Berlin immediately, because they were sealing off the east. I hopped into a taxi and drove to the mayor's office in Berlin. We started to do what seemed most urgent: calming people down, issuing protests, trying to contact politicians in the west. I tried to get some Jeeps from the Allies to patrol the border so the people in the East could at least see that we knew what was going on, so they wouldn't lose all hope.

That same night Brandt went to see the city commander. But it took him over 48 hours to issue even a mild protest. Everybody was surprised and absolutely puzzled. I think the west was content that they had secured their rights in the western part of the city and didn't care too much that the eastern part of the city had been amputated. You will not find in any document from those days a single official demand issued to Moscow or to Ulbricht to take down the Wall again. It was grotesque. The Soviets, I can imagine, were themselves surprised by the lackadaisical attitude. After that, Khrushchev steadily moved away from his demands for a 'free city' and presumingly was content with the assurance of having secured the existence of the GDR.

Thassilo Borchart

Officially, the Wall was built according to an order by Ulbricht to 'secure the border between the GDR to West Berlin and the FRG'. We in East Berlin didn't notice any changes on that beautiful

Saturday, 12 August. I remember it was a very nice summer day, with a clear blue sky. Many people had spent the whole day outside, swimming and picnicking. By the end of the day though, there were many more police around the train and S-Bahn stations leading to the west. Almost everybody was checked and had to show his papers. Then, around eleven o'clock at night the sirens started. As we learned the next morning, selected troops and members of the People's Police had been ordered to the border to start sealing off the sector. Soviet tanks were rolling towards the border. All traffic in East Berlin came to a standstill. For days, all of East Berlin watched as first the barbed wire was put together, and then the Wall was erected. At the Brandenburg Gate, the People's Police established small barricades. The asphalt was torn open and the noises of the drilling machines could be heard everywhere. The West was only a stone's throw away, but no help came. A group of people gathered at the Brandenburg Gate and started to talk to the police. We were attempting to take some of the wire down but were pushed back by their bayonets. The Wall grew higher and higher each day. First, people were speechless, then angry. Adenauer hadn't come to Berlin, nor had any of the other representatives of the Allies. Willy Brandt was the one who gave a speech from the Schöneberger City Hall. He asked the population to be prudent, but he also demanded more than just words from the western Allies—he demanded political action. Some newspapers started to print what everybody in the east thought. We had been sold off to the east to end a crisis and secure world peace.

Our family, like many others, was torn apart by the Wall. One brother was in the east, two in the west. Seeing them, or friends or other relatives, was made impossible. We were living in a large prison. A year after the Wall was built, the cruelty of the regime that had built it became very obvious to the world. Peter Fechter, an 18-year-old from East Berlin, had tried to escape from the east. He was shot down by eastern guards and bled to death. West Germans saw the killing and wanted to help but couldn't.

Ulbricht had got what he wanted: people who wanted to flee could try it only at great danger to their lives. In frequent statements after the Wall was built, Ulbricht insisted that the nation was divided because of the 'West German militarists and their Nato allies.' He spoke of a 'precondition for a time when Berlin would become the capital of a united Germany with no "imperialism", no dictatorship, but only the working class'. For many living in the west, the chapter on the East and West German conflict was closed. For us in the east, it really had only just started. I lost all hope along with the illusions I had clung to for so long.

Hannelore

Rita, a girlfriend, and I had decided to take our first vacation after several semesters studying pharmacology in Jena in 1968. Our decision on where to go was constrained not only by our limited money, but also by the list of 'loyal' communist countries—such as Czechoslovakia, Bulgaria or Poland—that were our only choices if we wanted to get a travel visa.

Before we started our trip we had heard through other students that Alexander Dubçek, one of the high-ranking officials of the Communist Party in Czechoslovakia, had come forward and proclaimed the introduction of a 'human socialism' that would end censorship and other harsh restrictions his country was suffering under. We were excited about potentially being part of, or at least witnessing first hand, reforms in a communist country. We arrived in Prague in the middle of August. Rita and I were immediately charmed by the 'Golden Town'. The bridges crossing the wide stream of the Moldau and the old Kings' Castle towering over the city reminded me of some of the romantic poems of Rainer Maria Rilke.

Wenzel Platz—one of Prague's main squares, dominated by the National Museum and the patron saint of the Czechs, St. Wenzel—was filled with people demonstrating for Dubçek's reforms. We watched for a while and took a few photos. I sympathized strongly. For a while I just watched the faces of the people. Pretty soon I joined the demonstration and I was not the only East German participating. For me, it was the first time I openly showed my opinion. Looking back, I now know that the only time I ever really felt young was during those few days in Prague. I had my own opinion, I was not afraid to say what I believed was right. At home, I played the role of the 'good daughter', the 'political student', so I could finish my studies.

The scene changed quickly, like a beautiful dream becoming a nightmare. Russian tanks and East German troops came rolling into Prague, firing at the demonstrators. East Germany's Ulbricht had for days consistently attacked reformers across the southern border and intimidated friends of the reformers. Dubçek had been a member of the Communist Party for a long time, but he had always been among the party members who wanted to follow a course independent of Russian Stalinism. The Russian and East German tanks put a quick end to the new ideas. What had been called a 'Prague Spring' was brutally stopped by the Warsaw Pact invasion. I had never seen overwhelming brutality of that kind before: East German troops marching through a neighbouring state, taking part in the occupation alongside soviet soldiers, firing into crowds and killing people who were just demonstrating for very basic political rights. Our East German regime had clearly developed in just a few years after the Wall was built into a model of 'people's democracy' loyal to the USSR.

Our sadness was profound. A planned romantic vacation, but more importantly, our hopes for change for East Germany as well as Czechoslovakia, had been abruptly halted by our own troops—supported by the USSR—and had been turned into a horrible nightmare. We were left with a feeling of total helplessness.

Coming home to our students' quarters after 21 August, our 'Prague adventure' did not end. The whole dorm knew that we had spent a fortnight in Prague and had witnessed the events of the 'Prague Spring'. East German media had denied any shootings and explained away the movement of soldiers as regular military manoeuvres of the Warsaw Pact countries. Friends had question upon question about what really had happened in Prague. Our pictures were passed around. An empty chocolate box became the designated hiding spot for all political materials we had brought back—fliers, petitions for reform, pictures of the Russian tanks on Wenzel Platz. I was so naive, thinking a witness to a political uprising would be left alone.

When I returned to my dorm from the first lectures of the new semester the next day, my room had been torn apart. Bedding was turned upside down, drawers opened, books were on the floor. The person who had stormed my dorm didn't even try to make a secret of the obvious. It was a strange, frightening feeling, knowing that a stranger had gone through even just a few of my personal belongings with such savagery.

It wasn't long before Rita and I were asked to report to the dean of the university. Fortunately, the dean was a well-meaning man who begged us to keep our mouths shut about what we had experienced in Prague. He ordered us to destroy any evidence of the events in Czechoslovakia and to leave the city for awhile. I can still hear him say, 'Girls, you cannot stay here; the People's Police will probably pick you up. Leave the university for a few weeks.'

Rita and I went to a small village close to the sea, frightened as two chickens being followed by a fox. We were silent for awhile, each aware that the regime once again had us exactly where it wanted us. Just like the three monkeys: seeing nothing, hearing nothing, saying nothing. As we learned later, during our absence the dean had to deal with several interrogations and finally had to sign a document attesting that none of his students had been in Prague during the month of August.

After we returned, we were lucky to be able to pick up our studies where we had stopped. Everyday life went on. In our little world everything seemed all right again. We had enough to eat, we were healthy, we had some money, interesting studies, good friends. But there was another reality: one of fear, isolation, oppression and the sure knowledge that whenever the regime decided to seek victims, any of us could be one of them.

Out of my 'vacation time' in Prague several friendships developed. One of them ended with a heavy personal blow. During the demonstrations in Czechoslovakia I met a young man from Mannheim, West Germany. We kept seeing each other in East Berlin for months after, meeting in an apartment of a friend. He did what I hoped for, yet feared at the same time: he asked me to marry him. Here I was an East German girl with a West German fiancé, and with a Wall surrounded by mines and watch towers separating us. After a while, his weekly visits were dominated by conversations about how I could leave the country. Silly ideas came up, such as swimming through the mined river Elbe, or working with a professional service organized by West Germans who tried to get people out through the few loopholes in the system. The latter had worked for some people, but most who tried to escape got killed or caught. Part of me desperately wanted to leave with him; the other part was scared and confused. And there was another problem: my old father. I remember one conversation particularly well. It started on one of those slow Sunday afternoons. My father was looking through some photo albums just letting the past slide by. There were his wedding pictures with my mother, who had just died, some shots of the few vacations to the countryside they had taken together, and pictures of me as a child.

After thumbing through page after page of the albums that had been carefully put together by my mother and written on with white ink, my father looked at me with his deep, sad eyes and said, 'There were some nice moments in my life.' I didn't say anything, but he knew what I was thinking. He had never lived up to what he might have achieved. My father had been a soldier during the Second World War. When he came home from the eastern front he returned to the eastern part of Germany, which was occupied by the Russians. While my grandparents had decided to go to Kiel, a harbour town on the Baltic Sea occupied by British troops, he stayed behind. Wisely, the grandparents had chosen the British zone, which soon gave back civil and political rights. He defended staying by referring to his 'Prussian discipline' and 'loyalty'. These two main pillars of his life also shaped my childhood education.

My father always knew that he had made a grave mistake by not leaving, but he expected me to make the same error. And I did. I stayed, passively letting go of my relationship, which ended on New Year's Eve 1969 at the Berlin Wall on Bornholmer Strasse. Fireworks were exploding and painted the sky in all sorts of different colours when, at midnight, all West Germans with a day pass had to return to the western part of the city. It was the last time I saw my fiancé.

Westerners ask today why we never told how bad the circumstances and living conditions really were in East Germany. I think the main reason was a sense of pride. The year 1949 was a new beginning for both Germanies. The west was lucky to have the 'right' political system opportunities for growth and prosperity; the east got caught up in filth, oppression and was headed by a criminal regime. We all knew that, but it is difficult to admit to a fellow countryman from the west, 'I'm a poor sucker and I'm living in a filthy mess'.

Part Three

Shifting Cold Fronts 1961–1989

The shortest way to ruin a country is to give power to demagogues.
Dionysius

Chapter Eight

The Honecker Era

In May 1971 the citizens of the GDR were stunned by the announcement that Walter Ulbricht had asked the Central Committee of his party to retire him. The departing party head proposed Erich Honecker, a long-time protégé, as his successor. Honecker, a model *apparatchik*, seemed to be a logical replacement for Ulbricht.

With Ulbricht's departure, a dominant figure disappeared from the political chessboard in the communist east. As a loyal servant of Moscow, he had survived three Kremlin leaders and had skilfully adapted to every new political direction suggested by the Soviet Politburo. When in 1945 Ulbricht assigned Honecker responsibilities for developing the Free German Youth (Freie Deutsche Jugend—FDJ), the communist young people's organization, Ulbricht did not know that he had found the man who would one day unseat him. For over a quarter of a century Ulbricht had controlled the GDR as an unchallenged dictator. Then in the spring of 1971, he found himself retired by a long-time political friend who had learned the ropes from him. Defeated by his own weapons, Ulbricht announced 'comrade' Honecker as his successor and chairman of the National Defence Council. Ulbricht remained as the nominal head of the Council of the State, but Honecker quickly made sure that this body lost much of its earlier significance. Ulbricht soon passed into obscurity, his once ubiquitous photograph vanishing from all the walls and his name from the press. Ulbricht was yet another communist dictator whose rise and fall symbolizes the triumph and tragedy of Stalinism.

Almost immediately, Honecker broke with Ulbricht's innovative interpretations of Marxism–Leninism and swung the GDR into a course of economic development aimed at 'perfecting' the system without losing party control. Steadily, he began to develop his own political style and to step out from under the shadow of his former mentor, Ulbricht. By 1976 he became general secretary of the party. Virtually every wall and publication was 'graced' with his photo and words. Once he consolidated his position, he began to reorganize the country's industries to bring research and development, production and exports and sales under one roof. Ulbricht's experiments with economic decentralization were abandoned, centralized planning and control were reinstated. Within months after Honecker's accession, the regime eliminated the few remaining private businesses and private participations. Only in retail and a few service areas did firms that shared ownership with the state—the so-called mixed-ownership businesses—survive.

The preconditions for all these changes were laid when Honecker and the GDR received diplomatic recognition from outside the Soviet bloc. Prior to the agreement with Bonn on the Basic Treaty in 1972, only 19 countries, mainly from developing parts of the world, had accorded recognition to the GDR. But once it became clear that West Germany would establish formal relations with the Honecker regime in 1972, the barrier also fell for other non-communist countries. By the end of 1973, 69 nations had established full diplomatic relations with East Berlin. Dozens of countries followed Bonn's example, including the United States in 1974.

Although East Germany's strong and absolute loyalty towards the Soviet Union was never questioned, the humble notion that 'learning from the Soviet Union brings victory'[1] slowly began to fade. Honecker's ego made East Germany yearn for its own identity, a yearning that found one outlet in athletic accomplishments. The GDR set out in concerted fashion to promote sports and to provide handsome incentives for international athletic success.

East Germany found another way of stressing its independence from the 'Big Brother' Soviet Union, by linking the GDR to the German past. The traditions of Prussia, including austerity and self-sacrifice on the part of the individual for the well-being of the whole, became part of the new appeal for a separate identity. The positive re-evaluation of Prussian tradition found expression in 1980 when a statue of Frederick the Great was restored at a prominent location in East Berlin. On the 500th anniversary of Martin Luther's birth in Saxony, the religious reformer who until then had been portrayed by the SED as a fanatic and an enemy of the common man, was suddenly celebrated as a hero and praised as a man of progress.

The new found admiration for German history nonetheless contrasted sharply with Honecker's campaign of 'Abgrenzung' (demarcation). The increased prestige the regime received from its acceptance in international circles and its policy of stressing the German heritage was accompanied by a propaganda campaign stressing the superiority of the GDR over the West German Federal Republic. The campaign was necessary because the Basic Treaty with Bonn liberalized restrictions on travel to the east, enabling many easterners to learn firsthand about the personal

---

[1] Siegmund Bernd, *Vierzig Jahre und so weiter*, official handbook of the GDR–Soviet friendship, pp. 41–8.

freedom and higher standard of living that existed in the west. Also, visitors brought valuable western currency into the east and, with it, the hope of increased trade and improved communication.

Like all propaganda, Honecker's campaign to combat this interaction was simple and consisted of one basic line: 'The two systems are irreconcilable; just as the GDR's future is bright and progressive, that of the Federal Republic is doomed and is shaped by unemployment, crime, inflation and difficult social problems.'[2] Soon other measures were enacted to decrease the number of visitors to the east. In November 1973 the amount of non-convertible eastern currency that visitors had to purchase with western money for each day spent in the east was increased drastically. In addition, 'about two million people classified as bearers of secrets', including all scientists in research and development and all military personnel, were required to sign a document that forbade them any contact with the west.

Economically, the East German system under Honecker ostensibly worked better than the systems of any other nation behind the Iron Curtain. With an annual per capita income of $8,000—twice as high as in the Soviet Union, four times as high as in Poland—it was a star performer. Nevertheless, the GDR's growing indebtedness and the resulting increase in the portion of goods produced in the GDR that had to be traded for essential imports, such as oil, hampered the overall performance of the economy. As in all centrally planned economies, lining up for food, shortages of familiar goods and long waiting periods for major purchases became part of the daily grind. In 1970 household income in East Germany was only two-thirds of that in the Federal Republic. By 1983 it had dropped to half.

Such numbers, however, convey only some of the frustration felt by East German citizens. A housing shortage had kept most of the population assigned to cramped, low-standard quarters since World War II. The usual wait for a car made in East Germany was 14 years. Ageing and obsolete industrial plants caused shortages and bottlenecks in other parts of the economy. Best-documented is East Germany's shortfall within the micro- electronic field. Because the west withheld technologies with military potential, East Germany spent billions on reinventing the wheel. Production of a 32-byte minicomputer, for example, started a decade later in the GDR than in western markets. Almost every East German citizen saw daily on West German TV how great the gap between the west and east had really grown.

Like other Warsaw Pact nations, the GDR had to start borrowing

---

[2] Heise and Hofmann, *Fragen an die Geschichte der DDR*, official handbook on the history of the GDR.

heavily in the 1970s and was very hard hit economically in the early 1980s. In line with Chancellor Willy Brandt's new eastern policy, Bonn and others accommodated the economically troubled GDR with an interest-free 'swing' credit for East German purchases in West Germany. Also valuable to the GDR was the duty-free access to GDR goods within the Federal Republic, which declined to apply import taxes in line with the western insistence that Germany was still one nation. To encourage road traffic to West Berlin and promote human ties, the Federal Republic had begun to make large lump-sum payments to East Berlin in 'hard' currency, which the regime then used to purchase needed items anywhere in the non-socialist world. Liberalized financial regulations also helped West Germans who had relatives in the east to send them West German marks. These came in handy for making purchases in certain speciality stores, called 'Intershop', carrying Western products that were unavailable elsewhere and originally reserved for high-ranking party members.

A plague afflicting all Marxist countries—the inability to meet unrealistic goals—was also starting to eat at East Germany. When in 1987 Honecker admitted for the first time that the GDR had failed to meet key economic targets, those familiar with the situation sensed the end of his career. But most did not anticipate his return to the Soviet Union, where he had been schooled by the party for his return to Germany to build the Communist Youth Organization. After returning to Germany in 1934, he was arrested for an illegal antifascist campaign by the Gestapo and imprisoned until 1945. A year after the Wall fell, the 78-year-old man who had ruled East Germany from 1971 to 1989 was taken to the Soviet Union without any prosecution for embezzlement, manslaughter and aiding terrorism. Although West German prosecutors had issued a warrant for Honecker's arrest after discovering written shoot-to-kill orders for guards at the Berlin Wall for people trying to flee the country, and after discovering that terrorists operating in the west had been given a safe haven in the east, West German authorities still were reluctant to enforce the warrant. Honecker's flight caused bitterness, especially among eastern citizens who for the first time were painfully given notice that democracy provides no guarantee of justice. The frustration among easterners deepened when Honecker later was returned to Germany, but his trial was dismissed because of health reasons.

Wolfgang Mischnick

Many West Germans used to say with an ambivalent pride that 'if anyone can make communism work, it's the East Germans'.

Honecker, the coal miner's son, was greatly responsible for this dubious success. I met with Honecker several times, the first time in 1972.

Herbert Wehner, long-time chairman of the Social Democrats, asked me if I would join him on an official visit to East Germany. The goal of our visit was to establish communication lines, not only between high-ranking party members but also between city councils and satellite parties of the SED. The Basic Treaty between the east and west had permitted brief visits by its citizens, particularly those over 60 years old, and in case of pressing family needs. The treaty, which stopped short of full diplomatic recognition, provided for an exchange, not of embassies, but of 'permanent missions' in Bonn and East Berlin. The coalition partners came to believe that only contacts, recognition and co-operation with the East German regime held prospects of improving the lives of millions of East Germans living behind the Iron Curtain and gave any possibility of reunification a chance.

I visited the GDR as an official of the West German government every two to three years trying to establish further contacts between cities and communities. During that time we reached a consensus with Honecker that the brutal order-to-shoot was to be abolished.[3] Travel easements became more common and the exchange of political prisoners was made easier than it had been before.

Wolf-Rüdiger Borchart

On all my visits to the east from the early 1970s, having left the GDR before the Wall was built, I was always depressed by the greyness of everything, by the obvious neglect. Now, the old street connections to the west are open again, and new routes are currently planned. Yet you still feel as though you've passed from sunshine to shadow when you enter East Berlin. The dreariness of this city is beyond description. The infrastructure has collapsed, but hideous former SED buildings still dominate the skyline.

Under Honecker, like in the early 1960s, the party strictly limited contacts with the west. Honecker's greatest triumph, the diplomatic

---

[3] Although this consensus was reached, 186 people have been recorded as dying at the Wall. Protests from the West German government usually resulted in the GDR's denial. The last victim shot at the Wall died in February 1989.

recognition of the GDR outside the Soviet bloc, resulted in the virtual elimination of the word 'German' from the constitution. Thus, the 'socialist state of the German nation' became the 'socialistic state of farmers and workers'.

Paradoxically, Honecker at the same time asked many intellectuals who had previously been denounced to invent a new communism divergent from the Soviet brand. He even allowed giants in German history, such as Frederick the Great, Bismarck and Martin Luther, to be mentioned in public. That's how I myself ended up working on the GDR's celebration of the 500th anniversary of Luther's birth.

My company had just received the Schinkelpreis.[4] I asked the East German Building and Construction Ministry if they knew of an East German firm that could help build replicas of cast-iron chairs originally designed by Schinkel. After four weeks I received an invitation to see a firm in East Germany specializing in cast iron. On the day of my trip to the east, I was asked at the check point to exchange the usual 25 West German marks for the non-convertible GDR currency that visitors to the east were required to purchase for each day they stayed in the GDR.

I refused. After an hour of checking and several hectic telephone calls between the ministry and the People's Police at the check point, I was angrily waved through and on my way to the little village of Görlitz. The firm I was to visit was the city's oldest cast-iron firm, established in 1900. As I arranged for my chairs to be delivered to the west, I discovered the feet, head and body of a statue of Luther under some sheets. I assumed it had been sitting there since the war. I remember thinking with amusement how Luther would have liked Honecker's socialism.

Later I was told that in 1861 Görlitz had invited several artists to submit designs for a Martin Luther statue. A Professor Rietschel had won the commission. His rather ascetic-looking Luther was, of course, removed from the town square after the war, since the regime preached atheism. Luther's 500th anniversary was nearing, and I thought I'd engineered a plan to return him to the little market square were he belonged. Although he was back in fashion, the bureaucratic problems were unbelievable. First, the statue could not be given by a

---

[4] Karl Friedrich Schinkel (1781–1841) was a German architect who built most of the outstanding monuments in Berlin.

western individual, it had to be an organization. Then there was quite a controversy over which currency was to be paid for the statue's restoration—East or West German marks. Every tiny decision required a meeting. But finally, Luther was repaired and once more standing in the town square. The mayor of Görlitz gave an impassioned speech on the vast achievements of socialism, to which the audience responded with scarcely a ripple of applause. The mayor was followed by a speaker from the west, who said a few words about Luther and the significance of his statue. When he had finished, 20,000 people who had come to watch the event applauded wildly. It was not the simple speech that set them off, but the opportunity to be in contact with the 'other' Germany.

Thassilo Borchart

As schoolchildren, and later as young adults, we were taught that capitalism exploits. That might be true, but no other political system compares in its degree of exploitation to that under which I have lived for the last fifty years. The exploitation of people by those in controlling positions is stronger here than anywhere else. I have had to listen to countless speeches about how everything belongs to the people. But the truth is that nothing and nobody is willing to take any responsibility. Communism is a religion that glorifies its goals, promising the unpromisable and perverting the truth.

It was sometimes amusing when the Honecker regime tried to link the GDR to the glories of the German past. One morning in 1980 I was among many who discovered to our very great surprise that the equestrian statue of Frederick the Great, the 18th-century soldier-king whose conquests made Prussia the major European power, had been restored to its former location, Unter den Linden, East Berlin's major boulevard. The last time I could remember having seen it was before the war ended. I had believed, like most, that the statue had been destroyed.

Why the same 'people's republic' that had blown up the Berlin City Castle because it was a remnant of bourgeois Prussia suddenly embraced Frederick the Great, I did not understand. But I soon understood how certain Prussian values were being appropriated by the communists. An article in *Neues Deutschland*, the party organ, praised the Prussian tradition of individual submission to the well-being of the group, and the Prussians' devotion to duty. Another surprise was the publication of a book on Otto von Bismarck in the mid-1980s. For the first time in decades the imperial chancellor was celebrated as a brilliant leader. The irony that Bismarck was responsible for unifying 19th-century Germany must have escaped the regime.

Many families were cruelly split up by the division of Germany, and the gap between the two nations and those family members grew bigger as time passed. The 1972 treaty did not change this fact. I'm the eldest of three sons, the only one who did not leave. Sometimes I feel I am treated like the 'dumb one who stayed behind'. I remember one Christmas a cousin sent me a box of hand-me-downs: 40 old ties, worn pajamas and some suits. I was glad to have them, of course, but it made me sad, too. It was humiliating. It was like charity.

I think it was Kafka who described it this way. Once there were two friends. One had spent six weeks in a hospital bed. The other had spent the same time travelling. When the traveller visited his friend, he would talk of nothing but the fabulous time he had. Although the two had been friends for a long time, they could no longer communicate. Their recent experience had made them strangers.

Wolf-Jürgen Staab

When I arrived at the permanent mission in East Berlin, Honecker had just announced that the number of 'bearers of secrets' who were not allowed to deal with the west had been greatly increased. In fact, it was increased ridiculously because his regime feared direct contacts between east and west. According to the treaty he couldn't deny entry to West Berliners nor to West Germans, but he could make contacting them very difficult for as many East Germans as possible. Then in January 1974, leadership instructions were passed out by Honecker. They stated that the Basic Treaty was not significant on its own but only in connection with Moscow and the Warsaw treaty. Additionally, the document made clear that the treaty was an agreement with a class-enemy. Pettiness and difficulties reached a level that even began to impinge on Soviet interests.

The first permanent mission in East Berlin was headed by a journalist, Günther Gauss, a friend and confidant of Willy Brandt and the Socialist Party. At his side worked the attorney Hans-Otto Bräutigam, who later became my boss, heading the permanent mission in the 1980s. Bräutigam was working behind the scenes in East Berlin mainly being responsible for all legal and administrative questions, while Gauss acted more as a socialite having already been a well-known journalist in the west. Bräutigam quite often told me about his first days in East Berlin. As I remember, he first moved into an Interhotel, a hotel chain that originally had been designed by the East German regime for foreign visitors and that supposedly represented all the luxury the east could supply. In reality, it was a carelessly designed concrete building at the corner of Friedrichstrasse and the main boulevard, Unter den Linden.

One of the first private invitations he received came from a prominent West German journalist, Lothar Loewe,[5] who had asked Bräutigam to join him and an attaché from Moscow for dinner at Loewe's home. The journalist was known to be quite bold in criticizing the regime and a good source of information about problems within East Germany for the mission. Bräutigam started to ask some piercing questions, but soon the dinner discussion began to resemble a scene from a Chekhov play. The evening had an interesting twist to it, since the Russian attaché was not only of a different opinion than Loewe, but was also his well-meaning friend. Loewe started to become increasingly nervous as he received warning signs and words from the Russian guest not to overstep his limits. The Russian attaché spoke about certain 'proprieties' that should be observed and noted that ignoring these could result in a situation everybody would regret. The whole evening was a new experience and a prelude to what we later called the 'tip-toe dance of communications' whenever we were in contact with the East German regime. Almost a year later, the same journalist who had been our host at that memorable evening called the Honecker regime a 'hare shooter'. He was immediately asked to leave the GDR.

During my early days in Berlin we were expected to participate in the cocktail-party circuit, involving endless invitations to receptions with diplomats of mostly communist countries and underdeveloped nations. I remember one incident when a rather ignorant diplomat

[5] Loewe was the first West German journalist admitted in East Germany.

tried to persuade me that Amsterdam was once the capital of a united Germany. I was unable to alter his conviction.

On a day-to-day basis I dealt with political prisoners and visited them in their prisons, if possible. The most difficult task was trying to establish a line of communication with the East German government and other high-ranking members of the Politburo.

The new relationship that had started so promisingly soon faded into a tiresome charade, where a little tension here and there or a carelessly spoken word could create a crisis.

We were advised to play our role of the friendly neighbours who watch to see that everything was in keeping with the terms of the 1972 treaty, but we were also told not to go beyond that role. Rituals took the place of real discussion.

Year by year we participated in the Leipziger Messe, the largest technology show in the east, raised our glasses to communist toasts with a smile, and shook hands with the highest functionaries of the regime. Another event that developed into a regular ritual was the traditional new year's reception, during which the diplomatic corps was welcomed and ritual protests were officially passed to the GDR. The protests usually didn't lead anywhere.

Throughout the existence of the permanent mission in East Berlin we had many daring visitors who asked us to help them to leave the country. As much as I would have liked to find a way for them to leave, as an official representative of Bonn I could only communicate 'official' advice, meaning they should apply to their government for a travel visa. Not only was the attempt in most cases hopeless but it was also usually punished with loss of a job or other cruelties. But nevertheless, the stream of refugees seeking shelter in our mission was sometimes not to be stopped. At one time, while we held a cocktail reception for official party members and some guests from Yugoslavia, a group of young families with small children had managed to get into the mission. Literally, everybody knew about the double play: the party members who had arrived in their dark blue Volvo state carriages were aware of the situation, as were the waiters who busily filled glasses, the young people who waited hopefully inside for a happy end, and the head of the permanent mission, Hans-Otto Bräutigam, who greeted everybody with a perky smile.

To a certain degree we already had adapted to what many East German citizens had got used to over the decades—the East German double standard of morals. We also used the mission's garden as a gathering place for East German writers, sculptors and painters. At the time Honecker entered his position, he had called for a 'broader and richer spectrum of cultural creativity'. By 1976, however, it became clear that the limits of ventures in critical art were very narrowly defined, and that the party's tolerance was minimal. We decided to regularly invite some of the less critical and well-known artists to our mission for a cultural exchange between east and west. For the purpose of encouraging 'alternative art' we had a small gazebo built, which after a while, became a meeting place for some artists who protested subtly against the regime.

While in the beginning we had been unsure about what could be done in the GDR and what couldn't, we now knew quite well that the only tone the Honecker regime understood was that of determination. The more we pushed towards an agreeable situation, the more attention we got from Honecker and his party.

After an irritating meeting with party members about the exchange of further political prisoners for financial help, I received an invitation to a weekend hunt with Honecker. First, I was surprised and unsure about the gesture's meaning. But as we learned later, those invitations for hunt weekends were part of a ritual to get to know the opponent—the class-enemy, as we were called officially. The atmosphere was stiff and cold in the beginning. I hadn't expected anything else. Everything was lavishly organized. Nothing was missing, from the caviar from the Soviet Union to china from Meissen and delicatessen foods from Poland and Hungary. The personal meetings during those weekend outings usually took place before and after dinner. While the first personal discussions I had with Honecker were dominated by a certain mistrust and lacked any warmth, later talks became more meaningful and sometimes even corrected political misunderstandings. During one of those weekends, during a walk through the forest, he told me an intimate story about how he had listened as a child to the tales of his father, who told him about Marx and Engels, and how he had helped his parents deliver the communist papers in the little town of Neuenkirchen in the Saarland. At that moment, I almost felt pity for the old man. I had to remind myself that Honecker and a couple of people in power were cold heartedly robbing their citizens off all essentials of life and covering the theft with an idiotic glorification of communism. He was also full of hatred for those who had been active during the Second World War and those who had put him in prison, and he was oblivious to the fact that he was giving his people exactly the same treatment. In a wicked way, Honecker deeply believed in the brutal system he and Ulbricht had built. He preached about the advantages on his side of the Wall, including subsidies for rent, public transportation, basic food and electricity. He was proud of his accomplishments and didn't want to have them tarnished by anyone or anything.

His foolish pride, I believe, was also his undoing. Honecker rejected Gorbachev's ideas for decentralization and liberalization and even refused to use the buzzword perestroika. Yet, while he had created his own political style over the years, he couldn't hide the fact that praise from Moscow was all he was waiting for. He told me once that he was tired but was very much looking forward to celebrating a personal triumph as one of the builders of the nation at the occasion of the 40th anniversary of the GDR. History thwarted his ambitious plan.

Francis Meehan

During my time at the embassy in East Germany there were quite a few daily chores mixed in with the high priority activities and emergency situations. Among those weekly chores was visiting the Stasi headquarters, a dreadful building. If you wanted to know somehow with whom you were dealing on the 'other side', you had to make a point of meeting East German officials. Of course, there were official cocktail parties and dinners where east met west, but the only other way to get to know some of the party members was by requesting an appointment. I usually had to wait for days to find out whether somebody on the other side was ready to meet with me. Then you had to go to that awful dark building on Leipziger Strasse. It was a real horror. I remember going up there and following those endless corridors, passing doors with no names on them, not even a number. Those doors symbolized the system, a regime mostly of nameless people, with only a few exceptions.

I met most East German officials in that building, including Honecker and Hermann Axen. Axen was in charge of international relations. He organized annual hunts in the forest of Thuringia or around the forest of Magdeburg for Honecker and all the ambassadors and other officials representing their governments in East Germany. It was well known that Honecker hunted almost every week during the season; once a year he invited the diplomatic corps to join him. Since it was considered a prestigious event, it would almost have been considered an insult for an invitee not to attend. So I went, albeit reluctantly in the beginning.

I remember one hunting feast in particular. We arrived by train in Magdeburg, where the regime's dutiful subjects were lined up to cheer us. Here we were, representatives of embassies in East Berlin with Honecker and company, being waved at by school kids and adults who had been ordered to come. Little girls brought flowers to Honecker, bands played, everything went as organized. Each ambassador was assigned a room in a hotel and was given clothes to wear for the hunt, since most of us weren't properly prepared or dressed. The overcoats that were given to us were old East German army coats: greyish, long and covered with all the emblems you can imagine. Although it was bitterly cold, none of the ambassadors wore the overcoat. One Italian representative, who was slightly built and had a cold, walked for hours alongside the hunt until after a while, he couldn't stand the weather anymore and asked for a coat. For the rest of the day he wore the East German Army greatcoat. I think he was the only Westerner I ever saw in one.

Usually there was one day of hunting. The ambassadors were asked to chase through the countryside while Honecker sat waiting comfortably in a blind. The diplomatic corps drove the game towards him so he could shoot it more easily. I think he had some of the highest-priced beaters in the world. Then at the end of the day, the hunters met, the horn and trumpets sounded and all the beasts were laid out. All together, between 250 and 300 deer usually had been killed. It was pretty awful.

Several hours later there was a dinner. This was the real reason most of the ambassadors came; it offered a chance to meet and talk to people and to develop a new sense of what the regime was all about. At one such event I happened to spend the whole evening next to an extraordinarily interesting person, Kurt Hager. He had joined the Communist Party in 1930 and had been editor of a major East German newspaper. He was made secretary of the Central

Committee of the SED in 1955 and ten years later became a member of the Politburo. He told me that he had become disillusioned during the Second World War, during which he spent his time mostly in England and later in the antifascist movement in Spain. He was one of those political rockets who returned from a self-imposed exile after the war and climbed the party ladder.

These hunts provided a way of meeting people in a quiet way and getting to understand one another better without ever discussing everyday politics. It was an old boy network on SED level.

Sometimes we had refugees at the embassy. Typically, East Germans coming off the street would ask us to grant them political asylum. But we couldn't do that. We simply couldn't help them to get out and we had to tell them that we couldn't even pretend that we could help them. Most would listen carefully; often they looked frightened. Sometimes we gave them Dr Wolfgang Vogel's name as a possible source of assistance, but that would cost the refugees' money.

I think some 'refugees' were sent by the Stasi just to see how the American embassy would handle a situation like that. I can't prove it, but from time to time there were people knocking at our door who just didn't seem to be real.

At other times, however, we had people who were so desperate they refused to leave. I remember three couples who came to us with a bunch of children. They were all afraid that if they left the American embassy in East Berlin they would be arrested immediately for contacting us. And they were very serious about wanting to leave the GDR. Again, we couldn't help them. But we couldn't throw them out, either. These people were under a great deal of stress. So we explained the situation as well as we could and told them that a prolonged stay at our embassy would raise uncomfortable questions and make them even more visible to the authorities. They still said, 'No, we are not leaving'. This produced the rather strange spectacle of a group of East Germans camping at the embassy for a day or two. We gave them a place to stay, several couches in a warm room with a fireplace, but we didn't have beds. The marines whom we usually had as security guards took care of them in their own way and brought them coffee or bagels. We were afraid that this situation could develop into a political confrontation with the east. I spoke on the phone to officials in Washington, but nothing was worked out.

Strangely, by the next morning the couples had accepted the fact that we couldn't help, and they let us know that they would try to leave the country via the official procedure of applying for a permit to travel. I later learned that, after spending a brief time under arrest, the couples and their children got out of East Germany.

Uwe Wunderlich

As the director of the Kombinat I had been responsible for almost everything—production, employment, inventory. Right after I finished my law studies in Leipzig, I controlled 30 small businesses. Then in 1981, I was asked to head up the Kombinat. That brought membership in the party, a certain lifestyle, more education and career rewards. Yes, the party used all these 'carrots'.

I knew from the very beginning—when I had decided to study law in Leipzig—that I would be asked to join. One's eligibility for advanced schooling was determined largely by one's 'political behaviour'. Some students were asked later, some earlier. There were about twenty students in my law class, five of whom were already party members. The rest, with the exception of one whose mother was a well-known communist, joined later. Membership meant hour-long interrogations about my attitudes, beliefs and goals. I have to admit that after a while I started to believe. I knew I was being brainwashed. For me, being a party member was a career decision. My motives were purely egocentric and opportunistic Yet it is difficult to stand aloof from what supplies your daily bread.

I believe many of the party members were not communists at heart—it was the only route to success. My wife was constantly pressured to join as well. As late as September 1989, she was called to an interrogation in which she was told that her obstinate attitude was hurting my career and our family's future.

Michael Bacher

I have to admit that for a long time I was among those members of the Freie Deutsche Jugend (FDJ), East Germany's Communist Youth Organization, who enjoyed going to party meetings and clapping my hands with 30,000 other young people. I shouted slogans such as: 'We want peace!', 'Friendship!' or even 'SED—FDJ!'

Looking back, it is a miracle to me how Honecker, who really doesn't have any charisma, was able to catch the enthusiasm of young people for so long. Egon Krenz summarized it by saying in his praise that no important event in the history of the FDJ would have taken place without Honecker. But at the beginning of the 1980s, when even the most apolitical people were becoming aware that Honecker's economy was leading the GDR into a catastrophe, many heavily engaged FDJ members—among them me—started to dream about an East Germany after him. I hoped that a new crew of able politicians would appear after the old man retired and lead East Germany out of the social and economic dark. Obviously Krenz, a protégé of Honecker, was not the man who could make the dream come true. After the Wall fell, up to 1.5 million members left the organization; they no longer needed to be in it for opportunistic or political reasons. On the contrary, if you were looking for a job in West Germany, admitting to membership in the Communist Youth could only limit your possibilities. Finally, the dream of a new GDR had died and with it the reason for a Communist Youth Organization. The 500,000 people left organized in the FDJ were mostly left-wing social workers or experienced functionaries who wanted to get their hands on the organization's funds.

Somehow the FDJ was a romantic debris from the past. Honecker had founded it in 1945–46 as an antifascist youth organization. At that time, the members loved to sing class-warfare songs while sitting around a camp fire. Honecker tells in his memoirs that, supported by his fatherly friend Wilhelm Pick, he convinced the Soviet occupation power to found a new youth organization that would bring a feeling for justice, truth and morality back to the German youth. All youth organizations, from amateur sports to bird watchers were brought under one umbrella, that of the FDJ. Eventually, everybody understood that the one and only goal was for Honecker to keep his romanticism for the class-fighting Weimar Republic alive and to control the youth by preaching Marxism-Leninism.

It wasn't too long before the repetitive political songs from the 1930s began to bore us young people to death. But there was also a certain enthusiasm among some FDJ members as subdivisions received honourable tasks. Probably, the best known by now is the project Megabyte-chip. Günther Mittag, a high-ranking party member and commissioner for the development of micro-technology, gave a well-trained group of FDJ members the job of developing a high-quality computer chip. It turned out to be a flop, and the general atmosphere within the FDJ was frustration. I can still hear a friend who worked within the development group saying, 'Honecker; the old guy gets his 40th anniversary party, but after that he really has to go.' That seemed the end to waving torches and the glorious youth organization, a semi-military group that from the beginning used young people's detestation of the Third Reich to its advantage.

When the enthusiasm for Honecker's idea started to fade, unwritten rules were made public that everybody who wanted to have a good education had to be a member of the FDJ. Party and FDJ members voted on who would get higher education, which itself became politicized. Every morning the class of students announced itself to the teacher, comparable to a group of soldiers saluting their officer. Often whole schools were asked to go to the airport or train station to greet arriving government guests from the Soviet Union.

In 1974 Egon Krenz took over the leadership of the FDJ. He didn't make the organization any more enticing, but we knew better than before what was really expected of us. His formula was, 'One who can adapt himself to the system doesn't have to be afraid of anything'. Four per cent of the FDJ were young students of high-school age; many more came from the police or military, and whoever wanted to study had to be a member of the FDJ. Over 20 per cent of all vocational trainees were wearing the blue shirt, FDJ's official uniform.

Not only education but also western concerts in East Berlin were controlled by the FDJ in the mid-1980s. Harry Belafonte and Bob Dylan concerts were sponsored by the FDJ; otherwise nobody would ever have seen a ticket sold in East Berlin. Originally, the concerts took place in the Treptower Park in East Berlin. Friends from the west tell me that sometimes the concerts could be heard in there as well. We were so close! But then by the end of the 1980s a new stadium was built away from the Wall close to an intercity park called Friedrichshain. I think Honecker must have feared even then that maybe one night after a concert the youth would shout, 'We are leaving now for the west.' At that time that thought seemed crazy and almost suicidal.

Chapter Nine

Ostpolitik

When Adenauer waited more than ten days before he visited the rising fortification that would become the Berlin Wall in 1961, the Germans asked, 'Is the chancellor playing boccia?' Even President Kennedy had promptly sent Vice-President Lyndon Johnson, accompanied by General Lucius D. Clay, as a demonstration of American sympathy for the German people.[1]

The other Allies were silent. Regardless of sympathies, the status quo of Berlin and the divided Germany had been decided and was respected by all four Allies. It was not Berlin, but the crisis in Cuba that brought the Soviets and Americans around one table again. Phrases such as 'Cold War' were replaced with 'containment', 'détente ' and 'peace politics'. In his famous address at American University in Washington, DC in June of the following year, Kennedy asked the American people to 're-examine their attitude toward the Cold War'.

The opposition party in West Germany, the Socialist Party of Germany (SPD), sought adoption of these same ideas for the internal German policies. In a speech in 1963, Egon Bahr, then head of the press information bureau of the Berlin Senate and a member of the SPD, laid the basis for what he called 'change through rapprochement' (*Wandel durch Annäherung*). The speech introduced a new language that would eventually provide the intellectual foundation for Bonn's Ostpolitik (eastern policy). The theory behind the new policy was that technological developments ultimately would force east and west to come closer together. The ruling conservative party, the Christian Democratic Union (CDU) and the majority of his own party members looked upon Bahr's idea with scepticism.

Even de facto recognition of East Germany seemed impossible at the time, but both world politics and the surprising Grand Coalition between the conservative CDU and the SPD following the 1966 elections in West Germany suggested that the winds of change might soon affect the

---

[1] US Government Printing Office, *Public Papers of the Presidents*, June 1963, pp. 459–64.

political relations between East and West Germany as well. Although Willy Brandt's 1969 Social Liberal Coalition between his Socialist Party and the Free Democratic Parliamentarians (FDP) is usually credited with the West German Ostpolitik and the rationale that made the breakthrough treaties of the early 1970s possible, the origins of the policy can also be found in the efforts of Christian Democrats such as Foreign Minister Gerhard Schröder and the Grand Coalition's Chancellor Kurt-Georg Kiesinger.

A first step in the direction Bahr had suggested was taken when in 1963 1.2 million West Berliners were allowed to visit relatives and friends in the east over the Christmas holidays. At the same time, West Germany was in secret contact with the GDR to arrange the first of tens of thousands of deals in which Bonn quietly paid for the release of political prisoners. Surprisingly, in 1966 the SED proposed an exchange of high-level speakers between themselves and the West German SPD. Herbert Wehner, head of the West German socialists, accepted, probably to the surprise of the SED. As the day of the exchange drew near, Erich Honecker, who would soon govern the GDR, convinced Walter Ulbricht of the danger involved in such a venture.

A year later, Grand Coalition Chancellor Kiesinger and his counterpart Brandt expressed their desire for better relations with the GDR and suggested a cultural and economic exchange. A number of letters were exchanged between Kiesinger and Willi Stoph, chairman of the Council of Ministers of the GDR, with no result.

Ulbricht, even more now than before, showed no interest in abandoning the idea of a united Germany under a democratic flag. During the Seventh Red Congress in April 1967, he announced a new citizenship law that eliminated all past references to a single German citizenship. Ulbricht himself declared, 'We German Marxists and Leninists have never written off the unitary, peaceful and progressive German state and will never do so.'[2] Internal polls among East Germans had shown that the citizens' attachment to West Germany was still strong. Ulbricht knew that the overtures and the new tone from the west could eventually determine the fate of his system.

Ulbricht was eager to establish his country's claims of distinction from the 'other Germany' in every area. Economically, he replaced an earlier Five-Year Plan with a programme of economic growth that funnelled capital into only the very strongest sectors of the GDR, such as chemicals and machine tools. After the 1968 uprising in Czechoslovakia, Ulbricht once again tightened the GDR's domestic cultural policy, and the party's watchdogs were put on alert. The GDR declared war on East

[2] Heise and Hofmann, *Fragen an die Geschichte der DDR*.

German intellectuals like author Stefan Heym, philosopher Robert Havemann and balladeer Wolf Biermann.

Ulbricht also strove to enhance the GDR's international role within the Warsaw Pact states by trying to shape Soviet foreign policies, particularly where the German question was concerned. He envisioned the GDR developing into a model of socialist achievement unparalleled in its economic efficiencies and socialist progress. In his stubbornness, Ulbricht had disregarded the changes taking place in the Kremlin under Brezhnev's rulership—changes from a rigid Stalinist-influenced foreign policy to a more open diplomacy of détente. He would eventually fall victim to his own presumptions.

Undoubtedly, Bahr, the father of Ostpolitik, transformed the confrontational vocabulary and relationship between West and East Germany into an atmosphere of reconciliation. But in the eyes of many, even today, his politics put the purported benefits of co-operation with the GDR not only ahead of Germany's national reunion but also ahead of the misery of the East Germans. As much as his Ostpolitik helped ease travel across the borders and improved communication between the two Germanies, there remain many who question whether, in the end, accommodating the communist bloc achieved the opposite of its intended effect by extending the life of the paper tiger GDR for years longer than necessary.

Egon Bahr

The origin of the Ostpolitik was the recognition that the Berlin Wall could only be overcome from our side, meaning we had to start to help ourselves. The principles of confrontation had to be changed into principles of co-operation. President Kennedy independently had suggested in several speeches given in 1962 that he would favour the risk of détente over the risk of war. He supported negotiating with the Soviet Union and he backed a proposed ban on nuclear weapons testing. I thought at the time, what wonderful timing; we can use Kennedy's reasoning to introduce our own policies in Germany. This insight was the first step toward co-operation.

The second step was the proposal, which surprisingly came from Ulbricht, to exchange high-ranking party members as speakers. I believe he thought that the West German SPD would never accept such a proposal. He was mistaken and when the time came for the first meeting, he cancelled. The reason was clear: he had promised that all speeches given would be printed in East as well as in West German newspapers, a promise he couldn't afford to keep. The East German leadership was horrified just thinking of it.

In the end, Ulbricht was forced to deal with Bonn's breakthrough after Willy Brandt had successfully initiated talks with Moscow. In his inaugural speech in October 1969, the chancellor had hinted that he hoped for a reconciliation with East Germany and Moscow. He spoke of a peaceful European order. Whatever was decided within the German relationship had to be advanced by talks with Moscow. That was why we first signed the reunification-of-force agreement with Moscow in 1970, and with Warsaw a few months later. Both were preconditions to dealing with East Germany directly. That same scenario came up again in November 1989. Helmut Kohl went in exactly the right direction when he first came to an agreement with Moscow and then approached his East German counterparts. The Soviet Union had the say both in 1970 and in 1989.

My personal motivation to push the Ostpolitik against all odds was that I could not believe that Germany would be divided forever. Second, I also believed that confrontation would divide the country even more. When the Social Liberal Coalition had its turn in 1969, it was time to try a new concept. The idea was that only through stabilizing the eastern regime could we be a catalyst for liberal political developments within the systems. Liberalization of systems like the one East Germany represented can only be accomplished step by step, not by radical change. That, of course, was a long-term perspective that was politically difficult to defend within my own party and within the opposition. I honestly didn't believe that I would experience a reunification of the two Germanies during my lifetime. I also didn't believe that the Soviet Union would fall apart. Our luck, Brandt's and mine, was that in 1969 the conservative West German opposition didn't have any feasible proposals for dealing successfully with the east. Yet it became clear even to those conservatives that *some* form of accommodation with the communist bloc had to be found. The West German public was demanding it, and in addition, the US had given its blessing to an east-west dialogue. Some critics, like Franz Josef Strauss of the conservative sister party in Bavaria, accused us of being naive in opening up discussions with the east. Worse, they accused us of running the risk of signing away any leverage West Germany might have on the national questions.

I strongly disagreed with this line of argument then, and still do today. Gorbachev would not have been at the summit in 1989 without détente, the Ostpolitik and the agreements we reached with Moscow in 1970, and without Gorbachev the Wall would still be standing. I believe that the agreements we made with Moscow and Warsaw were diplomatic masterpieces. We got what we wanted.

I went into the talks with a firm concept: we would promise that West Germany was ready to treat all boundaries within Europe—including the controversial Oder–Neisse Line between Poland and East Germany—as 'inviolable'. We gave that promise without negating the possibility that the status quo within Germany might change one day by peaceful means. The talks with Moscow and Gromyko were very difficult and intense. First, Gromyko was a hard-liner; second, we didn't have much clout, being a small country dealing with the superpower Soviet Union. Nevertheless, before all talks and discussions I marshalled my arguments. My main goals were to make East Germany an open gateway to the East and to ease at least somewhat the misery of the people living in the east.

My greatest strength was that I based my arguments with Gromyko on simple logic. For example, he wanted to set as a condition for any further discussions our recognition of the GDR as a separate and independent nation. First I told him that I couldn't do that because the rights of the four occupation powers wouldn't allow it. I added, 'If you want us to recognize the GDR as a separate nation, we have to put an end to the occupation status of East Germany and all of Berlin'. I continued, 'Get all the other allies in and start talking about a peace treaty'. That was obviously the last thing he wanted at that point. Second, I asked, 'How can I talk about East Germany as a separate and independent state if none of its representatives are here? If you want to treat the GDR as an independent state that's fine, but I cannot make any decisions about that without any of the East German leaders present.' Third, when Gromyko insisted that the borders of Oder–Neisse were not changeable, I told him, 'These are not the borders of West Germany; how can I discuss borders my government doesn't even share?'

After weeks of sometimes childish discussion like that, we finally were able to draw up the Soviet–West German Treaty on 19 August 1970. We continued to insist, as we had from the very start, upon a satisfactory four-power agreement to settle the status of West Berlin and by extension to define a relationship between the GDR and West Germany—I called it a 'regulated coexistence'. In general the talks with Gromyko were quite different from our later discussions with the leaders of East Germany, in terms of what we wanted to achieve and of the atmosphere. After I had met with Gromyko several times, even after just a few weeks, we told each other jokes. He became more and more relaxed as the meetings went on. At times Gromyko and I dealt almost on a friendly basis with each other. We never reached that level of understanding during the talks with East German leaders. Not only the opposition but also other world leaders were sceptical at times about my relationship with the Kremlin. I remember that when I told Henry Kissinger, whom I regard highly, about my talks with Moscow, he became quite nervous. He didn't trust Moscow at all, nor did he trust Bonn's ability to deal with all the issues he deemed important. But the Moscow treaty, which was signed in the Catherine room in the Kremlin, proved that the Kremlin was willing to opt for Brandt's offer of rapprochement and that Bonn was able to close a deal with the Soviets.

The Soviet–GDR alignment, which still seemed exceptionally close in 1968, changed after 1970. Ulbricht—who wanted to avoid political contact with West Germany—had little choice but to at least act as if he went along with the Kremlin's approach to détente. But the Kremlin had doubts about Ulbricht's domestic policies, especially with regard to economic affairs. It came as no surprise to me when Ulbricht was replaced in May 1971. For us in Bonn, that event signalled the go-ahead for our plans of Deutschlandpolitik (German politics). Ulbricht's successor, Erich Honecker, not only echoed Moscow's espousal of détente but was also ready for talks with Bonn.

The Berlin accord, signed in September 1971 by the USA, USSR, Britain and France, guaranteed the accessibility of West Berlin. The accord gave myself and my counterpart in the east, Michael Kohl, a foundation for working out a Basic Treaty. Major issues were a transit agreement and inter-German travel on a broader level. The talks with Kohl were slow and very tense. I always knew I was dealing with untrustworthy pigs. I knew that even as we talked Germans were being shot at the border, a fact that I didn't ignore but had to overcome in order to achieve our goal. I have been asked often if I trusted Kohl and his promises. I didn't trust him, but I trusted his promises since I was backed via Moscow. The Basic Treaty was in Brezhnev's interest, and Honecker and his comrades had to follow orders.

The Basic Treaty opened East Germany up to communication and an influx of visitors from the west. It was a one-way street, but as I argued at the time, bad relations are better then none. Sixteen million people travelled to the east in the mid 1970s. Two decades after the Wall rose, the relations of the two Cold-War Germanies had been transformed into a pattern of coexistence.

Wulf Rothenbächer

The policy of détente, which was started under Willy Brandt's presidency, operated from a platform that intended to put the interests of living human beings above the abstract notions of a reunited Germany. As is often the case, what sounded good actually had the opposite of the intended effect: the recognition of the GDR as an independent state as a result of the détente policy led to a strengthening of internal power of the Politburo within East Germany and other nations behind the Iron Curtain, and also prolonged the life of the East German regime—and the terror under which citizens had to live—for several painful years. To my eyes the politicians of détente are as guilty of maintaining communism in the eastern European nations as are the totalitarian rulers of those nations. The deathblow for the GDR would have occurred 15 years earlier if western politicians had not supported the GDR and the Soviet Union financially.

Money often has been used in the past to stabilize undesirable situations. At the beginning of the 1980s, West German politicians granted millions of dollars in loans to the GDR. The influx of hard currencies enabled the Honecker regime to buy new products, to keep the economy running at least minimally, and thus to keep social unrest down. The Honecker regime finally gave in to the pressure of its people mainly because of the enormously tight money situation the GDR had been in for the last few years.

My wife and I, after being let go by the GDR in the early 1970s, were disgusted by the treaties signed between the GDR and West Germany. We were dismayed by a democracy thinking that it could strike a deal with a dictatorship. It is often forgotten that communism is lacking one very important factor: respect for the human being. How can you argue as Egon Bahr so often has that you only deal with the other side for humanitarian reasons when the other side kicks humans whenever it can? The individual human being doesn't have a place or a role in communism. Yet not one single politician ever asked that the Wall be torn down at that time.

Politically, the policy of détente meant the acceptance of the status quo: a divided Germany. The quote of a Frenchman who said, 'I love Germany so much, I hope there will always be two of them', was frequently used as a protective shield by those who didn't want to rattle the cages of the communist regimes in the east.

Wolf Jürgen Staab

The head of the GDR's Council of Ministers, Willi Stoph—second in command to Ulbricht—met twice with Chancellor Willy Brandt: once in 1970 in the East German city of Erfurt, and two months later in West Germany in Kassel. Both meetings amounted to little more than a reiteration of each side's positions on détente. It became clear that Moscow held the key to successful talks.

Quickly, a sizeable minority in the FDP believed that some accommodation with the communist bloc was unavoidable—to what degree, many weren't sure. Others, the majority, thought any accommodation would end up in a sell-out of West German interests to the east. Of particular concern was the knowledge that East Germany's primary ambition in the talks was to secure the official recognition of the GDR by West Germany. As the Basic Treaty showed, the contract stopped just short of that. The discussions about the treaty and about the general idea of a tête-à-tête with the East German government were heated. Many believed that the concessions made by Brandt and Bahr threatened the constitutional right to reunite Germany at a later time. In passionate debates, Brandt's Ostpolitik was portrayed as an unconstitutional desertion of West Germany's obligation to free East Germany from the yoke of communism.

As the debates over ratification of the Moscow and Warsaw agreements began in early 1972, discussion of the treaties led to a request for a constructive vote of no confidence in the Brandt government by Rainer Barzel, the head of our party. Key Social Democrats

and Free Democrats who did not believe in Brandt's approach de-
fected to our ranks; however, two voters from our own party who fa-
voured Brandt's Ostpolitik kept the Brandt government from falling
and assured the passage of the treaty.[3]

Although the Moscow and Warsaw treaties thus passed the final
vote, it was a pyrrhic victory at best. The vote of non-confidence had
weakened the socialist government overall. As Bahr and Michael
Kohl, his eastern counterpart, began negotiations on a comprehen-
sive inter-German agreement over the following months, the issue of
détente became part of an emotional campaign to regain a parliamentary majority in the coming major elections. Political ambition was
linked to national policy. In a very self-serving manner, members of
the SPD exploited the dialogue with the GDR to their electoral advantage. It was no coincidence that Brandt had scheduled the initial,
but not the formal, signing of the treaty with the GDR eleven days
before the elections in West Germany. Voters had to pressure that a
vote for the social–liberal coalition was a vote for a new and promising relationship with the east, while a vote for the CDU–CSU was a
vote for a risky unknown. I believe that scenario gave the GDR
leaders more bargaining power with Bahr than was desirable.

In order to reach any accord with the east, many topics had to be
glossed over. As I later experienced myself while serving in the permanent mission in East Berlin, the treaty was full of ambiguities and
potential conflicts that the GDR exploited to its advantage. The two
sides still had opposing views on the national question., which the
treaty's preamble called 'different views'. In other words, Bonn and
East Berlin were in agreement that they disagreed. In the eyes of the
east, it was up to Bonn to demonstrate its respect for East German
sovereignty. For Bonn, on the other hand, the exchange of subam-
bassadorial 'permanent missions' and its success in attaching to the
treaty a letter of agreement affirming the commitment to national reunification sent a different message: Bonn safeguarded its claims to
treating Germans living in the east no differently from those living in
the west. On the other hand, East Germany was quick to pass out
East German passports to 'its' citizens.

All the changes—including favourable ones such as the transit

---

[3] It was later proved that the East German Secret Police, the Stasi, had bought
both votes. They paid parliamentarian Julius Steiner DM 50,000. Erich Mende,
the second vote, became successor of Barzel and is said to have received no
money. Also see, *Der Spiegel*, No. 29, 1991.

agreement granting women over 60 and men over 65 free travel from the east to the west—didn't much improve the overall conditions of the people. The East German system was always self-serving. For example, the only reason elderly persons could travel freely to the west was that if they stayed longer than their visas allowed, they were stripped of all their pensions. The agreement was a money-saving mechanism for the eastern government. West Germany picked up the tab, since such persons were clearly German citizens.

Bonn had conceded East Berlin full equality of status, and that no doubt contributed to the internal stabilization of the GDR. Equally important for the internal situation in the GDR was its upgrading elsewhere in the west. It now had a seat in the United Nations. East Berlin had gained international recognition by striking a political deal with West Germany.

A negative result for the GDR was that it had admitted into its camp an enemy that it had found useful in the past and had done so not necessarily on its own terms, but on terms decided between Bonn and Moscow. Perhaps the worst scene was played out before of the eyes of thousands of East German citizens when Leonid Brezhnev kissed Mrs Brandt's hand. Brezhnev had done no more than make a polite gesture. But his compliment to Mrs Brandt didn't support the characterization of Brandt as a class warrior, which was how western politicians had been portrayed in the GDR. How were easterners to be convinced that the treaty didn't increase the threat of 'Social Democracy' when Social Democrats were treated with respect?

Moscow's own interests demanded that no changes be made that could potentially endanger the existence of East Germany, which was a bargaining tool in Soviet hands. The GDR, above all, wanted to preserve itself and to keep East Berlin as far from the west as possible. But Moscow wanted to achieve as much co-operation with the west as possible, especially financially. I strongly believe that was the reason why the Soviets were willing to co-operate both then and in 1989.

Francis Meehan

The western countries and the NATO allies started to establish relations with East Germany in 1974. West German policy, which had been born in the early 1970s with chancellor Willy Brandt's Ostpolitik was to seek positive relations with the east, a policy that had been unthinkable under Adenauer's administration. I don't think the USA or other states would have taken the step if the West Germans hadn't taken it first. Once the Germans themselves moved, it brought a lot of consensus. In fact, it would have looked rather strange if West Germans alone sought ties with the east.

The motivation for Egon Bahr and Willy Brandt to introduce the politics of coexistence came from their deep belief that the only way to keep the two Germanies together would be by dealing with the GDR rather than by trying to isolate it. Whether the Wall would have come down sooner if the GDR had been subjected to more political pressure will continue to be debated, but it is a purely hypothetical question. Adenauer, Germany's first chancellor after the Second World War, had pursued a policy of isolation, and Brandt moved away from that policy. I think that made sense in terms of the realities that existed then. The Soviet Union at the time seemed prepared to remain in Central Europe forever. Almost everybody thought that the Soviet Armed Forces had become a permanent feature of the political landscape in the GDR. It was accepted as a reality, and at that time I didn't disagree. I strongly agreed with the policy of the West German Social Democrats. From the official US point of view, however, there were people who didn't like it, mainly those who wanted to follow a hard line and thought that Brandt and Bahr were getting too cosy with the east. But the debate always concluded with the point that West Germany was a crucial ally in Europe and its views on its inner political questions had to be accepted. So it all boils down to one fact again: the western world had simply accepted the status quo of a divided Germany.

Chapter Ten

What is a Political Prisoner?

The Berlin Wall and the fortified borders, the signal lights and the watch dogs were highly visible to anyone who visited East Germany prior to November 1989. What was not visible was the politicized criminal system that placed several thousand citizens behind bars for attempting to leave their country after the Wall was built in August 1961.

The exact number of people who suffered political imprisonment in the GDR has never been published and is difficult to estimate. Nevertheless, it is possible to arrive at a rough figure by looking at the number of prisoners whose freedom was bought by the West German government. Between 1963 and 1989 West Germany welcomed exactly 33,755 political prisoners from the east, each of whom had been released in exchange for DM125,000 ($75,000) paid by the West German government. All in all DM3,5 billion ($2 billion) were spent on the exchange of political prisoners. During years of economic slowdown, when the GDR's need for hard currency intensified, the International Society for Human Rights noted sharp increases in the number of political prisoners. Clearly the East German regime viewed its political prisoners, who were unwanted subjects in any event, as valuable resources, i.e., as a means of getting its hands on the valuable Deutsche Mark. This fact was known around the world but was largely ignored even in West Germany.

How easy was it to find yourself in a cell, for example, in the prison of Hoheneck? Very easy. Just being accused of committing acts of propaganda hostile to the state or simply of having a negative attitude towards the German Democratic Republic could be enough. Writing a letter to the city council expressing a belief that the GDR was slowly deteriorating into a developing country that one would not want to live in anymore could readily earn the author a year in prison. Among the most often punished 'crimes' was 'Republikflucht'—the attempt to leave the country without valid travel permits. Most people arrested in the GDR were never given a statement of the charges brought against them, however.

Both while working and at home, officers of the State Security Department (Stasi) were painstakingly cautious in their attempts to avoid public notice. They usually wore plainclothes and worked in groups of three to four. Most arrests were made on the pretext of needing to 'clarify some facts'. Usually, the person arrested was taken to a detention centre in an unmarked car. Interrogation started immediately and sometimes lasted for more than 12 hours. According to interviews with former political prisoners, the Stasi interrogators were all well schooled in psychological tactics and used them to take full advantage of the fear and confusion the detainee went through. Promises and threats were used to coerce the detainee into making self-incriminating statements. After three or four days, most arrested persons were brought to a magistrate who ordered imprisonment or, in some cases, issued a warrant. If detained, prisoners were first put in isolation for six to eight weeks, and then transferred to a three-to-four person cell. This tactic was based on the likelihood that a need to talk would surface quickly after isolation. Oftentimes, Stasi officers were placed in those cells as informers.

Once a day there was a 'recreation hour'. Detainees were led cell by cell into an area partitioned with barbed wire, giving the impression of a cage. Guards criss-crossed the area to ensure that no contacts were made between fellow prisoners. Books and newspapers of the Socialist Unity Party (SED) were distributed weekly, while reading materials for such purposes as studying in one's professional field were forbidden. After several months of living in a cell, prisoners were given a trial in which a determination of guilt usually was based on assumptions that the judge declared to be evidence. It was impossible to stage an effective defence. Court hearings were not open to the public. Indictments and verdicts disappeared into safes, lawyers were sworn to secrecy, and only international humanitarian organizations, such as the Red Cross, were allowed to see the detention facilities or penal institutions. The media, both eastern and western, remained silent about the facts.

Among the better-known prisons in the GDR were Hoheneck and Bautzen. Hoheneck, an old castle in the Erzgebirge,[1] became a women's prison in the 1950s and had been used previously as a Nazi camp. Female political prisoners, the majority of whom were 18 to 35 years old, were generally sentenced to spend two to three years in Hoheneck. The once-beautiful castle served for over 30 years as a women's prison and remained the most outdated, inhumane and unhygienic penal institution in the GDR.

Another prison that was used extensively as a Special Prison of the State Security Department was Bautzen. The T-shaped prison building had been built at the turn of the century, and was known as a particularly cruel and hard place. Since the summer of 1956 it had been used

---

[1] Erzgebirge is a mountain range in Saxony between Elstergebirge in the Northeast and the Elbsandsteingebirge.

predominantly for incarceration of political prisoners with long sentences and those described as 'especially dangerous enemies of the regime'.[2]

Countless demands by the West German embassy in East Berlin, by Amnesty International and by the International Society for Human Rights failed to limit the number of victims of political persecution in the GDR or to halt the violations of human rights. In 1987, stimulated by political pressure from the west and his impending visit to West Germany, Erich Honecker signed an amnesty agreement that applied to all political prisoners within the GDR. But little changed. Between 1987 and 1989 the International Society for Human Rights alone registered roughly 3,000 new political prisoners. The number of young people wanting to leave increased steadily and, within 18 months before the Wall fell, 1.5 million citizens had applied for travel visas that would have allowed them to stay in the west.

The number of political detainees who died in East German prisons is unknown, as is the number of people who were sent to other camps and prisons in the Soviet Union. Much of the documentation was destroyed by the Secret Police shortly before West German officials could follow it up. Even months after the Wall had come down, Honecker and other members of his totalitarian regime insisted that the GDR had never taken political prisoners and had never issued a shoot-to-kill order to border guards.

Wulf Rothenbächer

I'll start with the reason why I and my girlfriend, who now is my wife, wanted to leave. In the early 1970s I was practising medicine at one of the larger hospitals in East Berlin, specializing in ear, nose and throat diseases. The head of the department was a well-meaning guy, but he was also heavily involved with the party. I learned a lot from him about surgery and my medical speciality, but otherwise I tried to avoid him as much as possible. I was still a bachelor at that time and was pretty well-off, with my own apartment close to the clinic, a car and even a telephone. On the surface my life went well, but more and more I started to feel a depressing pressure resulting from life under 'real existing socialism', as Honecker called it. I felt cramped and limited in my personal rights every day. The system asked you to lie, to play a role you didn't want to play. Nobody could be politically active except within the boundaries of the

[2] IGFM, *Menschenrechte in der Welt*, 1987, 1988, 1989, 1990

system. I was aware that all the information we received via the East German broadcasting system and newspapers were lies to support the system.

Day by day I noticed how people around me lost colour, seemed to fade away, just waiting for the moment when they would receive a pension and would be able to travel to the west because of their age. But I didn't see how I could actively change the situation I, and everybody else, lived in.

I remember one key situation that annoyed me. It was a small incident, but it was very important in my personal development. I had come out of a successful operation, and the head of the department was patting me on the shoulder for a job well done. In the conversation we had while walking to the coffee shop he said, 'Rothenbächer, you are the only one on the list who hasn't signed up yet. Did you forget?' He was referring to a list of hospital staff who were supposed to give some donation to support the North Vietnamese. Some days before I had thought about the list and had decided I didn't want to make any more compromises and I didn't want to support the communist Vietnamese regime. I told him bluntly, 'I didn't forget; I don't want to donate to that cause.' He started an argument about how well I had been performing in the hospital and how I shouldn't throw everything away just because of a little donation. He even offered to give me 10 marks to donate in my name. From that moment on, I didn't applaud when I was expected to, I didn't sign any documents I didn't want to sign.

The moral pressure was increasing daily. The head of the department liked my work, but definitely not my political attitude. I was looking desperately for an opportunity to leave the prison I was living in. The opportunity came when I got some days off, which I had already announced I would spend in Romania on the Black Sea. Today I know I had planned the escape for me and my girlfriend, Gabriela, very poorly.

We travelled by train to Temeshvar in Romania and planned to get over the border to Hungary the next morning. The border between the two states was known to be watched less carefully and only sparsely fenced with barbed wire. Nevertheless, two Romanian border guards caught us. We were immediately detained and interrogated. Fortunately, at that point we were not separated. For several days we were kept in a cell, but were treated considerably well. We were given food and some reading material, but no answers about our further destiny. On the morning of the sixth day we were released. Two border guards accompanied us to a train and handed us two tickets to East Berlin. That was the end of that adventure.

I was terribly angry at myself, and during the train ride my girlfriend and I were already planning how to improve our next escape attempt. Back in Berlin, we decided to continue our lives as if nothing had happened. I went to the hospital the following morning and examined my scheduled patients while my girlfriend went to the office where she worked. By noon nothing had happened.

Nobody from the secret police had shown up. I called Gabriela at her office and asked if anybody had questioned her. We were unsure and greatly puzzled, wondering if the Romanians hadn't told the East German authorities about our unsuccessful escape attempt. We were stupid to think that our travelling to Temeshvar wouldn't have any consequences. The next day came and around noon, just as I came out of surgery, three men came walking up to me. I knew what to expect then. They took me straight to a detention facility, where I was questioned for several hours. I was questioned and questioned again. The officer who interrogated me wanted to know why and how and with whose help I had tried to escape. I didn't answer. Then he tried to bribe me with a cigarette and with a promise that I could return quickly to my girlfriend if I would tell him what he wanted to hear. Then he threatened me again. I managed to stay as cool as possible. Two days later I found myself wearing a prison uniform. It was an old army uniform with bright yellow stripes attached to the arms and legs. I still had some money on me with which I was allowed to purchase some toilet paper and cigarettes before I was taken to an isolation cell. For over seven weeks I was kept in that dark cell. Every other week I was permitted to request a thin book, which after several days I had memorized. I asked for a pencil and paper, but the request was denied.

I had been brought to Cottbus, a prison complex consisting of two large cell blocks, two production centres, and a separate facility for the detention of prisoners awaiting trial. Barbed wire fences with built-in alarms, dog runs, watch towers and a prison Wall that was about 80 feet high served as safeguards against escape. The building was in poor shape; many areas were unsafe and had walls that were starting to collapse. While I was there, around 500 prisoners were serving sentences. About 90 per cent were political prisoners and only 10 per cent had been arrested for crimes such as murder or theft. That ratio was unusual; most other prisons in East Germany kept closer to an even balance between political and other prisoners as part of an attempt to prohibit fraternization. The average age of the political prisoners, I would guess, was around 30 years old.

I was a newcomer and as such was taken to the 'catacombs', the basement of the cell block. I learned later that the commander who 'prepared' me for life in prison was called the 'Red Terror', or simply R.T. He was known for the beatings he gave.

During that first time in Cottbus my mother came to see me. I remember her first visit. I had just come out of the isolation cell and was standing in front of her in my striped outfit. She was shocked, although I saw that she really tried to pull herself together. During my time in isolation I had made a promise to myself not to lie or make any compromises for the regime I had suffered under. I was determined to be true to myself, to my wishes and desires. For the first time—and this may seem strange to an outsider—I really felt I was doing the right thing. I had protested for the first time; I was punished for it, but I had protested. I remember telling my mother that I never felt better, at least mentally. She obviously didn't believe me. She had made some progress in contacting Dr Wolfgang Vogel, an attorney known for his corrupt connections with Honecker and the West German government. A surveillance guard stopped my mother's visit when she started to ask me about my life in prison. She had to leave almost immediately.

Several days later, I was asked to work at a production plant stencilling metal. I refused and asked for some medical books. I was threatened with violence if I didn't perform and obey, but I was stubbornly persistent. A day later I was brought to a dark cell where I awaited my trial.

Dr Vogel visited me once before my hearing. He just handed me the charges that had been brought against me. When I asked him how he would defend me he simply said; 'There will be no defence. Keep quiet and maybe I can arrange that you'll be out of here within the next three to five years.' The punishment for attempting to escape from East Germany was ten to twelve years.

Handcuffed, I was transported to a building where my court proceeding would take place. The trial was a farce. I soon noticed that the only goal of the entire process was to criminalize the defendant's views and conduct. Like the examiners in the detention facility, the prosecutor and the judge work together to prove criminal motives and intent on the part of the defendant. There was no factual evidence for any charges against me or my girlfriend, but every insinuation and assumption was declared to be evidence. I didn't have a chance to reply, and Dr Vogel just agreed to whatever was said. During the whole trial, if you want to call it that, I was kept in handcuffs. After 10 to 15 minutes the farce was over and I was brought back to Cottbus, having been sentenced to three years in prison.

I was put in a cell with some other people. We had agreed that during the 'recreational hour'—about 20 minutes during which we were allowed to go outside—we wouldn't obey commands. We were told to walk in a circle to a drumbeat like soldiers. Each of us started to fall over his own feet or slipped. Five of us in the group were brought to Red Terror immediately. One of my cell mates and I were selected as the plotters and were put in a 'tiger cave'. We both spent several weeks in a wet cell enclosed with barbed wire, with little to eat and very little clothing. When the guard put me in the tiger cave, he told me that I would spend the rest of my sentence in that cell. I was crushed, desperate and totally disillusioned. During that time I started to keep my spirits up with autogenous training and with prayers. I tried to remember all the questions I had been asked during my medical examinations and to reproduce the answers. I tried to calculate how much gas a ship would need to get to the east coast of America leaving from a port in Germany. Of course, during all that time, I hoped that the GDR would need more hard currency and that maybe I would be among those who would be exchanged for DM100,000 and thus be free to live in the west. The days were endlessly long. I developed a feeling for the time of day and found my own rhythm of wake and sleep. My worst fear was that I would lose my thinking ability, that they would succeed in softening me and my mind.

After 15 months and some days, a guard came into my cell at an unusual time. I was surprised and didn't know what to think of it. He didn't say much. I was brought into a shower room and asked to wash myself and shave. Then I knew. At least, I hoped that what I had been dreaming about all the time was finally coming true. After I showered, I got a nice hot meal and was put for some 20 minutes under ultraviolet light. Following that I was asked to rest. The same procedure continued for three days. Then on the fourth day I was brought in handcuffs, but in civilian clothes, to a bus. With me were another 30 to 40 prisoners. After we had driven for a while, I noticed that we were approaching the border. I was free from prison, but not free from all the horrible memories.

My girlfriend Gabriela went through a similar treatment and followed two weeks later. My mother had also questioned Dr Vogel about her whereabouts and arranged for her to be on one of the freedom buses, as we called them.

Beginning a life in the west was difficult, not so much because of money or the difficulties of opening a practice—which I did just a year later—but because of the political ignorance I experienced. There were Germans in the west who didn't even know that East Germany kept political prisoners and that it was shooting people at the border. High-ranking politicians told me not to tell anyone about my prison experience, because doing so could easily disturb the west's 'carefully built' relations with the east. Nevertheless, soon after my professional life had settled down I began actively to inform the media and politicians about the machinations of East Germany. Many politicians knew exactly what was going on in the east but wanted me to keep quiet. When Honecker visited West Germany in 1987, I mobilized many people to use the occasion for a demonstration for human rights. Only a few of the conservative politicians wanted to know anything about my idea. I wrote up a petition to be signed by those in the west who knew that a member of their family was serving a sentence as a political prisoner in East Germany. The International Society for Human Rights was aware of over 4,000 people who had been put in prison for political reasons in 1987. After some back-and-forth discussion, the demonstration against Honecker and for human rights was allowed, and I was able to deliver the petition for the release of prisoners to an East German delegation in Bonn. Before then I had received anonymous phone calls and letters from people who threatened to kill me or abduct one of my children if I tried to disturb the harmony of the east-west German meeting. Just weeks after the Honecker visit, 60 per cent of those prisoners whom we had listed in the petition by name, prison and sentence were released.

I organized a similar demonstration in April 1985 when Honecker visited Italy and Pope John Paul II. Honecker was the first east European head of state to visit the Vatican. When I read the announcement that the Pope would grant Honecker a half-hour audience, I couldn't believe it. I was outraged. For Honecker the trip to the Pope was merely a PR effort. For years Honecker and his regime had imprisoned ministers and Catholic priests and had denied churchgoers the opportunity to receive higher education. He offered no promises or commitments that the situation would change after he talked to the Pope. I just couldn't comprehend why the Pope would grant Honecker, who had ruthlessly trampled on human rights, the chance to exploit the good will of the Catholic Church.

For days I tried to think of something my human rights group could do in connection with Honecker's visit to the Vatican. By chance at a party I bumped into an acquaintance, Dr Kurzjahr, a travel agent who specializes in pilgrim journeys from all over the world to Rome. After a brief chat, I asked him if he would organize yet another trip for the forthcoming Easter weekend, when the Honecker visit was to take place. He agreed to do it. When I told him he was sent from heaven, he laughed and said, 'I think you have something in mind I should know more about'. We met the next day and I told him about my organization and about six young mothers, ex-political prisoners who had been released for money in an exchange programme months earlier. Each of them had one or two children who had been placed either with foster parents or in an orphanage while their mothers served their time in a political prison. With one exception, all the women had been punished for raising their voices against the regime during a company outing. Right after they had been released to the west, all of them had demanded to be reunited with their children. There was little West Germany could do but pass the requests on to the East German embassy in West Berlin. The common answer, which usually came back weeks later from East Berlin, was that the children had either died or were missing. These mothers were in a horrible situation. They had been freed from their East German political prison, but were unsure about the whereabouts of their children. And as ex-political prisoners, the women were not allowed to visit the east for years to look for the children personally.

I suggested that we would try to arrange for the young mothers to talk to the Pope briefly about their problems with the East German government and their deep concern for their children. It was Wednesday, 24 April 1985. The Pope had seen Honecker in the morning, and there was to be a general afternoon audience in St Peter's Square. Through connections of Dr Kurzjahr, we arranged for all six women to sit in the first row during the afternoon audience. They held petitions in their hands and pictures of their children. The Pope, who had been informed who the women were, received them warmly and embraced them one after the other. The cameras of the whole world press were on them. Journalists and photographers surrounded them. Most of the women were crying while they talked briefly with the Pope.

At the same time, we had organized a demonstration in Rome in front of the East German embassy. We distributed in several languages the mothers' petition to be reunited with their children. Shortly thereafter, the small demonstration was dispersed and one or two people were put into prison for some hours. Within a week, Dr Kurzjahr became the victim of negative coverage in the West German and Italian press. He was accused of having interfered with a political process by using his connections with the Vatican. But within four weeks we heard that all of the women had been put in contact with their children. Some weeks later they were reunited in West Germany.

The general attitude of West German politicians and the media was not to touch an unpopular topic when visitors came from the east. They didn't realize that such silence was just what the GDR hoped for and expected.

The same avoidance of unpleasantness occurred when the GDR regime collapsed in November 1989. Nobody in the west dared to declare the party a criminal organization, which it really was. Only a few of the GDR's judges or lawyers have been put on trial. I have tried to recover my files and have asked authorities in Berlin to send me copies of my trial and sentencing documentation. I haven't heard anything from the government. The only mail I received from the West German government in Bonn recently was a document that I need to fill out to prove that I was really a political prisoner. If I fail to return that document within a couple of weeks, I will be registered as 'previously convicted'. It sounds absurd, but that's the truth.

Looking back, I often feel guilty for not having taken the steps I took in the GDR earlier. I lived half of my life with a lie, slowly being lulled into complacency and giving in to one of the most totalitarian and inhumane systems on earth. I almost wasn't living for the first part of my life, but instead was merely existing.

Waltraut Rothenbächer

After my children were grown, one after the other ran away to the west, all except Thassilo. The first to go was my daughter Renate. While she worked as a nurse at the Charite in East Berlin in 1959, she sometimes had a chance to visit our relatives in West Berlin. Before the Wall was built, travelling between east and west was difficult, but possible. One day, some months before 13 August 1961, she just didn't come home. She had decided to stay in the western part of the city for good. Shortly thereafter, the Wall was built. Miles and miles of fences and signal lights and watch dogs divided the two parts of Berlin and eventually the nation. The guards were ordered to shoot anyone attempting to cross the border to freedom.

My son Wulf tried to get out ten years later in 1970. He travelled with his girlfriend to Romania, in the hope of crossing into Austria. He didn't tell me his plan—only that he would be on vacation. I didn't hear from my son or his girlfriend, who is now his wife, for more than three months. They had been caught and imprisoned in Temeshvar, Romania, the city where bloody demonstrations resulted in the execution of Nicolai Ceauçescu in 1989. After more than six or seven days, both were released with a ticket to East Berlin. We should have known that this would not be the end of the story. After they returned to Berlin, my son and his girlfriend went to work as usual. The first day was routine. But the second day three men arrived at my son's hospital. They arrested him, claiming they needed to 'clarify some facts'. My son's girlfriend was arrested as well and brought to a different prison than Wulf. I sought out a prominent lawyer, who was able to get me special visiting privileges. I could see my son briefly a few times a year. Usually, as I later learned, anyone sentenced to more than two years was allowed one 60-minute visit every other month. Gifts worth less than 30 marks were permitted, but only if the inmate's work output merited a reward.

I remember well the first time I saw my son in prison. I was body-searched before the visit. Guards were present throughout. I had been instructed by my lawyer not to talk about my son's 'crime' or his future plans or lawyers or even about prison life. My son told me later that he and another prisoner shared a cell with one chair and a locker. He was perhaps fortunate. Some cells held as many as 30 people.

I tried desperately to remain calm when I saw my son, but somehow that wasn't possible. I wanted to ask so many questions—but just remembering what I was not to ask made conversation very difficult. My son tried to reassure me. 'Mother, don't be upset,' he said. 'For the first time in my life I feel good about myself. For the first time I told them everything I've always wanted to tell them.'

Hearing this, the guard who was present ordered me to stop the conversation at once. If I didn't, it would have terrible consequences for my son. I obeyed.

Desperate for his release, I arranged a meeting with the lawyer Dr Vogel. What could be done for my son and his girlfriend? I was amazed by the opulence of the lawyer's office. It was furnished with handsome desks, tables, chairs, carpets—things he couldn't have acquired in the GDR. He even had a fax machine. Another attorney from West Berlin had his practice on the second floor of the building. That was somehow suspicious, since at that time West and East Germany didn't have very good relations and no West German professional in his right mind would have had a practice within the boundaries of the GDR unless he was trying to do criminal business.

Dr Vogel treated me well. He was friendly, almost jovial. But one remark puzzled me. He said, 'Don't worry, I see the supreme court judge almost daily'. On the one hand, his remark suggested that he had connections, but on the other hand, I knew what kind of ideological concept he followed. At the time, I didn't much care how he made his money, or how he was able to buy furniture that wasn't even available in East Berlin. But today I have the inkling that he was engaged in trading East German intellectuals for their hard currency.

Some months after my son had been imprisoned, I was informed that court procedures for him would begin soon. The lawyer told me that my son would serve two and a half years altogether, a light sentence for a serious crime. Any attempt to leave the country was usually punished with ten years behind bars.

As trials were closed to the public, I was barred from my son's trial. Wulf later described the proceedings. Shortly before the hearing he had the chance to read the charges brought against him. He then had to sign some papers, which were immediately taken away from him after his review. A defence was impossible, or at least not attempted, as Dr Vogel didn't challenge the court. This farce was called a trial. Like most political prisoners, Wulf was brought to the trial in handcuffs. After the verdict was read to him quietly, he was transported to another prison.

Half a year later I received word that I could visit my son again. This time I was informed, before I saw my son, that he had been unwilling to work. I asked if perhaps he could practise medicine in the prison, treating his inmates. The guard just grinned at me and said, 'Mr Doctor first has to do some other work before he goes back to medicine.' It turned out that Wulf had been asked to stencil metal cups, and he refused. As a result, he had been imprisoned in a dark cell by himself for many weeks. When he was finally brought to the visitors' room wearing a black and yellow-striped uniform, he didn't say much, nor did I.

Six weeks later I was allowed to see him again. I was by now quite used to the body search and the endless filling-out of forms. The same guard to whom I had spoken the previous time intercepted me as I entered the prison. He said, 'Your son isn't here any longer.' At those words, I fainted. When I came to my senses again, my first thought was that they had beaten Wulf so badly that he was now in a prison hospital, or maybe even dead. I lashed out at the guard. 'What did you do with him? What did you do with him?' I cried over and over. Calmly he replied, 'What he always wanted. I can't tell you any more.'

I tried desperately to reach my lawyer without success. Days later, I received a letter. I was supposed to bring any documents I could find about my son and his imprisonment. I sat, nervous and impatient, as the lawyer thumbed through the papers very slowly. After more than five minutes he said, 'Have you talked to him yet?'

I later learned that the day I'd gone to visit my son, Wulf was on his way to the West German border in a tiny van together with several other political prisoners. The Red Cross met them on the other side. He was finally safe. My son's girlfriend was sent to West Germany several weeks later.

Many other young people in the GDR would have escaped to

West Germany, but feared the consequences of getting caught. My son knows many people who have served prison time in the GDR, their only crime being 'a negative attitude towards the German Democratic Republic' or 'acts of propaganda hostile to the state'.

Now that our family was suspect because of Wulf's imprisonment, it was just a question of time before the rest of my children would also decide to leave. The one I least expected to go was my youngest daughter. She had just married and moved into a nice area. But during one of her usual visits she said plainly, 'We also would like to leave the GDR.' I was shocked, even though I had always known this day would come.

In the late 1970s and 1980s it became easier for older people, women over 60 and men over 65, to move to the west officially. The regime let us old people go because then they wouldn't have to pay our pensions.

I had earned my retirement. I worked in the government-owned medical field for over thirty years. When I became a widow at 34, with four little children to take care of, I couldn't be very choosy. We are Christians, and I tried to make a point of going to church—a practice that, of course, wasn't viewed by some of my colleagues with great enthusiasm. I was sometimes teased on Monday morning because somebody had seen me entering the church. Because my younger daughter wouldn't go to 'Jugendweihe' (a ceremony at which children at age 14 pledge their loyalty to the system), she was not allowed to finish high school.

My job was strenuous. We were often short on medications. We ran out of x-ray films, even bandages. You had to be creative. Sick people were frequently sent back home without proper treatment. A person with my medical education should not have been allowed to give injections or handle minor surgery. But the GDR did not have enough doctors, particularly after the big exodus in the 1960s.

The hard work and the risks you had to take were bad enough—worse was the feeling of living in a huge prison. I always thought that showing the will to be stronger than the system was my only chance to survive emotionally. But the system was always one step ahead. I will tell a story to show how long a memory the regime had and how diligently records were kept. Shortly before my son Wulf tried to cross the Romanian border, he wrote on a piece of paper, 'Everything is shit here!' While he was imprisoned, I had to move his things out of his apartment so somebody else could live there. I found the note and stored it with all his other stuff. That was in 1970. In 1983 I applied to move officially to the west. After I had been called back four times to fill out the same documents, I told the official that I didn't know what other reasons I could give for wanting to leave the GDR. The official smiled at me and said, 'Well, Ms Rothenbächer, why don't you put down 'Everything is shit here'. Isn't that a phrase you are familiar with?'

Wolf-Jürgen Staab

My involvement with the GDR really started right after the Wall had been put up As a young government counsel to the Adenauer coalition, I was present during the first contacts with the Ulbricht regime. The initial meetings were extremely difficult to set up, because they were held without public knowledge. Our major concern was to gain the release of those dissidents and refugees who had tried to flee to the west and who were being held as political prisoners. We were well aware of one major concern: did we bargain for the 'right' political refugees, or would there be some among them who would be 'unwanted objects' for West Germany?

Ulbricht had just announced the abandonment of the Seven-Year Plan that had been launched with such great fanfare in 1959 and had proclaimed the introduction of a New Economic System. Market mechanisms such as interest rates and market-driven prices were introduced. Still, the role of central planning was so dominant that the Ulbricht regime had to fall back on West Germany to provide its economy with some essentials. Those essentials included bananas, oranges and other foods.

The predominant condition for the first meeting between the east and the west was that it had to be held in secrecy. Ulbricht's representatives had made it very clear from the beginning that a 'deal' could be struck only if the talks and the actual venture were kept secret from the press and the public. He feared that his own people would get wind of the food shortage.

The initial meetings took place in an atmosphere of scepticism and mistrust and moved slowly. We dealt mainly with an attorney by the name of Dr Wolfgang Vogel. Today it is widely known that he had been involved in the exchange of political prisoners for hard currency or other valuable goods since the day the Wall was erected. Vogel played a major role in providing the East German government with hard currencies through the years.

After further meetings, the representatives of the GDR laid down additional conditions for a possible exchange. A shipment of several million DM worth of oranges was to be delivered prior to the release of the political prisoners. We felt uncomfortable with the arrangement, as it didn't seem to reflect the idea of a typical exchange. We stood firmly by our demand to have the prisoners released first.

Finally, the day came. According to the arrangements, one day later we were to expect at least eight political prisoners. I was in charge of picking them up at the border. I had organized several Red Cross ambulances and some nurses who waited with me at midnight at the east-west border. Nothing happened until 30 minutes past the hour. I got nervous, thinking they weren't going to hold to their end of the bargain. Then lights went off and behind the border we could see the people at the watchtowers looking at us with field glasses. Finally, at a quarter to one in the morning we saw a truck. It was stopped at the gate, but after a short while it was quickly waved past the border. As I had hoped, it came our way and stopped just in front of an ambulance. Eight men quickly jumped from the back of the truck. A nurse passed out hot tea and little sandwiches. I remember that she offered a hot drink to the driver, but he refused and said in a heavy Berlin accent, 'I'm just delivering and have to return right away.' He turned his car around and headed back towards the border. I saw the man later on several similar occasions, and he always headed back.

The refugees were all in a healthy condition and were immediately brought to a refugee camp close by. Days later, there was some screening of the refugees' backgrounds. They received West German passports and some financial assistance. Those who had some family ties in the west usually had an easier time finding a job or a new home. Others had to stay in the camp for a long while until they created situations that enabled them to be on their own.

After this first successful venture, the West German government was involved in a series of exchanges of that kind, which usually followed a pattern like the one I just described. After a while they didn't even seem unusual anymore. We were able to keep those exchanges

secret from the public until the end of the 1960s, when the relationship between East and West Germany began to change dramatically
under the great coalition of Willy Brandt and West German Foreign
Minister Walter Scheel.

Francis Meehan

I met Dr Wolfgang Vogel for the first time in 1962. I was in Berlin
then, working for the US mission in West Berlin. I had arrived just
after the Wall went up when a rather famous case developed. American pilot Francis Gary Powers, whose U2 spy plane had been shot
down over the Soviet Union, was to be exchanged for Soviet spy
Rudolf Abel, a KGB colonel who had been convicted in New York
of running an espionage ring. Vogel and I worked on the details of
the exchange. As kind of an appendix to the deal, the East Germans
were also supposed to release an American student by the name of
Frederick Pryor, who had been imprisoned without being charged or
tried for five months.

The Powers case was a milestone in the Cold War. Nikita
Khrushchev used the downing of the U2 pilot to torpedo a Paris
summit meeting and to launch a series of crises that continued beyond the Eisenhower administration through the first year of the
Kennedy presidency. The negotiations that led to the Powers–Abel
exchange began months before the actual transfer. Another key figure was the New York lawyer James Donavan, Abel's court-ap-
pointed attorney. In arguing against the death penalty for Abel,
Donavan had made a prophetic plea, stating that, in the foreseeable
future, an American of equivalent rank might be captured by the Soviet Union or one of its allies, in which case an exchange of
prisoners could be of interest to the United States.

Abel and Powers became the symbols of an international crisis. I
remember the exchange. On the Glienicker Brücke, a steel-trussed
bridge that spans the river Havel between the former US zone and
the communist territory, a group of American cars awaited the approach of a Soviet convoy of cars from the other side. After the Soviets had arrived, two men walked from either side across the bridge.
Within minutes the exchange was over. Pryor, the 28-year-old student, was released at the same time and sent back to West Berlin.

I believe it was Vogel's first involvement in an international exchange. After that I dealt with Vogel on all kinds of cases, mostly involving American students who were caught trying to help East Germans escape Up to the late 1980s students in West Berlin had formed organizations to help Germans escape from the east. Unfortunately, those organizations were heavily penetrated by the Stasi. So these poor American kids would try to get someone out and then find themselves stuck in an East German prison. Because I was not as well connected as Vogel, we usually made use of him to get them out again. On critical cases we never dealt directly with the East German government but instead gave the job to a mediator, such as Vogel, to get some sort of leverage on the situation.

In subsequent years I was less involved in Vogel's main work, getting East Germans out to the west. That became strictly an issue between the East and West Germans. But I did get together again with Vogel on the Anatoly Shcharansky release. After nine years in prison and in labour camps in the Soviet Union, Shcharansky was released in an exchange over the Glienicker Brücke, just as the American pilot Powers had been released in 1962. Shcharansky's pilgrimage—which ended happily in 1986 in Jerusalem after his release—had started in the early 1970s in Moscow when he was working at an oil-and-gas research institute as a mathematician and computer scientist. The work allegedly exposed Shcharansky to state secrets, which is why he had been denied emigration to Israel. Subsequently, Shcharansky became active in a dissident movement and later married the sister of a fellow dissident who was allowed to emigrate to Jerusalem. Yet Shcharansky himself still couldn't leave the country. His reaction was even greater activism. He became the leader of the Moscow citizens group that monitored their country's compliance with the human rights provisions of the 1975 Helsinki accords. Shcharansky's activities became too disturbing for the Soviet regime, and in 1977 he was sentenced to prison. He remained there and in the labour camps until he was released in 1986.

For Vogel and the GDR these exchanges were extremely lucrative, a way of obtaining all kinds of hard currency and other products that were in short supply in the East German economy. The amount of goods and money—cash from hand to hand—was enormous. Prisoner exchange was a very useful source of financial support for the East German government, a kind of modern people-trading. Most political prisoners were exchanged for $75,000 and above. Vogel's fame really rose in the mid-1970s, when under a hush-hush program known as 'Kopfgeld', or head money, Vogel arranged for the ransoming of 1,158 political prisoners by West Germany. Two-thirds of these prisoners had been jailed for attempting to escape or for helping others to escape over the odious Wall. Others had been sentenced for speaking out against the regime in public. Some called the Kopfgeld money programme a 20th-century communist slave market. But for the west, for humanitarian reasons, there was no choice but to participate.

I remember Vogel as being kind of pudgy, in his fifties, and always well-dressed. How Vogel was paid, I don't know. He probably got fees, maybe a commission. He was a complicated man, and I somehow liked to deal with him. Things got done. He was obviously in a difficult situation, somehow sitting in between two chairs. Many people—including myself—have questions about Vogel, like who was he really working for? Much speculation was circulating. Some people said he was a Stasi agent; others believed he was a saint. I never really figured out what his background or official status was, but he obviously had good connections with East German officialdom. He always denied being a member of the East German SED, but he definitely enjoyed a cosy relationship with the highest-ranking party members, the Politburo and Moscow. He couldn't have functioned without such relationships As a conduit for hard currency, Vogel could hardly have been held in higher esteem by the East German regime. First he was awarded an honorary doctorate. Honecker also hung one of the country's highest awards on the lawyer's chest, the Order of Merit of the Fatherland, made of gold. Maybe Honecker had a sense of humour, since Vogel, meaning 'bird' in German, was definitely his chicken that laid the golden egg.

Ludwig A. Rehlinger

There were not many happy hours in the tasks I had in Berlin. Successful negotiations and delivery of political prisoners were always followed and contradicted by the wish to help more people to get out. It was and is particularly today a controversial issue if the dealing with the GDR to 'buy' political prisoners could also be called 'trading people' for head money and should be considered immoral. From the very first beginning in 1963, I interpreted the whole effort of operation as a human initiative to help political prisoners to freedom and support those 300,000 East Germans who were desperate to leave their country because of the unbearable political circumstances. Such initiative asked for uncommon and unbureaucratic methods.

The fact that people were imprisoned because of their political beliefs in the former GDR and were punished with year-long prison terms leads to nothing else but the fact that the system of the former GDR was brutal and detestable. A system with an ideology that kicked human rights with their feet.

Nevertheless, I developed an unusual, even unique, relationship with Dr Wolfgang Vogel. From the very beginning, the East German attorney acted as my counterpart. We met regularly over almost three decades and spoke on the phone almost daily. We dealt with each other for one purpose: to free people of the injustice done to them. Dr Vogel himself once declared to me that he is a Marxist, but the focus of his task is to help people out. It would have been senseless to start a political discussion with him at that point. But over the years, I got more and more the feeling that he really wanted to help. Up to 1989, the West German government regarded him highly. He was regularly invited to official functions in Bonn, such as the prestigious annual press dinner dance. Dr Vogel was accepted, just as the existence of the GDR was accepted.

The history of the human endeavour of the West German government which started on 14 December 1962, when Chancellor Adenauer restructured his cabinet, is closely tied to the personality of Vogel and his ability to deliver promises, which was unusual for the system he represented. Adenauer had asked Rainer Barzel to be the new minister for internal German political questions. His predecessor Ernst Lemmer had, until the Wall was built in 1961, as much contact with the east as possible. These contacts were literally cut off over night when the Wall was built. Barzel was young, new to his field of work, and a risk taker. His courage and his unbureaucratic attitude made the first exchange possible. Long before 1963 and as early as 1947, the churches had tried to get prisoners of war and political prisoners out of the Soviet occupation zone. The churches had worked through an attorney's office in Berlin. We later worked a similar way through an attorney by the name of Jürgen Stange. An attorney's office was for several reasons practicable to use as it was not a political representation of any government, but acted upon representing clients, in that case political prisoners. Since 1955 the West German government had also involved GDR attorneys in defending political prisoners. One of these correspondence attorneys between the east and the west was Dr Wolfgang Vogel. He was born in 1925 in Silesia and had studied law after the Second World War in Jena and Leipzig. From 1952 to 1953 he was employed by the GDR Justice Ministry. Later, he opened his own practice in East and West Berlin. After 1961, as normal traffic between East and West Berlin was no longer possible, and only people with a West German passport could pass the border, we used Stange as a representative to keep up the information flow on the East German political prisoners. As communication was extremely difficult, a middleman like Stange became extremely helpful. Stange, of course, came in contact with Vogel. After several meetings, Vogel hinted to Stange that the GDR was interested in an exchange of political prisoners for payment.

The young minister Barzel, newly in charge of the internal German issues, knew that trying to go the conventional way wouldn't open doors with the administration. He looked for a good contact whose voice had influence in Bonn. There was nobody better than the Berliner publishing magnate Axel Springer. After a private talk in Springer's office in Berlin, Barzel got the assurance that Springer would support an initial exchange of prisoners. The mood in Bonn changed and we received marching orders to meet with East German representatives to discuss the conditions of an exchange. As the operation was strictly secret and should under no circumstances be brought to the public eye, we acted without having an official government order.

Owing to my work with the law enforcement administration, I knew that there were roughly 12,000 files of political prisoners. Still, during this time over 4,000 Germans, who had been tried by the Soviet military tribunal in mass trials, were serving time in East German prisons. Among them were also people, civilians who had been tried because of 'anti-soviet propaganda'. These bogus trials had never taken longer than 15 minutes.

The first meeting between Barzel, myself and Stange had been arranged in the Easter week of 1963 in the Munich hotel Deutscher Kaiser. Preparation for the meeting was impossible since we had only a foggy idea under which conditions the exchange was going to be made. Stange could have been somebody who promised more than was possible. He could well have been a somebody who was just trying to throw his weight around. We didn't know. During the meeting, we showed our general interest in exchanging prisoners for payment. Stange and I would be the main contact through which the details would be arranged. At first, 5,000 prisoners were to be let go, then 1,000, then 800, and finally the GDR agreed to send eight prisoners. I had the dreadful task of selecting those eight people out of more than 12,000 cases. I was the one who had to play god. During the course of arrangements for the first exchanges, I had met Dr Vogel for the first time in Stange's office. I was initially amazed about the friendly tone. Both called each other by their first names and dealt with each other rather like buddies. What became most important throughout the following years in the dealings with Vogel was that he kept his promises. He never failed on any agreement he ever made with me, which were concluded only by shaking hands.

The most uncomfortable meetings were always those during which the amount of payment for each prisoner was discussed—the head money. In the early years, the head money was dependent on the political and human importance of the prisoner. An ugly process. I remember one incident in particular, where I got very angry and loud with Dr Vogel. We were to exchange two spies for each other. The East German spy had received a few years for industrial espionage serving time in a West German prison. Our spy had got a lifelong prison term in East Germany. Vogel didn't want to trade one for the other because 'they weren't equally valuable. Human life was worth nothing in the GDR system.

On 23 September 1963—I remember the date so well because it was my birthday—I travelled to Bonn to get the final green light from Barzel. I had spent endless, sleepless nights in order to select eight prisoners who had been imprisoned for longer than ten years, because of their connections to 'forbidden' parties such as the Christian Democrats, the Liberals and the Socialist Party. Among them were two younger people who were serving time because they had been active in the church of their community.

For good reasons, there was never an agreement or written

contract signed between East and West Germany to secure the exchange. It was purely a gentleman's agreement between Barzel, myself, Stange and Vogel.

During the negotiations, we had insisted that we were first to receive the political prisoners and then, upon their safe arrival in the west, the money would be delivered.

The prisoners were delivered in groups. It was an overwhelming feeling when the first three prisoners finally came. None of them had been prepared for their release. They had just been called out of their cells, dressed in old clothes, guided to the entrance of the prison where Vogel waited for them and then put on a bus. What must have gone on in those heads of the prisoners who had been serving time for years for no reason. Among the first three prisoners was an old man. He had been a carpenter who had been tried by the Soviet military tribunal for something nobody knew. He received a life-long prison term of which he had already served ten years. When he noticed that he was in the west, he uttered in disbelief, 'did somebody think of me,' and then collapsed.

After the first three prisoners were delivered to the east, Stange let me know that the other side was expecting to be paid. Barzel had arranged that the means were ready. Our problem was how to deliver the money without the public or the press being aware of the transaction. An official transfer from one account to another was not possible. How should the incoming and outgoing money be explained? What made the whole transaction easier was the fact that Berlin had its own independent pay office for all ministry and government representation. Barzel handed me a note which authorized me to cash DM340,000 from this pay office. The people at the pay office knew me and, for my own security and to prevent any rumours of misconduct, I took my secretary along when I picked up the bundle of cash. With the money under the arm I went back to the office and locked it away. Half of the problem was solved now. Yet, another hurdle to overcome was the delivery of the payment. At the height of the Cold War it was impossible for me or any other government representative to drive to East Berlin. So Stange was asked to do the delivery. According to an agreement of the four Allies the city train in West Berlin was run by the GDR train authorities. Particularly after the Wall was built, all citizens of West Berlin boycotted the S-Bahn as a protest against the division of the city. Most of the train stations weren't used anymore and were usually absolutely empty. Everybody coming from the west trying to use the S-Bahn had to expect to run the gauntlet. On the other hand, the S-Bahn, because of being avoided by West Berliners, was the best way for our delivery. Yet another problem was the border guards between east and west who usually searched every traveller thoroughly. What would a border guard suspect if he found Stange with that amount of money just wrapped in a brown paper bag? The press would have immediately picked up that something was going on. But there was no other way. I accompanied Stange to the S-Bahn station, the last stop before entering East Berlin. The border guards there hadn't bothered us and just before the train was leaving the east, I handed Stange the brown package through the window of the train. The first deal with the GDR was done. After the initial deal, a kind of a routine developed. Already in 1964 we exchanged 64 prisoners, then 500 the following year. From 1964 to 1986 the exchanges followed the same pattern. Starting in 1986, Vogel and I had agreed to release the prisoners one by one. That had the advantage that they could leave the GDR together with their families. Earlier, some of the prisoners had to wait months, sometimes years to be reunited with their families who were still in the GDR.

During one of the earlier exchanges—I think it was in 1964—I received a late phone call from Stange at home. His message was brief. He just told me, 'We need another van tomorrow'. I started to ask why, but he cut me off and just answered, 'We need another van tomorrow. I'll explain later.' I organized a second van, informed the border guards since it needed different licence plates for the crossing. I was pondering that night what we possibly could have overlooked, that we needed so much more space.

The explanation was what I call typically German. Many of the political prisoners of that exchange had been imprisoned for a long time. As the prisoners had worked during the time they were in prison, the GDR owed them money—East German marks, of course. It was forbidden to take East German marks out of the country; nevertheless, the GDR insisted on paying their political prisoners the money they had earned over time. As I later learned, 'The socialist government doesn't embezzle salaries, not even of political prisoners'. The second van was, therefore, needed for goods the political prisoners were able to buy in one of the buildings of the Stasi.

Already in the mid 1970s, the exchange programme, if you want to call it that, had become public knowledge. Since then I have heard the accusation that we also had spent government money on buying East German spies and that the GDR had implanted criminals into our society via the exchanges. That is absolutely wrong. From the files we had, I made the decision who was to be exchanged. After 1982 when the accusations mounted, I looked at the files and the biographies of the ex-political prisoners again in order to see if there was anything to the accusations. During my research, I found that the Stasi had yearly let go 20 to 25 criminals, among them even murderers, who passed the border of Friedrichstrasse to cross to the west. These criminals applied here for West German citizenship which we couldn't deny them legally. In other words, yes, there were criminals channelled into West German society, but not via the exchange operations.

It is true that for the GDR the exchange programme resulted in hard currency that amounted to roughly DM3.5 billion between 1963 and 1989. That amount was a drop in the bucket compared to figures of the overall GDR economy. What is true is that the GDR tried to put more people into prison after the initial dealings to have more 'commodity' to trade. Particularly, after 1984 the number of people imprisoned for political reasons rose dramatically in the GDR. During the mid-1980s more and more people had tried to get in contact with our permanent mission in East Berlin to enquire about ways to leave the GDR. Their intent to leave resulted in 400 to 500 more arrests and imprisonments than in the previous years. I wrote Vogel a harsh letter immediately, stating that we couldn't deal with him or with the regime he represented, if they didn't stop further imprisonments. They stopped.

What worried us was that we didn't have any control over what the GDR was going to do with the money. Of course, our intent was that the loads of oranges, bananas and other commodities we sent would end up in the hands of the people in the streets. For the lump sum which was usually arranged for the exchange the Protestant church signed a contract with Schalck-Golodkowski's operation, the KoKo,[3] on what was to be delivered. Sometimes it was cash, sometimes it was oil and gas, and diamonds for industrial use. The

---

[3] KoKo stands for 'kommerzielle Koordinierung'—commercial co-ordination. Erich Honecker created that term, referring to the lucrative and secretive party business of technology transfers and currency business.

shipment of these commodities was then approved by our Ministry of Economy. Of course, it was clear to us that among those commodities some could have been for military use. But on the other hand, the GDR could also have bought these commodities on the world markets if we had insisted on cash. This side of the deal was out of our hands.

Vogel once told me during a private conversation that he was the middle man between the all-powerful and the all-powerless. He also told me that he was glad he could play this role. He was the master broker in human lives, and we needed him.

Donald Koblitz

Vogel was notorious, not necessarily on the negative side, but very well known in the west as a kind of westernized representative of the Iron Curtain. Somebody one could do business with who was sophisticated. He was very much a charmer, but also genuinely a lonely person because of the status he enjoyed in the east and the west. He was kind of a hybrid. He was fun to deal with because things got done, but I was never under the illusion that he was on our side. He was clearly representing the other side.

Chapter Eleven

The Media

The importance of the media and their function within society, their right to develop ideas and information without political interference and their right to distribute information freely without regard to national borders were among the major points of contention during the Cold War. The results of the struggle between east and west concerning the free flow of information demonstrate that the right to communicate cannot easily be subverted, although no country behind the Iron Curtain seems to have understood that fact.

The conflict of interest between a free society and a totalitarian regime has never been better reflected than in the desperate attempts by the GDR to deny its citizens access to western radio and TV broadcasts. Just as citizens under the Nazi regime were punished if they were caught listening to the BBC or even to American jazz, East Germans who followed West German broadcasts had to fear imprisonment in the 1950s and 1960s. The vast majority of the population ignored the risk and listened anyway. Radio stations such as the West German Deutschland Funk, the BBC and RIAS (Radio in the American Sector) as well as Radio Free Europe became favourite sources for news and entertainment in the east. Fierce jamming was the only feasible way of preventing uncensored western news from getting behind the Iron Curtain. Despite intense efforts, however, the East German jamming system was never totally effective and left gaps in its coverage. East Germans learned how to make maximum use of their dials, adapting or moving their radio sets to try to receive an audible and intelligible signal.

The East German regime could not simply watch or do nothing. Specially designed East German news programmes were prepared to deny any information that had been broadcast by West German stations and had penetrated the east's attempts at jamming. The 'broadcast denial' developed into an elaborate series of programmes that portrayed the west—particularly the Federal Republic—as inhumane nations with high rates of unemployment, crime and inflation. The party organ, *Neues Deutschland*, even occasionally printed fantasy stories about East Germans who were vacationing in socialist Bulgaria being drugged and abducted by West German agents. Like their counterparts in other communist nations, East German newspaper, radio and television served the state and its ideology. Only news that matched the party line was published; other information was filtered out.[1]

Cultural creativity suffered, and the hunger of the East Germans both for uncensored news and for western entertainment increased. With the establishment of two television networks in West Germany at the beginning of the 1960s, electronic media reached almost all parts of East Germany. Antennas able to catch the signals of West German TV started to appear on rooftops like mushrooms. The regime put out an order for the arrest of any citizen who received West German broadcasts, but the state's ability to enforce the order was finally overwhelmed by the huge number of people who had arranged for reception of the broadcasts. The stodgy East German regime had no reply except propaganda.

The staff of the East German broadcasting system were generally *apparatchiks* and known to be dedicated party followers. Guidelines were given out every day on what was to be reported and what not. Journalistic creativity or 'digging' was not appreciated and often resulted in loss of one's job or arrest.

The media even remained faithful when the likely outcome of Honecker's and Krenz's defeat was becoming clear. Only church newspapers and secret newsletters were daring enough to test their limits, but many of them ceased publication as the increasing desire for reform made the regime even more restrictive. Once again, West German television was the only source of information for the protestors in the streets of Leipzig and Berlin to receive some feedback on how the regime might react.

With Honecker's resignation on 18 October 1989 came signs that media censorship might be relaxed. The official East German news agency reported by the end of October, 'Much still remains to be done', thus uncharacteristically suggesting that a change from the status quo was both desirable and necessary. Newspapers started to contain items that just weeks earlier would not have been published. Old party members suddenly became media turncoats, admitting that for years they had reported a distorted picture of reality. Stories about party members' summer houses, bodyguards and special privileges began to appear in the East German media. Still, by western standards the newspapers, TV and radio remained grey and unattractive, laden with communist jargon and items chronicling the ceremonial activities of party leaders. Little had really changed, except for the tone.

---

[1] Paul Lendvai, *Der Medienkrieg, wie kommunistische Regierungen mit Nachrichten Politik machen*, Frankfurt, 1981.

Behind the scenes a few faces changed. Some of the old party members who had worked in the media for the previous four decades were asked to leave and were replaced with elected personnel. The hopes were that East German newspaper, radio and TV services would survive unification. It turned out differently.

East Germans did not want to see the same old faces from the communist past suddenly reading uncensored news on television. They did not want to read the falsely upbeat commentary of old communist newspaper writers, and they definitely did not want to listen to the same radio announcers who, only a few months earlier, had asked them to participate in communist parades.

The broadcast systems of the east will become part of a unified east-west system only after they have undergone a good housecleaning of tough-minded comrades. For newspapers, unification seemed further away because of the striking cultural and social divisions between east and west. In the months following unification, East German curiosity led to a boom of West German publications. Influential western newspapers such as the *Frankfurter Allgemeine* or *Süddeutsche Zeitung* sold an average of around 350,000 copies a day in East Germany for several weeks after the Wall fell. Today, however, the circulation in the east is only about 10,000 copies. East German readers complain that West German newspapers are too voluminous and deal with uninteresting subjects. Most West German publishers seeking to establish a foothold in the east have been confronted with two choices: they could either bid for a former communist newspaper, or launch new products specially designed for East German tastes. One publisher experimenting with a new product called his glossy *Life*-style magazine *Schöner Leben* (Beautiful Living) in West Germany, but revealingly called the East German version *Leben* (Living).

Ferdinand Nohr

For over thirty years I was one of the leading journalists in the political department of the GDR's radio and broadcasting network. But because I left the SED in the 1970s, I was refused the job of heading the department. Working in East German media, of course, meant you were a loyal party member. But some toed the party line more eagerly than others. I was one of those who lagged a bit. I became rather cynical. In fact, an atmosphere of cynicism really permeated our radio station.

Presentation of the news and commentaries was tightly controlled. Certain words and phrases such as 'imperialistic West Germany' had to appear in every broadcast. We also had to use positive clichés and images of the GDR, and to report horror stories about West Germany's economy. No one at the radio station ever questioned this. Every morning our editor-in-chief received his orders from the 'Konti', a government agency that controlled all broadcasting activities within the GDR. His orders were called the ARGO, our 'argumentation guidelines'. The ARGO was always filled with news of terrible problems in West Germany, such as inadequate housing and sprawling slums. There was always lots of good news about the GDR. Every day the menu of acceptable terms was revised. I remember more than once that we were told to keep the word 'banana' out of our broadcasts. Why? It seems that the deliveries of bananas from Cuba had been delayed by several weeks. The banana bins at the markets had been empty for quite a while. People were growing impatient.

No one actually looked over your shoulder when you prepared the political commentary that always went along with the news. You simply got into the habit of censoring yourself. You knew precisely how far you could go in criticizing the regime in a commentary: not very far! You were very careful in your choice of words. But the fact is, I believed much of what I wrote. I couldn't have survived otherwise.

We were in a constant state of war with the western media. In the beginning, radio stations such as RIAS (Radio in the American Sector) and Radio Free Europe were heavily jammed. As their improved technology made jamming more difficult, our argumentation guidelines gave us a sketchy picture of what had been reported about the GDR. Based on these hints, we then had to hastily draw up a response. Usually the West German source was discredited.

I first got into this line of work when I started writing at the age of 26. Both of my parents were proud communists, and we children had been steeped in antifascist sentiments. I was born in 1930 in Magdeburg, just a few hours journey from Berlin. During the Third Reich, my parents fled to France and became members of the Resistance. My mother was particularly afraid of staying in Germany, as she was known to be not only a communist but also Jewish. After the war was over, I returned to Berlin and immediately joined the SED.

At that time, I would have supported any political system that had opposed Hitler and the Nazis. In the early 1970s I left the party in disgust. I felt suffocated by this pervasive ideology that didn't allow me to think or to do what I knew was right. Ulbricht's version of communism was the inflexible, brain-damaging ideology that evolved around the person and history of Stalin.

I became convinced that socialism, not communism, was the key to creating a new world order. But now I've changed, not only because I'm older and more cynical about politics in general, but also because I have lived for 40 years in a system based on socialist ideals. Unfortunately, the socialist model doesn't work. But I don't fully endorse the free-market system either; I simply don't have the answer. Theoretically, communism is a good concept, but it was always an ideology that could not deliver on its promises. What is the difference between communism and capitalism? In communist countries few goods are distributed unevenly, while in capitalist countries many goods are distributed unevenly.

We at the radio station were probably among the first in the GDR to learn of the exodus of refugees to Hungary. Though any mention of it was strictly prohibited, no one, not even the party hard-liners, believed that the silence could undo what had already been done. By August 1989 it was no longer possible to hide the many vacant apartments and the empty desks in schools. On radio we began to denounce the refugees as politically unfit and as 'criminal elements'.

The same strategy was used when someone wanted to leave the party, which usually arranged to oust the defector before he could announce his leaving. I was lucky to have left the party more than 20 years ago. The desire to control and misuse power seemed to have multiplied in the regime within its last 12 months. More and more people were punished as disloyal 'friends'. A colleague of mine decided to leave the party about five years ago. He was one of our finest journalists. His talent made it difficult for the party to find a reason to oust him, but they did. I think he ended up working as a gardener. Such incidents were not uncommon.

'Public figures' were routinely snooped on, and they rightly feared that their telephones were bugged—or even their bedrooms. When I discovered that a colleague had bugged my phone, I knew he did it for his career. He was simply jealous, and sought to advance himself at my expense. Snooping is not a political problem, it is a human problem. These unprofessional spies were uniformly over-ambitious, arrogant and troubled people. The GDR was nothing more than the biggest prison on earth.

My wife worked for an ad agency for a while. She represented the GDR at major trade shows in other eastern bloc countries and once in France. Of 20 agency people who were allowed to travel, three had never seen a marketing book or sat through a lecture on sales or any other related topic. It was clear that some were there to make sure that everyone found their way back to the GDR. Others may even have been secret agents travelling under cover.

Most of those undercover agents have lately been scrambling to get party money out to Swiss bank accounts. A friend of mine works at the *Morgenpost*, a daily morning newspaper. He interviewed a local truck driver who also chauffeured Stasi members. A few days after the Wall fell, he was asked to drive an old truck to a rural area outside Berlin. Half a dozen cars followed him to the field where he was supposed to stop. He observed bundles of money being removed from the rear of the truck and passed out to the six cars. He was paid handsomely to keep his mouth shut about the incident. My friend speculated that the party officials who divided up the money intended to buy East German companies.

Technically, the GDR is no more—but it would be foolish to believe that former members won't work to undermine our new democracy. Party members always got the right end of the stick before and they will again. They are already buying up hotels, stores and other businesses with SED money. They are emerging as the new entrepreneurs of the GDR. Most other citizens don't have enough money to pay their rent.

Ralf Matschat

The senses of an East German citizen received little stimulation. Everything—art, literature, even children's TV programmes—was strongly infiltrated by the dogma of the regime. Most secular music, such as pop songs, didn't promote love or trust, but instead screeched socialist ideals.

One of the few opportunities to escape the doldrums of everyday life was western TV, which we had received since the end of the

1960s in most parts of the country. The West German programmes were not only our channel of political information, but also one of our few sources of amusement. Probably no other nation followed the fortunes of the characters of the TV series *Dallas* more intensely than East Germans.

The SED's original attempt to restrict the flow of information by imprisoning any citizens caught watching broadcasts from the west proved unworkable. By the end of the 1960s, almost every third household had a TV that was, of course, tuned in the evening to the western channels. Until the 1970s it was an unwritten rule that you were not to disturb friends between 7:00 p.m. and 8:00 p.m., the time when the West German news was broadcast. To prevent the children from picking up on West German information, which could have created problems for the family, they were usually sent to bed or kept busy with homework in another room.

Seeing the western lifestyle depicted on the screen—starting with advertisements for things we couldn't get here—produced two distinct reactions. On one hand, they developed a strong longing to participate in a free and democratic lifestyle. But on the other hand, there was something appalling about what we saw. I believe the ordinary East German citizens were and are very politically sensitive and aware. They tend to be quite well-informed. Westerners are much more involved with themselves, busy with activities and feel uncomfortable when they are not moving around or organizing something. The cheerful, lively action in the ad or even in the news was attractive, but it was also repellent because of its superficiality.

Citizens of the GDR were prisoners not only in the literal sense, but also emotionally. They did not dare to show emotions or let off steam. Not being able to say what you think, or even feel what you would like to feel, resulted in strange behaviour. I have worked with people who were terribly depressed, men and women who were obsessed with food, or colleagues who were simply afraid to face the day. Forcing people to live under circumstances that suppressed personality, individual traits or whatever makes someone unique is probably the greatest crime the regime ever committed. The mind control started with the little toddlers in school. I remember coming home from school one day and watching my father listening to West German radio for a while. Every day our teachers were telling us that West German Chancellor Konrad Adenauer was killing little children and that he headed a Nazi country with which nobody wanted to be associated. We also had been asked to denounce anybody we caught receiving broadcasts from the west. Seeing my father silently listening to the western news and political commentary didn't fit in with my young communist-trained sense of propriety. Politely but firmly I requested that he turn the radio off, as otherwise I would have to give his name to the superintendent of the school. I can still see his face in front of me, smiling at me gently and just saying, 'I enjoy listening to this station'. That was the end of the discussion and I didn't know what to do.

Thassilo Borchart

I think the 40 years' separation will plague our communication for a long time, even though East and West Germans speak the same language. In the GDR we were used to speaking in 'codes' which only an initiate could understand. There was a time when I desperately wanted to leave the GDR—especially when the party barred me from working as a journalist. The only work I could find was as a bricklayer. As a journalist I had tried to stay away from politics, and, of course, I had to join the party—otherwise I couldn't even have written obituaries. Mostly, I reported on experiences of working-class people in an idealized and optimistic tone. The language should be simple, I was told, so that millions could understand and be inspired by our 'socialist heroes'. Almost everybody I interviewed was loyal to the government.

'Artistic freedom' is just not a concept familiar to East Germans. Painters and writers were controlled by the League of Culture. Failure to follow their guidelines was severely punished. Out-of-favour artists were not allowed access to galleries, concert halls or publishing houses. Some were sent to prison. Most artists, like myself, paid lip service to the government. We produced work to appease the 'ideological watchdogs' but privately pursued our own endeavours.

In the early 1970s I applied for an exit permit that was never granted. The authorities sought to make even the idea of leaving the country a crime. Usually someone who applied lost his job, as happened to me, or his apartment. You also had to think of relatives; they, too, could be punished for your decision. If you were to flee to the west, of course, you might either be shot at the Wall or, if caught, be imprisoned for at least ten years. The regime charged such refugees with the crime of 'flight from the Republic'—even though the right to emigrate was constitutionally guaranteed.

In one period of ten months, several doctors escaped in a refrigerator van. One of them knew a West German meat wholesaler who was allowed to trade in East Berlin. After the meat and other foods had been inspected and sealed, doctors in groups of five, sometimes with their children, hid in the cooled meat van. The GDR police didn't suspect anything until more than ten doctors from local hospitals were missing. The media never reported escapes; we heard of them through the grapevine or via West German TV.

A long time ago, I decided not to hang on to my old passion, journalism. Censorship and not being able to write what you want didn't leave me any other option. I have to say, however, that I was tempted to work as a journalist again just a year before the Wall. I was amused by an incident in East Berlin and actually angry that I hadn't thought of doing it myself. I was walking in the morning on East Berlin's main boulevard, Unter den Linden, when I heard a newspaper boy shouting, 'Socialist Party adopts reform.' I thought I was dreaming. Could it be true that Honecker was finally giving in to Gorbachev? I walked up to the boy, bought a newspaper and started to read while walking. The other pages were even more fantastic. There was a story about a contest on what to do with the Berlin Wall. Other stories said that the state archives of the secret police were to be converted into a public library and that Katharina Witt was to be seen nude in the next issue. I finally caught on. I looked again at the familiar layout of *Neues Deutschland*, the cheap paper it was known for, and then I noticed the format was a bit smaller. It was a spoof. A West German magazine publisher had made up several thousand copies and distributed them in East Berlin. I wished I had thought about producing a mock edition like that myself, but I probably would have been put in jail for doing it.

Lothar Loewe

Citizens of the GDR were the best informed of all Eastern Europeans, because they had access to West German radio. The radio station in the American sector, RIAS, started beaming its signal toward the eastern part of the country in 1946. Later came SFB (Sender Freies Berlin—Broadcast Free Berlin) and the West German TV broadcasters. By the mid-1970s, the regime was unable to stop the spread of TV antennas, which mushroomed up on rooftops all over East Germany. East Germans followed the political overtones of western broadcasts much more attentively than did their West German counterparts, and regularly compared the information received from the west with the broadcasts of their own manipulated media. The only programmes people *liked* to watch on East German channels were sports and pre-war black and white movies starring people like Marlene Dietrich, Heinz Rühmann and other older or already-dead stars. Poland, Czechoslovakia and the other communist-ruled countries had no source of information comparable to that of the East Germans.

The loosening of travel restrictions in the late 1970s and 1980s made it easier to smuggle popular western magazines and newspapers into the east. People brought them into the country placed under floormats of their cars or hidden in their coats when they passed through the border. Most of those newspapers, once in the east, were passed through the neighbourhoods. Even if the papers were weeks old, to the East Germans they brought news from the west.

My task as a correspondent in East Berlin was quite different from any other assignment I'd had. First of all, it was the place where I was born and the city that had been divided so cruelly in 1961, and I was the first West German correspondent to be admitted to work in the eastern part of Germany. I knew the eyes of all officials would be on me from day one.

It was fascinating to report from cities like Dresden, Leipzig, Strahlsund, communities that a whole generation of West Germans, born after the building of the Wall, knew about only from the map. But there was another, deeper fascination: everybody living in the GDR who came from the west—people like myself, diplomats, their staffs—we all tried to find out how the East German political system worked. None of us westerners really knew how things happened or why they happened. We didn't know when the Politburo met, or when or why it had fired a high-ranking party member. It was all a big question mark.

We were fully aware that we had to serve two audiences and fulfil two roles. The West Germans wanted to learn more about the people and the Germany behind the Wall. But the East German people looked at us as another source of news in their own country. When we reported about a flu epidemic, for example, the news was probably interesting to the western people who started to think about their relatives in the east possibly being infected. Yet this kind of information was far more interesting and relevant to East Germans, since we were usually the only network spreading such 'unwanted news', which the easterners otherwise would never have heard.

Within weeks after we opened our first office in Berlin we were getting tremendous feedback. People started talking to the camera teams on site. Some called on the phone to give me hints for stories. Our direct influence on the East German population made us very dangerous to the regime and raised even more questions about the east's dubious information system. Most of my work apart from news involved documenting the East German lifestyle. One series was a documentary entitled *People in the GDR*. Another one was called *For Me the FGR is Abroad*, which, of course, was a sarcastic play on the official theory of the division of Germany for the regime. All our work was aimed at bringing East and West Germans closer in their understanding and appreciation of one another. We were constantly looking for ties to maintain a bond between the two nations and their people. In co-operation with Manfred Stolpe, who was the head of the Protestant Church in the GDR in the 1970s and who today serves as government minister of Brandenburg, we developed a Sunday evening series that broadcast church services to West Germany from cathedrals in East Germany. Such series were not appreciated by the eastern regime. A bond between east and west, any feeling of team spirit between both sides, was exactly contrary to the regime's West German policy, which stressed differences and sought the official status of an independent separate nation. No West German government ever approved of that or agreed to that status, which is why West Germany never called its representation in East Berlin an 'embassy', but instead referred to it as a 'permanent mission'. Even in informal meetings, East Germany's officials stressed again and again their eagerness to continue the status quo: a divided Germany and a widening gap between the two sides. I once had lunch with a high-ranking bureaucrat from Saxony who was in the

SED and was a member of the Politburo. It was a nice, sunny day and we strolled along Unter den Linden, East Berlin's main boulevard. We were discussing this and that when he suddenly said, 'It must be difficult for a foreigner to find his way around here in the east'. My only reply was, 'I was playing here on Unter den Linden long before you were born, and here you are, coming all the way from Saxony to tell me that I'm a foreigner in the city I was born in.' He was speechless. He was not prepared for such openness.

The attitude of the regime toward the free press from the west was ambivalent. On the one hand, we posed a threat to the stability of the system; on the other, Honecker and his comrades were flattered that we thought the GDR important enough to have offices in East Berlin. In the end, the threat overcame the flattery, and I was expelled.

I would have liked to continue working in the eastern part of Germany, but I knew officials there were looking for a way to get rid of me. From the very beginning I had suspected that the SED was using every possible means to prevent me from working as the first West German correspondent in East Berlin. And after the fall of the Wall, I finally had an opportunity to look at files the GDR had kept on me and my family. Within these files there is a detailed documentation of my character, which is described as, among other things, 'dangerous to the people and to the regime'. My file goes back to the time I spent as a correspondent in Moscow. One incident described at length came back to me while I was reading through it. I had been present during a press conference held by Andrej Gromyko and West German Foreign Minister Walter Scheel at that time. Afterwards, the two politicians walked to an open corridor window. I sent my sound engineer after them to try to catch some of the conversation via his directional microphone. The security men, appearing within seconds, gave us a warning and pushed us back. For the GDR, that incident justified opposing me as a western correspondent.

Almost from day one I, the work team and my family were subject to abuse. Our cars were stopped regularly at the border and searched for hours before we could leave for the western part of the city. We were one of very few families who had two apartments in one city, one in the eastern and the other in the western part of Berlin. The children lived with us in the eastern part after I was transferred, but went to school in the western part. Therefore, we commuted back and forth frequently. The kids' school bags were inspected regularly and they also had to undergo body searches from time to time. After such treatment, I immediately went to the West German permanent mission to protest, but it didn't help much.

When I was expelled as a foreign correspondent, just two years after I had been admitted, the Stasi used different methods. It was shortly before the holidays, 21 December, and I was preparing a very critical and very political broadcast on the GDR. The impetus for the broadcast was the death of a young man who had been shot at the border while trying to escape to the west. Via TV, the whole world had watched East German soldiers carry the dead body away. At the same time, Honecker showed no intention of cancelling the order-to-shoot at the border. My wife had told me that morning that she was going to West Berlin for some holiday shopping. Later that afternoon, in shock and very irritated, she called from home to tell me that she had been in a bad car accident and had trouble with the East German police. A car had run into her at Leipzigerstrasse, just a few blocks away from our apartment. An East German policeman who was not wearing a uniform appeared immediately and asked her all kinds of questions, many not necessarily related to the car accident. She told me very explicitly that she believed that a car had followed her since she crossed the border at Heinrichstrasse and then had deliberately bumped into her. At first I didn't believe her and attributed the thought to her state of shock. But today we know from looking at our files that my wife was right. Somebody had orders to keep us on our toes, even if doing so required force or violence.

That same evening, the programme I had diligently prepared was transmitted from East Berlin. Pictures of the shooting at the border served to increase tension that had arisen between the two German neighbours days earlier when West German Chancellor Helmut Schmidt harshly criticized the GDR in a speech. Consequently, the state-owned newspaper *Neues Deutschland* attacked him and the West German government the day after the speech. The relationship between the two Germanies was at a low point.

My programme was aimed mainly at putting the political events of the previous weeks in perspective. I remember closing with the remarks: 'The strong reaction of East Germany, and its attacks on West German politics, could only have been possible with the permission and agreement of the Soviet Union.' I continued, 'That kind of reaction is symptomatic of the climate in this state, where artists, writers and other free spirits are oppressed. East Germany's writers and dissidents have been expelled, while ordinary people who were seeking to leave the country with an exit permit have lost their jobs or have been imprisoned.'

Minutes before I started to transmit, a couple called me from Leipzig and told me that they both had just lost their jobs because they had been applying for an exit permit, and the husband was afraid of going to jail, since the permit had been denied. I wanted to make very sure in my closing statement that people in the west understood how people had to suffer in the east and, in the spirit of the moment, I finished my broadcast by saying, 'Every little kid in the street here knows that people are getting shot like rabbits at the border'.

My closing statement was the highlight of the whole broadcast. People in the west were jumping out of their chairs. The phone wouldn't stop ringing in our offices. The officials in the east were enraged. I know today that Honecker gave an immediate order to expel me after watching the programme.

The next morning, 22 December, I had planned to finish undone business so I could start fresh in the new year. Within minutes after I entered the office, my telephone rang and East Germany's Foreign Ministry was on the line. Comrade Wehmann wanted to see me. I made it pretty clear to him that I already had my day planned differently, and I asked him if the meeting couldn't wait until after the holidays. His voice became very firm and assertive: 'Mr Loewe, I have to ask you strongly to appear in my offices today'. I responded, 'Mr Wehmann, you are not politely asking me to come, but you are ordering me to come?' He answered, 'That's your interpretation'. By that time, my driver came running into my office and pointed out six or seven cars that were parked in front of the office building, surrounding my limousine. Everything had been timed perfectly—the phone call, the Ladas that appeared out of nowhere. I asked my driver to pull our car up as close as he could to the exit door. I watched from my window as he walked towards the car and started it. At the same time, all the watchdogs started their cars as well. There were two or three people in every car. To see how many cars were following us, I asked my chauffeur to go around the block several times before dropping me off at the West German mission.

When we stopped in front of the gate at the West German mission, I could barely get out of the car, because two of the cars following us had positioned themselves tightly in front of mine, the others at the rear. As though I didn't even notice, I passed by and had my scheduled meeting with Günther Gauss, who was heading the mission at that time. From a window I showed Gauss the number of cars positioned around my limousine. He uttered aloud what I had been thinking for the last twenty minutes: 'They are going to throw you out!' Gauss and I decided that Bonn should be informed and that I should go to the meeting the East Germans had demanded.

I asked my secretary to join me at the meeting with comrade Meier, who was the head of press and media relations. It was always better to have a witness at one's side in such 'get-togethers'. When I had visited them before, there usually had been a pot of coffee and some cigarettes or, in the summertime, some cold lemonade standing on a small side-table. This time the table was empty; not even paper or pencils were on it. The table setting, as I called it, was usually a good barometer of the atmosphere the conversation would be held in. A man had silently guided us into the room, just nodded at us and showed us where to be seated. Within seconds Meier walked in. I rose to shake hands with him. Briefly raising one hand in a gesture that told me not to bother, he started reading a declaration informing me of my deportation. At the same time, about four o'clock in the afternoon, the East German radio announced that 22 December was the last day I would be serving as a foreign correspondent in East Germany for the west. The timing of the events was extraordinary. After Meier finished reading, I rose from my chair to defend myself. He interrupted me by saying, 'Your time to explain yourself is over'. He left the room and immediately two Vopos (Volkspolizisten or state police) guided us out of the building. The group of Ladas still surrounded the limousine, and from that moment until I left the Ladas followed me everywhere.

I knew that Meier had made one major mistake. According to the human rights declaration from Helsinki, deporting a foreign correspondent is illegal as long as he has not committed a crime. Even if there were criminal charges, the correspondent must be given an opportunity to defend himself against the accusations. The West German Foreign Office officially protested about my expulsion and asked for a second meeting between me and Meier. That meeting was granted. Meier met me again 48 hours after our first encounter in the same cold, empty room. We both sat down. He asked me formally to proceed. After I finished with my defence, he nodded calmly, saying, 'All fine and good. Mr Loewe, where did you learn that our soldiers have an order to shoot people?' His question was a trick and he thought I would stumble into it as into an open trap. I answered, 'Mr Meier, I cannot recite to you the exact words in which you advise your soldiers at the border to shoot at people. We only know it is happening. And if I knew the exact wording of that order, I wouldn't tell you, since you would immediately arrest me for political and military espionage, as so many East European countries do with foreign journalists.' He moved uncomfortably back and forth in his chair and asked me abruptly to leave. On Christmas Day my deportation became a fact.

I didn't know at that time that I would see Meier again, 12 years later in 1988. I had been in Washington as correspondent for ARD (Allgemeiner Rundfunk Deutschland—the first television station established in West Germany in 1961) for a while and later became the head of the SFB in Berlin. In that position I had to deal with Meier on a regular basis. The first time we met again, Meier was extremely friendly, asking me about my wife and children as though we had been the best of friends in the past. There was coffee and cognac on the table and Meier asked me what he could do for me to improve co-operation between the east and west.

Wolf von Holleben

After the reunification we took the initiative, as the largest public broadcasting system in Germany and Europe, to spread our activities to the five new eastern states that merged with West Germany. Of course, one condition for investing in new studios was free and uncontrolled media coverage. We could not get that, so currently the five new states are not part of our official government contract and treaty. Owing to the media monopoly in the Third Reich, the four Allies decided after the war that as long as just a limited number of frequencies are available, only public broadcasting which is controlled through a board should be allowed in Germany. I hope this situation will change soon.[2]

Through a partnership with other European German-speaking

countries, we made first contact with the BBF, the East German Broadcasting channel in Adlershof, near Berlin. The German-speaking western broadcasters met with representatives of the former East German TV and offered to arrange for available satellite channels. This first phase of meetings and discussions was made difficult by suspicion and finger-pointing among the easterners themselves. Doubts about the honesty of some eastern representatives who had been involved in Communist Party activities and about their possible crimes overshadowed and dominated the first meetings. Several times I was called out of the boardroom to listen to different people tell different versions of stories about who served in the party and who was responsible for certain functions. People gave me lists of former colleagues who were not to serve in any public position again, although at that point in the talks we were far away from any of those decisions.

After the Modrow government resigned and reunification came closer, a media council was installed which laid down general conditions for a restructuring of the old system into a free broadcasting system. A former cameraman by the name of Albrecht became the manager of the former East German TV, and the head of the Bavarian TV acts as his consultant. Albrecht, like many others who are now in management positions primarily because they were not active members of the SED, lacks experience. Like many others, he is not able to handle a manager's task. I don't say this to sound arrogant, but, unfortunately, that is the reality.

Albrecht was the successor of Hans Bentzien, who had been named general manager of the TV services by the former communist government months earlier. Bentzien was known to be a veteran of communism whose career had been marked by hanging on to Stalinism in East Germany. He was a forceful advocate for maintaining the broadcast services as independent and non-profit organizations. Bentzien's removal was really part of a political housecleaning.

The changes are especially hard on East German journalists. Their own people don't want to see the old faces who represented the system on screen anymore. Moreover, they won't be able to compete with the western broadcasting networks that will go east. The Second German TV took over one channel, the ARD took over another.

---

[2] This interview was conducted in the winter of 1991.

Journalists who are probably capable of doing managerial work are fired because they were party members. I agree that one cannot put a man who has been part of the SED apparatus for decades into an important media position, but the situation is not always as black and white as it seems. On the other hand, many of those loyal journalists and SED followers who are out of jobs now will never look for work again, but live happily on a West German unemployment payment or pension until they die.

Technicians such as cameramen are in a different situation. They can be retrained and they will, if they are capable, find work again. The rudest awakening will come for those who never were part of the system, such as radio orchestras and TV dancers. West German TV doesn't need them or cannot afford most of them. All those artists, however, see that those who were well connected during the regime's prime are still able to feather their nests.

In 1992 radio and television stations will become independent in the east and must finance themselves. Until then, the service will be given a certain period of time for adjustment to the new system. The other development will be that we, as a public broadcaster, will see increased competition from private ones. Already over 100 licence applications have been filed, mostly for radio stations. All were filed by West German broadcasters who want to extend their audiences to the east. I doubt if there will be applications from the east itself soon, although efforts have been undertaken to establish private radio and TV stations run by East German businessmen.

It is not only the West Germans who have an interest in broadcasting to the east. Asahi, the Japanese media conglomerate, already has its own facilities in the headquarters of one of East Germany's services. But many problems lie ahead, starting with technical ones. For decades the East German regime had dealt with broadcasting frequencies as a 'top secret' matter; now, someone has to solve the frequency puzzle.

Most people in the former GDR thought that reunification would lead quickly to paradise, in the form of money, status, good work, equipment, technology, everything the west stands for in their eyes. The disaster they are confronted with right now was not expected by any of them, nor even by most West Germans. The crisis in the Gulf region came as an almost welcome diversion, because, for the first time in months, the media reported in depth on something other than the east. Finally, there was something to talk about besides the billions it will cost to restructure the former GDR.

The situation has shifted from euphoria to pessimism also among West Germans. Disappointments, the harsh truth of the last forty years and the new taxation are all components of the current lack of joy about the reunification. The mood among East Germans is sad and probably best characterized by hopelessness. One cameraman I briefly talked to during my last visit told me that he felt like he just went through a big sale but didn't get anything in return.

I see more and more that Germany will have wide class distinctions between those who are well off and those who barely will make it. Most of the well-to-do will be westerners; those who barely survive will tend to be easterners. The situation was different after the big exodus in the 1950s and 1960s. The refugees were motivated to work hard and most of them had excellent educations. Everybody, even in the western zones, had started with little or no money after the war. Jealousy was non-existent. Almost everybody was glad to breathe freely again after the end of the Third Reich. Only 12 years had passed, and people could still remember what it meant to live a normal life.

Chapter twelve

The Role of Sports in the GDR

The following questions are frequently asked. For what should the German Democratic Republic be remembered? Should it go down in history simply as a failed communist experiment? Should it find its way into history books only because of its brutality, its elaborate surveillance system, its inhuman frontier that kept people prisoners of their own country? Or are there other less obvious and perhaps more positive aspects of the first workers' and peasants' state that are worth remembering and examining?

Sports is probably one such aspect. The whole world is aware of the Olympic and other international triumphs of such East German star athletes as the flawless, graceful figure skater Katharina Witt, the uncatchable runner Kathrin Krabbe and the unbeatable swimmer Kornelia Ender. But these are only three of the best-known names among a group of athletes who in Olympic Games between 1956 and 1988 amassed an impressive 582 medals.

In sports, the nation of 17 million people has ranked close to the vastly larger USA and the Soviet Union since the mid-1950s. The world has viewed this success with admiration mixed with perplexity and a tinge of envy.

Many claim that the victories were a result of doping. Clearly, some of East Germany's athletes used drugs, but the true secret of the country's success seems to lie deeper than the use of chemicals. The real roots of East Germany's success in sports were political. An official handbook identified a 'policy of the state, which has made it its concern to win over the whole population to a healthy lifestyle'. This concern was also affirmed in the constitution, and in youth and employment law. While few may attribute East Germany's profile output of world-class athletes to a systematic approach to searching for talent and training of young people, others stress that great athletic success is precisely what results when doctrinaire Marxism is crossed with Germanic pragmatism, organizational skill and physical culture. Seeing their flag hang higher than the US stars and stripes or even those flags from other Iron Curtain nations gave GDR officials yet another 'proof' of the quality of the state they had fashioned. For them, competing and winning internationally was viewed less as an individual triumph for the athlete than as an official triumph for and vindication of East German communism.

For athletes, on the other hand, competing successfully in international events was seen as a way to gain an acceptable future in a totalitarian society, money and—most importantly—trips abroad. A communist society might be classless, but there was nevertheless a rarefied level of elite athletes who were a bit more equal than others, and for whom the waiting lists for a car, an apartment or a vacation trip to Cuba was much shorter. If they were good enough, that is. Among the 'secret' ingredients that continually produced stars for the GDR were the athletes' point-payment system, coaching incentives, specialized training for female athletes and the alleged use of steroids.

To join that elite system in the GDR, a young person had to be identified early, trained intensively to have a reasonable chance of winning a medal. In most cases the athlete also had to embrace communism, a bad-tasting medicine that most swallowed, induced by an elaborate point-payment system that handsomely compensated champions. Clubs acted conveniently as a buffer through which athletes could legally be paid without violating their amateur status. For instance, the king of the shotput, Uwe Beyer, belonged to a club in Leipzig, but his so-called employment was with the state government as a member of the armed forces. Individual payments—salary—were made to him through the club's cashier, who also distributed special bonuses provided by the Ministry of Sport. Like Beyer, most GDR athletes were employed by either the armed forces, the secret police, the police or a ministry.

The centre of the Teutonic East German sports machine was the secret German Highschool for Body Culture (DHfK) in Leipzig. There, the athletes, who were chosen when young, were provided with everything they might possibly need and were overseen by a staff of over 750. Having set the athletes apart from the rest of society, the Leipzig officials cultivated excellence in much the same way race-horse trainers foster speed and stamina. At every level, the party played a major role in the process. All of the trainers and coaches and most of the athletes were party members, and many of them sat on the Central Committee of the party's Organization for Free German Youth. If a youngster was identified by a coach and thereafter sent to a sports school like the one in Leipzig, neither the parents nor the child could object. Any objection would have been considered unpatriotic.

Over 400,000 certified coaches, trainers, umpires and judges, plus 20 per cent of the population, belonged to the Sports and Gymnastic Union, which maintained some 18,000 sports clubs, all of which were official outlets of the party. Since reunification, those numbers have been drastically reduced. Also, the secret training, sports medicine and muscle-building techniques, including sophisticated biomedical analysis, that were developed at the institute in Leipzig and were once guarded as a national resource have become a commodity for sale. Athletes have also become saleable, especially the soccer players, who may now receive six-figure salaries for successfully putting the leather into the goal. Other athletes and coaches have become targets for angry fellow citizens who vent their anger about athletes' support of the former totalitarian system. Glamorous skater Katharina Witt has been a particular target of such criticism.

The last time the East German athletes appeared under their own colours was at the European athletic championship in Split, Yugoslavia in August 1990. There, worries about the future surfaced among those involved in sports on both sides of Germany.

Many fine athletes from what was West Germany will have to fight hard to hold their places against former East Germans in the new united teams. The arguments over selection have been bitter. Meanwhile, the system that created the East German sport machines has been dismantled. The cost of maintaining sports facilities like the DHfK in Leipzig was prohibitive, and the absolute priority of sports is impossible to maintain without totalitarian support. Most of the coaches and scientists who guided East Germany's athletes to victory have been dismissed. Many of the lucrative incentives the old system offered young people to join the GDR's sports force are no longer available, and the number of youngsters attracted to sports has declined accordingly. Formerly full-time athletes have to find jobs in order to live. With reunification, East Germany's love for athletic heroism, for flag-waving and for nationalistic image-building is fading and with it the communist sports machinery.

Gabriele Müller

Since 1955 I've coached all GDR skaters who have performed internationally. Before that, I competed in regional and national skating and roller-skating championships with some success. My daughter's talent convinced me to get more involved in coaching, and I started formal studies so I could train Gabriele properly. My daughter won the second place at the European championship in 1966. She won the silver medal in the 1968 Olympic Games. Then in 1969 and 1970, she won the world championship. Her success brought attention to my training methods, and I was asked to coach newcomers such as

Jan Hoffmann and Katharina Witt. Both later won world championships.

I coached many young skaters and helped the GDR win 57 medals in ice-skating competitions. My life has been consumed by the sport, and there is no way I would have achieved that success in any other state but the GDR.

Why was the GDR so extremely successful over the years in international ice-skating competitions? Mainly because of the generous state sponsorship we received. Young skaters were totally supported. Every possible obstacle was removed from their path. School and home life revolved around their sport. The most promising athletes had few concerns other than how they performed. They didn't have to fear that they might not make it into high school, or receive any vocational training. If you were lucky enough to be a good athlete, the system would accommodate you. If you performed, it was assumed you were loyal, and indeed most athletes were not as concerned about politics as about their next competition.

The privileges were kept within bounds, however. A successful athlete might get a bigger apartment or acquire a car earlier, but vacations in Spain or Italy, for example, were not allowed. Cuba instead was a reasonable compromise, which most athletes accepted.

Travelling generally was only permitted in a delegation—a group of athletes accompanied by a coach and two or three Party officials. The Wall between the east and the west existed for athletes just as it did for all the other citizens of the GDR. After a championship, our athletes were always the first to leave the hotel. They were packed into an aeroplane or train and sent back home. Travelling athletes from other nations could sightsee and spend time relaxing. Ours were forbidden to stop anywhere but at the location where the competition took place. A few still managed to defect during a sports event abroad. They must have had help from outside, or they knew the system inside and out.

Sports served the GDR as a PR tool. Success in international competition was supposed to reflect the virtues of the political system and of the GDR's leadership, as well as a sound economy. The success of an athlete was the success of the state.

But it would be wrong to condemn all athletes and coaches of the former GDR as puppets of the state. What counted for me as a coach was the success of my students. Katharina Witt, who skates professionally in West Germany now, couldn't perform for a while following some awkward political remarks she made after the Wall came down. I think these remarks were grossly misinterpreted. Unlike many others who saw and took advantage of an opportunity to desert the Communist Party, she has refused to throw away her party card. I still have mine and I'm sure going to keep it. I'm not a turncoat.

Here in the GDR, Katharina Witt was known as Katharina the Great, but she was often frowned upon because of her notoriety. Virtually overnight she found herself unexpectedly having to defend her privileged life. It hit the news that she had a penthouse apartment in East Berlin, a country retreat and a Porsche. The nation was frustrated and angry. But I have to defend her. We all, coaches and athletes, did something special and I think we deserved a better treatment. All of Katharina's life she was told she would be looked after, and now she has to look after herself. She is in the same position as many other athletes from the east.

In East Germany, sports was really the only alternative for someone who wanted to be special. The goal for many athletes was to use the opportunities that sports provided to travel, buy nice clothes, obtain an apartment. I think Katharina and I personified the message that East Germany had arrived. We were proud to be East Germans. Our athletes knew how to judge themselves.

For Katharina, as for all my other students, I was a substitute parent. I shaped and formed them, and all parents of the skaters accepted this diminishing role in their children's lives. Maybe some did so only because they hoped their children would attain the privileges associated with athletic stardom in the east. The privileges we enjoyed were based on our achievements. When there were shortages of certain items, the state had to choose who would receive them, and we were the ones who symbolized the country's political prestige and received domestic legitimation by outperforming countries many times our size. We were a mark of distinction.

Now, many very successful East German athletes will have a hard struggle, not only because of politics but also because the economy is so bad. The financial sponsorships and subsidies have been widely cut. We all have to get used to the idea that we have to earn our keep. Currently, I'm working with the Deutsche Eissport-verein (West German Ice Sports Organization) to keep our programme running. Under the Honecker regime we had 25 skating coaches looking for new talent. This number has been reduced to seven; I'm one of those lucky seven coaches who stayed. The same is true for the athletes. The stars were kept. The rest don't get any support from the state now. Their parents have to pay.

The GDR had a very disciplined network and system. Its sports regime can be seen as a pyramid. At the bottom, every citizen had the right to join the national Gymnastics and Sports Federation for a nominal fee that gave them access to athletic facilities. Coaches were trained to spot those youngsters with the greatest potential. Like Katharina, those youngsters were asked to enrol in one of the sports boarding schools, which often meant living some distance from their parents. If they continued to perform well, highschool-aged athletes were asked to join an elite sports facility from which our former Olympic team was chosen. Our system didn't raise false hopes. Those who performed rose to the top; others remained weekend athletes.

I'm curious to see how things work in this less structured system. In the GDR, all coaches were government employees and received a monthly pay-cheque. Since reunification, we have been paid by parents who have decided that their children have promising careers ahead in ice-skating. It is a totally new world for me.

The worst part of the change is that so many people will lose their jobs. Also, very little money will be available for promoting sports. Our economy has already collapsed since reunification. Nobody—even those who had the chance to travel—knew that our industries were so far behind. We now know about the terrible pollution, the outdated manufacturing systems, the hidden unemployment—but it is a great shock. Of course, when I was travelling with a group of athletes I noticed differences in architecture, and even in equipment and clothing. But we all thought that over time the GDR would advance. And we read daily in our newspapers that the GDR had the best economy of all the nations behind the Iron Curtain.

With all the free-speech demonstrations, the controls on security forces, the end to officials' privileges, and the exodus of people via the Hungarian border, everybody knew in the last months before the Wall came down that something was about to happen. But I never in my wildest fantasies imagined the reunification would happen so fast. Now there's disappointment that the current economic situation is so bad. Somehow we thought the west had an instant cure for the mistakes of the last forty years.

Jens Berndt

I started swimming when I was 8 years old, encouraged by my mother who thought that was the best way to channel my energies into something productive. After about two years of playing around and going to a nearby public swimming pool every week, I was asked by one of the lifeguards if I would like to participate in a race. That sounded just fine to me, and I felt pretty comfortable that I could compete with other swimmers my age.

What followed was what usually happened in the GDR if you were chosen to compete 'for the nation'. Systematically, I became involved in a schooling system that was a world of its own in the GDR. I visited sports school, which strongly emphasized athletic training. The ordinary schooling was a by-product. Children who were trained in sports schools were told they were the elite of the country and were usually taken away from their parents' influence at an early age. I liked the school because I loved to swim every day, but I was still quite often homesick.

When my mother fell ill with leukaemia, I wanted to live at home with my parents again. So I changed schools and spent my free time like all the other children, playing and doing homework. I completely stopped swimming.

When I turned 15 in 1978, I began to miss the daily swimming exercises. It probably also was related to being a teenager and wanting to leave home and to spend more time with other youngsters. I have to admit that, at that time, it also dawned on me that I would gain some privileges by attending a sports school. Anyhow, it somehow clicked in my head that I should start swimming again. As I had quit sports school voluntarily, I almost had to beg on my knees to get accepted again.

The boys I had originally trained with were four to five years ahead of me in technique and speed. I trained very hard every day, for as long as five or six hours. Because swimming came first in this sports school, it took us three years to pass the 7th and 8th school years and four years to complete the last two grades. We didn't have vacation like the other school kids; the time was used to keep swimming and to learn the stuff we had missed in school. We also had a separate curriculum.

Altogether, the GDR had 17 sports schools, separated by sport. Among the most prestigious and biggest was the Armee Sport Klub (Army Sports Club—ASK). The ASK had more money available and later, after we finished school, listed us as army members. Although we had never seen a rifle nor had any kind of army training, we were even paid like soldiers after we finished school.

Roughly two years after returning to the sports school, I had significantly improved my times in competition. I was being considered for the Olympic team that would swim at the Moscow Olympics. I didn't make the cut that year, but I became a member of the A league just a year later. In 1981 I ranked fifth in the European competition, and by 1982 I had made it to number 2 in the free style competition. In 1984 I swam a world-record time in the same event.

As the world-record holder, I was automatically admitted to the Olympic team that was to compete in Los Angeles. I was excited about going to America to compete in the games! For me it was the best of combinations: the free world and the games. Just a week after I had achieved the world record, the eastern bloc countries decided to boycott the games in the United States. Our whole team was crushed. I vividly remember discussing with a team-mate the frustration of working so hard over the years to reach our dream of being part of the Olympic games and then, with one single political decision, seeing everything fall apart. We were told in small groups that the Soviet Union had decided to boycott the games and as a brotherly nation, the GDR would boycott the them as well. We were also told it was unsafe to go to the United States.

In the same meeting we were told that we would receive 'material compensation'. It was the custom that for every medal won, the winner received money from the regime for his success. For a gold medal one was paid DM25,000, for silver DM20,000 and for bronze DM15,000. This premium was not official, but was awarded in a secret meeting. All sports people had an unofficial bank account. If you had won a competition, you usually got a note saying that 'Father Christmas' would like to see you. I usually met Father Christmas one-on-one. The money that was made available to us athletes was not to be spent on anything. Whenever I received money, I was interrogated about what I would use it for. The money definitely was also used as a way to put pressure on us. For example, if your performance was weak as a competition approached, you might be pressured into taking anabolic steroids or other drugs. I cannot speak for others, but whenever I was asked to take steroids, I refused.

Refusing the pressure was okay as long as your performance was good enough. Performance in sports had an extraordinary significance in the GDR. Because the GDR could not compete with superpowers economically, sports became the symbol for the status the regime wanted. Our performance, our training concepts and our techniques were almost treated as state secrets, like a secret weapon. George Orwell once said, 'Sports is war minus weapon'. That saying was definitely true in the GDR. As the athletes were the vehicles to gain status, we received special treatment and had privileges even beyond secret payments or better living quarters. The people on the street seldom had the opportunity to eat exotic fruits such as bananas, kiwis or even oranges. For us, those things were usually available. The ordinary citizen had to wait for 14 years to get a car; we only had to wait 2 years. We could travel and take at least a small look at the world. For most of us, that was the biggest advantage of all.

Six months after the Olympic Games boycott, I travelled to the US for a competition in Fayetteville, Arkansas. We travelled in groups of 10 to 15 people of whom probably five were 'supervisors', meaning watchdogs. Before travelling we were told again and again that we should not seek contact with members of other teams, and we were strictly forbidden from talking to natives of the country we were visiting. It was very strange, and to some extent depressing, to be able to travel to a country such as the United States but not be allowed to talk to Americans.

I was eager to try to use the English I had learned for five years in school, but every little contact one made, even if it was just with a waitress in the hotel, was looked upon with suspicion.

When we competed in Arkansas, everything was neatly organized by our supervisors: get up, eat breakfast in a large group, off to the bus for the stadium, and, immediately after the competition, back to the hotel. We had almost no opportunity to meet anybody. One evening I was able to sneak away. One of the American swimmers had told us about a party that was going on in the basement of the hotel, and I just couldn't resist going. I think the supervisors knew about it, but they accepted that we were eager to meet young people of other nations—as long as our performance was good, of course.

The morning after the party we were leaving for the airport to catch a flight back to the GDR. In the shuttle bus I had a funny feeling in my stomach and—really for the first time—when I looked outside I thought what if I didn't return to the GDR. What would that mean for me, for my family? Could I survive here? We caught a flight in Tulsa that brought us to Oklahoma City, and from there we were to go back to Berlin. We had a two-hour stopover in Oklahoma City. And that same feeling, the same thoughts came back. What if? Everybody was tired from the competition and the party the night before. Nobody was paying too much attention to who was doing what. During that two-hour stopover I struggled with myself with what to do. I decided to try to get away by hiding in the men's room shortly before take-off. If they found me, I still could say that I must have misunderstood when the flight was leaving and I was just late. So I hid in the men's room for roughly ten minutes, very scared of what would happen next. I heard the last boarding call for our flight and I became extremely nervous. As a teammate later told me, the supervisors noticed only after they got on the plane that I was missing. They tried to get off, but the flight attendant wouldn't let them leave them because it was time for take-off. The supervisor had me paged one more time. And I remember the announcement very well, as if it were yesterday. 'Mr Jens Berndt, please come to gate number 14.'

I waited about half an hour before I left the men's room. I was still very nervous, because now I had to decide whom to talk to. My English at the time was poor. I had no money on me, only a Walkman and a carry-on bag. I decided to talk to the airport supervisor. It was lunchtime, so he was out and there was only a friendly secretary. In broken English I told her, 'I'm from the GDR and I would like to stay in the United States.' Her eyes got big, her smile disappeared and she reached out for the telephone. I was in panic and I thought, 'Oh my god, now she is calling the GDR embassy'. Repeatedly, I said, 'Don't call a representative of the GDR'. She got on the phone anyway and my heart was pounding. I finally figured out that she was just calling her boss from lunch. When I met her supervisor, he assured me that my group had left and I was safe. He also called the Immigration and Naturalization Service (INS), the Central Intelligence Agency (CIA) and the Federal Bureau of Investigation (FBI). They questioned me for two days as if I were a communist, asking if I had family and why I had decided to leave. At that point I didn't care about my career in swimming. I was just hoping that I could find a place to stay and some work. What amazed me was that people were so extremely friendly and understanding. After two days I had a visa—and I'm still impressed about that. Today I have a green card.

For me those two days were very tense, but to some degree they were also enjoyable because people were so nice. At the end of the first day, two officers of the CIA and INS brought me to a nearby motel. The guy from the CIA strongly urged me not to answer any phone calls or let anybody in my room. We arranged for a certain code of knocking signals, and he promised to pick me up at seven o'clock sharp the next morning. All alone in the room, I was very exhausted and soon fell asleep. Shortly before dozing off I thought for the first time about the consequences my fleeing would have on my father. I toyed with the thought of calling him and letting him know, since my team-mates and the supervisors had been gone for only six or seven hours. I thought he should hear the news from me rather than from some official who would probably be knocking at his door at an ungodly hour. Somehow I couldn't bring myself to make a decision, and I fell asleep over it. Suddenly, at three o'clock in the morning, I heard the telephone ring. I sat up straight in my bed, wondering who could be calling me. The only people who knew that I was here were the INS and CIA, and they told me not to answer the phone or open the door. It rang and rang, probably over twenty times. I picked up the phone finally, without saying a thing. The voice at the other end just said, 'I must have reached the wrong number'. I became very worried and couldn't sleep for the rest of the night. Afterwards, oddly enough, I heard from my father that he had received a phone call before the plane with my team-mates had landed in Berlin. An anonymous caller told him that he shouldn't expect me back. Also strange was the fact that the radio station RIAS announced that I had decided to flee the GDR before the Americans made an official announcement. Nobody from the CIA or INS had contacted the RIAS.

While I lived in the GDR, there always had been rumours not

only that the Stasi was travelling with athletes, but also that a few had also been planted as waiters or bus drivers in the countries where the competitions took place. The phone calls at night and the time difference seemed to support that idea. I cannot prove it, but I'm convinced there was an undercover Stasi somewhere very close on my heels during that time. Fortunately, I must not have been considered very important, and nothing happened to me or my plans to stay in the USA.

After my first two days in the US, one gentleman from the INS asked me what I intended to do now. I told him the kind of schooling I'd had and that for most of my life I had done nothing but swim in competitions. He suggested I should talk to a college with a good athletic department. The head coach for the US swimming team at the time was Don Gambel, and he was also teaching at the college I was recommended to approach. Gambel was extremely helpful when I had problems in trying to swim competitively again. I had difficulties at college because of my poor knowledge of English and because I hadn't any certification of schooling. I was also much older than the rest of the college kids, having just turned 21. But somehow, with the help of some American friends, it all worked out.

After a while, I had my eyes on the Olympics again, but there were bound to be problems because I was not an American citizen, only a permanent resident. The normal time between receiving a green card and the possibility of applying for citizenship is five years. That timing would have brought my waiting time up to 1990, too late for me to participate in the games. Gambel and others asked senators and other politicians if I could receive citizenship. At that time Ivan Lendl had just received his citizenship more quickly than normal so he could participate in the Davis Cup team representing the Americans. I even got engaged in lobbying for my case and in the process was introduced to President Ronald Reagan, who endorsed the proposal. The Senate gave approval for my citizenship, but the proposal had to go through a committee headed by Senator Edward Kennedy, who opposed it. I had to make a swift decision thereafter, because I could still apply for West German citizenship and swim for that team—which I ended up doing. I was obviously disappointed, because I would have liked to swim for the American team after having lived and trained there. But on the other hand, I didn't want to be prevented from competing by a technical, or worse, a bureaucratic problem. I received West German citizenship and everything looked fine for my second Olympic games. Just days before the games were to start in 1988, the GDR officially protested against my competing. Their grounds for protesting were ridiculous. They claimed I hadn't paid my starting fee, which in the GDR was DM50. They also claimed that I was still a GDR citizen and had never given up my East German citizenship. Yet I knew at the time that my name had been deleted from all official record books. For the GDR I didn't exist from the day I left. The night before the games were to start, the Olympic committee decided in a 2–1 vote that I could compete with the West German team. There was an awful lot of going back and forth. I was also disappointed to a certain degree that the Olympic committee and the German representative didn't have enough backbone to prevent such a situation arising. I twice came in sixth in freestyle. After the games I returned to the United States to finish my studies; somehow, I was glad to get away from the battleground of the two Germanies. My host family, with whom I had stayed through the years, must have sensed my emotional turmoil and offered to adopt me as their son. I was overwhelmed by the idea, but gladly accepted. My father, whom I hadn't seen for four years, came to my college graduation and, to my surprise, understood my motives for becoming an American citizen. I finished my studies in Alabama in 1989, the year the Wall fell, and, luckily, a few month later I met Mark McCormack during an official function. I introduced myself and said to him, 'If you want to do marketing in the former GDR, I'm your man'. I'm one of those very, very lucky people who came out of the system early enough still to be able to make something out of my life.

Part Four

A Silent Revolution
Autumn 1989–January 1990

Great politicians owe their reputation, if not to pure chance, then
to circumstances at least which they themselves could not foresee.
Otto von Bismarck

Chapter Thirteen

The Role of Mikhail Gorbachev

Glasnost and perestroika, referring to the political and economic reforms in the Soviet Union, became two of the most widely used and publicized words in the world in 1987. Together with democratization, the ideals they represented became a powerful trio, potentially embodying fundamental changes behind the Iron Curtain, including freedom of speech, religion and assembly as well as governments chosen by and accountable to the people.

Mikhail Gorbachev was the political figure who had brought the newfound ideals for reform to his people's and international attention, not anticipating that the clash between the hopes of the Russians and the true face of the communist structure he represented would cause growing political tension in the nation, hasten his own loss of influence, and ultimately result in his resignation as president and last Soviet leader. Towards the end, Gorbachev lurched first to the left, ordering a radical '500 day' reform plan in the summer of 1989; next to the right, rejecting the plan and surrounding himself with party stalwarts whom he allowed to use force; then in spring 1990 back to the left, opening negotiations with the republics on a new Union Treaty. By then it was too late. On Monday, 19 August 1991, right-wing hard-liners placed Gorbachev under house arrest and tried to seize power by force. The coup marked a moment of truth for the democratic reforms Gorbachev had set in motion not only in his country, but also throughout eastern Europe. People on the streets of what had been East Berlin were as worried about the outcome of the coup as were the people in the streets of St Petersburg and Moscow. The thought of submission to a government that would seize power by using gunfire and tanks caused a chill in Soviet society and also in the west, whose leaders feared that the events could easily escalate into bloodshed, create internal chaos in the Soviet Union, and possibly even revive the Cold War. Backed by the party and led by Gennady Yanayev—who only weeks earlier had been selected by Gorbachev to serve as vice-president of the Soviet Union—the eight-man 'state committee' that had seized power quickly clamped down on the press, declared a state of emergency throughout the country, and finally sent tanks rumbling into the streets of

Moscow. As Boris Yeltsin, president of the Russian Republic, emerged as the leader of the opposition to the coup, standing on the top of tanks in Moscow and calling for a general strike, thousands of protesters joined him; within hours a group of army paratroopers and tanks switched sides and moved to protect Yeltsin. After three tensely absorbing days, the coup ended.

But the revolution that saved Gorbachev was now leaving him behind. With the defeat of the coup the republics had no more need for or faith in Gorbachev or the remnants of his union. Yeltsin, who led the resistance, promised in front of a cheering crowd to rid the government, media and army of communist influence, and he also guaranteed the independence of the Baltic nations. He promised the final break-up of the Communist Party regime. Yevgeny Yevtushenko, one of the Soviet Union's best-known poets, described Yeltsin at that moment, 'Around him there are no ghosts of past rulers, but real Russians.' Gorbachev missed the big rally in Moscow's Red Square. He stated in his first television appearance just days after he had been freed from house arrest on the island of Crimea, 'I'm convinced that socialism is right.'[1] In the same broadcast he offered an extraordinary defence of the Communist Party. Many people, including western politicians, were enraged and disappointed—not least because Gorbachev himself had brought into his government the eight men who had planned the coup, and because his reforms appeared too little, too late.

Most hadn't forgotten that, three years earlier, Gorbachev was the first Soviet leader to criticize the advantages party functionaries enjoyed and the first high-ranking Communist Party member to demand, in an address to the Politburo, the democratization of the Soviet Union. At 54, the youngest Soviet leader since Stalin, Gorbachev had electrified his country and the world with the introduction of glasnost. East–west hostilities evaporated. Dissidents emerged from labour camps and exile, hope filled the air.

Throughout the communist world Gorbachev had come to represent radical reform and a relaxation of the old ideology. He understood that, without the ability to criticize the controlling bureaucracy of his party, the military and the KGB, major change would be impossible and aid from the west unthinkable. He intended the most radical reforms in seven decades, a broadside that would reverberate through every facet of Soviet society. But his parallel attempts to reform the economy perished on the same shoals as all previous reforms—the large and privileged Communist Party apparatus.

[1] Mikhail Gorbachev, *The August Coup: The Truth and the Lesson*, New York 1991, p. 113.

Instead of enjoying reforms, the country was on the brink of economic catastrophe with a $200 billion budget deficit and a money supply out of control, and, faced with Baltic republics demanding independence, other regions barely under Moscow's control, and mounting pressure for reforms from hard-line voices in the United States, the Soviet government had to make concessions on arms control and political freedom in eastern Europe. The period also saw the virtual end of the Warsaw Pact.

The East German government under Honecker rightly feared that the news of democratization and perestroika would spread quickly throughout its own country. The regime thus tried to distance itself from Gorbachev's policy of economic and social restructuring, insisting that such programmes had no relevance for East Germany. Nevertheless, citizens were becoming restless for change. Seeking to quell growing unrest in the country regarded as Moscow's most strategically important ally, Gorbachev delivered a speech at East Berlin's 40th anniversary celebration in October 1989, in which he urged East Germans to be patient in their demands. In his speech he stressed the East German Communist Party's ability to lead the country through the coming changes.

At the same time, however, he warned Honecker in a now famous quote, 'Those who are late will be punished by life.'[2] The stubborn Honecker ignored the advice, not knowing that the silent revolution started by the citizens would soon put an end to the methods of his totalitarian regime.

Internationally, the voices praising Gorbachev became as numerous as those questioning his intentions. For many citizens of East Germany and other eastern European countries, perestroika and its economic benefits were the ticket to freedom. The Soviet Union under Gorbachev went only part of the way, however. Soviet leaders did indeed want the benefits of a market economy whose advantages they had seen widely demonstrated in major capitalist economies. But many doubt—even more so after the coup—that Gorbachev sought these benefits for the sake of a free market economy driven by consumer preference. Rather, he sought them because ultimately a strong defence depends on a strong economy, and because the increasing dearth of consumer goods had made the population restless. Before 19 August 1991, Gorbachev's vision of the Soviet economy was that of a market economy that would be regulated and planned, without private and transferable ownership of either enterprises or financial institutions.

Perestroika has successfully reshaped Europe's post-war geography, with most of the Iron Curtain countries having abolished the Communist Party and a reunified Germany struggling towards a thriving economy,

---

[2] *Frankfurter Allemeine*, 8 October 1989.

privatization and political stability. For the Soviet Union, perestroika meant compromises that led to a disastrous economic situation and growing political unrest that hard-liners could not tolerate. In the end, Gorbachev did not obey his own rule of 'Those who are late will be punished by life.' Perestroika brought Gorbachev fame abroad but little popularity in his own country. The leaders of Russia, Ukraine and Byelorussia pulled the plug on the USSR and proclaimed a new commonwealth of independent states. The Soviet Union was dead and with it Gorbachev's career as last president of a unified Soviet state.

Lothar Loewe

One of the key events in the reunification of East and West Germany was the speech Gorbachev gave at the UN in 1987. In summary, he stated then that communism was not the only way to happiness. I couldn't believe my ears when he said that while the Soviet Union believed communism was the right solution, Soviet politicians also had to accept the opinions of opposing systems. He also noted that military encounters wouldn't solve political conflicts and he recognized the international supreme court in The Hague as a mediator for political disputes. Gorbachev was the first leader from the Soviet Union who opened up to the west and started to promote a philosophy other than communism.

A second milestone leading to the end of the division of Germany were the happenings in Hungary in the summer of 1989. When the Hungarian soldiers at the border started to dismantle the chicken wire and let people pass to Austria, I knew it was the beginning of the end. The wave of refugees from the GDR were not to be stopped anymore. It was like an avalanche. I had a meeting with Manfred Stolpe[3] during late spring of 1989. We both feared a repetition of 17 June 1956, when demonstrations in the east were stopped by rolling and firing tanks. I never would have believed that the Soviet Union would watch silently as the GDR fell apart.

I often recall the view out the window of the apartment we lived in when I was working as the West German correspondent in East Berlin. It overlooked the ruins of the French dome in the middle of the city just a few blocks away from the main boulevard Unter den

---

[3] Stolpe was a church representative in the former GDR and is now the minister president of Berlin–Brandenburg.

Linden, and the border, and Checkpoint Charlie. The view was so melancholic. I used to think while staring at the ruins, 'When the third world war starts, I'm going to be right here in the centre where American tanks will be rolling and where the Russians will be heading towards Zehlendorf'. The thought is absurd in view of today's circumstances, but at the time it seemed quite realistic.

Otto von Habsburg

In my view, the role of Mikhail Gorbachev has been greatly exaggerated. It is true that he has shown much more flexibility than have past Soviet rulers. But I don't trust Gorbachev. He is a man who received his political education from the KGB. That does not recommend him to me. Most people forget that the current financial and political situation in the Iron Curtain countries were too much for Gorbachev to handle. The Soviet Union is no longer concerned about the satellite states. It is no longer a superpower. That was demonstrated again during the Gulf War. All the Iraqis' equipment came from the Soviet Union, and none of it was really effective against the modern US weapons. Moreover, Gorbachev must deal with political unrest at home. The Soviet Union is the last powerful nation that is structured as it was during the last century. Gorbachev has manoeuvred himself into a corner. The only chance he has of remaining friendly with the Baltic states and with other regions seeking independence is to give in to their demands and to try to develop a new political framework.[4]

The communist system really started in 1956, when Russian tanks rolled into Hungary. Then came the Prague Spring in 1968. Piece by piece, communism is fading away. It is a senseless ideology.

Wulf Rothenbächer

The turning point was the Iceland summit in 1986, when President Reagan rejected Gorbachev's proposal to sharply reduce ballistic missiles. It was the start of a totally new relationship between the

---

[4] This interview was conducted in 1991 before the August coup.

Soviet Union and the USA and the beginning of a utopian vision becoming reality. Reagan's posture of powerful strength and determination was what really led the Communist Party of the Soviet Union to finally give in to the democratization process at home and in the satellite states. The enormous economic pressure Gorbachev was exposed to forced him to take the leap into democratization.

The Soviet Union, the military superpower, was and is in serious trouble and is unable to compete with the United States or any other nation. After four years of economic failure, Gorbachev had no choice but to plead for help from the west. The price he had to pay was the freedom of the countries behind the Iron Curtain.

It was to my great advantage that I know the east as well as I know the west. The tumbling of the Wall was, to my mind, quite predictable. It really started with the soft tones that came from the Soviet Union after the Politburo had begun to feel pressure from the Reagan administration. By strengthening American military forces, tightening restrictions on transfer of technology to the Soviet Union, and launching the Strategic Defence Initiative, which potentially could neutralize the enormous Soviet investment in nuclear missiles, President Reagan created the context for communism's terminal crisis. Reagan challenged the Soviet Union as had no other president before him, rhetorically branding it the 'evil empire' and describing communism as a bizarre, sad chapter in human history whose final pages have already been written.

Most European politicians were surprised to see the depth of yearning for democracy among Romanians, East Germans and Czechs. They all asked for a free press. And they made it clear they wanted not an enlightened ruler but free elections, not a reformed party but a multiparty system. They understood the essence of democracy, even though their rulers attempted to blur the vision of democracy, an effort that seems to have borne more fruit among western politicians and publicists than among eastern Europeans.

Since the October revolution in 1917, the western world often has looked upon the east and its new ideology, communism, with a great deal of illusion. Well-known writers such as Franz Werfel, Thomas Mann and Klaus Mann strongly supported—even glorified—Stalinism and communism.

Communism has always held a fascination for certain types of people. It is in theory a perfect, very simple, well-functioning system that takes into account many important economic and historical factors and categories. It is a system that even uses the cover of socialism to appear just. But communism fails to account for one very important factor: the infinite variability of human abilities, wants and needs. Human beings simply don't have a place or role in communism. People who are unfamiliar with and don't care about human interests and interactions—the petit bourgeois—these are the people who have been fascinated with communism.

Since the end of the 1970s, it has been pretty clear to me that socialism and communism don't have a chance of surviving within the eastern European countries. In 1982 I wrote an article for the *Deutschlandfunk* in which I predicted that the Wall would fall soon. It was called 'Reunification will happen tomorrow.' Reading this article today, I have to say that I was wrong on only one point: I had never thought that east and west could be reunited with the Soviet Red Army still present in East Germany and Berlin.

Most people thought I was crazy because of my conviction that Germany would be reunited soon. For many reunification was politically undesirable. It was often argued that a unified Germany would undermine an integral aspect of a stable Europe. The quote of a Frenchman who said, 'I love Germany so much, I hope there will always be two of them', was frequently used as a justification for not rattling the cage of the communist regime in the east.

In the end, the changes were brought about by the courage of the people in eastern Europe, who sensed the time for reforms had arrived as the Soviet Union lost its control over its own destiny. The awesome upheaval under way in the communist world is the response by citizens to the recognition that Marxism has failed.

The human rights organization I had formed after I lived in West Germany received notice that within the last few months before the Wall opened, over one million East Germans had applied for exit permits. Even for the well-organized GDR, that number was too overwhelming to prompt a repressive reaction by the government. The people's courage was born of despair. Not even the Socialistic Unity Party (SED) could stop the people's desire for freedom and change, nor could the threat of terror, imprisonment, or discrimination. To halt the open disagreement and the shouts for change, the GDR government would have had to open concentration camps just as the Nazis had during World War II.

For some time, even civil war seemed possible in Hungary and East Germany as the old party leaders were caught between the necessity of introducing reforms and the possibility of losing control over their nations altogether. One question that was asked over and over again and spun around in the heads of the East European people was: would Gorbachev mobilize troops, after already having pulled 5 per cent of the Soviet Army, or would he stand by and let the Warsaw Pact alliance crumble? But Gorbachev couldn't really afford to intervene; if he did, his already shaky support at home would have faded altogether and, more importantly, his hopes for acquiring western economic aid would have vanished completely.

Step by step Gorbachev signalled to his party members that, without the willing help and co-operation of the west, the internal problems of the Soviet Union and its satellite states would produce a disastrous situation that could end in a nightmare. This was the first time that a Soviet leader had asked for any help. The request was extended to his own citizens as well: a 15-foot sign went up on Kutuzovsky Prospect, a main thoroughfare leading to central Moscow, asking 'What are you going to do for perestroika?' Gorbachev admitted openly that he couldn't remake the Soviet Union alone.

Caspar Weinberger

I think Gorbachev is becoming increasingly irrelevant.[5] He won't be in power very much longer. The important thing for the United States is trying to help the groups that are definitely opposed to communism and socialist economics. Gorbachev is not one of those.

He has never repudiated communism and he is doing a lot of things now that indicate he still considers either that he is under the thumb of the Stalinist group or that he needs to make concessions to them. He is also not above using repression in places such as Lithuania and Georgia. I don't think we should continue to support him the way so many people do.

Much of Gorbachev's popularity in the west is a result of the positive image he was able to create with the media. He has absolutely mesmerized the western press. He is the first Soviet leader who is available for interviews and has the knack for dealing with

---

[5] This interview was conducted in 1991 before the August coup.

journalists. And because that's so different from many of his prede-
cessors, he is perceived as being a great man who turned the Soviet
Union around. Gorbachev realized that because of the disastrous
economic situation in his country he had to get some western support. He knew he would not get it with threats or intimidation. He
had to do it by appearing to change.

But I don't think he has changed politically. His attempts for
moderate reforms perished as did all previous reforms—the thick
Communist Party apparatus stood in the way. The more glasnost
flourished, the more perestroika was floundering. Gorbachev, in the
end, did too little too late. For that reason I believe, he is terribly
overrated. He is much more form and shadows than substance. He
was smart to recognize that he couldn't win by military strength
alone, although he is trying to use all of that against the splitting
Baltic states.

Towards the west he changed his rhetoric, trying to demonstrate a
different political atmosphere in the Soviet Union, one in which the
cults of communism had ended. He allowed a few demonstrations, a
little bit of freedom of the press and travel easements, not imagining
that the little freedom he allowed would get completely out of control
and out of his hands. The deep hatred that his people had for
communism made them march in the streets by the thousands, holding up signs until quite literally the whole lid blew off. People like
the rough-hewn Boris Yeltsin, who got a terrible press in the United
States, or a man like Anatoly Subtschak, the mayor of St Petersburg,
or the scholarly Edvard Shevardnadze represent the new feeling in
the Soviet Union and have fought against prolonging the life of the
Soviet communist system for a few more years. Gorbachev has not.
He had enough intelligence to change certain things, but not enough
to see that everything he and his party represent will eventually be
destroyed.

I cannot predict who is going to end up formally in power. It's
doubtful—but not impossible—that a Stalinist who is far more decisive than Gorbachev could be installed as part of a coup or
something of that kind. The enormous Soviet military capability cannot be underestimated and with it the strong influence of the Red
Army. I believe the influence of the army has been diminished over
the last couple of months as the troops are suffering from serious
morale problems, but they aren't stopping developments and

deployment in the design of new nuclear weapons. On the other hand, the really horrible chaotic economic conditions are going to lead a lot of people, including the army troops, to the conclusion that they simply cannot live under communist rule the way they have. I strongly believe that leaders such as Yeltsin and others can change the conditions in their nation. The Russian Republic now is practically an independent country already. Others will follow. Then you have other states that are moving towards independence by trying to consolidate. The least effective and most irrelevant leadership is at present the so-called national government of the USSR.

Ota Sik

What I called the 'Third Way' in my book—which was published in 1973—was never anticipated as a political revolution against the communist system in eastern Europe. At the time, I saw no chance that dissidents or even the majority of the eastern European population would be able to win against Russian tanks. From the start, I believed in reform. For that reason, the title of my book suggested a compromise—a capitalism-oriented, planned market economy. In a sense, Gorbachev's attempt to moderate the influence of the party in the Soviet Union can also be considered as a compromise between the more radical groups that supported the total abolition of the party apparatus and the power of the party itself. I know today such a compromise is not possible, not in a dictatorship. Nevertheless, Gorbachev's effort started a chain reaction. He was the first Soviet leader to ban the Brezhnev Doctrine, thus stopping the direct involvement of the Soviet Union in the political problems of its satellite countries. His political detachment from other nations of the Council for Mutual Economic Assistance (COMECON) created a vacuum that made room for a democratization process in his part of the world and made possible for the first time a strong engagement by the political opposition. The Hungarians and the Czechs were among the first to recognize their opportunity to move away from the influence of the Soviets, and they pressured for additional human rights, including travel permits and a less planned market economy. Unfortunately, Gorbachev's Prague visit at the end of the 1980s left the wrong impression, since he met only with the official party representatives such as President Gustav Husak. Deeply hurt and disappointed, the Czechs interpreted his visit as a step back and a confirmation of the old party system. On the other hand, Hungary, which had already tried over the years to reduce the influence of the 'Big Brother' Soviet Union with stronger ties to the west, took the opportunity to adopt more radical forms immediately. What happened can be compared to the domino effect or an avalanche: once started, the process could not be stopped anymore. As GDR citizens fled to Hungary, where they found a friendly welcome and the freedom to leave for West Germany, it became clearer and clearer that the Soviet Union had lost its sphere of influence and its status as the watchdog over eastern Europe. Groups of dissidents formed to create a new political forum, and free elections followed in almost all of the former eastern European countries that were once under communist influence.

Starting in the mid-1980s, the Soviet Union itself was in the process of reformation. The reason for that process was the miserable economic situation and the ever-increasing gap between the technological developments of the west and of the east. Already in 1986 Gorbachev announced a radical economic reform that was supposed to replace the old bureaucratic and centralized system. At the same time, he announced his concepts of glasnost and perestroika. To most of the outside world it became apparent that this reform process was intended to go much further than mere economic reform. Within the Soviet leadership, it had been conceded that economic reform could not be isolated from other political reforms. According to Gorbachev, the parliament should play a larger role in the political decision-making process as well as in defining the civil rights of the population. For the first time, open discussion of political and economic problems was demanded. The reform process gathered momentum, taking the original economic reform far beyond its intended limits. Glasnost and perestroika undoubtedly made the reforms in Hungary, Czechoslovakia and Poland possible.

I often have been asked why, with the exception of Romania, the democratization process was so peaceful. First, the communists had no other choice, since their economy was weakening daily and all of the former communist nations in the east needed western financial support. Second, the leading communist politicians in the reforming nations struck a deal with their non-communist successors guaranteeing that none of them would be put on trial. Finally, Gorbachev significantly influenced the development of reform into a peaceful, almost silent, revolution in those countries by not giving hard-liners any prospect of help.

Gorbachev was among the first Soviet party members to notice that communism was a historical error, a political development that did not take many human or economic facts into consideration. Starting with the uprising in the former GDR in 1953, followed by the Prague Spring in 1968, communism faded and could be kept in place only by a strong dictatorship using force and a finely tuned system of spying. Communism is an enemy of reality, and among the first to notice were the economists. In 1956 I was present during the first meeting of the Economic Organization Commission, and witnessed the insane nonsense which the commission planned for the Czech economy. Theory and practice are as far apart in communism as possible. Starting in 1957, I tried to find ways to make the system work and ended up suggesting in the *Third Way* a compromise which was at the time not acceptable to the system. Excepting a few romantics, none of the economists' thinking was shaped by Stalinism; they were convinced that a market economy couldn't be replaced with a planned economy. The Prague Spring was an early attempt to replace the party thinking, but it ended unsuccessfully because the timing was wrong. The old *apparatchik,* such as Brezhnev and Ulbricht, could not allow a change and sent the tanks in. Gorbachev's timing, however, was right, both politically and economically. Honecker was old and sick, all of the east's economy was literally in shambles and there was nowhere to seek help but in the west.

The democratization process in the Soviet Union itself will take much longer owing to the size of the country, its different ethnic populations and the distance between the radical reformists and the strong party apparatus which includes the military, the state security system and the KGB.

Observers speculated that Gorbachev himself was not fully aware of the process he had started by letting the satellite countries break away from the Soviet Union. Some also suspected him of secretly working with the old party hard-liners once more. I myself believed that Gorbachev could envisage a peaceful way to end the influence of the Soviet Communist Party, but that the pace of change bypassed him.

Harald and Elke Zimmer

We acquired much courage to protest on the streets from the actions of Soviet President Mikhail Gorbachev that we viewed as symbols of hope for reform. We didn't know if he would send troops to stop us. I believe even he himself didn't know at certain times. For us, Gorbachev's apparent openness to change represented an opportunity that would be foolish to give away after 40 years of tyranny. I'm not sure what his original intentions were when he became the youngest leader since Stalin in 1985. Maybe in the beginning all he wanted were mere cosmetic changes, which only later developed into dynamic movements that couldn't be stopped anymore. Gorbachev chose not to interfere with that development. I remember that in the mid-1980s Gorbachev described the Soviet changes as an extension of Red October, the 1917 Bolshevik Revolution.

I don't think he was planning the dissolution of the Warsaw Pact or the fall of the Wall. But he was wise enough to follow the events of the times and to support them within the satellite states of the Soviet Union.

When he said in his 1989 speech in East Berlin that Moscow would not interfere in East German politics, we interpreted the comment as a go-ahead. Of course, the thought of over 300,000 Soviet Red Army troops sitting right here in East Berlin scared us, but our hope for change was stronger than our fear. We followed the Gorbachev speech very carefully. His whole address seemed to be designed to avoid embarrassing the Honecker regime, for which the mass exodus of people was the gravest challenge yet to its authority. Gorbachev was treading very cautiously, trying not to disappoint us while at the same time supporting the East German communists by expressing his belief in their leadership role. He repeatedly told us to 'be patient'.

Honecker strongly showed his different opinion by attacking the west, which he referred to as 'our enemies'. Honecker's most stinging shot came when he said that the appearance of neo-Nazi groups across the border—meaning West Germany—was food for thought. Obviously, this was his way of trying to discourage any more people from leaving the country.

Thousands of people were gathered shouting 'Gorby, Gorby', although the East German press had made it a point not to print

Gorbachev's schedule and the local TV didn't broadcast his arrival. Riot police were everywhere, carrying tear-gas canisters and water cannons, and the passages between East and West Berlin were closed. The area around the Brandenburg Gate, the symbol of Berlin's division, was sealed off, as was the area around the US embassy. It felt to us like the Honecker regime's last-ditch effort to make the uninvited guest, perestroika, leave. Honecker and his hard-line communist friends had given up any pretence of jubilation and were bristling with defensiveness, since they had hoped to present the GDR as a showcase of communist progress.

During the parades of the 40th anniversary celebration, I was less afraid of the Soviet troops present than of the hundreds of Free German Youth (FDJ) members, who marched down East Berlin's main boulevard, Unter den Linden, carrying torches and singing patriotic songs for the celebration. We weren't there to celebrate at all. We only wanted to see and hear Gorbachev. Being there shouting 'Gorby' was our way of showing support for his reforms. But at the time of the 40th anniversary, in the autumn of 1989, we were sometimes unsure about what an open border, more freedom and different leaders would bring. Opposite us were those true believers in communism and socialism and admirers of its theory. Many of them feared they would lose their privileged status if East Germany were to disappear. The situation could easily have got out of hand, since the audience was about equally divided between supporters of Gorbachev's reforms and the East German hard-liners who were looking for confrontation. The members of the youth organization had lined up to parade while some of us held signs asking for 'Freedom!'. Others carried banners asking for the right to emigrate.

Two days earlier, thousands of East German citizens had occupied a train station, hoping to jump onto one of the trains carrying East Germans who had occupied West Germany's embassy in Prague on a special journey to West Germany. West German Foreign Minister Hans-Dietrich Genscher had arranged in a dramatic dialogue between Poland and East Germany that all the refugees of the West German Warsaw embassy could leave on a special train to the west without being checked in East Germany. Many of the East German citizens had hoped to be able to jump on the 'Freedom Train' as it passed through their territory. More than 2,000 police pushed the crowd out of the train station, imprisoned several hundred and used water cannons to disperse the crowd. Honecker probably did not want Gorbachev to see such an incident, so he left the shouting Gorby supporters alone.

The atmosphere in Berlin for the anniversary was surprisingly dull and not festive at all. There were few flags, and hundreds of plainclothes police patrolling the centre of East Berlin. I remember seeing a press photographer trying to set up his camera when he bumped into a policeman who hovered behind a bush. Obviously, he was not pleased to be detected. He immediately put on his dark glasses and before he left he tangled his walkie-talkie in some branches of the bush. I kept a low profile and wandered off as if I hadn't seen anything, but the press person was just giggling.

One day after Gorbachev's visit to East Berlin, notices were posted in neighbourhood government offices saying that anybody who wanted to leave the country would receive permission to do so. The one condition for departing was that one had to leave within 48 hours after applying. Honecker still thought he could solve his problems and keep perestroika from happening in East Germany by getting rid of all the protesters. It would turn out the other way around. Just a month later, Honecker was replaced by Egon Krenz, a loyal member of Honecker's Politburo, under whose leadership the pressure of demonstrations led to the fall of the Berlin Wall. I'm very sure that the leadership change at that moment had something to do with Gorbachev's trip to East Berlin and was a decision made by him. In the end, Honecker's forced withdrawal from his position was the result of his arrogance, his distance from reality and his insistence that the orthodox communist course was the only correct one, ignoring reforms adopted by the Soviets, Hungarians and Poles. Honecker, unlike Gorbachev, was inflexible and still believed that East Germany was a showcase of socialist and communist progress.

Chapter Fourteen

The Hungarian Way Out

A squad of Hungarian soldiers, descending on the Austrian border on 2 May 1989, started to tear down the 160 miles of barbed wire that formed Hungary's Iron Curtain. Within a week, more than 15,500 East German refugees crossed the newly opened Austrian–Hungarian border to flee to West Germany. The number of people joining the exodus had grown to 130,000 by the day the wall fell in November 1989. In August that year, Dr Otto von Habsburg, head of the Pan-European Parliament and grandson of the last emperor of Austria and king of Hungary, initiated a 'walk along the Austrian–Hungarian border', demanding a Europe without borders. During a symbolic picnic celebrating European unity, border gates were opened to mark the increased access across the frontier as a symbol of the reduction in east-west tensions, with Hungarian border guards present to stamp the passports of European participants. The walk triggered an additional haemorrhage of 900 GDR citizens pouring into Hungary. Each day dozens of families arrived in Budapest, taking the desperate step of holing up in the West German embassy. Just a day after the walk on the border, the East German government accused Bonn of meddling in its internal affairs by not evicting the East Germans from the West German embassies. Meanwhile, hundreds of refugees had found their way not only to the German embassy in Budapest, but also to the missions in East Berlin and Prague. East German émigrés reported that East German and Czechoslovak authorities had begun seizing passports in an effort to stop the flood of refugees to the west.

Nevertheless, the number of people arriving in Budapest became so overwhelming that West German Ambassador Dr Alexander Arnot finally had to close the doors of his mission, asserting that the 180 people inside had exhausted its capacity. Still, the number of refugees coming over the 'green border' to Hungary from the GDR amounted to over 100 people daily. The Red Cross and the Maltese Service, under the supervision of Csilla, Baroness von Boeselager, arranged for tents to accommodate refugees and arranged for Red Cross passports that enabled a majority of them to leave Hungary for West Germany and Austria.

The change in the Hungarian policy did not occur overnight. A year earlier, reformers had ousted Communist Party General Secretary Janos Kadar, ending his 32-year rule. The reformers hoped to lessen ties with the eastern bloc and establish a country with neutral status, much like that of Austria or Switzerland. Within months, rising opposition to the old regime forced the Communist Party to make concessions, including acceptance of a multiple party system, independent trade unions and a new constitution that no longer reserved a leading role for the Communist Party.

Among the countries behind the Iron Curtain, Hungary more than most managed, with its characteristic charm, to make the best of communism. Having been part of the Habsburg monarchy, Hungary remained, within the eastern bloc, the nation with the greatest cultural sophistication and the greatest relative autonomy from Moscow. Hungary, in a style that was unique among members of the Warsaw Pact, had begun a revolution. The process had gone so far that by the end of 1989 the Communist Party had begun to commit political suicide; it changed its name, lost 90 per cent of its official members, and became a distinct minority party. Today, Hungary vigorously promotes private enterprise; despite a shortage of capital, the structure of a market economy is in place, from private banks to a stock market.

At the same time that Hungary was moving inexorably toward democratization, the GDR signed a document at the KSZE Conference in Vienna in 1989 that guaranteed to GDR citizens the possibility of leaving the country for family reunions and other travel.[1] But the new document did not change the situation for most citizens, since the decree was subject to interpretation by the authorities. And even though East Berlin had withdrawn standing orders to shoot on sight anyone attempting to flee across the Wall and had signed the KSZE Conference documents, it was not until the Hungarians dismantled their border fences that East Germans unwilling to wait for a visa got a chance to flee.

Mario

I had planned a holiday for quite some time. Hungary was a favourite vacation spot for us East Germans, as it was among those eastern bloc nations with better food supplies, freer lives and some western atmosphere. Budapest was also known for its charm and for certain details—such as the lavish use of academic titles, hand-kissing, the

---

[1] Konferenz über Sicherheit und Zusammenarbeit in Europa (Conference on Security and Co-operation in Europe)

passionate interest in opera and theatre, the afternoon coffee and cake—that represented parts of what I imagined the west to be like. Within Hungary, a favourite area to go was Lake Balaton, where you could swim, hike and backpack. As most GDR citizens either didn't have a car or had only a plastic-bodied Trabant, for which the route would have been too rough, most came in specially arranged tours.

For most GDR citizens, June and July 1989 weren't much different from any other summer months, since the East German media hadn't televised or printed anything about the exodus taking place at the Hungarian border. I heard about the large number of refugees via the west German TV, which I regularly watched at night. It was reported that ever since the border fence had been removed in May, GDR citizens were crossing at isolated points along the frontier, sometimes sprinting past guards at road crossings; the instruction from Budapest was not to shoot.

Perestroika and the news of Gorbachev's visit to East Berlin had led me to look for changes even within the rigidly controlled East Germany, but generally I had the feeling I was wasting my life.

It was not only the scarcity of clothes and food. Generally, life in the GDR was grim, with little prospect for advancement. Even though I had never been convicted of a crime and had passed the age of 18, I had no chance at all of getting a passport in the GDR. I felt like I was under constant watch, imprisoned. As a second-class citizen, I had to live in a nation where people who wanted to be free to travel were put behind bars or even murdered. The uncertainty and the psychological burden of the whole process of applying for an exit and travel visa were heavy. In the end I had to admit to myself that leaving illegally via the Hungarian border was probably the only possible way out. My prospects if I remained in East Germany seemed nightmarish. The society in the GDR was tormenting and confining. I didn't believe in the ideas on which the GDR constitution was based. The thought of government institutions using their distorted definition of freedom to put me into a strait-jacket was unbearable. I felt like a bondsman. The worst was the omnipresent East German state security agency, 'the Stasi'.

The Stasi had even planted 'ears' in our factory. Mostly, these were people who had committed minor crimes but had got off by promising to listen in discos and factories to what people were saying. I had announced my travel plan in the plant even before I knew about my opportunity to flee to the west. Two days before my vacation, when I was still unsure if I should use the opportunity or not, a co-worker came up to me and asked, 'Just between you and me, tell me, are you going to leave for good?' I had seldom talked to the guy before and immediately knew what he was up to. I kept my mouth closed and just smiled. At that moment my decision was made. My planned vacation to Hungary was my way to escape to freedom.

Prior to the time that my bus tour would bring me to Hungary, the East German government had mounted a disinformation campaign against the Hungarian-Austrian escape route, stating that people had been shot and killed at the border. Nonetheless, I decided to stick to my plan. It was difficult to get away from the organized bus tour, but one morning I told the woman sent by the organizer to accompany the tour that I wasn't feeling very well and would pass up the sightseeing tour. I made my way to a small border village on a local bus. As a foreigner I obviously drew some of the attention of the village people to myself. An older man came walking up to me and asked if I needed help. He spoke in the charming way German is spoken by Hungarians. I liked him and dared to tell him that I was here for the sole purpose of finding my way to the Austrian border. The villager told me he would help me in the morning by taking me to the border in his car. After a night of drinking with him and his family, I was brought to a forest where my host explained as well as he could the route I should take. I saw dozens of abandoned East German cars that obviously had been left behind on the way to freedom. I somehow made my way through the forest and avoided watchtowers. After an hour I saw a woman on a bicycle, who said, 'Welcome to Austria'. She knew exactly where I was coming from when I had asked her where I was. I contacted the German embassy and was finally brought to a refugee centre in Giessen, where I got a passport and some initial orientation about life in West Germany.

Otto von Habsburg

We knew the walk along the border would be provocative, but we had no idea we would unleash a mass emigration.[2] August 20th was

---

[2] This interview took place before the break-up of the Soviet Union.

chosen as the date because it is a national Hungarian holiday. The German embassy in Budapest had become a favourite enclave for over 130 East Germans. The thousands of newcomers hoped to find their way there.

In early May the foreign ministers of Hungary and Austria had presided over the dismantling of the barbed wire fences at the East German–Hungarian border, followed by the eyes of TV cameras. I believe the Hungarian President, Miklos Nemeth, sent President George Bush a piece of the wire to show how open Hungary now was. But the hopes of the many East Germans who crossed the Hungarian border were abruptly dashed. Nemeth found his hands tied by an agreement with the GDR that would have forced Hungary to send all GDR citizens back.[3] The West German embassy could also do nothing.

The 'walk along the border' was to be a demonstration for the removal of all barriers within Europe. Gates were opened to mark the greater access across the Austrian–Hungarian frontier as a symbol of lessening tensions between the east and west. Hungarian border guards were present to stamp passports of European participants in the demonstration. A picnic had been planned by the Pan-European Parliament and the Hungarian Democratic Front, an opposition group under reformer Imre Pozsagy. The climax of the walk was to have been a symbolic crossing of the Hungarian–Austrian border near the city of Sopron.

In the late afternoon, Hungarian border guards opened a gate between the city of Sopron–Puszta and the Austrian village of St Magarethen that hadn't been touched since the war. As the gates were opened, some East German citizens who were on holiday in Hungary and had come to witness the event seized the chance to step on Austrian soil. The border guards were pushed aside and hundreds of people crossed the border with nothing more than the summer clothes they were wearing and perhaps a camera. Some 300 East Germans pushed their way through the gates as they were opened and another 200 followed a few hours later the same day. Soon it became clear that most of the latter group were campers who had stayed at a nearby campground and had heard over the radio about our 'picnic at the border'. They had rushed to the border leaving everything behind in order to walk into freedom. This was the

---

[3] The agreement was subsequently suspended.

catalyst that triggered a series of historic events, one after the other. There were demands for free speech and travel, and mass rallies in Leipzig. In addition, the exodus from East Germany aggravated the worsening economic and political conditions in that country, which had rejected reforms introduced in other eastern bloc countries. Hungarian police still patrolled all road crossings days later with the instruction to seize East Germans and send them home with their documents stamped as would-be border crossers. But East Germans —oftentimes with the help of Hungarians—continued to hike through the woods to get across.

Csilla Baroness von Boeselager

There I was in the camp, on 10 September 1989, standing side by side with the Hungarian Minister Gyla Horn, who had just announced that, starting at midnight, all East Germans would be permitted to leave Hungary without a travel permit. This was four weeks after I had agreed to take care of the East German refugees. People were crying, hugging each other, hugging me, hugging Horn. Everything had started two years earlier in 1987, when I became the most persistent panhandler in Europe. At a cocktail party I'd met Imre von Ugron, a member of the Order of the Knights of Malta, who told me about the miserable conditions in Hungarian hospitals. I was flabbergasted. While other eastern European nations such as Poland and Czechoslovakia were well-supplied with money and food, Hungarians received few donations. This was partly because the western world perceived Hungary to be one of the more well-to-do nations living under communist rule and thus believed, erroneously, that Hungary needed no help. In addition, Hungarians are very proud people who would never bring their misery to the attention of the world. The story of the Holy St Martin typifies the Hungarian mentality: 'The knight didn't have much for himself, but, on that wintry snowy night, he cut his coat in half and gave it to the poor and shivering man on the street.' I decided to help. I told my husband that same night, 'I believe God calls quietly when he calls'.

In 1987 I met for the first time Father Imre Kozma, a Catholic priest who two years later played an important role in putting together the camps for the East German refugees. Meanwhile, I began seeking contacts inside the Hungarian government and looking for ways to route used medical equipment to Hungary from Germany and other western industrial nations. During my first meetings I felt uneasy. I knew I had nothing in common with these representatives of the Hungarian government. They were hard-line communists and I was a faithful believer in Catholicism and the Church. During the talks I somehow overcame my resentments and asked straightforward questions such as, 'Why don't you allow priests in hospitals?' I remember one occasion when I got so angry about the communists' bureaucracy that I said to the Hungarian Minister of Health, 'You want my help for your hospitals because then you won't have to spend your own money to buy new equipment from the west. That's fine, but people need more than medical supplies and instruments to become healthy again. I'm not a communist; on the contrary, I'm a Catholic and I believe that sick people also need treatment for their souls, which only a priest can provide.' I demanded an exchange: I would get medical supplies for Hungary if the Hungarian government would give the Church greater influence within the hospitals.

At the time I knew that the Franziskus Hospital in Budapest had an adjacent chapel that was being used for storage. I pointed this out to the Minister of Health and said, 'Before I'll organize a delivery of several incubators and x-ray machines to that hospital, the chapel must be rebuilt and must again be used for its original purpose'. As I spoke, he reached for a book. He opened it and read to me that only in cases of death would priests be permitted in Hungarian hospitals. I replied, 'That's not good enough'. He glared at me and said, 'You can have your chapel'. It was just a start, but I clearly had got my point across.

Initially, I approached Father Kozma in Budapest to help me deliver the equipment and supplies to the hospitals. To the outside world it probably looked like Baroness Boeselager's private initiative to help her native land. But I had bigger ideas in mind. Upon my return to Germany, it had become clear to me that I needed an organization in Hungary that could oversee the delivery of the goods and channel them into the right hands. This, of course, was a problem because only communist organizations were allowed to exist. Within 12 months my project became well known in West Germany. My initiative had developed into a major aid programme to Hungary. Over 500 trucks called 'Hungario caminos', which for years had entered

Germany to deliver Hungarian salami and duck breasts and then had returned empty-handed, now returned to Budapest loaded with hospital beds, x-ray machines, computer tomographs and surgical instruments. In February 1989 I founded, with the help of my husband and a friend who is also a member of the Knights of Malta, the Hungarian Maltese Caritas organization, not knowing that just a few weeks later East German refugees would need its help.

I journeyed to Budapest on Friday, 11 August 1989 simply to check on recent hospital deliveries and to participate in a procession that Father Kozma had planned. The German Ambassador, Dr Berg, whom I had met several times on my visits to Romanian refugee camps, invited me for the first time to stay at the embassy. I was picked up at the airport. It was mid-morning hours when I arrived at the German embassy and, after being introduced to a number of embassy people and some German politicians who had just flown in from Bonn to discuss the refugee situation at the Hungarian–Austrian border, I was seated at a table on the veranda with a cup of coffee. I could see and hear how they were discussing and arguing about what to do with the refugees who had been standing in front of the embassy for hours, some maybe for days. What the outside world didn't know at that time was that the German ambassador had taken it upon himself to accommodate a large number of refugees in the embassy, but his capacity was limited. He was skating on thin ice, since the treaty of 1972 between West Germany and East Germany prohibited the West German embassies from giving asylum to East German refugees. It was also a breach of contract with the embassy's host nation, Hungary. Some of the refugees within the embassy had quietly received West German passports and were ready to leave for the west the next day. Nobody mentioned this within the embassy, nobody talked about it.

When I returned on Saturday afternoon from meetings, Ambassador Berg and some others where standing in the kitchen, looking at each other with rather pale and dissatisfied faces. Somebody said, 'It sounds as if the only option we have is to close the embassy tomorrow.' Another voice said, 'And what happens to the refugees who have been gathering day and night in front of the embassy to apply for political asylum?' 'I will take them,' I said calmly. Everybody stared at me disbelievingly. Berg, however, knew I was serious. He placed a phone call to Bonn and after he finished his conversation it was agreed that I could take care of the refugees. I didn't know how many there were, but I knew that more would be coming in thousands as soon as the news spread that there was an organized effort to take care of them.

On Sunday, 13 August, the embassy was closed. The information that Father Kozma was ready to give out free meals to some 250 to 400 refugees was passed around quickly. Father Kozma had opened up his church, located in Zoqliet outside of Budapest, and had set up tents in front of it to provide shelter for the refugees. On Monday morning there were already 580 people staying at the camp. By lunchtime the number had increased to 700. Members of the embassy offered their help; I had them wear red and white Maltese ribbons around their arms so they would be identifiable. After three days, the first convoy of trucks with goods from Germany for the refugees reached the camp. They were supposed to come daily until the middle of September.

Whether they are in Hungary, Cambodia or Romania, refugee camps are the most desperate places in the world. The scene is always the same: desperate people, uncertain about their future, show haunted looks on anxious faces while children cling to their parents. Many refugees wanted to talk, to learn how the west functions, and what they would experience once they reached it.

After a week, the flood of refugees threatened to exceed the camp's capacity. We had to look for a second camp, which we found in the hills of Buda. Also, Father Kozma had appealed to his parish to care for the East Germans. Many came forward and offered to share their three-bedroom apartments with one or two refugees, even though the apartments were already filled by families of four or more. Communication was difficult. The older generation remembered their German from the Habsburg years, but the younger ones, who had learned Hungarian and Russian in school, could hardly speak to their guests.

During the first weeks, I noticed a change in composition among the refugees. For the first week we saw mostly political refugees. The first refugees who came from East Germany were usually single or young couples without children. I would describe them as intellectuals, some of them extremely religious and shy. They looked upon Father Kozma and me as leaders who could show them what to do and where to go next. In the second and third weeks, the number of families with small children and babies increased immensely. They had seen the opening of the Hungarian border as an opportunity to escape not only East German politics but also the disastrous economic conditions there.

Within a week, a representative of the East German embassy visited our camp. He demanded to know the names of all refugees and offered to house some of them. Father Kozma and I politely but firmly explained that the refugees had chosen to stay here, but if he chose to he could open an office in a van a block away from the camp. The refugees were upset that we allowed him to do that and one night they vandalized the van. Soon thereafter the East German consul realized that he was wasting his time in a fruitless effort. The van left two days later.

We also knew from the beginning that there were several Stasi people among the refugees, snooping around and trying to undermine the morale of the refugees. By the end of August, some of the refugees threatened to start a hunger strike to try to force the Hungarian government to allow them to travel to Germany. The strike was instigated by the Stasi members who had disguised themselves as refugees. A strike would have been very damaging to the talks between the Hungarians and West Germans that were underway. The East German government and the Stasi knew that and were trying to undermine any effort for a successful and happy ending to the refugee question. I jumped on a ladder and addressed the refugees pretty harshly, reminding them that those who were threatening a hunger strike were probably people sent by the Stasi who were working against the refugees' best interests. For a day or two the atmosphere in the camp was tense and filled with mistrust.

During those late August days, two men came forward and asked if they could talk to me in private. In a storage room behind the church they told me that they were Stasi members sent by the East Germans to sabotage Father Kozma's and my efforts, but now they wanted to leave East Germany with the others. They begged me not to let anybody know about their past, for fear of being lynched by the refugees. I informed Father Kozma and a few people from the German embassy about this incident. There was nothing we could do, either for them or against them. After 10 September they quietly left the camp for West Germany with everybody else.

We knew about other Stasi members in the camp. I remember the face of one who couldn't hide his astonishment when Horn and I announced that everybody would be free to leave for West Germany as of midnight, 10 September. I even saw reruns of the scene, which had been taken by a West German broadcasting network. His face froze for a moment while people around him cheered. A few seconds later he automatically threw up his arms like everybody else, and then slowly disappeared into the crowd.

The camps stayed open until 14 November. Some people were too weak to leave immediately, some didn't have a contact in West Germany and didn't know where to go, and some didn't want to move to another refugee camp in West Germany. Within three months over 36,000 refugees stayed with us for periods ranging from days to weeks.

The world probably has already forgotten that if it hadn't been for the Hungarian people and government, the Berlin Wall would still be standing. It was the Hungarian decision to allow the refugees to leave for the west that gave the rest of the East German citizens hope for change and the belief that a new era of freedom was around the corner. Without that historic decision, the wave of freedom would have stopped before it started to unfold.

Janos Fekete

In the early 1960s we came to the conclusion that central planning was no longer acceptable to Hungary because it was impossible, even in such a small country, to make every important decision in one building, even if the people there were the most intelligent in the world, which, of course, they are not. We decided to put the plan under the control of the market. To be sure, Hungary's economy has strong state direction; with the central bank, we put a system in place that exercised a tight rein on credit. Hungary's concession to the free market economy, on the other hand, included allowing people to make some profits from family farm plots. Because Hungary relied so heavily on short-term bank deposits, we were especially vulnerable to the credit squeeze that hit eastern Europe after Poland's near default. But unlike the rest of the Soviet bloc, we were able to raise new loans in the west. We joined the International Monetary Fund in 1982, and since then have tried to meet the organization's stiff loan requirements. We succeeded mainly through an austerity programme that included a cutback in imports and a sharp increase in prices for consumer goods. As a result of those actions, which are of course easier to apply within a communist nation, Hungary laid the foundation for growth and was once more able to raise money from the west. We signed agreements with a consortium of financial institutions that included the Bank of America and the Chemical Bank. Moreover, the World Bank granted us a generous loan. Piece by piece I tried with some supporters to use more western financial methods to keep the Hungarian economy running. I proposed the issuing of bonds. Everybody told me that is capitalistic. I asked, 'Why is it capitalistic to issue bonds? There are a lot of people with money who do not use it, and there are others who need money. Why not let them change positions?' My long-term goal was always to make the Hungarian currency, the forint, convertible into western currencies. I am proud that I could help Hungary live within its limits, so that by the end of the 1980s people here could buy cars and holiday houses, travel to the west more freely and purchase food without standing in queues of other communist countries. For more than two decades I have advocated more and freer east-west trade. Also, I have always pointed out to Moscow that the east has over 400 million people who are interested in buying western goods, and for exchange we could offer our goods. Hungarians have actually been very successful already in the 1970s and 1980s at selling items to the west—from the original Rubik's cube to Crown Ikarus buses that are used in Portland, Oregon, and parts of California. Few other eastern bloc countries adopted our programme because of pride and vanity. I believe that of all eastern bloc countries we have the best chance of adapting to political pluralism and freer markets.

One of Hungary's first steps in showing the west our willingness to open relations with western Europe was the decision to dismantle the border fences in May 1989. Hungary was not yet ready to be a fully fledged member of the EC, but in our humanitarian concerns we are close to the west. Foreign policy represented a kind of flashpoint for the changes and reforms. Human rights were the key. We hadn't expected thousands of East Germans to use Hungary as a gateway to Germany, but we simply couldn't turn away from our commitment to the democratic values of the west.

I know that in early August, Deputy Foreign Minister Laszlo

Kovacs and Gyula Horn met to review the options for solving the refugee problem. Kovacs, now 50, has worked with Horn for more than a decade. They were a close team. The two options they had were, first, to send the East Germans back, an option dropped immediately as politically and technically not feasible. Politically it would have been contrary to Hungary's human rights concept, and technically it was impossible because by the beginning of August there were between 1,000 and 2,000 refugees in Budapest alone. In the rest of the country there were around 10,000 East Germans, and we didn't know what they were planning to do. In addition, over the next months or so, thousands of East Germans holidaying in Romania and Bulgaria would be crossing through Hungary on their way home or wherever they were going. There was just one solution that could be defended in Hungary and to the world: we had to let them go.

The obstacles to this decision were examined. The legal barrier was a 1969 bilateral agreement Hungary had signed with the German Democratic Republic. By the terms of the agreement, Hungary was not to let East German citizens proceed to any third country for which they did not have valid travel papers. Legal experts examined the treaty and decided that it could not be cancelled because it provided for a six-month advance notice of cancellation. The much quicker solution was to suspend the treaty on the grounds that conditions had changed since the signing of the document.

The next issue was how to break the news to the East Germans. Prime Minister Nemeth sent messages to the West German government in Bonn and the East Germans in Berlin suggesting a meeting to discuss a solution. The East German minister declined, pointing out that Party Leader Honecker and Prime Minister Willi Stoph were both ill. Honecker had departed abruptly from a meeting in Budapest in early July, reportedly suffering from a gall bladder illness. The West Germans, on the other hand, responded eagerly. Horn and Nemeth flew to Bonn on 25 August. There were legal and logistical considerations, and the Red Cross had become involved. The refugees were moved to a church in the Buda Hills, the historic side of Budapest, and two more camps opened. When Horn returned from Bonn, the West German government announced that reception stations were being set up in Bavaria to receive an indeterminate number of East German refugees.

There was still no word from East Berlin. Horn waited until 31 August, when he decided to fly to East Berlin to meet with Oskar Fischer, his East German counterpart. The session didn't go well at all. Horn's approach with the East Germans was to urge that an agreement be reached between the two Germanies. Hungary, Horn said, had been caught in the middle. He reassured Fischer that Hungary didn't want to cause discomfort to an ally, but the country was in an uncomfortable position and only action by the East Germans could relieve the situation. Horn stopped short of a threat, but he suggested to Fischer that if the East Germans failed to arrive at what we thought would be a reasonable answer, Hungary was going to look for its own solution. Then the East Germans asked that their consulate in Budapest be given free access to the camps where the East Germans were waiting for further decisions. We didn't have any objections. A pitiful exercise followed. The East German consulate dispatched a small trailer and a team of police officers to a street corner near the Holy Family Church, where the officers spent most of their time fending off the jeers of fellow citizens.

On 7 September, at a regular meeting of the Hungarian government, the decision was officially taken. At the time, there was a rumour that the Hungarian parliament was split between hard-liners who opposed the decision and liberals who supported it. But that was not true. No one spoke against it, and the decision was unanimous. The East German embassy received a diplomatic note saying that if there was no further response from the East German side, the Hungarian government was suspending the 1969 bilateral agreement as of midnight, thereby allowing the East German citizens to leave for any country. A few hours later, Horn received an urgent message from East Berlin to reverse the decision. Horn declined. Later that evening Horn publicly announced the Hungarian government's suspension of the bilateral agreement. The buses to carry the East Germans to Bavaria and Hessen were already waiting, and four hours later they rolled towards the West German border. Earlier that year, in May, we hadn't been aware of the reaction we might cause within the East German population, but in autumn we fully realized that what the Hungarian parliament did would have a profound influence on the GDR. Hungary had opened a kind of hole through which thousands of people could leave.

Chapter Fifteen

The Role of the Church

The Castle Church in Lutherstadt, Wittenberg where Martin Luther posted his 95 Theses in 1517 was refurbished in 1983, the year of the 500th anniversary of the reformer's birth. Near the top of the tall church tower is a gold band inscribed 'Eine feste Burg ist unser Gott' (A mighty fortress is our god)—the first words to the battle hymn of the Reformation. When local leaders of the SED saw this impressive statement they asked representatives of the church what words from Luther might be appropriate for the adjacent building. They suggested the beginning of the second stanza of the hymn, 'No strength of ours can match His might'.

Lenin said, 'Religion is a kind of spiritual alcohol in which the slaves of capitalism drown their claim for a human-like existence'. But neither punishment nor scorn, atheism nor new rituals, such as 'Jugendweihe', which was the communist substitute for the first holy communion and confirmation, could stop the democratizing influence of the church, which since 1957 the SED had called 'the last organized enemy'.[1]

The system nevertheless took its toll on the churches, at least in terms of numbers. When Germany was divided, there were 17 million church members in the east; by 1989 there were only 4 million left. Church membership in heavily Protestant East Germany declined from more than 80 per cent of the population to less than 30 per cent during the communist era. The government thought it had dealt religion a fatal blow by enforcing strict church–state separation, eliminating state funding, and teaching only Marxism and Leninism in schools. Added to that was a heavy dose of oppression. Until the Berlin Wall was erected in the summer of 1961, the East German churches had close ties with the better-financed, state-supported churches in West Germany. In 1968 these formal ties were severed and the East German churches, after a period of confrontation, moved toward being a church *in* socialism but, as its leaders pointed out, not a church *of* socialism.

But still, churches were meeting places for dissidents and the incubators for the 1989 peaceful revolution in the GDR. What happened in the

---

[1] Swoboda, Die Revolution der Kerzen, p. 22.

churches of the GDR in the years before the Wall fell, culminating in the events of autumn 1989, is the result of the continuing function of a religious institution in a dictatorship. The church in the GDR was a quiet force of opposition with a clear vision of the distinction between what belongs to the church and what to the state. The church played, and still plays, a critical role in the reformation process of the former GDR.

Pastor Johannes Neudeck

> But I say unto you, Love your enemies, bless them that curse you, do good to them that hate you, and pray for them which despitefully use you, and persecute you. Matthew 5:44)

The church was packed that night and my friend, Pastor Lehmann, had chosen Christ's Sermon on the Mount to open the service. For days we had witnessed discussions among the congregation on who was an enemy and who was a friend. The images of 'the enemy' had played a role in the East German society since the communist regime came to power in 1949. In schools and newspapers, and on radio and television, the news had been spread for decades that the west and all people with a different opinion than that of the regime were enemies. I felt that the communities in the east had started to split openly into two groups: bad people with power and good ones without any influence. And the anger and frustration on both sides were rising. Hundreds of churchgoers had to deal with disadvantages of one kind or another because they had not been members of the Communist Party and had been visiting churches. November 1989 was the time when the majority of the population who were not part of the organized party apparatus started to question what had not been questioned openly before: why does anybody have to accept living without freedom? Like most other pastors and priests, we feared that the population was ready to fight with their bare fists against the overwhelming communist apparatus.

During that time, the clergy in the east saw their biggest task as calming people down without diminishing the momentum of the political movement—the most determined one in East Germany since June 1956. Lehmann continued the sermon, 'Jesus is asking us to love exactly those who make our lives difficult, those who practise such questionable politics'. He was saying, People, stay calm and moderate; do not use weapons or fists, but prayers and candles. The

213

church played the most influential role in the peaceful revolution in East Germany. Every priest and minister in the churches of Leipzig and later in Berlin and other major cities were trying to communicate that those who had tyrannized the country for so long had to be made to understand that the people demonstrating were not against them as persons, but against their beliefs and what they stood for.

The people of the GDR won in the end, without using force. With their peaceful actions they broke off their chains and brought a weary system down as the world watched in wonder. Why did the peaceful revolution win? Actually, the roots of the protest movement went back years, even before the first time I had travelled to the east. The SED regime's fear that its system would crumble was clearly demonstrated by the precautions taken to prevent any criticism or if criticism was stated openly, to prosecute it immediately. In the mid-1960s, Robert Havemann, a party member himself, demanded that parliamentary opposition be permitted in the GDR. He was immediately expelled from the SED and the Academy of Science. Later he confined to his house. In 1976 song writer Wolf Biermann was expelled from the GDR because his songs criticized the regime.

In August 1977 Rudolf Bahro, a member of the SED, was imprisoned for eight years after criticizing socialism in his book, *Die Alternative: Zur Kritik des real existierenden Sozialismus* (The alternative: a critique of the existing socialism). Bahro said GDR society was governed by a despotic group of bureaucrats, noting just days before his arrest, 'I have not started a new process with my book. A silent movement against the party has long been under way.'

Many priests and clergy men in the east compared the party to the Pope who governed during the years Luther reformed the church. Then, abuses of power and influence produced mistrust and disbelief among the populace, and propaganda and economic and social concepts lost their effectiveness. The party, like that Pope, sowed the seeds of the revolution that would undermine its influence.

It was a silent cultural revolution that was under way for years. An East German illegal organization, the Democratic Union of East Germany's Communists, in 1978 wrote a memorandum that was broadcast by the two West German radio stations in Berlin, RIAS (Radio in the American Sector) and SFB (Sender Freies Berlin —Radio Broadcasting of Free Berlin) and published in *Der Spiegel,* the major political journal in West Germany. The authors of the manifesto surprisingly came to the conclusions that they were against a one-party dictatorship and against a dictatorship of the proletarians, but for party pluralism and for an independent parliament. In addition, the authors noted in a chapter entitled 'German politics' that the two Germanies should seek a common future.

From the end of the 1970s, apart from the inner party quarrels, the Protestant church in East Germany functioned as a vehicle for political dissidents. The introduction of the 'Wehrkundeunterricht' (military training) into schools prompted the first open rebellion against Honecker and his apparatus. The churches led by Protestants opposed the training in open letters stating that the conflicts of the world could not be solved with weapons and furthermore that schoolchildren should not be exposed to military training. Almost automatically the churches became the haven for the dissenters, although priests and churchgoers were arrested more frequently.

In summer 1981, Pastor Rainer Eppelmann wrote an open letter to Honecker demanding that the Wehrkundeunterricht and other military training in schools be abolished along with school books that glorified soldiers and guard posts at the Wall. A second letter was published by Eppelmann under the title 'Frieden schaffen ohne Waffen' (peace without weapons). Four months later, he organized a peace workshop in Berlin. More than 3,000 people participated. When in March 1982 Honecker announced that in case of a mobilization women would have to serve as well as men, another wave of protests was initiated by members of church organizations. The artist Bärbel Bohley called hundreds of women protesters to the streets. The following four years were difficult for churches. Some started newsletters for their congregations in which Honecker and his regime were criticized rather openly. Shortly thereafter, the clergy and their helpers who were responsible were arrested, or, in lesser cases, their paper, printers and copy machines were confiscated. During those years, many of them relied on their western colleagues to smuggle in paper, maybe even a copying machine. This was a very difficult task, since even sending Bibles to the east was forbidden until recent years, and such items were usually confiscated by the border guards.

In September 1986 the Church of Zion opened a library called by the apolitical name 'Umweltbibliothek' (environment library), which later developed into one of the important centres of the opposition movement. One year later, newsletter editor of the Church of Zion and one of his assistants were arrested. Churches throughout the country organized day and night vigils to demand freedom for the arrested pair. In addition, on 10 December, the anniversary of the UN declaration of human rights, several human rights activists were arrested. Most of them were picked up at home or at work. Over 500 people openly protested about the incident in the Gethsemane Church in Berlin. Then in January 1988, several members of the peace movement participated in a demonstration for Rosa Luxemburg and Karl Liebknecht, two major German socialists who were shot without trial in 1919. Hoping to beat the SED with its own weapons, the protesters carried banners emblazoned with one of the best-known quotes of Luxemburg, 'Freedom is only freedom for those who think differently'. Within minutes all the protesters were arrested and accused of high treason. A week later, more than 3,000 people gathered in East Berlin's Gethsemane Church to protest the arrests. The Bishop of the Protestant Church of Berlin–Brandenburg, Gottfried Frock, read a declaration in favour of the opposition movement followed by an evening prayer. He ended his prayer with the words, 'We wish that Jesus Christ will fill our hearts with love so we have good thoughts to convince those we must deal with in this state of the power of love of Our Lord Jesus. Amen.'

His prayer was the starting point for the demonstrations against the oppression of the state. The church increasingly spurred the movement. Although many activities started in East Berlin's Gethsemane Church, it was no coincidence that Leipzig with its proud revolutionary heritage was the centre of the first organized and regular demonstrations. Since late August 1989, prayers for peace were held in the Nikolai Church in Leipzig. Every Monday more people were drawn to the event until it developed into the biggest demonstration against the regime in East German history. Thousands of people gathered every Monday to demonstrate against the regime. It was here in Leipzig that people first shouted, 'We want to leave!'

Leipzig was the voice of the citizens of East Berlin. In autumn 1989, there was fear that the SED would take revenge for the embarrassing demonstrations during Gorbachev's visit. A small group of well-known artists, among them the conductor Kurt Masur, pressured the regime with a public statement to maintain calm and prevent the use of force. By midnight, no shots had been fired. The next morning's issue of the party organ *Neues Deutschland* stated that only the goodwill of several high-ranking members of the party had prevented a blood bath. On the same page, a meeting between Party Leader Honecker and a member of the Chinese Communist Party was announced for the next day. Honecker, seemingly unimpressed with the events of the previous days, stressed that 'especially during shaky days like these, the values of socialism will have to be maintained stronger than ever'.[2]

On 16 October, over 100,000 people walked through the streets of Leipzig, which was by then known in both the east and the west as the 'Heldenstadt' (city of heroes) without being interrupted by security forces. A week later, another 300,000 people joined in. Nobody knew yet that within less than four weeks their courage would be rewarded and the Berlin Wall would fall.

Pastor Friedrich Schorlemmer

The role of the churches in the GDR didn't differ much from that in other countries: its primary task was to spread the biblical message and exegesis. But the church also had a special function in the GDR because it filled a void. It was the only independent institution able to criticize the regime, within certain limits. In this sense, the church turned into a shelter for those whose thinking differed from what the regime expected. For the most part, however, the church's role in toppling the monolithic communist rule has been ignored compared to the litany of other factors: Mikhail Gorbachev's policy of glasnost, Hungary's decision to open its border, the great number of East Germans fleeing to the west, the opening of the Berlin Wall, and the country's woeful economic, educational and ecological situation.

Since the hierarchic structure of the church is very similar to that of a political party, the SED saw similarities between the power and influence of officials in the party and those in the church. The regime respected the representatives of the church as enemies who had to be dealt with and lived with in coexistence. On the other hand, the SED feared the church and tried to confine it to a purely religious role. The SED wanted in particular to avoid political scandals involving the church or its representatives. For example, party officials knew that arresting a pastor or priest for his militant Sunday sermon

---

[2] *Neues Deutschland*, 10 October 1989

would attract a lot of attention, perhaps even internationally, while prohibiting a student who regularly attended church services from receiving a higher education was a common punishment that received little media attention.

I have always believed that man is a political being, and that for the church to deny itself a political role would be to negate its Christianity. I was 16 when I noticed that connection. My father had been a pastor for a long while and consequently his children—myself and my six sisters and brothers—were not allowed to attend high school. The outlook of having the same future as my father, living as a pastor in very poor circumstances with little or no personal freedom, was distressing enough for me to announce to my family that I planned to leave the GDR. My mother was mainly concerned that I would get shot at the border, while my father stressed over and over again that the family had to stay together. Night-long discussions followed, with very little support from my parents. Although as a teenager I wouldn't have had the backbone to disobey, I actually stayed because I was persuaded to stay. My father must have noticed for the first time my deep frustration, and he managed through some of his contacts to slip me into an adult education class where I later earned a degree that allowed me to enter university.

In kindergarten, school and later university, I was always considered an outsider. In the elementary school, teachers sent me home regularly because I wasn't wearing the expected blue shirt and scarf for the weekly consecration of the colours. Later in school I had to share a room with a 17-year-old boy, a member of the FDJ, the youth organization of the SED. He was frank about his tasks concerning me. The very first day he told me, 'Listen, I'll report any religious propaganda I hear coming out of your mouth. I'm staying with you in this room so somebody has an eye on the "Christkindl" (child of Christ).' But the Christkindl, as I was always later referred to in university when I had decided to follow my father's footsteps, had understood something from early on: the church in the east provided some opportunities despite all its repressions. My decision to study theology was influenced less by my father's career as a pastor than by my eagerness to become politically involved. I had understood that the church provided the only shelter to those who act and think differently. My decision to become a pastor was clearly politically motivated. First, I became a pastor in one of the first satellite cities, Halle-Neustadt. The architecture there was nothing but ugliness and coldness. People living in that kind of community soon started to feel like bees in the honeycomb. It was the end of the 1960s. The Wall had been up for eight years, and all our hopes for a free East Germany had been shattered. Russian tanks, with the help of East German troops, had dispersed the groups of protesters in Prague. Officially, there was a celebration under way for the homecoming troops. Tanks returning from Prague were rolling proudly through the streets while most people felt a deep sadness and anger. I remember jumping onto a tank and shouting at the soldier behind its controls, 'Are you proud? Were the Czechs happy when you arrived, or were they happier when you left?' It was a wonder that I wasn't arrested immediately.

The year 1968 was also an important one for the churches in the GDR. Until then the West German and East German Protestant churches were unified. But the East German church leaders decided, partially because of pressure from the regime and partially because they wanted to coexist with the SED, to separate from the western churches. Manfred Stolpe, who serves today as the minister president of the state of Brandenburg, was one of the forces who worked towards the separation of the churches and the establishment of a separate East German Protestant church. The newly founded church was officially described as 'a partner in socialism'. Stolpe soon became the representative of the East German church who not only worked together with the regime, but also ensured a certain freedom for the churches. Christians were no longer enemies but 'socialist citizens with a Christian belief'.

But the relationship between regime and church was a difficult one. Stolpe was often referred to within church circles as the 'crisis manager' as he tried to remove all possible conflict between the church and the regime. He was the mediator during the historic 60-minute meeting between Erich Honecker and Superintendent Bishop Schönherr in 1978. During this brief talk, Honecker granted financial help for the renovation of churches and travel visas for pastors and priests to visit the west. Still, the regime kept a close lid on other church activities. Church newsletters were constantly confiscated, and people who had been involved in preparing them were arrested. People like myself, who had drawn some unfavourable attention to themselves, were smeared. (For example, rumours were spread among students and the community that I was crazy and living in a religious delirium. My church and private rooms were bugged and some of my closest friends were denounced.) But still, by the beginning of the 1970s the church and its representatives had found a niche in society that later grew into a full-scale spiritual and political movement. We called it a 'Freiraum' (free room) where church and non-church people discussed issues rarely brought up outside the church walls.

Around the same time I became interested in the peace movement. People in Germany, particularly in the east, have always been concerned that, in the event of a military confrontation between the eastern and the western blocs, the country would be the battlefield. We were the communist world's buffer state against the west. We felt the dramatic tension building up in 1973, when the armament race started all over again.

Honecker had succeeded in having the GDR recognized as a full member of the UN, separate from West Germany. I remember watching a television programme in December 1973 that showed two German flags, one with black, red and gold horizontal bars and the other with the same coloured bars but with a hammer and sickle in the middle, being raised for the first time next to each other at the UN headquarters in New York.

At the same time, Honecker started within the GDR an ideological campaign to prohibit any thought of a possible reunification of the two Germanies. The East German constitution was changed by eliminating all references to 'Germany' or the 'German nation'. That same year Honecker in collaboration with Erich Mielke, the regime's chief ideologist, had worked on a plan to sabotage any influence the East German churches still had on the population. The confiscation of newsletters increased, the appearance of watchdogs in the church grew from Sunday to Sunday.

Unlike Poland or Czechoslovakia, East Germany never had one major charismatic opposition leader such as Lech Walesa or Václev Havel. Different groups formed to push forward a series of divergent demands ranging from a better environment, free elections and a cleaner political apparatus to a free choice on unity with West Germany. The East German communists sabotaged these early attempts at reform by stealing and adopting our positions to make themselves seem like a new and more trustworthy force. During the time this was happening, the symbol of the church in East Germany was the ploughshare, which Honecker had declared in 1982 to be the symbol of a public enemy.

Strangely, Honecker had discovered during the 1980s an appreciation for German history, which presumably was why he allowed the celebration of the 500th anniversary of Luther's birth in Wittenberg in September 1983. The city where Luther nailed to the church door his reformist theses had often been antiestablishment. First, there was Luther, who fought against the hypocrisy of Pope Leo X. Over 400 years later, in September 1933, the 450th anniversary of Luther's birth, the first 'brown bishop' resided in the city and the Nazi flag waved in the wind from the top of the church's tower. Again, it was time to protest. Pastor Martin Niemöller and Dietrich Bonhoeffer distributed pamphlets warning the population not to listen to the Nazi regime. Both were arrested and put into a concentration camp, where Bonhoeffer later died.

In September 1983 it was my turn to organize a protest. I wanted to plan something for the anniversary of the reformist's birthday. Secretly, I got together with a few people whom I knew I could trust. We prepared some defiant texts and songs and arranged to meet by dusk around the old fountain in front of the church. But that wasn't enough. In my group was a blacksmith, who, during a ceremony of two and one-half hours, reshaped a sword into a ploughshare, accompanied by our songs. The news of our gathering spread quickly and within minutes the whole town gathered in the courtyard—more than 3,000 people. I was told the next morning that the Stasi, in the guise of an anonymous caller, had tried to get the local fire brigade to interrupt by reporting that the courtyard was on fire. Luckily, the brigade learned what we were doing and didn't respond to the call.

The presence of a West German camera team prevented our arrest that night. I had given a Hamburg TV channel a call and informed them of my plan and the ceremony, not really knowing if they would show up or not. I know that at least 50 to 100 Stasi people were among the crowd in the courtyard, ready to follow orders to arrest us all. The western cameras that reported live from the courtyard that night made the Stasi reluctant to issue or follow the orders. Not one single person was arrested as a result.

Just a year earlier the ploughshare symbol had been the focus of a conflict between regime and church, which was once again quietened by Stolpe. Opponents of East Germany's paramilitary education in high schools had started wearing an emblem featuring a ploughshare on their lapels. After acrimonious discussions, Stolpe publicly announced that the ploughshare symbol was not to be worn in public anymore, in order to 'regain a normal and quiet community life'.

A few years after the protest in the courtyard, the well co-ordinated relationship between the party and church representatives such as Stolpe stopped functioning. People like myself wanted more than a coexistence between church and party. My determination to work on changes grew stronger after the event in Wittenberg. Maybe I also felt safe. By the end of the 1980s the regime was no longer quite so omnipresent or powerful. Church members like myself dared to make suggestions about peace and about the environment for the 11th Party Conference of the Central Committee. The number of open letters of criticism increased from year to year. But the reaction of the regime remained a stereotypical 'received and filed'.

Nevertheless, peace groups discussing east-west tensions and the deployment of missiles in the two Germanies met more openly. These discussions led inevitably to discussions of human rights issues, the environment, freedom of travel, freedom of the press and free elections. The regime had lost touch with reality and greatly underestimated the church's importance in East German society. Most people who met on Monday night in my church before they went out to demonstrate hadn't been in a church for a long while and had only a passing acquaintance with God. But there they sat, young, old, left-wingers, socialists and conservatives. They had recognized the church as the only 'free-room' in society that offered the space for a peaceful revolution. Maybe there was an awful lot of candle wax spilled from prayer vigils on the streets of Leipzig, Wittenberg and all over the country, but better drops of wax than one drop of blood. The revolution was so peaceful from the side of the demonstrators because of the spirit of the church. Luther once said that the church is only the church when it always reforms itself and lets itself be reformed.

Chapter Sixteen

The City of Candles and Prayers

During the 18th century, Wolfgang Goethe called Leipzig 'Little Paris'; in 1830 and 1848 the revolutionary movements that pointed Germany toward democracy came from Leipzig. Some travellers know the capital of Saxony through its annual fair, an event that in the mid-1970s made possible the first exchange of technology between west and east. It was no coincidence that Leipzig—not Berlin—was the East German city where the first demonstrators voiced their anger over the country's regime. No one except the citizens of Leipzig believed that Saxonians would reaffirm their proud revolutionary heritage, which had been repressed by the communist regime for over four decades.

On Monday, 18 September 1989, following a prayer for peace in the Nikolai Church, about 100 citizens gathered to demonstrate for political, social and economic changes. Eleven of the demonstrators were immediately detained and put under arrest for up to six months. A new political group called Neues Forum (New Forum) applied for official recognition, but the East German interior secretary turned down the application and called the party a public enemy. A week later, on Monday, 25 September, over 8,000 people congregated in front of the Nikolai Church demanding freedom of speech and press.

Just five days later, West German Foreign Minister Hans-Dietrich Genscher engaged in lengthy and dramatic talks with the Polish government that resulted in the release of 7,000 East Germans to the west who had fled to the German embassy in Warsaw.

While this was happening, the East German government was proudly planning the state's 40th anniversary. Honecker hoped for the support of Soviet President Gorbachev, who was expected to attend the celebrations. Because the stream of East German refugees trying to find their way to freedom via Hungary and Poland couldn't be stopped, Honecker found himself in an increasingly embarrassing situation and agreed to have an extra train filled with refugees from Hungary and Poland pass through the East German territory without passport control.

During the third Monday demonstration in Leipzig, 25,000 people were dispersed by the Secret Police, using gas and water canons to end the peaceful demonstration. Meanwhile, citizens of other East German cities, including Dresden, the old university city of Jena, and East Berlin, joined the weekly demonstrations in their urban churches. At the beginning of October, once again the brutal power of the state was used to forcefully interrupt the demonstrations. The Karl–Marx Platz, a big meeting point in the middle of Leipzig, became the showplace for the largest demonstrations in East Germany since the uprising in 1953. The demonstrators gathered after a service in front of the Nikolai Church. Nearly half a million people stood eye-to-eye with the East German People's Police. Hours in advance, hospitals had been advised by government services to be prepared for the worst. Blood banks from all over the country were asked to bring their reserves to the city. The fear and uncertainty of the citizens could be summarized in a single question: 'Will this demonstration end like the one on Tiananmen Square?' The courageous citizens who walked hand-in-hand along the streets asking for 'Freedom' and shouting 'We are one nation' had to expect the worst.

Johannes

Shortly before I put on my coat to leave for the Monday demonstrations, my brother reminded me to be careful, since he was on duty and my parents were visiting an aunt in the country. 'Be extra careful today,' he said. 'There won't be anybody home before Tuesday night to bail you out if the Stasi gets you!' I had never thought about what I would do if I were arrested, put on a truck and questioned about my intentions. I had heard about people being missed for days, maybe even months, and a week earlier I had seen the Stasi going after those who weren't quick enough to run away. I had escaped on 18 September, when eleven out of 100 people who had prayed for freedom and peace were arrested in the Nikolai Church.

As I put on my running shoes and got my poster ready, an image from the previous Monday popped into my mind: Stasi carrying weapons, wearing protective shields and chasing people through the streets until the crowd dispersed. I was sure the same thing would happen this week. Maybe the first Mondays I had just walked along because it was something new to do, something to get me out of the doldrums. But the more I spoke to my parents and other young people, the more I began to feel that those demonstrations were not just a game; they hit the very nerve of the system. Either our shouts for freedom, the churches' suddenly stronger role in the movement, and our open rebellion were going to succeed now or we would end up as China after Tiananmen Square—worse than ever before.

On Sunday night the SED party member and head of the city of Leipzig, Wolfgang Heiland, had stated in a broadcast that the party would handle counterrevolutionaries and all others who challenged his government in the same way that the students in China had been dealt with. Everybody was fearfully aware of this message. But I asked myself, was our fear based on facts, or were those broadcasts carefully planned to prevent more people from joining the demonstrations? We knew the media had always been the mouthpiece of the party, but what had happened since May 1989 was surprising even to us. We were betrayed as never before. A faked election that gave the regime a 97.5 per cent majority had been called by our local newspaper 'a powerful show of support by the people for their government and the party'. Just months later, the same newspaper claimed that the East German refugees in Hungary and Prague had been kidnapped by professional traders. All refugees, stated the newspaper, had been doped and then had been brutally brought over the border. Further, the newspaper reported that all these actions had been planned for a long time by spy organizations in the west who wanted to undermine socialism. I wondered, how stupid did the regime really think its citizens were?

Then we heard via the West German news that church newsletters increasingly were banished in various cities in East Germany, and the famous monthly publication *Sputnik* had been stopped. Protests, smaller gatherings in churches, arrests and imprisonment were altering and dominating our daily lives. I heard from a friend who delivered petrol to the main police station in Leipzig that, by mid-June, the police had already used up their allocation for the whole year. The demonstrations in Leipzig were more than a thorn in the side of the regime; they were destroying the carefully constructed international reputation of the East German government.

The bus that brought me to the Nikolai Church on 9 October was moing slower than usual. As we approached the city centre, there were more and more security police. Tanks had been called in. I was afraid, and those none-too-encouraging words of my brother popped into my head. At that moment, an older man sitting next to me on the bus punched my side and said with conviction, 'The worst mistake you could make now would be to sit in your chair watching the events on TV and feeling happy with yourself'. His remark put me on the right track again. It was probably the courage and enthusiasm of the many people around me who were all going to the same demonstrations that wouldn't let me quit at that moment. The churches had announced that they would leave their doors open after the evening service to give demonstrators a safe place to hide. And that had been exactly my plan. But somehow it turned out differently.

An unbelievable number of people had gathered on the Karl–Marx Platz. I was impressed by the peacefulness of the demonstration. The citizens seemed to be at ease with themselves and to have no doubt that they were doing the right thing. There were little children holding their mothers' hands and people like myself carrying posters. It was already dark, but the city's lights had illuminated the streets. Then the church bells started to ring. The atmosphere was surprisingly calm among the demonstrators, and the security police seemed to watch us with disbelief. A lady next to me must have noticed when I stared at a policeman carrying a Kalashnikov, standing just yards away from me. She was in her mid-forties. She hooked her arm through mine and said, 'We don't have anything to lose. It only can get better than what we have now.'

I felt much better and more secure as we got closer to Nikolai Church. The service, broadcast to those outside who couldn't squeeze in, began with a message from six artists, among them our orchestra conductor, Kurt Masur, and a high-ranking party member, Dr Meyer. The message asked for peaceful dialogues and prudence. People started to cheer. Was that a turning point? I hadn't been to church often, but I remembered a story my mother told me: I thought of the Israelites when they were chased by the Egyptians through the desert with no chance to turn the situation to their advantage. Since 9 October I have understood better than ever the kind of feeling the Israelites must have had when the sea suddenly opened.

Marisa Müller

Here I stood as a mother of four sons, ready to go to my first demonstration. I was fearful, although my children had told me over and over again that there was no reason for concern, since the 9 October demonstration had ended without intervention from the secret police. Still, my heart was full of fear.

The preparations for the demonstration were already under way during the weekend. My sons had asked me for an old bed sheet, on which they painted 'Freedom can't be divided'. Two poles were attached to either side. They planned to carry it on Monday through the streets of Leipzig, where this time over 250,000 people were expected.

Monday, 23 October came. With a beating heart I got on the train around two o'clock in the afternoon to be sure I would get a seat in the church. The service was supposed to start around five o'clock, but usually the church in Leipzig filled up one to two hours early. A large crowd was already in the Nikolai Church when I arrived. Latecomers had to wait outside in the cold. I had noticed that many who had already taken their seats probably were not regular churchgoers. I had quite some time to study the people around me. In many faces you could read desperation, yearning for change and for justice. The group was mixed: young, old; men; mothers with children. Finally, the service started with a canon, Dona nobis pacem. A group of ministers read messages to the community and also gave their understanding of the current political situation in Leipzig and Berlin. Listening to their words made it clear that this group was determined to force the government to change. The presiding minister spoke of the injustice that we all had lived with for so long, and openly criticized the regime. I hadn't heard anybody speaking so frankly in public before then. Although I felt his determination, I also sensed tension and exhaustion in his voice.

Outside, the crowd was roaring, waiting for the end of the service and ready to walk the streets of Leipzig. I met my family in front of one of the church entrances. My sons Tobias and Florian were already holding the poster. I had felt very safe in the church, but started to become very emotional once I left the building. The police were everywhere, staring at the overwhelming crowd.

For the first time I experienced the feeling of walking in a big crowd of people. There was little pushing, although people started to sing and shout, 'We are the people'. After about 15 minutes the demonstration passed by the Stasi headquarters in Leipzig. All of a sudden people got nervous or angry. Some started to throw rocks, others whistled. I was afraid the demonstration would get out of hand. The shouts for 'free elections' could be heard louder and louder. I heard voices singing, 'We are not going to leave, but Honecker has to'.

Police started to push the crowd back. They didn't use water or gas as they had in earlier demonstrations. I think if they had used force, a situation like civil war would have developed. I managed to get out of the crowd and ran into a small side street. I had lost my family somewhere out there. Late, around midnight, I managed to get home. Almost all the people on the train had been participating in the demonstration. You could recognize most demonstrators because they were wearing especially warm clothes, parkas, hats, gloves and running shoes. Some still had posters in their hands. I was proud of myself. I had participated.

Kurt Masur

I knew that leading SED members intended to crush the Leipzig rallies that Monday. Columns of tanks and trucks had been strategically placed. After rehearsing with my orchestra all morning, I called the SED Regional Secretary of Culture, Dr Kurt Meyer, and expressed concerns. A blood bath would have disastrous consequences. He called two other SED members while I contacted two other friends who were not party members—a theologian and a cabaret artist. The six of us met in my living room and wrote this statement, 'We are writing in our growing fear and sense of responsibility. As part of this city's cultural establishment, we beg you not to use force. We ask you to govern with prudence.'

The appeal was read aloud to church congregations and was broadcast to thousands of people by radio in Leipzig. I never wanted to be a political figure, but I recognized that as music director of the Gewandhaus Orchestra I had a certain clout. Over 70,000 people gathered that night on Karl–Marx Platz. There were many well-known faces. Our hope was that the police wouldn't start shooting when prominent people were among the demonstrators. I was in the front row of the protesting crowd. Most were frightened, but they still came to demonstrate for freedom. I had heard that hospitals had stocked up on blood, a sure sign of what was planned. The Honecker government had ordered the local police commander to use force if necessary. But no shots were fired. Monday, 9 October in Leipzig was the turning point. The following Monday, more than 150,000 people gathered at the same spot where just a week before we had been fearing the worst. They shouted, 'We are the people'. The SED finally agreed to talk to the opposition groups. I served as chairman of several such meetings in the concert hall.

Yes, the 'Six' played an important role in preventing the use of brutality and in the eventual fall of the Honecker government, but, in the end, it was those thousands of people who came Monday after Monday who made the difference. The Six was a group quickly organized for one reason only, to prevent bloodshed. Our reasons were as varied as the group itself. Dr Kurt Meyer acted out of purely humanitarian instinct. The two other party members were more practical, fearing the consequences if shooting started. We learned later that one of our Six was a member of the Stasi.

Where did the East Germans get their inspiration and courage? I believe that without Gorbachev the 'peaceful revolution' in East Germany would not have happened. I cannot accept criticism of Gorbachev now. Even if he loses some of his control, neither his stature nor his greatness will suffer. As for the west, it bothers me that all of a sudden there are people who fancy themselves to be of higher moral and intellectual superiority. They think they know everything better than we do. People ask me now if my musical work had suffered under the East German regime. People ask me why I enjoyed privileges and others didn't. It's of course true that if you were talented, the regime used you as a showcase for its success. But other political systems do that as well—maybe in different forms, but they do it. For my part, frankly I feel much more confined now, as I have to fight to keep my orchestra solvent. I never had to do that before.

It's also true that SED members will go unpunished. But as the reunification came so quickly, and it had to move fast, the opportunity to conduct anything like the Nuremberg process was lost. The politicians had to act speedily. Still, most East Germans are upset and frustrated that they did not get a chance to create their own political system. It feels like the West German Republic benevolently forced its system upon us. One young man summarized it pretty well, 'We all didn't get where we wanted to be'.

It's a little like a man building his first house. He is excited to express his own visions, taste and personal style. Then somebody comes along and sells him a plan with all the details. The homeowner has to admit it is a good plan, but still it is not his own. We wanted freedom, but we also have other dreams, still unrealized. I think the younger generation was robbed of that chance.

Chapter Seventeen

The Fallen Symbol

The Berlin Wall began to rise menacingly during the early morning hours of 13 August 1961, after the GDR regime, under the rule of Walter Ulbricht, decided to seal East Berlin off from the western part of the city. Ulbricht dissemblingly called the structure an 'antifascist, protective wall'. The fortification that would soon symbolize totalitarianism to the world went up all around West Berlin, spanning hundreds of miles around the Soviet occupation zone and cutting across Germany in a gash of barbed wire, concrete and guard-towers.

During the next 28 years, the rest of the world witnessed hundreds of frantic escape attempts by East Germans. Some desperately tried to scale the Wall, others tunnelled under it, and still others tried to smash through it with cars and trucks. Some attempts had happy endings, others did not. Probably the most spectacular escape took place in 1979, when two families took off in a hot air balloon in Thuringia and landed safely in Bavaria several hours later. The last of those desperate attempts to reach freedom was made by Martin Notev, who escaped by swimming the River Spree in February 1989. He was picked up by East German guards in a patrol boat while he rested on the west bank, which he had reached successfully. Allied protests about Notev's kidnapping finally resulted in his release to the west. The exact number of GDR citizens who were caught by guards while attempting to flee to freedom is unknown, but estimates run as high as several thousand. It is known that 78 people were shot and killed at the Wall by border guards; an additional 119 were wounded and died later of their injuries.[1]

In 1963 John F. Kennedy became the first American president to visit the Wall, during which he reinforced the United States commitment to Berlin in his famous 'Ich bin ein Berliner' speech. Ronald Reagan visited the Wall in June 1987, demanding in a speech broadcast to the east that it be torn down. West Germany's President Richard von Weizsäcker said, 'The German question is open as long as the Brandenburg Gate is closed'.

---

[1] IGFM Bericht, *Menschenrechte der Welt*, Frankfurt, 1988.

How beliefs and hopes can become reality is demonstrated by the dramatic events of 9 November 1989. At seven o'clock that evening Günther Schabowski, a Politburo member, announced in a televised news conference that henceforth only an easily obtained pass would be needed for emigration or travel to the west. Spreading like a fire, the news made it immediately to thousands of people at home as well as to the demonstrators in the streets of East Berlin and Leipzig.

Checkpoint Charlie, one of the most famous Wall crossings in Berlin, became the scene of hundreds of East Germans walking for the first time to the west, where a cheering crowd was waiting with sprays of champagne for new arrivals. By midnight a huge traffic jam stretched from east to west. East Germans waited for their chance to cross over and get their first taste of the west by visiting West Berlin's main boulevard, the Kurfürstendamm, where stores were passing out free Coca-Cola and food.

Kristina Matschat

You could feel the tension in the air. The excitement was mounting among the crowd of thousands who had come to Friedrichstrasse in Kreuzberg, Checkpoint Charlie. I was in the front rows. People were pushing towards the Berlin Wall, pushing me from behind, pushing toward the 'antifascist, protective Wall', as it was officially called by the East German regime.

I had never before been so close to soldiers of the Volkspolizei (People's Police). Ever since the Wall went up in 1961, they'd been under orders to shoot to kill anyone attempting to flee to the west. Nobody—neither those pushing towards the Wall nor the soldiers themselves—knew if they would shoot now. Nobody knew if the Soviet tanks were already lined up, just as they had been in June 1953 when a similar uprising had been quickly squashed.

I shivered—not from the coolness of that November night, but from fear. Most of us were wearing running shoes. Hours before, as I laced up my shoes, I planned my route to safety—how I would somehow escape the crowd and flee when shooting began. Others must have had similar thoughts. Everybody was full of fear—but also full of hope.

I had followed closely the recent developments in the Soviet Union, the reforms made possible through glasnost and perestroika. Via the West German TV and radio channels we heard about the elections in the Soviet Congress. For the first time in Soviet history, several candidates were vying for positions. We also knew about the strikes that were not instantly put down by the police. We heard about books, such as Anatol Rybakow's *The Children of Arbat*, which had been banned in East Germany but were published in the Soviet Union. We heard about the reforms in Hungary and Poland.

On the 40th anniversary of the GDR, Gorbachev sent a clear signal that the Honecker regime would have to loosen its grip on East Germany. We knew we might all be kidding ourselves, grasping at straws, but this is what gave us the courage to come together in Berlin's Friedrichstrasse on the evening of 9 November 1989.

My whole life I had lived by the party rules. I was never allowed to study what I chose, because my parents and I myself had not been willing to play politics. Admittedly, I'm still relatively lucky; I was at least able to study something. This was a luxury since my parents were not 'workers'. One of many conditions in the First Workers' and Farmers' Republic was that workers or farmers could automatically send their children to college. As with most Stalinist regulations, this seemingly just concept was not based on humanitarian goals but on fear; intellectuals were a real threat to the regime.

Anyone who was not closely allied with 'them', not actively involved with the party, was perceived as an antagonist and treated as such. Some who did not join the party now ask themselves if they should have surrendered their principles for a better life and become part of 'it', even if it was all a pretence. Of course many people did just that, going along with the party line and living a double standard, believing that they could play along and still be happy. But it seemed the party always knew. 'Hypocrites' had to endure a humiliating ritual of 'public self-criticism'. The intent was to erode your self-respect, to belittle you and make you humble. People without self-respect look for a haven and cling to what they know—in this case the party. A human being without dignity will do anything for anybody. It is that ritual of self-criticism combined with fear that made the system last so long. Open rebellion was out of the question. The obstinate felt the arm of the ubiquitous beast immediately.

We had a friend, a talented chemist who worked in research and development for the military, and who openly refused to join the party. He thought they would not dare touch an important scientist. But one day he did not show up for work and nobody knew where he was. Months later his mother told us that he had been taken to a prison—or 'mental rehabilitation clinic'—outside Berlin. When she went to visit him in prison, she asked him if she could talk to him without the guard present. Her son snapped back, 'That's not a guard, that's my defender.' Obviously he feared for his mother's safety. After four years he was released—one of the few people in such a prison who was allowed to go to West Germany. He was labelled an 'unwanted element'. We have not heard from him since.

The only viable form of rebellion was a work slowdown. The East German government did not want to be dependent on western goods or raw materials, and boasted that the system was economically self-sufficient. But it doesn't take much intelligence to figure out that, in a country the size of East Germany with a population of 17 million, self-sufficiency is simply not achievable. Our economic ups and downs since 1949 are proof of that. A dictatorship seeking to control all areas of life cannot survive. The slowdowns at work were partly the result of individuals rebelling against the system. But they were also caused by shortages of materials.

The 'Beschaffungsproblem (difficulty in procuring everyday necessities, from fresh fruit to coffee) occupied up to 70 per cent of a working woman's free time. Nobody left the house in the morning without a string bag in her purse—just in case she heard of fresh groceries available somewhere in the town. You might, for instance, hear on the train to work that a load of fresh oranges had just been delivered to a certain store at the other end of the town. You had to decide between being on time to work and running the risk that after work no oranges would be left for you and your family, or being an hour or two late in order to secure a week's supply of oranges. I still have the habit of buying too much and hoarding it. I can't get used to the idea that I can always get whatever I want.

Sometimes we received parcels from relatives in West Germany. In the late 1960s all packages were opened at the border. Food, silk stockings, soap, chocolate and other items we could not get were often missing when the package finally came. Shortly after I married my husband, who held a sensitive position in a physics research and development facility, I was forced to sign a document that prohibited further contact with family members living in the west. Any form of contact with the west was feared. Gatherings of more than eight people—even small parties at home—had to be registered with the

police. Just sitting in a cafe could become a risky situation if someone at another table picked up from your conversation a word here
and there that was not 'party proven and safe'. After a night with a
group of friends you always asked yourself, did I say too much?
Should I trust my friends? Anyone who felt vulnerable or afraid was
likely to belong to the Stasi. Some were in it for the travel privileges
and hard currency. Still others were former Gestapo or SS members,
stupid people content to follow orders blindly.

I cannot fully explain why in autumn 1989 I felt emboldened to
say things I would not have dared to say just a few months before.
We knew perestroika had put pressure on the Honecker regime. On
the other hand, there were still those pictures of the 40th anniversary
in my mind, pictures of Honecker and Gorbachev hugging and kis-
sing. When the Hungarian border guards demolished the barricades
at the Austrian border, they unleashed a mass exodus comparable
only to the one that occurred shortly before the Wall was built.
Thousands of East German citizens took refuge in Austria, Germany
and other western European states.

The regime blamed the 78-year old Honecker's 'poor' health for
its decision to pass his 'duties' to Egon Krenz, his protégé. Krenz,
like countless SED members, feigned flexibility. For ten years he had
been responsible for state security. He had supervised the phony
elections in May 1989, and had congratulated the Chinese government for the massacre at Tiananmen Square. His idea of flexibility
was to allow talk shows on state media. And while 85 per cent of all
GDR citizens lived in assigned three-room apartments, Krenz lived
in an embassy villa just minutes away from Alexanderplatz.

But despite all this, I felt hopeful for the first time in my life.
Krenz remained a puzzle to most of us. Perhaps he too had merely
been playing along with the Honecker regime. It was hard to tell.
Krenz spoke of 'humanitarian socialism'. This was not a new idea.
Czechoslovakia had tried to end the rule of the communist techno-
crats, as had Hungary. Both movements were stopped by the Soviet
Union. We feared the same end. But we also knew that the USSR
had lost its status as a superpower, which until now had been the ce-
ment that held its satellite states in place.

Now, as we stood before the Wall together, everyone shouted,
'Tear the Wall down! Open the gates!' Everyone, that is, except one
man, old and weak, who shuffled along almost as if in trance. I later

learned that he had lost his job as a teacher ten years earlier, after refusing to join the SED. The Stasi had denounced him until no one would hire him except to shovel coal into a truck.

People carried posters and banners calling for 'free elections' and 'an end to Stalinism and 40 years of torment'. Far away, on the other side of the Wall, I saw several camera crews. A massive crowd of people had assembled in West Berlin, joining us in the east who had been demonstrating for days. The first rallies were in Leipzig a month earlier on 9 October; ever since, I had been glued to the TV and radio, listening to the West German stations that told about the hundreds of people already across the Hungarian border. Until the evening of 6 November, our own media never covered any of the uprisings. There had been no mention of the half million people demonstrating in Leipzig or the flood of East Germans to Austria.

The rush of East Berliners to the Brandenburg Gate was actually instigated by the turncoat regime of Krenz himself, who wanted to prove his 'openness' and commitment to a new political climate. Krenz had even allowed rallies of protestors demanding his immediate resignation to be shown live on East German TV. Then came the news of the much extended travel provisions. But there was confusion about those. Nobody wanted to take the responsibility for allowing East German citizens to travel. No one was prepared for the moment when, at about midnight, border soldiers opened the gates, terrified of what we might do to them when they were stripped of their menace. They began to assist people crossing to the west. Strangers embraced, laughing, crying. The word I heard over and over again, shouted out loud was: 'Wahnsinn' (ecstasy).

Until three or four o'clock that morning the Brandenburg Gate, the symbol of the German people, was open. Some people climbed onto the Wall to dance. Suddenly we were seeing the west for the first time, the forbidden Berlin we had only seen on TV or heard about from friends. When we came home at dawn, I felt free for the first time in my life. I had never been happier.

Wolf-Rüdiger Borchart

A friend of mine called me from London on the evening of 9 November to tell me he had just heard on the BBC that the Wall would be coming down. I first thought, what an odd canard coming from England. Then I remembered that horrible week the Wall went up in 1961. It was the second week in August. I had been studying architecture in Berlin, and decided to bike to the Baltic Sea for the weekend. My friend learned via the radio that the Ulbricht regime had sealed off the Soviet occupation zone. We immediately returned to Berlin. More than 150,000 East Germans had fled to the west, bringing the total number of refugees from communism since the end of the war to over 3 million. Why a Wall to stop the exodus? For the East German regime it was simply an economic necessity. I left for the west the day after the workmen began running barbed-wire barricades across the streets and through houses located along the route leading from the eastern to the western part of the city. The barrier, which would become the Berlin Wall, also circled Berlin. Minefields, watchtowers, machine gun positions, towers and spring gun constructions were added over the years. Public transportation between east and West was stopped except at a few checkpoints, probably the best-known being Checkpoint Charlie. Those were tightly policed. 'Unauthorized people' were returned to East Berlin.

Ulbricht succeeded in stopping the flow of people, though a few desperate souls risked death by crawling through barbed wire or jumping from the roofs of houses adjacent to the Wall. Later different routes were attempted. Some swam through minefields in the Elbe to reach the west. Others tried to escape in hot-air balloons. Most failed to make it to freedom, however, and perished.

Ulbricht said the Wall was necessary to halt infiltration by western spies who were planning an invasion. Pravda said the people had asked for the Wall. Though my mother and two brothers stayed in East Berlin, I had to leave to continue my architecture course at the University of Berlin (West). When I first applied, my graduation papers from the east had not been accepted and I had to earn a second degree in West Berlin, which took a full year. I was just 19 and more afraid of being unable to go freely back and forth than of leaving everything behind, including family. I borrowed the papers of a West German cousin, dyed my hair blond like his, and passed illegally through a transit point. Nobody seemed too interested in me or my phony papers, although many others did not get through.

After settling in West Berlin, I formed an underground network with friends. Our system worked pretty well until the autumn. Those of us with western papers would go to East Berlin and lend our own passports to others who wanted to get out. A third person would return the documents. It was fairly intricate. Soon the GDR changed the rules, issuing passports and day-passes with special marks visible only under infrared light. It was impossible for an amateur group like ours to get round that.

Now, with escape routes cut off, the SED really cracked down on dissidents. Slacking off on the job became a punishable crime. Also, for the first time the SED instituted conscription for the National People's Army. There was no longer any concern that a reluctant draftee would flee to the west. Those unwilling to bear arms were forced to serve in army construction units. Those who refused to wear a military uniform were imprisoned.

My younger brother Ingo, who had stayed with my mother, now had to get out before he was drafted into the People's Army. I secured forged papers for him, paying quite a large sum of money, and he escaped just in time. Throughout the 1960s and early 1970s the desperate escape attempts of East Germans made headlines around the world. Some spent years digging tunnels. Others threw themselves at the Wall and were filled with bullets. Such horrible scenes took a heavy toll in human misery.

My children wondered why, when we visited my family in East Berlin in the 1980s, the People's Police would always search the car when we returned to West Berlin. Once Jonathan asked the officer, 'Why are you poking into the petrol tank with a long stick? Do you think we'd drive with "bad" fuel?' The officer, of course, didn't answer. I decided to level with my son. I explained that the officer was checking to see if we had hidden anybody else in the car—for example, his uncle. Jonathan looked blankly at me and mused, 'But he would sit up front with you, not hide in the gas tank'.

Harald and Elke Zimmer

For years we kept a low profile, because I was one of the few people who owned a house and a shop. But shortly after the Monday demonstrations in Berlin and Leipzig we started to openly oppose the system. More and more people now found the courage to protest. The fall of the Wall was only the first step. We also wanted to take revenge on those who had tortured us for half a lifetime. More importantly, we believed that Germany should be one country again.

Every day the SED had to give in a little bit more. They knew that the eyes of the world were on them. They knew they could not, as in other times, rely on the Russian Red Army to brutally silence our demands. A little bit more each day we felt that the moment of truth had arrived. On 1 December 1989 the SED announced that it would remove from the constitution the paragraph naming it as the one and only legal governing party. The next day came the shocking revelation that Secretary of State Alexander Schalck-Golodkowski's firm, IMES, was in fact a weapons and ammunition depot, which we had suspected all along. The man was notorious for his extravagance. Like many party members he drove big cars, travelled frequently to the west and to the Crimea in the Soviet Union. Still, his corruption was mind-boggling.

What was also upsetting were the attempts of some easterners and westerners to make money out of the fallen symbol. Only hours after the Wall tumbled, crazy-minded people began to hammer at the Brandenburg Gate. I saw a young man hammering and hammering, not looking left or right, almost bewitched, and he was not the only one. Pieces of the Wall were traded on the Kurfürstendamm like fake jewellery New York's Fifth Avenue. Obviously, souvenir hunters couldn't tell whether the pieces they bought were from the wall or not. After a few months, even the old East German hard-liners realized there was money to be made by selling the 'protective wall' they once had erected. They set up Limex Bauland Export–Import which sold bits and pieces to Japan and the US, and one bit, I heard, went for over $500,000. It almost sounds as though the last corpses of East Germany are the hottest export items the country has to offer.

Lothar Loewe

I spent 9 November 1989 in Warsaw with West German Chancellor Helmut Kohl. A German delegation was visiting the Polish government and the press, myself among them, followed the events of the visit. I hadn't had time to listen to any news, since I was busy preparing a programme and interviews on Kohl's visit. I remember returning to my hotel to change for an evening event and listening with one ear to the news. I stared unbelievingly at the TV set when I saw people sitting on the Berlin Wall with champagne bottles in their hands. Kohl had planned a press conference after the official dinner. A bunch of press people had gathered several cases of champagne for the press conference, to celebrate the fall of the Wall. When Kohl entered the press centre, I could sense that he didn't feel comfortable appearing in front of the press that moment. I was among the first to ask questions addressing the events in Berlin. 'Chancellor, what is happening in Berlin today is a historic moment. We are just days away from the Christmas holidays and as the situation presents itself momentarily, this Christmas will be the first in a long time that Germans from both sides will be able to celebrate together. Do you have a special message for the German nation?' Kohl didn't say much. He almost ignored the question and mumbled something about Europeans celebrating the holidays in peace. I asked a further question, 'Chancellor, with all respect to the importance of your journey to Warsaw, wouldn't it be appropriate for you to leave Poland tonight to go to Berlin? Shouldn't the chancellor be in the middle of events at this historic moment?' He ignored the questions again. Kohl was in a difficult position. It was not yet clear how the Soviets or even the Polish government would react. Kohl had briefings all night and then left the following morning for Bonn and Berlin. I took an early morning flight to Berlin as well. It was 10 November, and after landing I immediately walked to the Brandenburg Gate and the former border crossing, Invalidenstrasse. Some of the East German border soldiers recognized and greeted me, 'Hello, Mr Loewe, nice seeing you again.' They all smiled. The dream of my life had really come true. The city I had grown up in was free and open again. I walked back and forth several times across the former border. It was a fantastic feeling. I bumped into three dentists from the East who had driven through the night to come to Berlin. It was their first time in the West and they didn't know their way around. They sat squeezed into their Trabi car, rolling with a thousand other eastern cars through the streets of Berlin. For days Berlin was one enormous traffic jam. In the following days I bought street maps that I passed out to strangers who looked like they were lost. To a family with little children I gave 100 German marks. The majority of easterners coming to Berlin within the first days after the Wall fell didn't have any western money. Some of the stores in West Berlin just started to pass out drinks or hot dogs to them. It was amazing to see how people who didn't know each other just came together because their nation was one again.

A year later—in October 1990, the day of the official reunification—I was in Dresden. There were fireworks bigger and more impressive than any I have ever seen on New Year's eve. People ran around in the streets in coolish October weather with bottles of champagne in their hands, embracing each other. Everybody celebrated so vigorously that the next morning all the streets were empty. I got into my car to drive back to Berlin for a welcome celebration for the German Admiral Wellershof at the airport, Tempelhof. That drive on a clear blue day was a very emotional experience for me. Remnants of the border crossings and the Wall were still present, evidence of the last decades of a separated country; but there were no more soldiers around; the minefields had been cleaned up and the barricades and wires had been partially dismantled. For the first time, it was clear to me that Germany was one again, reaching from Dresden to Flensburg in the north and from Frankfurt-on-Oder to Aachen. After a two-hour drive I got to Tempelhof. American, Russian, British and French admirals were present. Then, for the first time in 43 years, a German aircraft, a helicopter, approached the airport from the distance with Admiral Wellershof aboard. I remember the American Airport commander greeting Wellershof with the words 'I welcome you to the free German city of Berlin'.

Chapter Eighteen

Who is Mr Krenz?

On 18 October 1989, eleven days after Erich Honecker had celebrated the 40th anniversary of the GDR, he was ousted. Health reasons were given for his resignation. The end of the Honecker regime was what many called a revolution in the East German communist palace.

Egon Krenz, a protege of Honecker, became his successor and sought to cast himself as a born-again reformer heading an internal revival of the Communist Party. He promised reforms similar to those that Gorbachev had introduced in the Soviet Union. Indeed, just hours after it was announced that he would take Honecker's position, Krenz appeared on talk shows that were broadcast on East German TV promising political and economic changes. But East Germans did not forget that Krenz not only was closely identified with Honecker, but also was responsible for ordering violent police actions against protesters and for praising China for sending tanks against student demonstrators. In a desperate attempt to regain legitimacy in the eyes of the doubting population, Krenz adopted western-style openness with both citizens and the press.

Krenz and others had clung to the idea that if only they could distance themselves from the discredited leadership of Honecker, they could retain control over the government. And although Krenz was born in a Baltic town in an area which is now Poland and had dedicated his life to the party apparatus, at first glance he even impressed aides around West German Chancellor Kohl, who argued that Krenz probably would be open to fundamental changes. But the East German citizens knew better and doubted his intention to be a true reformer.

The demonstrations for reform continued under Krenz. Every Monday more people showed up for the traditional demonstrations in Leipzig and Berlin. Having been lied to for over 40 years, they finally demanded that some promises be kept. Increasingly, demonstrators asked for the resignation of Krenz, who promised but did not deliver. The public power and the party's reformist wing around Hans Modrow, Party Secretary of Dresden, were too strong. Modrow himself scrambled to save a place in a more democratic system by disassembling the party and unloading the heavy baggage of politicians associated with the Honecker regime. On 3 December 1989, six weeks after his election, the 52-year-old Krenz was forced by public pressure to resign, and with him other members of the Politburo. Krenz's removal had become one of the rallying cries in a wave of anti-government sentiment sparked largely by revelations of abuse of power and financial mismanagement. Günter Mittag, the country's economic czar, and Harry Tisch, chief of the Communist Trade Union Federation—both Politburo members—were arrested for heavily damaging 'socialist' property and the economy through abuse of power. They were accused of, among other things, squirrelling away $54 billion of hard currency in Swiss bank accounts.

The collapse of communist authority left a large power vacuum, which many East Germans clearly hoped to fill with democratic structures. Modrow became the interim leader who wanted East Germany to remain independent of its more prosperous neighbour. Only a handful of people had started to talk about a possible reunification of the two Germanies.

Wolfgang Mischnick

Until the end of the 1980s, Honecker and his surrounding party members tried to prohibit Gorbachev's glasnost and perestroika as much as possible. The reform process that already had begun in Hungary and Poland had been kept away from the GDR. Although Honecker agreed to ease restrictions on travel to the west, no sign of other reforms emerbed before 1989. His cultural politics, the pre-eminent role of the party, the election system as well as the dissident role of the church remained unchanged.

While Hungarian border police took down watch towers and machine guns, East German police were still shooting. Honecker even declared at the beginning of January 1989 that the Wall would stay in place for least another 50 or 100 years.

Yet the events in the countries surrounding the GDR didn't leave any doubt in my mind that sooner or later reforms would also come to it, and with them the opportunity to improve relationship between the two Germanies. The obvious economic and technological problems would provide the initial impetus even though East Germany was still doing better than the Soviet Union or Poland. As in all communist-ruled countries, economic reform could not be realized without involving the whole system: the participation of the population at the political and social levels improved civil rights and the free flow of information, and a more tolerant attitude towards the role of the churches had to follow.

Also, for the first time in communist history a reform process became a chain reaction through east European countries. The GDR leadership increasingly felt the pressure. Thanks to glasnost and perestroika, the East German people began to act more openly and freely, asking for rights they never had dared to ask for earlier. And all the pressures were focused on the ageing men surrounding Honecker: Honecker and chief ideologist Kurt Hager were both 77; Ministerpresident Willi Stoph was 75; Hermann Axen, who was responsible for international affairs, was 73; and security chief and head of the Politburo Erich Mielke was 81.

Today it is known that Gorbachev pressured Honecker to select a successor during his visit for the 40th anniversary of the GDR. As we also know now, during his visit to East Berlin Gorbachev had sent messages to the local Warsaw Pact commander to force Honecker to withdraw. Gorbachev and Krenz had been personal friends for quite some time, as were Honecker and Krenz, so the choice of Krenz as Honecker's successor didn't come as a surprise. Gorbachev's longstanding personal relationship with Krenz had led to a certain amount of trust. Gorbachev's traditional way of doing politics was to select a couple of people whom he regarded highly and could listen to. He wanted Krenz to become his source of information and the opinion-shaper of the GDR.

For Gorbachev, the GDR was something like a trump card, something I believe he eventually wanted to play. There is no question that he thought the average East German was much more socialist than was in fact the case and that he thus believed East Germany would be the last domino to fall. What came as a surprise to the party hard-liners was that Krenz was unable to fulfil his dual role of representing the party on one hand and appeasing the East German population on the other.

Everything happened very quickly after Honecker and the whole Politburo stepped down two days before the Wall fell. Just ten days later, the East German population experienced another satisfying event: the new party leader, Hans Modrow, promised political and economic reforms and better relations with West Germany.

The developments during the last months and weeks before the

Wall fell were extremely quick. Still, in May 1989 I had planned to hold a seminar in Dresden on the politics and economy of the co-existence of two Germanies. It was the first seminar I had planned since the early 1970s. Two weeks before the deadline in May, I received an official letter from the Politburo that I was not to come to the seminar. At the time, I suspected that inner political difficulties as well as the increasing pressure resulting from Gorbachev's glasnost had caused the cancellation. The seminar, by the way, was given a month after the Wall came down; I changed the theme of the seminar to 'Opportunities of a common German economy'.

Between May and September, the wave of protests within East Germany and the number of refugees who had come to Hungary had increased daily. While part of our government was dealing with the Hungarian refugee question, a group of government members and I met with Krenz in autumn. While we were discussing the arrests that were taking place of protesters, Krenz suddenly indicated, almost out of context, that soon we could expect the announcement of travel easements for all citizens. I had listened to similar promises many times before and asked him, 'When, Mr Krenz, when? What time period are you thinking of? A year?' He answered, 'No, no, people like to plan and I think it should be announced during the Christmas period'. Krenz apparently wanted to ease some of the pressures that greeted him when he had taken over as Honecker's successor.

After the discussion we were both invited to a talk show broadcast in the GDR. Krenz's media friendliness was a new personal touch he had added to convince his population that changes were really under way. During the TV show he didn't mention any commitments concerning the changes which he had hinted at to ease travel. Before we parted after the show, Krenz accompanied me to a waiting group of reporters in front of the building, a gesture that was uncommon among SED members, who usually shied away from journalists--particularly those from West Germany. Krenz must have had the feeling that what he had said during the talk show was not enough to appease either the demonstrators or the nagging questions of the media. Faced with the reporters from around the world, he announced that within days GDR citizens would be allowed to travel whenever and wherever they wanted. The news was a turning point in events whose ultimate results were still uncertain at that time. One journalist asked if he really had heard correctly that the travel restrictions would be lifted. Krenz answered, 'Yes.' He still believed at that time that his decision to lift the ban would help to save his position within the party; he wasn't aware that he had just provided the means for a totally new democratic development in the east.

But the protests against Krenz didn't stop in the streets of Leipzig and Berlin. People perceived him correctly as a typical turncoat, adapting quickly to whatever political attitude was in vogue. People were carrying signs and shouting such phrases as, 'Krenz, we are your competition! Who lied once will lie again.'

Two weeks after the borders had been opened, over 2.5 million people from the east had visited friends and families in the west, getting their first personal impressions of the world on the other side of the fence. As the easterners started to get a picture of the west, westerners also started to understand the realities of the east. Horrible environmental sins became evident, as did an economic situation that was worse than ever imagined and unheard-of political circumstances. Within days, a majority of people polled in East and West Germany had come to the conclusion that the only way to end the misery and to normalize relationships between the two halves of the divided fatherland would be reunification. On 28 November, West German Chancellor Helmut Kohl introduced the 'ten-point plan' in which he suggested a confederated structure of both Germanies under the condition that the east would be governed by a democratically elected government. At the end of his speech Kohl said, 'What a reunified Germany will look like, nobody knows today. If the people in Germany want the reunification, I don't doubt it will come.' Three days later, on 1 December, the SED declared that it would no longer be the only governing party in the GDR. On 3 December, Krenz and the Politburo withdrew from their positions and within hours Honecker and 12 other high-ranking politicians were expelled from the party. On 6 December, the LDPD (the liberal sister party of the SED) replaced Krenz with chairman Gerlach, who announced an immediate amnesty for over 15,000 political prisoners.

Harald and Elke Zimmer

We knew from the beginning that Egon Krenz was a phony. The unbelievable results of the quick community elections, with 99.85

per cent of the votes selecting him, made it even more obvious that he was a typical chameleon. His children used to live just across the street from us. We would see them working on their house, using products and tools impossible to find in East Berlin at that time. Shipments from West German catalogue companies arrived almost daily. One morning Krenz's little granddaughter stopped by to talk to my wife, who was busy in the garden. She was about six, a sweet little girl. She said to Elke, 'You have a nice house, but you won't be living in it much longer'.

We knew immediately what that meant. According to GDR law, anyone could be forced to vacate his home if a higher-ranking SED politician fancied it. The buyer determined the price. Usually you were moved to a much smaller apartment far away. I was furious— but helpless. All the skill and labour I had put into the house to fix it up to our liking would be lost simply because a Stasi coveted the place I proudly called my own. Well, in the end the short career of Mr Krenz as general secretary allowed us to keep our house.

My wife's aunt wasn't so lucky. She inherited from her grand-mother a collection of antique dolls, which she built into one of the finest collections of its kind in Europe. About a year before the Wall fell, she got a phone call about her taxes, followed by a letter inform-ing her that the tax authorities would be coming for an audit. As she earned little, she was suspicious, but by then it was too late. The 'tax authorities' walked through the apartment, looking not at the tax papers but at the dolls. A day later a big van pulled up in front of her house and she was handed a letter saying that her taxes hadn't been paid and as collateral her dolls had to be confiscated. My aunt over-heard one of the men saying that this 'shipment' would go to an auc-tion house in Cologne. I found out months later that our fine Secretary of State, Alexander Schalck-Golodkowski, was an art and doll collector. He probably kept some dolls he liked and sold the rest to the auction house.

Wulf Rothenbächer

East Germany slipped deeper into political chaos as ousted Commu-nist Party boss Egon Krenz gave up the ceremonial post of the presi-dency. The Communist Party had underscored the urgency of the need to react to the people's demand for democracy, but even advancing the date for a party congress couldn't help anymore. The promises announced through the government-owned press agency ADN—according to which the party would be radically reformed into a modern party committed to democratic socialism—came too late as a last-ditch effort. The most visible target of the public was Krenz who, dogged by his cosy relation with Honecker and a reputation as a hard-liner, was rightly not able to regain the trust of the citizens.

In the beginning some GDR citizens may have been puzzled over Krenz's intentions, since at first he appeared to be a copy of Gorbachev, willing to push reforms through. His tendency towards openness particularly impressed some West Germans. But the other side of Krenz was too well-known to be ignored. Krenz may have projected a smooth image, but soon almost everybody doubted that he was a real reformer. Even if he were, he would have had very limited room to manoeuvre within the Communist Party's ruling Politburo. The Communist Party even hoped that chastising some scapegoats—such as Harry Tisch, Günter Mittag or Alexander Schalck-Golodkowski—for their horrible mismanagement would make the party more believable.

Suddenly it seemed that the mood within the Communist Party had changed, and everybody, including the party's voice, the newspaper *Neues Deutschland*, was trying to salvage tarnished reputations by commenting, 'This is all the more painful and incomprehensible in that these people for decades handed out to others the bread of poverty'. It was clear that many tried to save themselves by pretending to have opposed the party for a long time. Soon the word 'turncoat' could be heard everywhere, and it appeared in all the headlines of western newspapers.

I travelled to Berlin on 22 December. A long-awaited dream became reality, the Brandenburg Gate had been opened for good. For 28 years it had been the symbol of the German division. Now it was the scene of German reunification.

Part Five

Do the Two Germanies Share the Same Planet? Spring 1990

Greatness is a road leading towards the unknown.
Charles de Gaulle

Chapter Nineteen

Smoother Than We Thought

Just a month after the Wall had fallen, there was a remarkable change in the public mood among East Germans. The wording on posters changed from 'We are the people' to 'We are one people'. The initial reason for the rallies to reform the GDR had quickly been replaced by the goal of re-uniting the two Germanies.

The people of East Germany were not satisfied with the promises by their rulers—Egon Krenz and Hans Modrow, the SED's nominee for prime minister—to reform the GDR politically and economically. A few weeks earlier, East Germans and westerners alike would have applauded speeches such as the one Modrow gave at his inauguration on 17 November, in which he promised to 'assume a closer relationship with the European Community, and to work towards a cooperative coexistence'with the FDR.[1] The Central Committee's 'action programme' called for free elections and media freedom and promised an overhaul of the collapsing economy. But Krenz and his comrades had greatly under-estimated East Germans' acquired mistrust of political promises which had not been kept for the past four decades, just as they failed to realize that the citizens' outrage was no longer limited solely to the domestic situation. For all those who had been silent opponents of the regime, it was time to put an end not just to that but to the GDR as a whole. Although within a week Krenz had sacked the cabinet, shuffled the Politburo and promised reforms, to the majority of East Germans he was nothing but a puppet of the old regime, a hard-liner trying to survive. During the Monday demonstrations, which by that time were known worldwide, the East German flag with the hammer and compass in the middle was replaced by the West German flag of black, red and gold. Voices were shouting, 'Germany, united fatherland'. One heard not only cries for freedom, but also demands for unity. Chancellor Kohl's reply was a ten-point plan which he presented on 28 November 1989, taking the initiative in providing a cautious framework for reunification. The reunification of one Germany was under way.

---

[1] *Neues Deutschland*, 18 November 1989.

Within a few days, all political parties in both Germanies, as well as all neighbours and Allies, had formulated their own ideas about which path should be taken. For the people in East Germany, only one thing was clear: reunification had to come quickly. The lengthy realization of a multilevel confederation plan or a step-by-step ten-point plan was not what they were hoping for. People were leaving the east by the thousands daily. The SED still held all the power in its hands, but it had lost authority. Modrow had put together a coalition government that nobody really wanted or listened to. Bonn was ready to pump aid into East Germany, but refused to do so until free elections were held. In the face of the GDR's total collapse, elections originally scheduled for May were advanced to 18 March; these were the first free and democratic elections for East Germans since 1933. The old SED party presented itself in new clothes as the reformed Partei des Demokratischen Socialismus (Party of Democratic Socialism—PDS) and hoped to profit from the rescheduling of the elections, since none of the smaller parties formed by the opposition had been able to formulate a clear programme. With the exception of Neues Forum and Bündnis 90, small parties that campaigned for an independent East Germany, all other parties, Free Democratic Party (FDP), Christian Democratic Union and the Socialist Party of Germany, were carbon copies of their western counterparts. The socialists had formed the SPD just before the Wall fell and had merged with the sister party from the west. The same happened with the liberal FDP. The situation was more complicated for the Christian Democrats, who over the years had served as a 'front' party for the SED. With Lothar de Maizière, an attorney from Thuringia, it was able to revamp itself and clear its tarnished image with the East German population.

The star speakers at the campaign rallies were mainly experienced politicians from the west. Kohl, Brandt and Genscher were not only more familiar faces than the parties' new local leaders, but they also were politicians who, in the eyes of the people of East Germany, symbolized the hope for freedom and democracy. Polls taken shortly before the election seemed to indicate that the SPD would be the clear winner. Surprisingly, the newspaper headlines on the morning after the election read differently.

The Christian Democrat, de Maizière, had won with 48.15 per cent of the vote. The Social Democrats were placed second with 21.84 per cent of all votes while Bündnis 90 and Neues Forum together obtained merely 2.9 per cent. Even though de Maizière seemed the clear winner, it was Kohl and his party's reunification plan that people had been voting for. The majority of voters were attracted to the chancellor because he was most inclined, and best situated politically, to force through such difficult steps as unifying currency and removing the remaining Allied constraints on Germany's sovereignty. De Maizière, by being elected prime minister, had also received a clear mandate—to start negotiations for unification with the four Allied powers and his West German counterparts. In other words, his main task was to prepare for his own disappearance.

Kohl himself had done his homework well. By February he had already met with Mikhail Gorbachev in Moscow to rewrite history and assure the Soviets' agreement to a unified Germany. A very moved chancellor announced on 10 February from Moscow that the Soviets had given up on resisting unification. The chancellor ended his statement by saying, 'It's a very happy day for Germany and for me personally.'[2]

Kohl was eager to press ahead with full reunification, since national elections were to be held in December 1990. The first hurdle was to create a single currency for the two Germanies, a step that seemed essential to any kind of economic recovery.It was clear that unity would come, but how it would come was still a big question mark. The Basic Law still governed the Länder of Baden–Wüttemberg, Bavaria, Bremen, Hamburg, Hesse, Lower Saxony, North Rhine–Westphalia, Rhineland–Palatinate, Saarland, Schleswig–Holstein and West Berlin. The law would be binding in other parts of Germany as soon as they acceded to the Federal Republic under Article 23 of the West German constitution. Another option was thought to be made possible by Article 146, which said that a new constitution could replace the Basic Law if the German people were to decide to do so in a referendum.

The parties began to argue almost immediately. Minister of the Interior Dr Wolfgang Schäuble argued for taking the fastest and most elegant route to reunification, according to Article 23. That would require making additions to the Basic Law before the two Germanies could formally reunite at midnight on 2 October. Socialist law did not recognize private ownership of property and protected tenants differently than did laws in the west; abortion rights were much more lenient in the east than in the west. There was some question as to whether any of the 'old GDR identity' was worth including. Should the treaty retain *any* of the legal system, education, welfare or local government created by a tyrannical system? The prewar Länder, which had been abolished by the communists in 1952, were re-established. The five new 'Länder' corresponded with former kingdoms, dukedoms or provinces. Saxony, like Bavaria, had been a kingdom until 1918, as had Thuringia and Mecklenburg–West Pommerania. All, including Brandenburg and Saxony–Anhalt, had their almost-forgotten traditions that they started to rediscover.

---

[2] Chancellor Kohl and Foreign Minister Genscher met with Gorbachev in Moscow on 11 February 1990.

Though US Secretary of State James Baker, French President François Mitterrand and EC Commissioner Jacques Delors strongly supported unity under Article 23, the Soviets threw in another problem that delayed quick success. They demanded that a united Germany be militarily neutral. Obviously, Gorbachev's yes to unity had not come without strings attached. For the majority of Germans, neutrality was unthinkable. Germany could only be a safe haven if it were reunified as a member of NATO. Yet a vigorous debate started within the German parties as to which action to take. Gorbachev, obviously amused by the ring of fire he had started with his request for a neutral Germany, remarked jeeringly during a televised interview that the problem could be solved easily if the Germans would just enter the Warsaw Pact.

West German Foreign Minister Hans-Dietrich Genscher brought the solution to the table with his formula, two plus four. 'Two' referred to the two Germanies, and 'Four' meant the four former Allies. The Soviets had proposed a four-plus-two formula that would have put international questions ahead of issues related to German reunification. Genscher successfully turned the formula around and even found a solution to the question of Germany's military alliance. Germany was to belong to NATO, but NATO troops could only be stationed on former West German territory. Throughout the European press, Genscher was praised as the man who had achieved a 'European Yes' to Germany's reunification. US Secretary of State James Baker let the Germans know in an interview with the German press, 'This is Germany's reunification; tell us when and how, we'll support it.'

On 3 October a little more than a year after the Wall had tumbled down, and subsequent to the economic unity that had been achieved on 1 July, the political reunification was formally celebrated in Berlin. At midnight, a young German hoisted the black, red and gold flag in front of the Reichstag building in Berlin as several hundred thousand people watched. De Maizière, who would step down and be replaced by Chancellor Kohl as a result of the first all-German elections on 3 December, announced that 'The German unity is not concluded by the joining of the two Germanies. This will remain a common task for all Germans. This is not only a material question, but also a question of practical and mutual solidarity. Unity will not only have to be paid for, but it also has to be wanted within the hearts of all Germans.'[3]

---

[3] *Frankfurter Allgemeine*, 4 October 1990.

Wolfgang Schäuble

The main task of the authors of the Reunification Treaty was to find a way to introduce West German law to the new Länder in the east. Originally, when the West German government got what was then a conditional go-ahead from Moscow, members pondered various schemes for a contractual community established through a network of treaties and confederate structures between the two Germanies. Soon, however, in spring 1990, it became clear that a political unification was the only desirable solution.

To understand and appreciate the treaty that led to unification, it is important to look at the conditions under which the treaty was drafted. The treaty reflects the historical uniqueness of the moment as well as the problems that were inevitable in a country being reunited after over 40 years of separation. How do you rejoin parts of a country after one part has been ruled by totalitarian socialism and the other by democracy, democratic law and a social market economy? How can similar lifestyles be obtained in both parts?

There are three main issues that one must consider to begin understanding the Reunification Treaty from a historical perspective: first, a very short time elapsed between the fall of the Wall and developments within the former GDR resulting in demands for unity; the treaty was drafted under great pressure of time. The second issue concerns the fact that after autumn 1989 the former GDR went through what I sometimes call an 'unfinished revolution'. And third, one must look at the results reunification had on Germany's foreign policy, such as the two-plus-four talks as well as on the EC.

Some people have accused Chancellor Kohl and his government of rushing reunification and selfishly supporting developments leading to the formulation of the treaty. I think the people in the east who didn't want to wait any longer for democracy were the only ones rushing and demanding action. The fall of the Wall had started a chain reaction that could not be stopped. The thousands of people who poured into the west every day were probably the best sign that a slow reunification of the two Germanies was impossible without risking instability in both parts of the country.

When I speak of an unfinished revolution, I refer to the fact that, parallel to the demonstrations in Leipzig and East Berlin, Honecker was replaced by Modrow. Those events led finally to the first

Germany-wide free elections in March 1990 from which Lothar de Maizière emerged as the winner. But unlike other revolutions, this one did not undo or put on trial 'the illegal actions of the GDR'. During the 'Wende' (turn), the constitution of the GDR was never totally replaced; only in certain circumstances were former regulations newly formulated. Not 'finishing' this revolution was probably the only way to ensure its bloodless and fortunate outcome. Many people have already forgotten that while the demonstrations were taking place, over 400,000 soldiers of the Red Army were present.

Another fact that must be explained in order to understand the reunification is that it was based on Article 23 of the West German Basic Law. This meant that the GDR would gain access directly to the Federal Republic in conjunction with the reconstitution of the five Länder which had been abolished in 1952. East Germany's joining under Article 23 ended a series of arguments that had taken place both in East Germany and, to a lesser extent, in the west. The issues were whether unification might instead be achieved through the convocation of a new Constitutional Assembly, and whether at the moment of reunification West German law should immediately govern the east, as opposed to a step-by-step adaptation to western laws. I argued strongly for a step-by-step, evolutionary adaptation, on the ground that the immediate and total replacement of the East German legal system would create a heavy burden on and shock in the former GDR. The argument for immediately replacing the whole legal system was that it would create confidence among western investors who might be interested in making substantial investments in the east. I think the discussion about which way to go was in the end also decided by the demands implicit in the slogan, 'We are one people'. One people with one and the same law.

It was necessary to make some exceptions to the rules, meaning that a number of areas would be covered by law that did not coincide with the West German Basic Law. Among those exceptions were issues ranging from abortion rights to the permitted alcohol level for drivers. Abortion was a particularly stormy issue; the former GDR allowed free abortion until the 13th week of pregnancy, while in West Germany the timing was much more restricted. After a long debate in Bonn and discussion between the two German delegations, the negotiators finally agreed that, for a transitional period, each part of Germany would keep its own 'ruling', pending drafting of a new law. Many such compromises were required to accomplish the goal of reunification.

The treaty itself was formulated quickly, despite very complicated conditions, including two delegations that were widely known to have brought very different ideas to the table.

We met regularly, sometimes until dawn, in East Berlin in the building of the ministerpresident. I remember well the time a delegation of 30 people from the west met the delegation from the GDR for the very first time. That was a moving moment for me; even amidst all the stress and pressure of work, I felt the beat of the clock and sensed the importance of that historic moment. With all the legal complications, disagreements and arguments over political issues, exhaustion was a constant companion for the people debating and drafting this unique document. Up until just six or seven hours before the treaty was to be formally signed at 12:30 p.m. on 18 May 1990 in the Kronprinzenpalais in Berlin. None of us had slept for days and we were physically exhausted, yet we shared a feeling of great accomplishment.

The most difficult issues in the treaty involved property rights, what to do with the almost 2 million people who worked in the public sector under the old regime, and questions concerning the Stasi. We touched on the property rights issue when we put the currency union together in June 1990, and additional legislation has made step-by-step improvements. Of 2 million people who worked in the public sector, 700,000 were let go by 1991. But rebuilding government in the east was not only a quantitative problem concerning the vast number of people who were employed by the former GDR's bureaucracy, but also a qualitative concern. The job descriptions for government employees in the east and west do not correspond at all. It was necessary to find people in the west who were willing to give up their jobs to go east, and at the same time to retain qualified government employees in the east.

Obviously, questions about the political past of many of those ex-GDR government employees play an important role in attempts to integrate the two Germanies. It is a two-edged sword. We in the west must be very careful not to generalize and blame people for 'aligning themselves' with a system they knew they had to live with and, for all they knew, might never end. On the other hand, citizens of the former East Germany have been hurt by many of those who represented the system, who spied for the regime. These citizens are understandably appalled when a representative of the old regime now represents the West German government, wearing a different uniform. Recognizing this problem, we included in the treaty a regulation that gives every employer the option of firing a former member of the Stasi if the work relationship becomes a burden for the employer. People from the public sector can also be fired if they are found morally unfit for their jobs. Many such cases have occurred when party members occupied high-ranking positions in organizations of the public sector. Yet there are difficult decisions. What does a minister of the interior do, for example, if his police force consists entirely of former members of the 'weapon-carrying organization', but he can guarantee stability and security only by keeping that police force on hand?

Generally speaking, the treaty tried to consider all different scenarios. A full and complete judgement of its quality may be possible only by the next generation. But I believe that the treaty provides a fundamental element of the new unity as well as a basis for restoring the environment, reconstructing buildings and rebuilding the infrastructure. The treaty has created conditions that I hope will soon produce similar standards of living in east and West Germany. Although the treaty was put together under heavy pressure of time, so far only three lawsuits have been filed, two of them concerning service in the public sector. I strongly believe the path we chose to unity was the only path we *could* have chosen. It is a path fraught with many obstacles, fears and difficulties. The price all of us are paying is high, but not too high if one considers that, with the fall of the Wall, the Iron Curtain fell as well and the east–west conflict has come to an end. Germans in the east and west lived through very different developments during the last 40 years. As long as many in the east could only compare their standard of living with the conditions in other eastern European countries, they were satisfied. Now, the only comparisons are with West Germany's standards. A chance to relive what has been missed has started, and patience is a word that is not used too often. Without doubt we are asking a lot from the people in the east—flexibility and willingness to change. Those two qualities are also needed in the west.

Donald Koblitz

The American delegation under George Bush and James Baker set the tone in the two-plus-four talks from very early on. They were not only in favour of the German reunification, but they also wanted it as soon as possible in terms of acceptance into West Germany. Nevertheless, there were concerns. Adding the two Germanies together was a big controversial issue in the beginning even with members of the US Congress, who raised the question as to what degree the USA would benefit from a reunited Germany. From Washington's standpoint we also had legitimate concerns, genuine concerns that the Kohl administration would be so anxious to be unified that they would agree to unreasonable demands from the Soviets such as the neutralization of Germany. The European Allies, the French and the British, interpreted a reunited Germany as a threat, an overwhelming economic force in the European economy which would have an unfavourable influence on the French franc and the British pound. The British opposed any type of reunification of Germany in the beginning.

The integration of a reunified Germany into Europe, the economic, political and defence question which arose with the topic were initially looked upon very skeptically. Many European politicians, among them Margaret Thatcher, argued that a rapid reunification would bring a period of instability to western Europe. She demanded an international framework which would make the reunification of Germany possible. François Mitterrand, on the other hand, argued that a reunified Germany would be of importance, but would really be no different. So why the rush? Under pressure, German Foreign Minister Hans-Dietrich Genscher came up with the formula of two-plus-four in February 1990. The only issues to be debated at the negotiations were the German external affairs which were influenced by the reunification. Internal affairs were to be covered by the German Basic Treaty.

Looking back, reunification of Germany seemed natural, but in its details and negotiations the two-plus-four talks were intense and tough. The negotiations took place on at least two to three levels. The presidential and ministerial level exchange, which tended to set the context, sometimes decided major issues. The next level down were ministerial meetings to which each country sent its ministers during which agonizing over each and every sentence and word became a daily chore. And then there was the third tier, the staff level which was headed by the United States. Secretary James Baker ran most of the under-secretary meetings between all six parties involved. They were represented by Baker and a state secretary of Bonn, East Berlin, Paris, London and Moscow. During those six or seven meetings there was a lot of back and forth even on the issue of should Germany be reunited at all. When Chancellor Kohl reached the agreement to the Germany treaty between the two Germanies, our negotiations also took a turn. We came under a lot of time pressure to produce. I think only then all of us involved became aware of the historical importance of the negotiations. I had seen a fair amount of meetings in Berlin, but nothing on that level. Many of us were thoroughly exhausted during the negotiations. The travelling back and forth was exhausting—more so the endless meetings, discussing clauses with Russian negotiators who tried to niggle on every issue, important or insignificant.

What the two-plus-four agreement was meant to do was to cut away all of the baggage, the inheritance of limitation on Germany, and to make the Soviets feel that they are part of it. I consider the whole process a great triumph. Two-plus-four was simply a sort of symbolic crown on the process that had became fairly inevitable; because two-plus-four ended up being somewhat of a symbolic act, it is hard to say outright if things should have been done differently. The treaty that has more consequences not only historically but also in terms of individual people's lives is really the reunification treaty.

Once the basic trend was clear that the two Germanies would be reunited the Soviet demand for the neutralization of Germany appeared on to the table. In the end, we agreed that no NATO troops would be stationed on the territory of the former GDR. The neutralization of Germany would have been an unacceptable price to pay for the western former Allies. I think the Kohl administration might have been ready to pay the price, not the former Allies.

In retrospect what seemed so critical in 1989 and 1990 has vanished from the table. There is no longer a Warsaw Pact. We have different threats in Europe, the treat of civil war, and NATO has the challenge of being a useful administrator.

After the reunification, Germany's role changed. I don't share a lot of sympathy for the Cold-War Berlin nostalgia which has been a trend in the city. Reunification changed Germany from the one of three or four very important powers for the United States to the most important. I think when you look at the political influences in the world, one must also say Germany is probably number two now. It should be the Japanese, but they don't exercise the political power.Germany is not ready for the new role and it would be frightening if they were. Germans are criticized for not participating more in NATO and the UN, but they have their own burden of history, and they will not shake that off soon.

Robert W. Becker

In 1990 nobody was sure how long the transition between the fallen system and the re-establishment of a democratic system in the former GDR would take. Kohl was still talking about a kind of coalition or confederation for five years, which would then result in a possible reunification. The goal changed rapidly when the March elections were advanced and political parties were founded. During that time, in early spring 1990, one could feel an excitement and enthusiasm and dedication among the people in the east as well as in the west. I also felt even then an immediate and growing awareness that times ahead would be harder. At that time, I wasn't really struck with how run down the place was. The attitude of the people impressed me most. Many people had been influenced by the hostile propaganda and educational system, which under the GDR regime didn't represent the USA in its best light. Nevertheless, a great number of people came up to me confessing that they had always looked to the United States as a beacon of hope. They were very open to say so. I had people coming up to me saying, 'we want to thank you, Mr Becker, as a representative of the USA, for all you have done'. I said, 'I don't understand, thank me for what?' I was told that they thanked me for the Marshall Plan, for overcoming the Berlin blockade, for the support of human rights, and for the support of German reunification. And I asked, 'But did you experience, did you take part in all of that?' The reply was, 'Oh, yes, we did. That was our hope for the future.' It was very moving.

After the initial excitement there came frustration, particularly among the easterners. I can't characterize the entire people, but most of those I have been talking to went through kinds of curves, emotional peaks and valleys. The valleys came with the monetary union, which had a very depressing effect on people's emotions. They were of course excited to get the Deutsche Mark, they were excited to be able to buy goods, but the monetary union was 'western'. By summer 1990, easterners started to feel they were losing control. They had a growing awareness that reunification wasn't going to quite take the form that some people had hoped for. The hope was for greater participation, just like in the Round Table discussion. Probably two-thirds of the people were just glad that the unification process was underway, but the other third were disappointed. This one-third had the greatest time of their life from November 1989 until the monetary union; during that period, many said, there was an unfettered expression of thoughts and a flowering of new ideas for all sorts of new forms of government structures. It was a very creative and spontaneous time. Later, these same people from the grassroots felt left out. People in the east wanted a round table type of town meeting, a participatory democracy—which is great at the small local level, but becomes impossible as size and progress move forward. With freedom of movement and the west offering tremendous economic opportunities, it was clear that the east would have been deserted very quickly without a rapid change to a stable political system. Toying with new governmental structures was a wonderful dream, but simply an unrealistic hope. The reunification treaty was the only feasible solution. It was negotiated by a democratically elected government, but one that was under tremendous pressure. Reunification was carried out properly, correctly, and to the best of everybody's abilities.

People tend to forget how delicate the discussions were on the two-plus-four talks. The results of the reunification treaty and the two-plus-four talks were in reality the best of all possible worlds. The participating parties, Chancellor Kohl, President Bush, Secretary Baker and Foreign Minister Shevardnadze, showed great leadership and courage and vision. It was one of those wonderful moments in history when co-operation worked.

Chapter Twenty

Revolutionaries Left Behind

They were called the children of the silent revolution. They served time in prison and feared the Stasi, but they were courageous and determined to obtain freedom and democratic changes within their nation, not only for themselves, but also for everybody. They were the first ones to shout 'Stasi raus' (Stasi out) during demonstrations. They mobilized thousands of people to demonstrate and led the crowds in the streets of Leipzig and Berlin.

Now, the veterans of the revolution are still activists, but they no longer send a clear message. They have numerous demands, but the demands are often divergent, ranging from calls for a better environment to insistence on a free choice on unity for the two Germanies. Some even disagree on reunification and on whether the previously state-controlled economy should become more market-oriented. The New Forum is the largest group, with about 200,000 members who are mostly young street protesters. Other groups include the 150-member Green Party, the Social Democrats, Democracy Now, and Lutheran Pastor Rainer Eppelmann's Demokratischer Aufbruch, (Democratic Awakening).

After the Wall fell, many activists criticized the fact that the subsequent elections were totally orchestrated by the western parties. But what else could they have expected of the first free elections since 1933? Only a handful of East Germans had any experience at all of democracy, let alone of political campaigning. For most voters in the east, Kohl, Brandt, and Genscher, rather than the local heroes, were the star speakers during the election rallies. Prosperity, freedom, reunification and currency union were the keywords during the political rallies. For West German leaders, reunification couldn't come fast enough; the old regime and system had to be denied any chance of reinstating a network of power. While leaders of the former opposition to Honecker were still discussing 'finding processes for democracy in the former GDR' and a 'morally correct pluralistic spectrum', the Christian Party with Chancellor Kohl on the ticket had already won the elections.

Resignation and disappointment set in, accompanied by bitter attacks from the east that reunification had come too fast. Some of the former revolutionaries stated bitterly that all the ideals of their silent revolution had died during the election campaign. Many still contend that the Germany they see now is not what they were fighting for during all those years. A few former dissidents, however, look beyond the initial disappointment of not being able to shape the future of the former GDR with their ideals. After being imprisoned (for many years in some cases) for those ideals, after not being allowed to work in their professions, those few interpret gaining the freedom that they fought for so desperately as imposing a duty to make politics their profession. Some of them have built a reputation for being constructive East German leaders, but most are looked upon as naive ex-freedom fighters who, in the wake of developments that they no longer controlled, turned into starry-eyed environmentalists or dreamers.

Ulrike Poppe

We reformists never thought that we could get the masses behind us. We were totally overwhelmed when the Wall fell as we always had thought that our silent revolution would end up in very long-lasting and gradual reforms, but not in a collapse of the whole system. Consequently, we weren't prepared to talk to the masses either. We didn't have a leader unlike our fellow dissidents in Czechoslovakia and we weren't used to political campaigning. We had made the reform possible, but we never wanted to be involved in party politics. For me and other dissidents and reformists, 'power' and 'influence' had always been associated with something dirty. Parties for us represented the establishment, which in turn represented the misuse of power. Government and parties as we knew them were unacceptable, and so we transferred our experience to the new situation as it presented itself in the spring of 1990.

After 9 November 1989, nobody listened to us anymore; instead, everyone looked towards the west for help and for buzz words. Our utopian dream of creating a new democratic Germany in its own right couldn't withstand the temptations of western prosperity. I had always hoped we would have more time to develop our own thoughts about how the GDR should be integrated into the west. I looked upon it more as two people walking towards one another with mutual respect than as one taking the other by the hand and going in the direction that only the one wants to go. With the fall of the Wall, every reform movement within the GDR died. You could say that the fall sabotaged any chance for the GDR to follow a democratic path of its own choosing. Now we are just part of a bigger but homogenized Germany.

Most people living in the former GDR never had an identity of their own since the Wall was built in 1961. We were trained to think one way or the other. Our move to go out into the streets was a protest against the Honecker regime, but it was also an attempt to form an identity. As people look west, we are losing our voice. Reunification, nevertheless, was unavoidable, because Germans are one nation, one culture and one people. But I believe that not all of socialism should be thrown out. We succeeded in speaking out against a hated order, we fought official lies and we also overcame the fear that accompanied day-to-day life. We got rid of the fear that governed us, so we should also be able to find our own identity. Yet I cannot blame anybody who favours the proven western democratic system over an unproven system such as 'democratic socialism', which I would have preferred to see installed in the former GDR.

For over 28 years we knew nothing about the west other than what we heard via the regime-controlled media. We heard about the high rate of crime, drugs, unemployment and prostitution. Now, for the first time, we can go see the west for ourselves. Of course, after experiencing the real standard of living in the west after having lived in terror for so long, most people are fed up with illusions. They want to start living and stop sacrificing their lives.

Still, it is depressing to see how many give up their ideals. With the border open, I fear that many people will no longer want to deal with politics at all. Most are unwilling, at least for now, to look in depth at the problems we are going to face. I believe we will almost have to go back to 1945 and start over again—go through the whole process of rebuilding and hardship again. Most are not willing to do that, they are closing their eyes. But we cannot simply copy the system in the west. We will end up being a no man's land.

Egon Bahr

Citizens' organizations and their initiatives for peace and human rights in the former GDR were caught up in the illusion they could build a democratic socialist East Germany. That was the whole intent of the revolution, right up until the appearance of the first signs and posters asserting, 'We are one people'.

In the spring of 1990 I had met with the writer Stefan Heym,[1] a tragic figure of his time. His thinking always made the Americans uncomfortable and his ideas unsettled the West Germans as well. He told me that he didn't believe he was wrong in wishing for a third way for the GDR, the way of democratic socialism. He really still believed there would be an opportunity to create an independent socialist, but democratic, GDR. I warned him, saying, 'Dear Stefan Heym, do you really think that after 40—no, 70—years of experiments, failed experiments, people are ready to say, "Let's try another experiment; let's spend another life and waste it"?'

It's true that many people in the GDR liked the first Round Table, a quasi-parliamentary body created in December 1989. That organization ultimately failed, too, while other opposition representatives were making the natural passage to legitimacy. The people of the GDR liked the Round Table because it exposed the crimes and corruption of the SED and prevented Modrow's attempt to reconstitute the Ministry of State Security in early 1990. But in the end, the Round Table deprived the GDR of its reasons for existing, and it never developed into a body that legally represented the citizens of the GDR. The majority of people in the east didn't want anymore debates; what they wanted was the West German Mark and a higher standard of living. Kohl was wise and saw these developments and—very coolly, bravely and even brutally—he pushed the whole movement towards reunification. He saw the 75,000 people coming from the east to the west creating instability in both places. There was only one reasonable possibility: reunification.

Robert Vogel

Reunification came not too early, but a year too late. It shouldn't have taken place on 3 December 1990, but instead right away in the same year that the Wall fell. We Germans lost a year waffling around about 'their' government and 'their' say. Meanwhile, billions

[1] Heym, born in 1913 in Chemnitz (former GDR), writes political and social essays and reports. Because of his criticism of the Honecker regime, he had been punished with house arrests.

were fed to an incompetent East German government, including party hard-liners such as Hans Modrow, who made rather unrestrained use of his power. The peaceful revolution was not turned into a democracy quickly enough or forcefully enough. East Germany could have been a model for the rest of eastern Europe by being the first pearl in a string of wealthy and well-to-do democracies.

The German reunification was delayed not because of difficult political reasons but because of pusillanimity. On that very special November night in 1989, people from the east and west fell into each other's arms. Germany should have been united there and then, but politicians hesitated. With the fall of the Wall the communist vision, a monster, collapsed, but some people have not yet adapted to that fact. Delaying reunification a year gave the old regime a breathing time which they shouldn't have been allowed to have.

Even after the first free elections, the East German administration is full of appointees from the former communist government. They sabotage privatization and reinforce the still-existing fear of the former secret police, the Stasi. Now the question is, will people, after a year in limbo, jump at the opportunity reunification offers, or will the socialist slovenliness continue to rule? It is time for people to get involved and participate actively in the process of rebuilding their country. It reminds me of the saying, 'You can lead a horse to the water, but it has to drink by itself.'

Kristina Matschat

We Germans call what happened during 1989 the 'Wende', a turnaround. It was more than a turn-around; it literally was a revolution, though fortunately one without bloodshed, without guns. Those who were actively involved in bringing about this revolution came from all kinds of backgrounds and political ideologies, but they all had two things in common: courage and the willingness to put an end to the totalitarian regime. There are many disappointments now that it has become clear that the west is not a paradise where grapes and honey are fed to you freely. There is not only economic disappointment, but also political disillusionment with the discovery that even life in and with the west can be unfair. A few people are quick to put the past behind them and, like a fallen gymnast, get up again and make a fresh start. The younger people in particular will grasp opportunities with both hands and will forget the tragedy of the last years; the older ones won't be quite so able to do that. The majority will take some time to adjust, will ponder their options and maybe will even withdraw for a while. I think the group that promoted the combination of democracy with socialism as a political form for the east were hoping to appeal exactly to those people who view the changes with a somewhat reluctant attitude. This attitude reflects more the pain of the past than any resentment of reunification, I think. On the other hand, the reformists who cling to their model of an independent East Germany with a political system of its own were wrong when they believed any form of socialism could have a chance over here. We had enough of trial-and-error in the political arena over the past 40 years.

Chapter Twenty-one

Champagne, Bananas and Burgers

Many East Germans were shocked after they got their first taste of the west. What had looked like paradise on the TV screen—the way most GDR citizens under 60 had experienced the west so far—had become a nightmare for more than a few. For example, the fact that liberty's blessing can also be a curse was felt first-hand by those East German citizens who got cheated by some West German salespeople selling them insurance policies for outrageous prices.

After all the champagne corks had been popped and some West Germans had taken a chunk of the Berlin Wall home as a souvenir, the realities of the tremendous changes began to settle in on both sides. The mood changed from initial euphoria to anger and bitterness. 'Why were we lied to for so long?' and 'why have we wasted all those years?' were among the biting questions asked by the ex-East German citizens. The bitterness increased as the truth started to come out about the Stasi brutalities and its operation, the true state of the GDR and its economy and corruption.

When, around midnight on 1 January 1990, a young student died and over 300 people were injured during the first New Year's Eve that the east and west celebrated together, it should have been seen as not only a tragedy, but also a symbolic event reflecting the state of mind in which Germans on both sides of the Wall would soon find themselves. Euphoric about the current events and also somewhat intoxicated by alcohol, dozens of youngsters had climbed the Brandenburg Gate via a metal scaffold. The scaffold collapsed and buried more than 300 people. Like an oracle, the Brandenburg accident announced a headache between the two Germanies instead of a national delirium. The expectations that had been built up as highly in the east as in the west would soon come crashing down.

The new decade was approached with mixed feelings on both sides. Nevertheless, that the fall of the Wall would result in reunification of the country became more apparent every day. It was only a question of when and how.

For the first East German revolutionaries, who in October 1989 had risked their freedom and even their lives, the approaching reunification ended the dream of an 'independent', democratic second German nation. From November 1989 to spring 1990, the number of East Germans who opposed a reunification with the west had dropped dramatically, from 23 per cent to 3 per cent. During the same time frame, 2,000 newcomers from the east arrived daily in West German cities. Tents and temporary housing for the thousands of people who poured in from the east were set up in the parks of almost every larger West German city; the tent cities soon seemed to become a part of daily life.

For many, prosperity and happiness seemed possible only in the west, not in the east. Between October 1989 and February 1990, for example, over 9,000 doctors left the east. As a result, many hospital departments had to close. Similar developments occurred in other areas of the country's industries and services. Posters with such slogans as 'We stay if the Deutsche Mark comes, we leave if it doesn't' made it clear that only a swift change and a democratically elected government could reinstate confidence. West German citizens and politicians watched the exodus anxiously. How many more people could the west swallow and support?

Even if Lothar de Maizière the attorney from Thuringia and head of the CDU in the former East German states appeared to be the winner of the advanced election on 18 March, Chancellor Kohl was the real winner. The citizens of the former GDR had voted for a Germany independent of confession, profession or education. The party leader of the leftist environmental party, Otto Schily, had only one comment on de Maizière's apparent victory. During his first TV interview after the elections, he simply held a banana in front of the camera for several minutes. Bananas were seldom available in East Germany, but they were very popular. They were among the first 'exotic' items easterners had shopped for in West Germany after the Wall fell. Schily's message was clear: easterners had been voting not only for reunification, but also for materialism. Who could blame them after 40 years of subsisting on almost nothing?

Because the election results had provided a clear mandate for reunification of the two Germanies with each other as approved by the four Allied Powers, the main task of the de Maizière government would be to orchestrate discussions which became known as the two-plus-four talks. The next hurdle to overcome was a monetary union between the two Germanies, which was essential for economic recovery in the east. Chancellor Kohl promised in public that 'No one will be worse off as a result of the monetary union'.[1] The devalued Ostmark was to be replaced

[1] Speech in German Parliament, September 9, 1990.

by the valuable Deutsche Mark at a 1:1 rate. The black market rate at that time traded the Ostmark against the Deutsche Mark for 5:1. The former Bundesbank president, Otto Pöhl, argued that 1:1 would increase inflation and would discourage outside investment in the country. On 1 July 1990, people partied to the theme, 'Dance to welcome in the night of the Deutsche Mark'. Just as all border controls had disappeared, so the Ostmark had disappeared overnight as well.

Almost immediately, East Germans were buying out former border villages. They went on a shopping binge, as long as it cost less than $54, the amount that the West German government passed out to every East German as 'welcome money'. West Germany's shopping malls quickly and delightedly noticed that the hottest items were exotic fruit such as bananas, video games, TV sets, hamburgers and walkmans. McDonald's managers were desperately waiting for emergency patties and a new load of beef to satisfy the 'Ossi's' (easterner's) appetite for western fast food.

But at the same time, West Germans started to feel overwhelmed by thousands of easterners accompanying them shopping and creating traffic jams with their often broken-down cars. West Germans with modest incomes started to eye jealously the long lines in front of banks where the welcome money was passed out. Many average West Germans became frustrated at having to finance the undoing of evils the East German government had caused. The anger at Bonn rose when West German taxes were raised to cover parts of the exorbitant costs of economic recovery in the east. For political and economic reasons, Chancellor Kohl was eager to press the issue of reunification. A treaty of unity was drawn up between the two German governments and a formal approval of the four Allied Powers was obtained. Under Article 23 of the West German Basic Law,[2] the East German parliament voted to accede to the Federal Republic and the two Germanies were united at the stroke of midnight, as 2 October became 3 October. Ten days later, the voters in the east were called to the polls for the third time in less than seven months. Five new Bundesländer were established—the so-called 'Neue Bundesländer'—with each presided over by a semi-autonomous government similar to that in the west. In December, the first pan-German elections confirmed Chancellor Kohl as the first leader of a reunited Germany.

Just a few months later, almost everyone had come to realize that the adaptation process would be more difficult, more traumatic than they had thought. Almost every easterner had seen the west and many westerners had visited the east during the first days after the Wall had fallen, so the initial curiosity and excitement were gone. The huge differences in wealth

---

[2] Article 23 of the German constitution states that the West German law will be binding in other parts of Germany when they accede to the Federal Republic.

and education and value systems were becoming increasingly apparent. East Germans had to deal with inferiority complexes and doubts about their independence. To them, many West Germans appeared arrogant and anti-social. West Germans, on the other hand, believed that most Ossis were lazy, inflexible and unable to bear any pressure.

Westerners became increasingly concerned that their East German neighbours would soon be second-class citizens. How differently the two Germanies had developed within the prior four decades, not only politically but also economically and socially, is illustrated by the story of a young Red Cross assistant who watched an East German woman trying to wash a disposable diaper. For many on both sides, euphoria was replaced with the realization that 40 years of living in a different world cannot be wiped out in months or even years. Today the majority of East Germans know that the new world they have been merged with is better than their old one. Unfortunately, however, many do not feel as though this new world belongs to them.

Klaus Bölling

In general, expectations on both sides were too high after the reunification. Westerners thought Germany would live through a boom like the one in the 1950s, and many easterners expected to make up within months for what they had missed during a whole lifetime.

The opening of the borders between east and west produced a clash between two economic systems that couldn't have been more different. West Germany, one of the most developed countries in the world, loaded with goods and known for its prosperity, exports and hard currency, had to be merged with a deficient economy designed after Karl Marx's unworkable utopian theories. Planned production and 'people-owned' property were supposed to prevent the 'chaos of a free market' and produce a 'workers' paradise', but what they had produced instead were cars working as if they been built during the 19th century and a telephone system that one had to wait ten years to be connected to. A once-thriving and famous East German machinery industry had been surpassed twentyfold by Taiwan. Generally, one could say that before the Wall fell, the former GDR had reached the industrial standards of a Third World country. In other words, economically and socially we are trying to bring up to date a part of German history that stopped dead in 1933.

At the beginning of the 1980s, 2.50 Ostmarks were needed to earn the export value of 1 DM; today that figure has almost doubled. The GDR had an economic system in which the prices of apartments, bread, energy, transportation costs, even the prices of flowers, were determined by the regime. Production costs were seldom even known. Rigid plans, not consumers, determined production. So, for example, because subsidies made bread cheaper in the stores than corn, chickens came to be fed on bread instead of corn. Any initiative to produce and work hard was taken away because nobody had the right to own. These are just titbits of facts how the East German economy worked, or better, didn't work.

The difficulty we face now is to turn a non-functioning economy into a working market. Without resources and production facilities, the former East Germany might easily slide into a state of receivership and become a part of the country that only consumes, but doesn't produce or manufacture. The west, on the other hand, looks upon the east as a new market with consumer potential not seen since the 1950s. The obvious question is, can the simple desire for champagne, bananas and burgers on the one side, and the desire on the other to expand western markets to the east, provide a sufficiently strong platform for giving freedom a chance to survive in hard times?

Werner Meyer-Larson

In 1990 West Germans discovered in the eastern part of the country a deterioration that exceeded their worst expectations. News started popping up about a dangerous psychological and moral deformation of the eastern society. The west learned more about the old production systems, which were totally outdated and often run and operated by unmotivated, slow and sometimes lazy workers. There was no communication system except for the one that had for the last 40 years helped the Stasi to control people's lives and intrude on their privacy. Disaster reports on the environmental destruction—of air, soil and water—that had been sanctioned by the communist regime became part of everyday life.

Everyone who visited the former East Germany with the thought of investing there became a first-hand witness to the total lack of equity in housing, the crippled infrastructure, the poor distribution network and the low productivity. Visiting the former GDR was like leaping back in time 40 years.

Very few East Germans had any real understanding of what the post-war culture had brought to the west. The lack of modern amenities shocked West Germans: there were virtually no electronics, few computers, no cost calculations, no marketing. To nobody's surprise, official statistical data produced by the Honecker regime had been falsified. The combination of 12 years of fascism and 45 years of Soviet communism had pushed eastern Germany back to the mid-1930s. Nevertheless, the common social consensus in the west was that the process of rehabilitating the east had to start immediately with the greatest possible financial power. Kohl and others declared a determination to bring East Germany up to western standards within the decade. Looking at the reality today, it will take up to three decades.

I believe that West Germany made some pragmatic decisions that may be questionable today. For example, West Germany introduced the Deutsche Mark as the united currency at a comfortable exchange rate of 1:1 for consumers, but not for producers. An exchange rate of 1:2 or even 1:3 would have been a far more economical and realistic decision. For the first few months, the improvement of the infrastructure became a top priority. Germany introduced its own legal system, promised to compensate people for their property losses during the communist years, and made East Germany part of its social net—mainly by compensating many unemployed easterners.

The Treuhandanstalt was given the task of selling or transforming the 90 per cent state-owned economy into private ownership. West German trade unions agreed to adjust East German wages gradually within a five-year time period, without prorating the wages to increase productivity. It all sounded fine until the bill was presented to the West Germans. Chancellor Kohl announced to the West German citizens an increase in personal taxes for a limited time to fill up the reunification fund. In 1990 the volume of new net debt in the federal budget reached 54 billion DM, amounting to 11 per cent of the budget and 4 per cent of the GNP. By May 1992 West Germany had transferred over 200 billion DM to the eastern areas.

This infusion definitely had an impact, some of it positive, some negative. The whole operation at first had an enormous Keynesian effect, like that of the Reagan armament programme during the 1980s. East Germans spent and consumed, the deficit was in the West German budget, and the profit taker was West German industry. Factories could serve the expansion without additional investment, just by using more of their existing capacity. It was a bonanza for the free market system. As a consequence, the stream of refugees into the west slowed and became almost invisible. A limited number of predominantly West German companies started major investments and built new factories in the east. Volkswagen was among the first. Additionally, the Treuhand tried to sell many companies in order to stabilize the job situation in many eastern areas. Generally, one third of the payment from the west was used for investment, two-thirds for consumption, so unemployment became a typical sign of the structural changes—and it grew and grew. The East German population on the one hand was admirably patient, but on the other was not motivated, following the old-style passivity learned during the Ulbricht and Honecker regimes.

What we have learned now is that the budget deficit of 11 per cent is a mere window dressing. The Treuhand's deficit alone, which is not part of the federal budget, has already reached DM300 billion, which is more than 60 per cent of that budget. Another twilight zone of deficits has been hidden within social security.

What was surprising, even to optimists, was that, during the first 18 months following the reunification, there was almost no financial damage to the West German system. The introduction of the Deutsche Mark in the east happened very smoothly. The inflation rate remained moderate. The enormous transfer of money was hardly felt in West German pocketbooks; it simply slowed the rate of increase in individual spending.

Some of these facts resulted from the special situation of the German economy at the time. After a long consolidation process, in 1990 Germany was in the best financial, technological and economic shape in its history. The starting point for taking on Project East Germany couldn't have been better. The consequences of the additional taxes and high social security rates didn't hit most employees until 1992. Likewise, the consequences of the unavoidable interruption of technological and inventive processes in 1990 are only now starting to become apparent.

Considering all of these factors, I believe that an immediate success story in the German joint venture is highly unlikely, and that at best the reunification will be very expensive. My guess is that, five years after the start of the take-over process, East Germany will be able to operate under market economy conditions. But it will take at least a decade to boost East Germany to a western standard of living. Even within such a generous time frame, a complete transition from communism into a western-style society would represent an enormous success.

Is this a model for all the other transformations? My answer is no. Why not? First, there is not enough money in the world to bring the same capital investment into the whole of the former Soviet empire, which holds roughly 350 million people. Using the same ratio we applied to East Germany, the G7 nations would have to raise between DM20 to 30 trillion. Additionally, in contrast to the German take-over style, there would be no effective money control. The rest of the eastern world consists of independent nations with no desire to be controlled. Hence, we will have to combine the money factor and the time factor. The former Soviet Union, with all its turmoil, will become a decent business partner by the second half of the 1990s. To bring things up to western standards will take half a century.

Today, the fear of many Europeans that 78 million united Germans will dominate their neighbours economically and monopolize trade to the east proves to be unfounded. If anything, we overwhelm Europe with our unexpected weakness. The costs and the social and economic upheaval involved in absorbing East Germany have been a sobering experience for us Germans. We didn't expect inflation, nor did anybody believe that the German Bundesbank would have to impose the high interest rates that have been choking the rest of Europe. The reunification of Germany didn't just create a mess for Germany itself, but also, for the time being, for Europe and the Maastricht Treaty. Currently, we are farther away from a monetary union and Maastricht in Europe than before the Wall fell.

Eberhard Diepgen

The decision to adopt a 1:1 exchange rate for the currency union was a difficult one, but in the end I believe the only one possible. It was the only way to keep easterners from migrating to the west and to motivate them to work on getting their part of the country back into shape. Nobody knew what a horrible shape the former GDR was in at the point of reunification. We in the west had been blinded by a paper tiger, as we now know. Between the fall of the Wall and the first elections, the interim government under Modrow had calculated that the 'people-owned capital' amounted to more than 1.3 billion Ostmarks. Today, we know that the debits were much higher than that. If the reunification hadn't come as quickly as it did, the former GDR would have fallen apart economically.

On the other side of the coin, nobody was prepared to make big sacrifices. The east thought it would be easy to attain our standard of living, and we thought they wouldn't need a lot of help from us. The results were frustration and disillusionment. This frustration together with the rising unemployment rate are the reasons for the incidents that made headlines throughout the world. I am talking about the acts of violence by some Germans against foreigners living here. These acts are horrible, and I as mayor of Berlin am trying to curtail such extremism. Thousands of Germans have demonstrated against these right-wing extremists, and I hope the world also recognizes these efforts to encourage solidarity. Understandably, the world looks upon Germany with a special focus, as this violence brings back memories of the Nazi dictatorship. For the sake of fairness, it must also be mentioned that within recent months Germany has taken in more refugees from crisis regions than any other nation of the EC. This is a difficult situation for a country that had never before been a nation of immigrants.

The giant social upheaval we are experiencing now—between East and West Germans and between Germans and refugees from other countries—is a direct result of the economic clash of two very different systems. The Treuhandanstalt is planning to complete privatization and restructuring in 1994. Ideally, the Treuhand would then be replaced by an international agency supported by western Europe, the USA and Japan. This international agency could bring western know-how to eastern Europe as well as assist in transforming state-controlled economies into free-market systems. I envision something like a Marshall Plan for all of eastern Europe. Nevertheless, West Germany will have to be the driving force in helping East Germany develop living standards comparable with its own. East Germany and the existence of the communist system is a result of the

Second World War, an aftermath of the war for which Germany is responsible. From that viewpoint alone, economic support from West Germany for the east is undeniably justified.

Robert Vogel

There are major differences between those Germans who lived under tyranny for 12 years and those who lived under a totalitarian system for almost 50 years. The time difference produced different under-standings of social and economic concepts. The citizens of the ex-GDR have lived through two dictatorships since 1933. The first, the Third Reich, fortunately lasted 12, not the 1,000 years once pro-claimed by Hitler. And we can thank the Allies that they freed us from that pestilence. Rebuilding West Germany was easier after those 12 years than it is now for East Germany. First, except for the Jewish community, the income conditions were unchanged after the currency reform in 1945. And second, there were many people and politicians left who knew how to build a democracy and a free-market economy. In the former GDR, however, all income conditions have been restructured during the last four decades. Also, people were politically brainwashed for almost two generations. They'll have to overcome many psychological hurdles. Additionally, the west, unlike the east, lived according to the 'surplus value' theory, according to which profit comes from the value added to a product during production. This profit, which could be given wholly to the workers, is partially retained by the employer. There is no doubt that this theory motivates both employers and workers. Our favourable economy, which has been sustained for decades, is driven by this economic motivation. Even wage agreements with unions and em-ployees have not reduced the motivational force of the idea of pro-ducing a surplus value. It is a concept of building, paying wages, building more and paying even more wages.

This theory of added surplus value is a concept most easterners are unfamiliar with. It is probably more than a concept, it is an atti-tude to which one can't adapt overnight. For years, East Germans were taken care of in a basic way by the government. The majority of GDR citizens are still thinking of the government as an institution that takes care of them, as a problem-solver. They are looking towards the west as a sugar-daddy. It will take a full generation until the majority become actively involved in our economy.

Kristina Matschat

Unemployment may hit 30 per cent to 40 per cent of the workforce here in the east before the economy turns around. My husband, a physicist who worked for the last decade for the Akademie der Wissenschaften, was not a party member (though he was a 'carrier of government secrets'), and so he could have found work in Munich or somewhere else in the west. But we don't want to leave East Berlin. Our thinking is that if we weathered the storm of living here for the last 40 years, during which we opposed the regime and fought for reunification, we can also weather the aftereffects of the storm. Many of our friends have gone to the west and I think they are better off than we are, at least economically.

I think reunification was a great moment, but I don't know what we are going to make out of it. Are the West Germans really willing to integrate the east, or will they just rule over us? Some West Germans treat us as if we freely chose to have that terrible kind of government. Many forget that we are in a kind of shock. We are just now learning to what degree we were cheated; we are facing great economic difficulties and we fear the future. We are going through an identity crisis. First, we fought a regime we couldn't relate to; then we joined an economic and political system for which we've had almost no preparation. Although we never identified with the old system, we nonetheless felt some solidarity in opposing it. Now we are asked to be flexible, to be loose and not take life so seriously, but that is just not the way we were educated. I think even the West Germans kids themselves think that they are not uptight or compulsive. They just have had different objects for their compulsions.

Francis Meehan

What is currently going on in Germany is a typically German debate. Germans are great at debating among themselves. Angst rules. Central to the debate is the psychology of the workers who for years toiled to produce things that could only be sold to Azerbaijanis on a bad day. The question now is, how can we get former East Germans to produce goods that work in Norway or any other European market? The answer is elusive. Many of the workers were happy to produce worthless things, which I call stupid things. It was a chain reaction; as eastern workers only produced stupid things, they could only buy stupid things for whatever stupid prices prevailed.

How do you change people's minds when their views have been entrenched for more than 40 years? Most people in the east will miss the security of their old system. Of course, they all want BMWs, but most of them only want to work the way they did under the old regime. I believe that if a whole nation has been taught not to use their brain for such a long time, it is difficult to try to make them start thinking again. The Treuhandanstalt is trying to do just that: make the East Germans think again. The problem it faces is exemplified by the strikes of the shipbuilders in the cities on the Baltic Sea. The sad fact is that today Koreans can build better ships at lower cost. I now live in a place in Scotland that used to produce ships like the *Queen Elizabeth* and the *Queen Mary*. People there still speak of skilled shipbuilders, but they don't build ships anymore, because you can't build them if nobody wants them.

What Germany is dealing with is a revolution in people's minds. I'm sure the Germans will be able to handle it in the long run, but will they have the patience—both easterners and westerners—to weather the very stormy first years?

Robert W. Becker

I was surprised to see that the GDR and the former SED regime were very successful in turning this part of Germany into a working-class society, which meant, among other things, driving out all the bourgeois and with them their value system. The middle-class people who didn't leave in the early 1950s and 1960s were pushed into a corner and no longer had much influence on the culture.

A lot of what I think of as 'German' is heavily marked by the value system, work ethics and aesthetics of the German middle class. Yet here in the east one can see abandoned Trabi cars at the side of the street; things are trashed here, the houses are in a disastrous state. Only a few people care about their belongings, fashion, looks. People here in the east have been educated to be more pragmatic, more utilitarian. I think that is one of the great misunderstandings that led many investors and economists in the west to believe that, with the right work ethic, East Germany could soon experience the same Wirtschaftswunder (economic miracle) that revitalized West Germany in the 1950s. It was not considered that many in the east had priorities other than to rebuild, because they had a different outlook on life.

One definite mistake that was made during reunification was the exchange rate of 1:1. Kohl's argument was that any other exchange rate would be inhumane. The people in the east also pressed awfully hard for a 1:1 rate. In the short run, yes, 1:1 benefited the easterners; but in the long run, the even exchange rate forces prices up and means that the quality of work and products must reflect the buying power of the German Deutsche Mark. The cost factors, for example, of the companies which the Treuhandanstalt is trying to sell were presented in their opening balance sheets in West German Marks and are, therefore, totally misrepresented. The East Germans outfoxed themselves by demanding a 1:1 exchange rate.

Uwe Wunderlich

In the spring of 1989, I was a director of a metal-processing Kombinat. How much has changed. Our family were on holiday in Hungary when we learned about the exodus of thousands of East Germans to that country. I can't deny that I was tempted to leave myself, even though I was one of the more privileged citizens. My wife and I had a car and a nice apartment. My wife had not been forced to join the party. We were allowed to go on holiday once a year. We had some sleepless nights, but finally decided against leaving, maybe because we are too deeply rooted in Dresden. Frankly, we were also afraid. We didn't know what to expect on the other side.

Like toppling dominoes, one pillar after the other collapsed. It began with the opening of the Hungarian border. Returning from our vacation, we were shocked by the silence of our media. The Hungarian newspapers had been full of pictures of couples helping each other over the barbed wire, of cramped embassies, of crying children and mothers. We were deeply shaken that none of this had been reported at home. Nobody seemed to know anything about the exodus. It hit me then that this system could not survive. How could a government ignore an exodus of thousands of its own people?

Right after the Wall came down, I suggested breaking up the Kombinat. Recently, some bankers, insurance people and representatives of other West German industries had visited us, and during our brief talks it became obvious that I worked for an obsolete institution. It seemed senseless to keep this insane administrative organization alive—even though in dissolving the Kombinat, I was putting myself out of work. Co-workers in similar positions to mine disagreed. They wanted to keep the Kombinat going. Nevertheless, I closed it on 31 March 1990.

As the director of the Kombinat I had been responsible for almost everything—production, employment, inventory. Right after I finished my law studies in Leipzig, I controlled 30 small businesses. Then, in 1981, I was asked to head the Kombinat. That brought membership in the party, a privileged lifestyle, more education and career rewards. Yes, the party used all these 'carrots'.

I knew from the very beginning—when I had decided to study law in Leipzig—that I would be asked to join. One's eligibility for more education was determined largely by one's 'political behaviour'. Some students were asked later, some earlier. There were about twenty students in my law class, five of whom were already party members. The rest, with the exception of one whose mother was a well-known communist, joined later.

Gaining membership required hour-long interrogations about attitudes, beliefs and goals. After a while I started to believe. I knew I was being brainwashed, but being a party member was a career decision. My motives were purely egocentric and opportunistic. Yet it is difficult to stand aloof from what supplies your daily bread.

Christian, Count von Wedel

My mother's family came from a little Prussian village near Zeitz, where my grandparents owned a large piece of property and a small castle. They were dispossessed by the communists after the Second World War. Shortly after 9 November 1989, my aunt—she is over

81 and has lived in West Germany since the war—decided to show me and some cousins the origins of the family in Prussia. We got into the car and drove to the castle, which was in a dreadful condition, and the nearby family cemetery.

My aunt remembered that the graves were attended by the family's former cook, Mrs Posart, a lady now in her seventies. For the past few years, Mrs Posart had been in contact with my aunt, who sent her care packages with coffee and chocolate from the west. After asking around in the village we found her house. My aunt had not actually set eyes on Mrs Posart in 45 years, and I knew of her only from the many stories and memories of my parents and aunt. She was so delighted to see my aunt again that she asked us all for lunch and then dinner—the hours of talking passed very quickly. We all sat in her living room discussing the recent events, future plans and a lot of pleasant memories.

Later Mrs Posart's son started to interrogate me about how to become a self-made man. He wanted to know everything about the free-market system, sales, accounting and the process and problems of becoming self-employed. He told me he planned to put together a stereo business. He was working for a VED, a state-owned company which repaired TV sets, radios, and other electrical appliances.

Weeks after our visit, I received a letter from him. He had talked to a group of his colleagues and they all agreed that they needed some marketing and financial assistance from a westerner, and he asked if I would be willing to help. Two days later we met again to discuss the plans in more detail, and in February 1990 I decided to form a corporation as a limited partner, since that was the only possible set-up for a West German citizen before reunification.

As the reunification drew nearer, I grew more fearful that this venture would not be successful. I knew little about radios and TV—only that a button turned them off and on. There were two other big problems: where would we get the space for the shop and, more importantly, how would we get a decent supply of radios and TV sets into the store in East Germany?

Despite such questions, Mrs Posart's son and six of his colleagues quit their jobs at the state-owned company. We managed to purchase an old supermarket close to Leipzig, which we converted into a stereo and repair shop. This was a small miracle. It was extremely difficult for the electricians who worked for the VEB to purchase the store. At that time GDR officials were not interested in promoting free enterprise.

After the summer of 1990 it became easier for us to travel to the east. We no longer needed visas or travel permits. But building materials were hard to get, so the finishing touches in the store were still missing when we opened in July. One weekend I rented a big truck in Frankfurt and went from building-supply stores to carpet stores to tile stores. I loaded the truck up to its roof and started towards Leipzig. The border between east and west was still in existence and, being a good citizen, I stopped at customs and showed the receipts for the materials I had. I needed the customs official's approval to export the materials to the former GDR. After a long discussion, he decided he couldn't give me the needed permit. He suggested I write to the customs department or directly to the city to which I wanted to export the materials. Waiting for the answer most likely would have taken three or four months.

This whole episode got utterly ridiculous and I became very impatient. Finally I decided to turn around and get into the line where only small cars were supposed to pass. The customs officer at that gate was so astonished by my boldness that he waved me through. I had behaved like an 'arrogant West German'—and it had worked! It was interesting to observe how helpless and confused the official watchdogs of a totalitarian system become when their system has lost its power and scope.

Our second problem was keeping radios and TV sets in stock. As you can imagine, the appetite among East Germans for news, information, and entertainment was voracious. Our original supply of AEG radios and Telefunken TVs was exhausted within hours. I came to understand that the TV means much more than information —it means freedom. Fortunately, I knew a former board member of AEG Telefunken who was able to help out. After our initial success we decided to divide the shares in our company three ways. I was the major stockholder. I arranged financing for an additional 41 percent. Although the equipment sold like hotcakes, we partners didn't make much money at that point. A quarrel started about how the shares should be distributed. With the exception of Mrs Posart's son, all the easterners believed my share was too high. After all my work, financing and enthusiasm, I was deeply disappointed at their obvious greed.

I decided to pull out of the project, as did Mr Posart. He was devastated by the belligerence of his friends. He and I decided to start a similar project with only a few shareholders. We formed a company called Merkur Electronic, following the same plan as our first project.

My East German partner, Mr Posart, turned out to be a super salesperson. Since none of his family had been party members, he had never been allowed to study or to attend an advanced school. Now he and people like him have a chance to begin again, to do what they want to with their lives. I feel fortunate that I am among the few West Germans who are not anxious about doing business in East Germany. My business is going very well thanks to dependable partners.

Many West Germans are disappointed by the slow rate at which businesses are developing in the east. They complain about the inflexibility of the East Germans and the lack of a work ethic. But travelling to the east is a hell of a lot different than it was just months ago. The streets are alive, and here and there you find a splash of colour because houses have been painted. The mood generally is upbeat, especially among the young. It is true that unemployment has risen, and the suicide rate has reportedly doubled. Yes, in certain regions, particularly in rural areas, pessimism is rife. Unfortunately, people on both sides thought reunification would solve all of their problems. But those who are patient, who understand that they will have to work hard and listen and be creative—those people will thrive and prosper. Most East Germans know that they lack education and knowledge about business, but they are eager to learn and they learn quickly.

Henning Prenzlin

My expectations about the speed of development in the GDR have changed drastically within the last couple of months. In the beginning, right after the Wall came tumbling down, I, like most other westerners, was extremely enthusiastic about helping to rebuild the east. I even felt a duty to do so; because the people on the other side of the fence had suffered for so long, they deserved a break and our help. At first, when Chancellor Kohl drew up his ten-point

programme, everybody hoped for a dramatic Wirtschaftswunder
—an economic revival like the one that followed the currency reform
in 1948. Now, we are disappointed.

As I drove towards the border on the night of 30 June 1990,
when the currency reform happened, I expected to find thousands of
people celebrating in the streets, and a major traffic jam on the auto-
bahn. Instead, there was nothing; nobody was there. For a long time,
mine was the only car moving towards Dresden. I thought perhaps I
had missed the party, that I was just late. Maybe everybody is busy
filling the empty shelves with West German products. Wrong! The
stores were still empty in Dresden. All of a sudden it dawned on me
that since the borders were open, the shelves must have been empty
because very few West German firms had any management present
in the east and the easterners weren't able to handle management yet.

While the salaries in East Germany have risen almost 8 per cent,
the productivity there is still only two-thirds that of West Germany.
That is at least true for the construction business. From that standpoint, Ireland and Portugal might be more attractive for investment
than East Germany. We in the west are also growing tired of the
East Germans' complaining, and we are extremely angry about the
tax increase resulting from reunification.

However, communication between easterners and westerners—at
least in my office—has improved. In the beginning, there was much
staring at each other, at each other's clothes and gestures, and listening to the different dialects. We westerners are sometimes a bit
off-balance when we come to the east. There is a certain insecurity
about how to deal with the people, and there is a totally different
lifestyle in the east. Adding to my own discomfort, I usually don't
get enough sleep, since I want to get things done and leave again,
and I don't follow a good diet. I mostly have the feeling I'm in a
prison camp that I can leave at any time. I think that for many, East
Germany is interesting to invest in because they believe that the
market will inevitably expand into the other East European markets
such as Poland, Hungary and eventually into the former Soviet
Union.

Of the many business people who have thus far visited cities like
Dresden hoping to be able to contribute to the restructuring of the
former GDR, only a few have actually invested, and those who have
are now frustrated. But like me, they are willing to finish what they

started. Since 1 January 1991 many West German government officials have moved to Dresden or to other major East German cities.
Unfortunately, most of these are not the most effective. They are put
into situations that require them to make quick decisions, or, sometimes, just to keep things going for a while. Most of them are not
capable of doing either. I have the feeling that many of these government employees who had a hard time in the west are going to the
east, hoping for another career opportunity.

Janos Fekete

I believe the political decision-makers in the western world who are
now considering ways to help the countries of central eastern Europe
will first have to answer the following questions:

>1. Do they intend to launch a mostly altruistic aid programme which
>is based on political considerations?
>2. Alternatively, do they want real business—medium- and long-
>term investment that is by no means a free give-away, but investment
>based on the principle of mutual economic interests in which the
>strong economic position of the west is used to finance the transi-
>tional period of the east until the latter's recovery?

The first approach may alleviate some problems, but it cannot offer
any long-term solution that would be beneficial to both west and
east. Only if the west is thinking in terms of a realistic perspective,
with fruitful economic co-operation as its objective, is there a need to
specify what the needs of the east are, and how they can be harmon-
ized with the interests and economic potential of the west. The east
will have to transform its central planning system into a market
economy; the difficult transition will require a strong and effective
social welfare network that can guarantee at least a minimum standard of social services to the low-income social groups.

The establishment of market economies in central eastern Europe
could pave the way for European economic integration. The US,
Britain, Canada and Australia entered into a state of economic
stagnation or even recession in 1990, and this is likely to have an impact on the world economy for a longer period of time. Increasing
purchases by the east of both capital and consumer goods improve

the chance for boosting economic growth. Yet the east, in its present condition, is not able to function as a real market should. The question is whether the west is prepared to inject capital into the east—in the form of short- , medium- and long-term credit and direct investment—to create this real market. If the answer is yes, what are the necessary conditions to develop the east into an export market with sufficient purchasing power and into an export market with reliable suppliers? First, the east will have to produce an annual growth of 4 to 5 per cent. Second, to attain this goal it will have to liberalize restrictions on imports, a step required to create real competition in the domestic market. The third condition is to have a single, uniform exchange rate and at least the external convertibility of the national currency, so that it is possible to compare prices in the domestic and foreign markets.

One of the major preconditions for a healthy and consistent economic policy is to have a selective development approach. This is where the OECD member countries can play an important role, especially since the most obsolete equipment of the industries of the east will have to be replaced by up-to-date machinery.

At the same time, a healthy economic development is inconceivable without the gradual improvement of the standard of living, which would then encourage increased demand for consumer goods. This is where economic development and politics are linked. If the west cannot—or is not prepared to—act fast, then the process of democratization in the east may come to a standstill. The temporary but drastic decline of the living standard is a painful but inevitable consequence of the adjusted market conditions. At some point, however, the deterioration of the standard of living may no longer be tolerated by the people in the eastern countries, and their lack of tolerance may lend support to extremist political trends that can lead to dictatorial systems, which unfortunately have long traditions in this region of the world. *Periculum in mora*—peril lies in delays.

To produce a system of intensive co-operation capable of achieving the desired goals, the east could be transformed into a group of democratic states based on a multiparty system and on a market economy in which private ownership is dominant but which is protected by a social welfare net. A genuine western policy of financial assistance for the east would also have to include helping the former Soviet Union to shape its own market economy. Including the former

USSR in this process can be justified by both economic and military considerations. It would be very difficult to count on a substantial reduction in military spending—a reduction that could be used as a significant source of additional revenue—without a Soviet Union that is democratic and is on its way to developing a market economy. With east-west relations improving and likely to continue to improve, it is quite feasible to substantially cut military expenditures and to direct the money saved into business-oriented loans.

The recovery of the east and its restored links with the world market would create a new Europe with 500 million people and a total GNP of about $6 trillion, a Europe that could be an equal partner in a triangular world economy balanced among the US, Japan and Europe. What the countries of eastern Europe need is not free aid, but cash and credits under favourable conditions. If the east can attain these two conditions, it can reasonably expect private foreign capital to start flowing into direct investments in this region. The more private investors from abroad enter the region, the more the amount of support provided by government agencies and international organizations can be reduced. An economic recovery in the east can also help curb the oncoming economic recession in the world, which is just another indication of mutual global interdependence.

Chapter Twenty-two

The Treuhandanstalt

Since its formation, the Treuhandanstalt, the East German privatization agency,[1] has been Germany's favourite punching bag. East Germans mostly think it is a heartless institution while West Germans believe it is a pompous, bureaucratic monster that moves too slowly and too inefficiently. The Treuhand's task is to finish converting 11,000 formerly 'people-owned' companies to private ownership by the end of 1993. Even when it appears to have done a good job, it may end up in litigation, and it is often accused of being anti-competitive.

The Treuhand, the world's largest holding company, was founded by the last communist East German government before the Wall fell. Given its public mandate for privatization conferred by the democratically elected government in 1990, however, the agency interpreted its task more broadly than that of a private company when selling subsidiaries. For example, when selling an industrial company, it is not unusual for the Treuhand to accept an offer that it believes will save jobs and promote investment, rather than the higher cash offer of a speculator. Still, the agency sometimes failed to explain its actions clearly. The argument of 'broader interest' has angered many western managers when the Treuhand has used the phrases as rationale for granting or denying deals to certain bidders.

Both its history and its mandate—to radically transform the East German economy from estate ownership and centrally planned production into a free-market system—have made the Treuhandanstalt one of the most controversial institutions of the reunification and a symbol of the very difficult relationship between the two Germanies. But even more disconcerting than all the frustrations and failed illusions related to the business dealings of the Treuhand was the April 1991 assassination of Detlev Karsten Rohwedder, the agency's

---

[1] Literal translation is 'Holding Trust Company'.

charismatic director, who was shot and killed at his home over the Easter weekend. Although German terrorists of the Red Army Faction were charged with the murder, the symbolism of losing Rohwedder disillusioned many Germans in the early months after the reunification.

Yet the Treuhand had come a long way since 1990 when howling demonstrators fearing for their jobs besieged the agency's headquarters at Alexander Platz, in what used to be East Berlin. At that time, the Treuhand had nothing in its favour except the brainy Rohwedder. Rohwedder had left the Hoeschel Steel Group to step in as a temporary replacement for Reiner Gohlke, the first Treuhand chief who had resigned from the job after only a couple of weeks; he was immediately faced with many loose ends and seemingly impossible problems. The Treuhand was in desperate need not only of a modern communications system, starting with telephones and fax machines, but also of a competent staff. During the early days of the Treuhand, a number of communist party hacks still operated within the organization trying to secure parts of East Germany for themselves. Rohwedder fired a number of the former staff and brought in western managers, many of whom took voluntary leaves of absence from high-ranking and well-paid positions, to help out at Alexander Platz. The staff totalled 3,000, one third of whom were westerners who filled senior positions and mostly ran the show under the eye of a supervisory board comprising leaders from business, trade unions and politics. Rohwedder also decentralized the Treuhand, forming 15 regional branches that handled sales of companies with fewer than 1,500 workers.

Rohwedder tried to give the Treuhand a new image by moving its headquarters from Alexander Platz to Berlin's biggest office block in Leipziger Strasse, close to where the Berlin Wall had stood. The agency issued an offer catalogue—both in print and on computer disk—with East German communist properties for sale ranging from run-down industrial firms and textile businesses to makers of hunting guns and even of yachts.

After Rohwedder's assassination, Birgit Breul stepped in. The former Christian Democrat and economics minister of West Germany's Lower Saxony confirmed her no-nonsense, Margaret Thatcher-like reputation by presiding over the sale of nearly 3,000 industrial firms for almost $7 billion by the end of July 1991 and getting pledges of roughly $30 billion for further investments. Nevertheless, those successes were overshadowed not only by disgruntlement with the Treuhand's selling process, which to many seemed more than opaque, but also by the fact that most of the 'people-owned plants' were totally outdated—some called them museums, to be polite—debt-ridden, polluted and generally staffed with unmotivated workers. Breul herself summarized the job of the Treuhandanstalt as a three-pronged task: 1) sell the few good firms that would find buyers easily; 2) restructure companies with some potential for success in a free market; and 3) close the hopeless cases. Of course, the first task was easy and brought in cash, but not enough to cover the second and third points.[2]

During the first months of the Treuhand's existence, after the currency reunion, the agency gave struggling companies guarantees of liquidity, as long as they could come up with a balance sheet and a survival plan. Though many of the former managers were willing enough to try, only a few could handle demands like that; baffled by western accounting, most handed in useless management plans. Others, like former members of the Stasi, often tried to cook the accounting records to ensure their positions within a formerly state-owned company.

A bubble that burst quickly was the Treuhand's initial dream of showing some profit. The small number of good companies on the East German market became even smaller after the initial bidding, while the bills for firms with environmentally damaging products started to rise beyond what was reasonable. Theodor Waigel, Minister of Finance in Bonn, had put a cap of DM21 billion on the deficit the Treuhand would be allowed to build up. By the end of the first year of the its activities, the agency had sold communist property for DM12 billion and had saved 554,000 jobs, but had incurred restructuring investment costs of DM12.8 billion, liabilities inherited as a result of sales of DM4.8 billion, and interest payments of DM11.6 billion. By the end of 1993, the Treuhand had roughly 300 companies left to be sold and had sold property for roughly DM50 billion.

The Treuhandanstalt, which called itself a privatization agency, was often ironically referred to as 'private, *perhaps*'. Companies already in the free market criticized the tax breaks, loans and other

---

[2] *Deutschland, ein Jahr danach*, SMH & Co, November 1991.

subsidies the newly privatized companies enjoyed. Desperate to save jobs, the Treuhand had developed not only a privatization agency, but also a support system for those companies that provide most of industrial employment. There are numerous instances in which the Treuhand rejected the highest offer and accepted a lower one in order to save jobs, in the process creating competitive problems that many bidders—especially those from abroad—resented. Indeed, although the Treuhand wanted to boost foreign investment by setting up offices in New York, 90 per cent of all the companies sold have gone to Germans; the remaining 10 per cent have been sold to British, French and American bidders.

A large number of companies that had been acquired by their East German managers were in danger of going bankrupt within the first 12 months. The Treuhand offered them an extra year in which to pay the purchase price and in some instances even took over some of the companies itself. The agency that proclaimed as its goal selling all of the communist portfolio by 1994 set up two holding companies in 1992 to handle restructuring work and management tasks that were beyond the agency's responsibility. As often happens with large government agencies, the Treuhand initially looked reasonably successful, but it greatly underestimated the effort it would take to reach the finishing line. In November 1990 Rohwedder had stated that he would remain in the job only if the Treuhand were given a high degree of independence from the government. He overestimated the extent to which a clear distinction could be made between the agency's market role and the state's regional support and political roles—a dilemma with which the Treuhand will have to deal and from which it will suffer until it finally is dismantled.

Wolf Schöde

After the collapse of the Honecker regime in November 1989, the reformers within the SED recognized that the centrally planned economy, in which production was tightly controlled, had proved its inefficiency. The reformers intended to install a new economic concept, a third alternative with its foundation somewhere between capitalism and communism. By December 1989 there already had been attempts to abandon central planning and all 'people's enterprises'.

The desire for a modern economy, a functioning economy with legal forms such as holdings, corporations, property rights and privatization was and is strong. In the Modrow government such thoughts played a major role in the decision-making process leading to the formation of the Treuhandanstalt, an institution that manages the total assets and properties of the former SED regime.[3]

In its role as owner of the shares of corporations emerging from the transformation of the state-owned Kombinates, companies, and organizations, the Treuhand is responsible for helping to construct a market-oriented, competitive private economy and for preserving existing jobs and creating new ones. The Treuhand is, therefore, concerned with a radical reconstructing of the state economy of the former GDR.

Well, as you might have noticed, that all sounds good enough on paper but is a rather difficult task in reality. Every day there are people on our doorstep protesting that we are too slow or too greedy, too money-oriented or not entrepreneurial enough. Right now, the Treuhand is the largest, most complex and most heterogenous holding company in the world. It has responsibility for over 8,000 companies comprising about 40,000 individual firms and extending throughout all sectors of the economy. Retail shops, public houses, chemist's shops, cinemas, individual businesses and real estate are included, as are community properties such as lakes, forests, Red Army barracks and food reserves for catastrophes. These responsibilities make the Treuhand more than a manager—really the heir to the people's economic assets.

Our priorities are privatization, reconstruction and closure.

In the first phase of our operation, between December 1989 and January 1990, our first priority was to bring capital into the country via joint ventures. The joint ventures procedures that were valid before the reunification allowed foreigners only a 49 per cent participation; the rule held true for West Germans, who, according to the Two Germanies Treaty of 1972, were also treated as foreigners in the GDR. For most West Germans joint ventures were not acceptable because of the 49 per cent clause. The Treuhand had to think of new ways to bring some money into the former GDR. Direct foreign-controlled investments, even totally owned, seemed the only option.

---

[3] Schöde was interviewed in March 1991, a few weeks before Detlev Karsten Rohwedder was assassinated.

To be historically accurate, the Treuhand was a baby of the re-formers of the SED regime. In the beginning there was not one West German economist, bureaucrat or consultant represented within the organization. Yet between January and May 1990 more than 3,000 businesses were founded. I only mention it because most people be-lieve the Treuhand is something the 'capitalists' brought along. But in reality it is, like the whole silent revolution, a creation of the people of East Germany. In my opinion the revolution had two roots: within the party, some of the wiser members knew that the economic and social system that had held the apparatus together for over 30 years could not exist any longer; also, the citizens sensed that, for the first time in several decades, the time was right to be daring and brave.

Looking back at the usual state of the economy in the GDR, the system can best be described as insolvent. There were shortages of products, East German Marks had to be traded for hard currencies, and there was high hidden unemployment, so the GDR was unable to compete outside the Iron Curtain. Production in the GDR couldn't begin to be competitive internationally. Production was driven by a concept that linked East Mark investment to the return of dollars or West German Marks. In other words, something like a value analysis was an unknown concept. Additionally, the GDR had few natural re-sources. For that reason, it had to trade high-tech products for other resources within the Council for Mutual Economic Assistance (Comecon).

Don't forget that owing to restrictions on technology transfer be-tween the west and east, countries like the GDR did not have the ad-vantages of developments such as micro-electronics. As you know, because of well-founded western fears, technologies that could be used for civilian and military purposes could not be exported to the east by most western companies, such as IBM and Microsoft. So, during the last ten years, the technologies which drove the western world either were not available or were very limited behind the Iron Curtain. In 1989 the GDR was economically dead; maybe it could have survived for another year or so, but not much longer.

The GDR's only chance of economic survival, as understood even by Modrow, was to switch to more free-market conditions and closer relationships to the west. Suddenly, phrases such as a 'social-ist free market' and 'socialist enterprise' could be heard. Well, now

I'm back where I started, at the initial phase in which SED reformers were controlling the path of the Treuhand. During the first unified elections the idea of the old cronies sitting behind the wheels became less and less attractive. The CDU won the elections, the SPD lost and it was understood that dramatic changes had to be made within the organization. On the 15 June a new Treuhand law was passed that brought the institution into its current form and reshaped its tasks and priorities.

The Treuhand in its present form was established at the same time the West German Mark was introduced within the borders of the former East Germany. The initial fiction was that the Treuhand could be a black box, financing itself either through sales or through reorganizations. The general thinking was that through reorganization of companies their value appreciated, so that when they were liquidated, costs such as those for unemployment and modernization could be recouped. Some even thought that eventually, using funds that accrue after ten years of selling off people-owned properties, money might be paid back to the East German citizens who had to exchange their money 1:2 to receive West German money.

With the new Treuhand law the structure of the organization changed as well. West German managers, bankers and administrators came to assist in the effort to divest the former people owned properties. Mr Vogeler served initially as the chairman of the board. He came from the board of Hoesch, one of West Germany's largest companies. He is really the man who shaped the organization in its new form. Soon people from Price Waterhouse, Deutsche Bank, and McKinsey came as support.

The first meeting of the board of directors can almost be called historic, as the mixture of top managers together with politicians from the east and west was unusual. On the board sat members of the people's council, the ministers of finance, economy and employment, environmentalists, representatives of IBM, Phillips, Grundig and many others. None of the new emerging states were represented, since they hadn't been formed yet.

Looking back at the year 1990, the concept of the Treuhand is only understandable as long as one treats every month as a new phase of development. Every phase was so intensive and important. Many of the people working here now gave up their ordinary tasks to help out. Most of them are professionals, high ranking-managers who asked for sabbaticals from their companies to assist in putting all the loose ends together. The first president of the Treuhand, Dr Reiner Gohlke, worked hard, but the chemistry wasn't right with many people and there was very little success in the beginning. Gohlke was then replaced with Rohwedder.

Rohwedder simultaneously served as the chairman of the board for Hoesch Steel Group. A very American-oriented man, he was quick, self-determined and loved challenges. He was born the son of a bookseller in Gotha, East Germany. His parents left early, so he grew up in the west, but he was one of a few who were able to work on their childhood dreams of reunifying Germany. He also served under Otto Graf Lambsdorff as secretary of state in the Ministry of Economic Affairs for more than ten years. Rohwedder changed the Treuhand from a bureaucratic institution into an entrepreneurial organization.

The problems we are dealing with are mounting every day. The Deutsche Mark was literally introduced overnight to the eastern territories and with it the free-market economy. This drastic shift of monetary funds was made against all better judgement and previous experience. In Latin America, Australia and everywhere else, those important decisions were carefully prepared and introduced step by step. But there were two major reasons why the currency exchange couldn't be done more slowly in Germany. First, the dominant political topic in 1990 was not economics, but rather the moral and political impulses of the reunification for Germany. Here was a historic chance to free East Germans, to free Berlin of its island status, and to send several thousand Red Army soldiers home. It was the only chance for us Germans to finally close the post-war chapter. The desire for unity was much stronger than any reasoning about economics. Second, the brain drain between neighbouring cities, such as Magdeburg and Hanover or Berlin and Frankfurt, could only be stopped if German Marks could also be earned in the east.

The expectations for developments in the east were very high among westerners, whose optimism was fuelled by memories of the Wirtschaftswunder—the economic miracle that took place in West Germany after the war. Citizens in the east, on the other hand, were waiting desperately for some improvement in their lifestyle. That required relatively little in the beginning since for most, an improvement in lifestyle meant acquiring a car, a radio, a new TV set and maybe taking a trip to Italy. The appetite among the easterners for travel in particular was almost insatiable in the beginning. The Alps, the Mediterranean, anywhere you could think of was crowded with people from behind the Iron Curtain. I talked to a 60-year-old man from East Berlin who told me, 'When I was young I couldn't travel because of the Second World War. Then I couldn't travel because I wasn't allowed to under the recent regime. But now, before I get sick and can't move anymore, I would like to see the Alps.'

Some people ridicule comments like that, but there is nothing laughable about them. Such comments represent a sad and a very significant socio-psychological problem.

The fact that the western German Mark became the currency for the former GDR almost overnight resulted in a liquidity problem. Within the first eight days after the currency exchange, the Treuhand had to guarantee liquid assets to 7,000 GDR firms. The Treuhand worked with the banks which gave loans directly to the companies with the agency functioning as guarantor, backed by the German government. Someone here at the Treuhand said, 'The GDR is the country of unpaid bills'.

At the same time these economic developments were producing unrealistically high financial expectations on both sides, the major December elections were in preparation. The Social Democrats' candidate, Oskar LaFontaine, coined the phrase, 'hot autumn'. He was convinced that the shock of the introduction of the West German Mark was too much for the voters, who would make him the favourite in the elections based on his suggestion that the two Germanies should form a two-state system that would eventually grow together. The 'hot autumn' never happened, and the eastern unions still had contracts with the major companies that made firing workers impossible until 30 June 1991. It happened that many people were already out of work at the end of 1990, but they continued to receive their salaries and were legally still employed. Furthermore, the German government heavily subsidized GDR exports to the Soviet Union during that period. The psychological effects of unemployment, and the resulting social unrest, could not be felt yet, and LaFontaine's hopes for a 'hot autumn' were never fulfilled, at least not during that important pre-election period. LaFontaine lost in the first nationwide elections by a big margin to Chancellor Kohl and his Christian Democratic Party (CDU).

Shortly before the election the Treuhand was increasingly criticized for its methods of granting loans to GDR firms. The public criticism resulted in a reduction in the number of loans guaranteed. The agency's next priority became the privatization of the East German economy. We were confronted with two diametrically opposing opinions. Many economists believe that one cannot privatize an economy unless it is healthy; others suggest that an economy such as the GDR's cannot recuperate unless it is privatized. As in so many cases, the truth lies somewhere in between. For private housing, it is true that the best repairman is the owner himself. Generally that is true for all consumer-related industries, such as transport, energy and construction. Lufthansa showed some interest in buying the government-owned GDR airline, Interflug. But the international media immediately spoke of a German monopoly and feared unfair competition.

Generally speaking, the privatization policy of the Treuhand follows three guidelines: (1) sell businesses for reasonable prices, (2) require a business plan from investors, and (3) clear up restitution claims.

In principle, evaluations are made according to the rules common in western industrial nations—asset value, income value and other value-creating factors such as goodwill and know-how. The evaluation of returns on investment or of future earnings is more difficult in centrally controlled markets, because one can't build on valid experience from the past. A market for resources does not exist, so market values for long-term development are missing. The real-estate market is still subject to inexact valuations. Consequently, land often must be evaluated by neutral experts; but buyers may sometimes pay premium purchase prices for real estate based on market values fixed by outside experts.

Usually, we expect an investor to present a concept, a business plan that shows his management strategy for the continuation of the business, the investment he has planned, and possibly his approach to preserving jobs.

Problems that became apparent by the end of 1990 were the environmental burdens and damage that have occurred and the influence of old cronies and party connections. Additionally, the question of claims by third parties for refund or indemnification became a bigger burden. The law of clear title obliges the Treuhand to ensure that there is no known declaration of claims by a former proprietor. We can only handle restraints on transferring title pragmatically, on a case-by-case basis. Should a former owner successfully enforce his claim, he now can only demand financial indemnification by the agency, not the return of his land.

By the end of 1990, the initial West German euphoria was gone. The Wirtschaftswunder hadn't happened, and the press was full of examples of lazy easterners who were only looking for the quick buck. Many 'explanations' were offered: the easterners can't work; they haven't been used to work; their education is bad. Of course, such assertions are based on personal impressions and experiences, but I believe the real problem lies much deeper. It starts with the endless list of complications that arise when communally owned property and companies must be transformed into private properties and companies. It is less an economic problem than a legal one. The reunification treaty proposed that restitution comes before business. Within the first few months we received over a million claims from former property and company owners. It will take more than a decade to go through all of these claims. Some will make privatization impossible, others will help to speed up the process. There is a great uncertainty among GDR citizens about what will happen in the future because most of the property titles are not cleared and won't be for a while.

In addition, westerners are angry about the current tax increases. Chancellor Kohl had said, during his election campaign, that higher taxes wouldn't be necessary. After the taxes are raised this summer [1991], Germany's tax brackets will be among the highest in the world. The tax problem occurred partly because, at the time of the election, the five new federal states had not yet been established; essentials, like a government, still needed to be put in place. The Treuhand has served as a scapegoat, ever since the discussions about higher taxes started.

I feel as if we are in a pressure cooker. Today everybody looks towards the Treuhand to make tough decisions on controversial issues such as the sale of Interflug to Lufthansa, and the disposition of historic castles such as the Wartburg. The priorities of West Germans have shifted from dealing with issues of political and moral responsibility to addressing problems of an economic nature. Viewing issues strictly in terms of black or white is a typically German attitude. So the Treuhand's task is a little bit like trying to answer the question, 'Are you with me or against me?'

Germany always has lagged behind the social developments in other nations, and structural changes come very slowly. Once they are broadly accepted, it is difficult to change them. For the first time Germans have experienced what it means to witness and undergo a very rapid change in structures. Accomplishing the dramatic shift we're facing now will take patience, time and a lot of money. A change in social structures is mostly to the advantage of the next generation. The hard work of the Germans in the 1950s and 1960s benefited people in the 1980s and 1990s. Similarly, the beneficiaries of the present historic changes will be the next two generations.

Waiting for a booming economy for East Germans based on West German goods is no help. We need research and development to help us create new, competitive and intelligent products.

We must try to speed up privatization, but not at the expense of social unrest or the destruction of the social fabric. Never before have all components within one system changed at the same time: while switching from socialism and communism to capitalism, we are changing economic, political, cultural and social conditions. Changes for most humans are very difficult to comprehend. We should make loans available not only for winding up the affairs of companies and disposing of their equipment, but also for developing human capital.

I see the task of the Treuhand as being broader than that of a mere money manager and trader. It should also be an advocate for social responsibilities at the same time. The Treuhand is an agent of change that is trying to be successful as quickly as possible.

The organization is clearly eager to strike deals. Just as the Resolution Trust Corporation in the United States manages the assets of failed savings and loans and arranges for their disposal, we are responsible for making East Germany's companies more efficient and competitive and selling them off. Nearly half of the companies for sale are in heavy industry, ranging from printing press makers to railway car, brake and gear manufacturers. So far Volkswagen and Mercedes Benz have invested heavily in automobile manufacturing. Opel, a General Motors subsidiary, has also started to produce cars in the east. Almost 30 per cent of the companies sold are in the luxury food sector. Coca-Cola, for example, is the ninth largest investor so far in East Germany. Philip Morris locally produces one-third of the tobacco supply to the former FDR. Siemens has invested $60 million in the electronics and communications sectors. BASF, the world's largest chemical company, purchased Synthesenwerke Schwarzheide in a particularly interesting negotiation. BASF struck a deal with the Treuhandanstalt regarding its potential environmental liability; BASF would be responsible for any environmental or pollution problems that were known to exist when the plant was purchased, but the government would be responsible for any problems found thereafter.

The future poses three questions. When will the economy hit the bottom in the five emerging federal states? How big will the change of structures really be within the former GDR? And how stable are the political conditions?

The mood among the people is worse than the reality. In autumn 1990 it was exactly the other way around, the mood and the outlook were better than the reality. I don't think we'll have to contend with a social disaster as long as we can create a strong belief that the future will improve and there can be a happy ending. A happy ending means that within ten years the eastern part of Germany will be highly modernized, will have a stable infrastructure, and will be able to compete within the international market. The magic words are high-tech, high-culture, high-quality.

For the first time since the Third Reich, there is a trend towards upward mobility within the boundaries of the GDR—the old system did not allow any pluralism for 60 years. Nevertheless, Germany won't be able to handle all its future problems by itself. It will need the support of Europe.

The EC, Bonn and the individual states have created programmes ranging from loans targeting particular industries to investment and grants. The European Recovery Programme, which dates back to after the Second World War, is offering loans derived from interest collected from Marshall Plan funds. These loans, called ERPs, are available primarily for the establishment of new corporations in the tourist industry and for investments in environmental protection. East German investment is not routine; it requires careful and thorough planning, patience and diligence. Essentially, investors will have to design plans and strategies for guiding back to profitability industries that have been held back by decades of centralized planning. These tasks reach far beyond just negotiating sales and determining favourable prices with the Treuhand. However, investments in the east promise unprecedented long-term opportunities inside the European market as well as a clear access to eastern Europe.

Henning Prenzlin

In all my mostly unfortunate dealings with the Treuhandanstalt, I have found that the agency is not very keen on selling the small and medium-sized companies that really are the backbone of West Germany's economy. The agency is too big and too bureaucratic to handle the needs of smaller West German entrepreneurs who are really willing to invest their money in the east. The Treuhand has forgotten that West Germany didn't build its wealth on big Fortune 500 firms, but rather on entrepreneurial, often family-owned, businesses.

In the summer of 1992 the organization advertised its sale of small, East German, formerly people-owned businesses. The ad campaign was clearly aimed at smaller West German investors. It was a roaring success and over 1,600 inquiries came in, most of the serious. The Treuhand reduced them down to 300 candidates, but three months later not a single deal has been completed.

If I make inquiries at the Treuhand about a business I'm interested in, I usually spend hours on the phone unsuccessfully, because nobody can give me an adequate answer. Its officials usually know very little about the companies they are trying to sell, particularly if the deals are smaller ones. I sometimes even have the feeling the officials shy away from West Germans' questions, thinking they might uncover some uncomfortable or difficult issues. I feel, therefore, that many of the small businesses in the east have been sold to East German managers. I believe that is very good as long as they are capable of running the business and have access to financing. Of course, for the Treuhand it is easiest to sell to East German managers. They are typically not trained to ask discriminating questions, so the transfer goes quicker. Many people, like myself, fear that a lot of businesses that went to easterners will fail again because of lack of skills and lack of experience in a free-market situation. The late Detlev Karsten Rohwedder warned at his last news conference that

303

handing over cash to East Germany's current managers could be equivalent to flushing it down the drain. Today not too many people want to be reminded of that remark.

Apart from the administrative problems one faces with the Treuhand, there is one major issue that makes investing in the east very difficult. It is the possibility of reconveyance of restitution claims by former property owners. The possibility of claims by former owners makes real-estate deals almost impossible, for example. Typically, you acquire a piece of property, start building an apartment house, and then somebody shows up and says, 'I have proof that this is my land. I was dispossessed in 1956.' The property rights have not yet been clearly defined. I believe, that so far, the Treuhand has received nearly 1 million claims arising from illegal property confiscation by the communist government. One case became particularly famous: a West German claimed ownership of the property on which the 26-story International Trade Centre now stands in East Berlin.

The deadline for former owners of expropriated property to file claims was October 1990, but late filings are still blocking sales— even acquiring assets that are currently free of any claims might not buy security. Bonn has now passed a law that permits sale of a property to a third party even if a claim has already been filed by a former owner, if the sale is necessary to protect the labour force or to supply housing; however, the transaction still can take years. And because the law allows for monetary compensation to the claimant, in place of restitution, getting a firm decision on the value of property can take forever. Besides the possibility that you might never obtain a clear title to the property on which you want to start construction, Bonn has unfortunately passed a new law, which applies to all of Germany, that prohibits a building's owner from raising the rent more than 20 per cent within a certain time frame. Given the average monthly rent for a two-bedroom apartment in the GDR, there is not an awful lot of money to be made. I fear that eventually a two-class system will develop between the east and west. I recently heard about a divorced woman who had to stay in the same one-bedroom apartment with her ex-husband because she couldn't find a new apartment. That is a situation unheard of in the west. I believe that, with so little incentive for construction investment, the situation won't change.

In addition to the restitution claims, investors deal daily with environmental liabilities and potentially with employment obligations. Upon reunification, the five new states adopted German labour laws that require the purchaser of an East German company to assume the obligations of existing employment contracts. Lay-offs are only permitted if you can prove that they are essential for conducting business.

I admit that we Germans tend to see things blacker than they are in reality, and I really hope that operates as a motivating factor so things won't work out as badly as they present themselves right now.

Walter Momper

It doesn't make any sense to talk about past mistakes, but in the case of the Treuhandanstalt many people, including myself, wonder why there is just one big Treuhand. Wouldn't it have cut bureaucracy, boosted competition and speeded privatization if several independent regional agencies had been set up? The Treuhand as it exists now should have been dissolved, because its monolith structure is too easily identifiable with the centralization of the communist system under which it started to exist. Another alternative, which I think wouldn't have worked, would have been to put East German firms up for auction and let the market do the rest. That kind of hands-off politics would have created an even higher unemployment rate and more social tension than we have now.

Today the Treuhand is kind of a buffer between government and business; it's a difficult role, and I'm sure nobody will mourn the disappearance of this colossus after it has done its job. In particular, people from the east resent the fact that it has not fired all employees who were communist party members, but only those who were proven Stasi agents or senior party members. Even that was sometimes hard to prove, since, during the chaotic months between the fall of the Wall and the first elections, thousands of party officials had time to shred files and papers related to their past. Although the Treuhand had dismissed 400 out of 1,000 managers for political reasons, for the majority it was easy to change from communism to capitalism overnight.

Robert W. Becker

Every American firm that successfully purchased a company from the Treuhandanstalt is happy with the agency. I will say, however, that no organization as big as the Treuhand could successfully avoid mismanagement in some areas and less-than-honest dealings—corruption if you like—in other areas. It is much too big a company, much too much money is involved, and there is of course the human factor, which shouldn't be underestimated. Many times the Treuhand, when given the choice between a German and an American investment proposal, will decide for the German one because they understand how a German company functions but might not know how an American firm works. I have argued repeatedly with both the Treuhand and with the German government, that there are cartel-oriented and monopolistic tendencies in German industries, particularly in the power-generation industry. Whether you are talking about Telecom as a monopolistic market or you are talking about the three major western power producers who had monopoly rights granted to them, these are areas where the agency gets a black mark.

The real problem of the Treuhand lies in the scope of its task. Can you really privatize that many companies in three years? It's my observation that many companies will be lost in the process and that, Kurt Biedenkopf, minister president of Saxony, was right when he said that some of those firms don't have to go down the tubes. The Treuhand is a *Behörde* (bureaucracy), not an enterprise, and it functions like a bureaucracy. It received its marching orders and said, 'That's what we are going to achieve in three years'. It will fulfil its tasks whether it makes sense or not.

Chapter Twenty-three

Reclaiming Family Property

Between 1945 and 1961 over 3.5 million people left East Germany. Many of them fled the communist-run country with little more than the clothes on their backs, some papers, and maybe the family silver hidden in a baby carriage. There are many well-known tales of families leaving at night with children and babies in their arms abandoning their homes as though they were just walking off to a casual dinner instead of turning the key to lock up for the last time. Those who left relatives behind sometimes managed to get some personal effects to the west by having small items and valuables sent out by mail. But many of those parcels were confiscated at the border and never made it to the west. Typically, the property and valuables of those who turned their backs on the East German regime were confiscated immediately and either auctioned off among party members or just made available to them for the taking.

From the very beginning of its presence in the Soviet occupation zone and later in the GDR, the communist regime was determined to put its Marxist definition of property into practice. 'Socialist property' would be owned and administered for the benefit of all people. Private property would be strictly for non-productive use by individual citizens. The first reform to install these practices was the *Bodenreform* (land reform), which took place in 1945 and 1946 and during which land holdings over 250 acres were brought under Soviet jurisdiction. Collectivization, which started in 1952, merged, first, farms and, later, industrial sectors into large entities that were supervised and controlled by the government. Owners who were not expelled became employees of the state (owners were not compensated for collectivized property) and had to fulfil state-imposed annual production quotas. Smaller businesses fell on hard times in the mid-1960s, when their supplies were cut off or their loans were denied. The final act against private property came in 1972, when the remaining privately held businesses were 'nationalized' for cash that was paid to owners in ten equal annual instalments. These companies were merged into *Volkseigene Betriebe,* (People-owned plants—VEB) and in 1980 they became Kombinates.

Property belonging to citizens who 'fled the republic' for the west immediately came under state control. Most such property belonged to people who had left the GDR before the Wall was built in 1961. In addition, some West Germans had owned second homes in the east before the GDR came into existence in 1949; these, too, were confiscated.

Naturally, after the reunification the question of how, if at all, to restore lost property arose, along with masses of claims. The 1972 nationalization was reversed immediately. But more difficult issues were presented by farmers who had been forced to collectivize the houses and properties taken from them. In 1990 the reunited Germanies decided to try to redress the property-related wrongdoing of both the Nazi regime and the communists. Germany passed a law that any property confiscated after 1933 would be returned if proof of ownership could be shown. Property seized in the Soviet occupation zone between 1945 and 1949 is exempt from this law, however, since the Soviets agreed to the German reunification only on the condition that those expropriations were to be excluded.

Furthermore, the law concluded that property cannot be given back if its former owners have already been compensated. Of all the eastern European countries where democracy is taking root, Hungary and the former Czechoslovakia have enacted the strictest rules for returning property or compensating former owners. To qualify in Czechoslovakia one had to be both a citizen of the country and a resident. Additionally, for property to be returned, it must have been seized after 1955 and there can have been no previous compensation. The Hungarian parliament will only provide compensation bonds for confiscated property.

Both compensation through payment and restitution of property have their problems. In the first case, where will the money come from to satisfy the millions of claims? In the second case, what happens to buildings and properties that are currently occupied? The German government established an October 1990 deadline for filing of all claims, but property owners who failed to file by that date did not automatically waive all their rights. According to the German law, a claimant is still eligible for financial compensation and moreover, so long as the agency handling property claims has not sold the property in question, a claimant who files after the deadline may still seek restitution of the property. Considering the wave of problems related to transferring property back to its original owner, as well as their inhibiting effect on investments from the outside, many argue that Germany should have limited itself to compensating legal owners rather than giving them back the property itself.

Most of those who were dispossessed for ideological reasons after they left the former GDR had never even dreamed of getting back what they once left behind. For many the reclaiming process is very emotional and time-consuming, since title registers were destroyed and records were mismanaged or simply not kept by the communist regime. Many who finally get their property back feel a responsibility to rehabilitate buildings or clean the often heavily polluted property; others, for whom the surprising fact that they owned property 'in the east' became a financial and emotional burden, sold that property—often run-down factories and orchards—to interested developers who were mostly West Germans.

What does that mean for the 17 million former East Germans? For many it means they have a West German landlord, ideally one with deep pockets who will repair the sins of 40 years of neglect. Eventually, this rehabilitation will result in higher rents, which currently still average around $70 per month for a one-bedroom apartment, almost matching pre-reunification levels. The few who were living in houses in East Germany may have to move or to pay rent to West German owners. Many East Germans who are living in property being claimed by former owners have difficulty understanding the meaning of 'private property' and the responsibility that comes with it. In some tragic cases where East German families have to move out of what they thought belonged to them, West German claims are disputed. Even East Germans who didn't believe in communism absorbed some of its ideological constructs, among them the illusion that their land belongs to 'the people', as communist law said it did. In reality, they merely had the right to *use* apartments, farmland and company premises. The meaning of real estate and the battalions of West Germans coming to the east to reclaim it are for many quite difficult to understand. Many East Germans think that ownership of 'their' property should be their reward for 40 years of work and suffering.

Wolfgang Schäuble

Among the most difficult issues we had to deal with during the period of reunification were those involving property rights. Governments in both the east and west had already made declarations concerning this topic at the time of the currency union. On 15 June 1990 there was no question on our side that property rights had to be guaranteed in the former GDR in keeping with Article 14 of the Basic Law. One major exception had to be made in accordance with the dispositions of properties which had occurred between 1945 and 1949 under the occupying powers. This exception, which was defined during the two-plus-four talks was for property seized during the occupation by the Soviets after the Second World War.

It was clear from the very beginning that the availability of land and buildings would be a key to the rebuilding effort in the former GDR. Endless quarrels about property ownership and rights of restitution would only further delay the effort. The reunification treaty, therefore, included a programme to promote investment in the east that not only guaranteed indemnification for property liabilities, but also gave the creation of workplaces through outside investments a higher priority than redress of lost property rights.

The almost innumerable cases of property rights claims makes this issue the most complex and touchy one in the whole treaty. What's more, questions like these on property confiscated before 1945, for example from Jewish citizens, are tied up with questions of what to do about expropriated property that no longer exists, as well as with non-property issues. For example, how do you indemnify people not only for damage of material goods, but for loss of freedom or physical harm?

To my mind, the regulation sets the right priorities in principle by generally trying to reinstate property rights while weighing the interests of both original owners and current users, and by giving priority to investment and creation of jobs. In reality, unfortunately, this regulation often has not brought satisfying solutions.

Margarethe Fuchs

We returned to the east for the first time 29 years after we had left the GDR. We went back with very mixed feelings. The political events during autumn 1989 were already very emotional for us, but returning 'home' again for the first time was very touching. Throughout the years, my husband had missed personal belongings such as books and portraits of his family. We knew we wouldn't find those, but my husband still hoped to go back to his family's past.

The villa we lived in as a young couple had been converted into an apartment building with 14 tenants living in it. Originally, different family members had occupied it, and the house lent itself to being subdivided among several different parties. We found a parking spot within walking distance of the house. As we came closer, we saw half of a balcony lying on the pavement and people walking around it. The house was in a disastrous condition. All of the balconies from the old stucco facade had fallen off. The rubble from the one in front of us must have come down recently. Nobody had enough pride to clean up the remains. The heads of the art deco figures on both sides of the house had long been missing. The whole house, which once had been painted light yellow and grey, was black from the coal-polluted air. My husband, who had inherited the house from his mother, stood in tears in front of the wreck. He couldn't understand how people could let beautiful things deteriorate like that, even if they didn't own them.

Above the outside doorbell we noted that the housekeeper lived on the top floor. When we rang the bell, there was no answer, but we could see movement behind the curtain. My husband wanted to leave, but I pushed him inside. He is not a person who looks for confrontation, and I sensed that he was feeling uncomfortable. After some arguing, we decided to walk up to the third floor and talk to the housekeeper. Literally, none but the most essential repairs had been made during the previous 30 years. In the entryway we saw signs warning of rat poison. The iron railing of the staircase was missing, and only one lamp—which had no shade—lit the spiral staircase leading to the upper three floors. Some people had painted their entry doors white; others had chained their bikes to the iron staircase. One could still appreciate that at one time this had been a charming villa, yet I didn't feel as though I was going through a house in Germany. The house had been so badly neglected that I sensed that I was paying a visit to a Third World country. We both had a hard time identifying with the house or with the feeling it gave us.

When we reached the third floor, we rang the housekeeper's doorbell several times again. An old woman opened. She was friendly but not very talkative. We asked her how long she had been living there and she answered, 'Twenty-eight years'. She must have known intuitively that we were the legal owners, because she immediately ran off a list of things that wouldn't work, starting with the heat and the hot water. Her voice was demanding.

I believe it was then that my husband, for whom a sentimental attachment brought him back to the house where he had grown up, started to distance himself from his boyhood home. Before we left we walked up and down the street where he used to ride a bike and play. Like his old home, all the houses had been sorely neglected. Weeds grew out of the walls, balconies were missing, side staircases lay in rubble, paint peeled, leaves from years before rotted in the yard. Although it was a crisp January day with a clear blue sky, the street seemed grey and colourless. Here and there one could recognize in the windows the logos of West German pastries or other consumer goods that had found their way into the east since the opening of the Wall, but that was the only colour present.

I don't know what we expected of that 'homecoming'. We definitely didn't want to move back, but maybe we thought at least the house and the neighbourhood would look like we remembered them. We had hoped that somebody had taken care of what we had left behind.

On the five-hour drive back, my husband was very quiet. We were almost home when he said, 'I don't want to see this house again. Let's reclaim it and then sell it as soon as possible.' My husband had made an emotional, not a financial, decision. Not selling it would have meant to take responsibility for it. Had we been younger, maybe we would have done it, but it became clear that day that when we left the east in 1961, we really left everything behind. It took this journey into the past to realize that East Germany was no longer home.

The reclamation process was difficult and cumbersome, almost impossible to deal with without a local attorney. All claims for family properties went through the local mayor's office. Most larger cities now have elected mayors from the west, but secretaries and assistants are local. In the early days after the reunification, the junior positions were filled with the same people who had served under the communists. So people from the west who had fled and now came back to reclaim weren't treated with much friendliness. The first incident occurred when the lady who was in charge of comparing my husband's mother's will with her title registration said, 'A will won't prove anything and you don't have a title to the house, or did you take that along with you when you fled our republic in 1961?' She was obviously one of the old hard-liners who hadn't noticed that the wind had changed. It took an awful lot of restraint on my behalf not to jump at her. What worked was asking for her supervisor. It's awful to say, but it must be a German trait that asking for a supervisor makes people jump. It took days and weeks to find the title. The title register usually was a carefully kept log of property and ownership, but not under communist rule, when all property was turned into *Volkseigentum* (people's property). Either many of the old registries are missing, or if they do exist, certain lines have been crossed through. We were fortunate eventually to obtain our title. We had employed a lawyer who specialized in reclamation of East German property; almost a year after our first visit we actually had the house back. We received the title, put the property on the market, and in a matter of days sold it to a West German construction company, which is renovating the whole house. I hear it looks nice. Most of the old tenants are still in there, with the exception of two families who left the east to try their luck in West Germany.

Part Six

United yet Divided 1991–1993

Chance never helps those who do not help themselves.
Sophocles

Chapter Twenty-four

How Different Are We?

When the first curious West German tourists visited the East, most of them returned deeply depressed. The economic crisis, the pollution, the miserable housing conditions confronted them everywhere they went. But one impression hurt most. 'Over there' they are different. Although Germans on both sides of the fence have been speaking the same language and have shared the same culture for hundreds of years, the division of the country during the previous 40 years has left recognizable imprints not only on the standard of living in the east, but also on the minds of most easterners. Far more alarming than the economic crisis is the difference in how people on opposite sides of the Wall looked at life.

'We are still divided' is a truth that many have to discover for themselves—divided no longer by the Wall, but by experience, expectations, attitudes and value systems. Though communist propaganda has been unsuccessful in driving an emotional wedge between easterners and westerners, within months after the Wall fell many West Germans have developed a sense of a separate identity. Throughout the years after the Wall had gone up, the majority of East Germans viewed West Germany and the western hemisphere in general as a beacon of hope for democratic change. West Germans tried to stay in contact with relatives on the other side of the Wall or if they had no family in the east, with friends and acquaintances. Ironically, the two Germanies seemed to feel closer while they were separated than after the Wall had fallen.

The differences between the two Germanies are partly the result of living apart for nearly a century, but even more so they are the product of separate post-war experiences. West Germans, aided by the American Marshall Plan, built their famous Wirtschaftswunder literally out of the ruins of the Third Reich and the Second World War. They developed one of the strongest economies in the west. Their East German cousins, meanwhile, were ruled by a neo-Stalinism that not only suppressed any kind of democratic development and free market planning, but also stifled personal initiative and individual thinking. The system imprinted most people's minds with the horrors any tyranny leaves behind. The regime

317

kept the former GDR alive by using massive repression and fear to control its citizens. The vast majority of the people didn't approve of the political and economic conditions they had to live under, but they could not avoid being profoundly shaped by those conditions any more than they could escape the GDR itself.

For example, after the Wall had tumbled, West Germans trying to arrange meetings in the east were puzzled when East Germans frequently suggested meeting in public places which could not be bugged. But for most easterners it was and is difficult to shake off behaviours and fears that were nurtured over decades. Psychologists have found that because many East Germans kept their anger and their frustration under rigid control by simply playing the roles the regime wanted them to play, split personalities and blocked emotions are common among them.

Ironically, East Germans often complain about unfriendliness and a lack of warmth when they meet West Germans. While such generalizations are often wrong when applied to individuals, there does seem to be a pattern in the way easterners and westerners think of each other and of themselves. The very words used to differentiate East from West Germans, *Ossie* and *Wessie,* have only been used since the fall of the Wall. They are short labels for stereotypes for the naïve, sometimes confused, friendly but inexperienced Ossie and the slick, impatient, money-driven and know-it-all Wessie.

'One nation, two different worlds' is how the current German situation is often summarized. The misconception, particularly on the western side, was that a 40-year-long tyranny wouldn't leave any emotional legacy at all. Both easterners and westerners lived under the false assumption that when the Wall fell and the communist system ended, they would share the same values and attitudes again. But everyone, including those who were not part of the system and those who rejected and opposed it, was shaped by its rules and demands.

How differently the eastern and western mentalities developed is reflected in language, concepts and value systems. Of course there are different dialects, but more importantly there are certain words and vocabulary that reflect a socialist culture, such as *Schokoladenhohlkörper*—a word whose meaning most West Germans would not know. The word, literally meaning 'chocolate hollow space', was commonly used in the east for 'chocolate Easter bunny', since religious terms were forbidden in everyday language. The kind of cuisine that was available in the former East Germany is best suggested by the word *Sättigungsbeilage*, meaning 'filling dish'. Side dishes in the former GDR were usually exactly that, tasteless fillers. As unfamiliar as West Germans are with such words, East Germans have equal difficulty with terms that refer to concepts outside their experience, such as 'marketing' and words such as 'hardware' and 'software'.

In the few days after the Wall came down, teenagers from both sides were eager to intermingle. In recent months, the enthusiasm for meeting youngsters of the same age from the other side has faded. Westerners complain that their eastern counterparts are boring, obsequious and avoid eye contact; the eastern teenagers, on the other hand, say their western acquaintances are too aggressive and too strong-headed. Easterners, who complain that westerners are superficial, point out that they in the east spend their weekends more productively. People there are proud that they don't need 'toys' like tennis rackets and surfboards to keep themselves busy in their free time. They are happy to spend the time reading, talking to friends or going to the theatre.

Obviously, how free time is spent is also related to the economic gulf that splits Germans. Average income of former East Germans is less than 40 per cent of that of their western counterparts.

According to recent polls, East and West Germans have very different opinions on topics of concern to both. Asked which city should be the capital for example, 70 per cent of all former GDR citizens say Berlin; only 46 per cent of West Germans give it their vote.

Of course, every German's household has a TV set, an electric drill, a bicycle and maybe a piano; however, very few dryers, video recorders or home computers are found in the east yet. While over 60 per cent of all West Germans live in spaces with more than four rooms, only 25 per cent of the former East German population enjoy that luxury. Most East Germans still live in houses that are older than the GDR and have not been repaired since 1945.[1] Others live in one of the 'achievements' of the Honecker regime, so-called *Trabantenstädten* (satellite cities). Most of the buildings in a *Trabantenstädte*, where thousands of people live in tiny quarters, are badly built and in shocking disrepair. Many high-rises will have to be torn down within the next few years.

West Germans travelling through the East look with disgust upon the living conditions, the dirt and grey façades of the cities. Those cities are now slowly beginning to brighten up, but only with the help of some billion Deutsche Marks that are being pumped into infrastructure improvements and the renovation of historic buildings and private homes. Even well-meaning West Germans can be heard complaining, 'If we had only known what we are getting into!'

While it probably should not be taken too seriously, the message printed on a T-shirt that recently sold out in both the east and west hints

---

[1] See *Spiegel Spezial, 162 Tage Deutsche Geschichte*, pp. 98–102.

at the frustration felt on both sides: 'I want my Wall back'. A cabaret comedian in Berlin gets laughter from his audience with lines such as, 'I would have preferred Germany being divided in a way that would end the battle of the sexes as well as the Cold War: one Germany for men, one for women, and Berlin for transsexuals'.

Many West Germans were shocked by a series of polls made in the east from 1990 to 1992. Answering the question, 'Do you think communism is a good idea, but was badly realized?', 53 per cent of former GDR citizens said yes. Asked if they think socialism is a good idea, but was badly realized, 63 per cent said yes.[2] The poll results are a definite sign that, after 40 years of living in a dictatorship, many find it difficult to admit that they had lived for an idea that proved wrong, whether they supported the system actively or passively. West Germans, on the other hand, have grown impatient about the bill for reunification, the small signs of economic improvement, and the potential instability in the east that might very well influence the political scene throughout Germany.

How long it will take to overcome the differences in the rocky marriage between the two Germanies is far from clear. But it seems unlikely that a solution will come quickly; instead, it looks like resolving the differences in the emotions and thinking between the east and west is more a long-term social and political problem which could take at least a generation to overcome.

Egon Bahr

Once we swore devotion to the nation's unity despite its division: today, despite reunification, we have realized that the nation remains divided. We all made the same mistake, the West German government and the opposition: we underestimated the differences in mentality between east and west. Forty years cannot just be wiped out.

Walter Momper

For the people in the west and even more so for those in the east, the fall of the Wall began a cultural revolution. The changes affect every aspect of life. For people in the east, an economic, political and social house of cards collapsed overnight. People in the west must

---

[2] Ibid, p. 120.

also adapt. We have 17 million more German people to live with who been living in another world for 40 years. Their system, their lifestyle and their habits have been totally uprooted and rapidly replaced with what we in the west have to offer.

In Berlin especially, where the former Germanies are in closest proximity, there is more tension than anywhere else. Easterners speak of colonialization, while West Berliners complain about the exploding costs in 'their' city, which is suddenly overcrowded and filled with crime and uncertainty. The level of competition since the Wall fell is higher in Germany, not only in the workplace, but also for apartments and in traffic. There is something paradoxical about the whole process of reunification. In 1990 East Germans could vote and exercise democratic rights for the first time in more than half a century. Yet both sides, east and west, found and still find plausible arguments that no one had ever really been asked what kind of a Germany the reunited Germany should be. Nobody was prepared for the speed with which reunification happened. That is probably one of the few things Germans would agree upon. Otherwise, reunification has brought a collision between confident, open, upfront, sometimes cut-throat and market-driven people from the west and more passive, uncertain, bewildered, mostly introverted East Germans, who tend to avoid conflict and withdraw when challenged.

Kristina Matschat

For the west, reunification has not brought any turbulence into everyday life. The 30 per cent unemployment rate, the dying industries, the polluted rivers and the job retraining are all in the east. Conversations in most eastern living rooms start with discussions of who is working, and how to pay for this or that.

We are probably the only region in the industrialized world where a soap or detergent commercial trumpeting how one brand can outperform another can be the sole subject of a dinner conversation. There were no choices under communism, not even in soaps. Simple things like utility bills look totally different than they did under the communist regime; food shopping is a new experience. Now we can really buy what we have seen advertised over the years on western TV. It may sound ridiculous, but for many the choices are so overwhelming that shopping has become a burden. Jobs and fixed rents are gone, crime has spread, schools are reorganized, banking, health and the legal system are new, and even the newspapers carry 'real news'. In 1945 Germany experienced a visible and bloody collapse; now the eastern region has lived through a bloodless destruction. As fortunate as we were to have had a silent revolution, it is much harder to understand.

I think a lot of the personal misunderstandings between easterners and westerners result from people in the west being too presumptuous and then being perceived as arrogant. I remember when a friend brought a girlfriend along from the west soon after the Wall had fallen. She just confidently flopped into a chair in our living room and started to chit-chat with everybody around her. She probably didn't mean any offence, but for many in the room her behaviour was a demonstration of arrogance. People here in the east are not used to opening up very quickly to strangers. During GDR times, you didn't know if you could trust the person or not. I think many of us have developed an instinctive response that asks whether it is all right to reveal yourself, or whether whatever you reveal might be used against you.

To a certain degree we easterners lived schizophrenic lives. Daily newspapers told us fairy tales and lies while we heard the truth on the streets and sometimes via West German TV. On the outside, many of us acted one way; inside, and with very close friends, we acted differently. I think what many westerners don't understand is that most of us have no problem fulfilling a task or learning how to work a computer; rather, the hard part of adjusting is looking at life differently and changing a set of behaviours that had unconsciously been implanted over the past 40 years. Changes like that take time, yet many people in the west grow noticeably impatient around East Germans.

Many East Germans, including myself, resent some of the West German advisers who come into the east to help us rebuild, but have no sense of our need to keep at least a certain GDR identity alive. We are glad that we have some help, but you cannot just put 40 years in a dustbin and start from scratch. Maybe one can do that with infrastructures and buildings, but not with people. I cannot survive as a person if I reject all that has happened for several decades.

I have watched closely to see who deals with the changes best.

It's the younger generation, of course, the people between 18 and 30 who are ready for a new start and have not been shaped too much by the regimentation of the party system. Also adapting well are many in the older generation, those over 55 or 60 who lived before the GDR came into existence and are familiar with life without communism. I know an older couple who have a small neighbourhood office-supply store. Just after the 'Wende' (change), the woman complained that the changes came too late for them, since they were too old to enjoy them. Then he became the only person in his corner of the city to invest some of his money in fax and copy machines. Queues were lining up in front of their little store, because everybody needed résumés, or old documents copied or faxed to the west. She just told me with a smile on her face, 'I have never worked more and never have been more happy'. So you have those stories, too.

The other group of people who deal relatively easily with the changes are the turncoats, functionaries and opportunists, who have already switched from being Nazis to communists, and have left communism to become good capitalists. That is very frustrating for people my age. We stayed as clear as possible of the system; we were not opportunists, yet now once again we are falling between two stools. We are aware that we lived half of our lives under miserable conditions; we tried to build our own little protected world where we felt comfortable, but we are now trying very hard to learn the ropes of the West German system.

Robert W. Becker

How do people feel now? Press here and you get one reaction; press there and you get another. For six months after the Wall fell, many people went through an emotional shock—a combination of moving too fast and then too slow. People in the former GDR experienced something like a future shock. They love it on one hand, and they are frustrated on the other. It's undoubtedly wonderful to suddenly stop in the street looking at an ad in a travel agency window and realize, yes, you can really take that trip to the south of Europe and buy the book you want to read and read the newspapers you like. It's simply experiencing freedom. But the freedom of choice also requires more responsibility, planning, alertness, knowledge.

One woman here in Leipzig told me just some days ago that she saw the first Coca-Cola can in November 1989. She drank her first Coke in January 1990, but now she says that she wants Pepsi. People here absorb things very quickly. They want all the choices in goods, that's easy. Decisions are harder to make when matters get more complicated. A large number of people are very insecure because of the changes. Many of their sentences start with words that suggest a subjunctive thinking and that leave a back door open, words such as 'perhaps', 'possibly' and 'if possible'. Most people, particularly those who were not *Wendehälse* (turncoats), are much more careful about deciding on unchangeable issues. Because of the unthinkable conditions people lived under for decades, they have grown very close to those whom they trust. And I believe that people in the east who were not organized during the communist years were once more welded together during the events of autumn 1989. They had to survive. Anybody who is persecuted and always under the gun finds his own little core of friends and relatives with whom he establishes a very deep relationship. It's what keeps people together in coal mining regions such as South Wales or West Virginia. You feel that certain kind of togetherness when you meet in the evening with friends, usually at someone's home. The discussions are deep in small circles, very political, with very little superficial small talk.

Without trying to sound moralistic or overly philosophical, I must say that many times, the better off we are materialistically, the worse off we are in terms of meeting spiritual challenges in life. I'll let my daughter's words speak for me. We were returning from a weekend trip to Munich driving back into Leipzig. As we drove along the dark, terrible, unbelievably potholed roads she said, 'I'm glad to be home'. I looked at her and asked her to tell me about that. 'Here things are real', she said. 'Munich is a beautiful city, but there is a kind of smugness and softness that goes with it', she continued. 'But here it's very exciting and challenging. It's more exciting to build something than just to maintain it'. Everybody here is dealing with the essence of life, with core issues. It's obviously easy for me to say, since I'm leaving after my four years are up. Leipzig is a phase in my life that has shaped me, but I don't have to stay here. Leipzig was and is pioneers' work for me.

Uwe Wunderlich

Now I'm practising law for the first time. Generally, an attorney in the east has about two years less legal education than his western counterpart. I'm confronted daily, not only in my work but also personally, with things I never have faced before. I catch myself being overly nervous, preparing legal arguments over and over again, feeling knowingly anxious whenever I am expecting a phone call from a partner in Stuttgart. I know that I will have to work hard to catch up. Competition and making real choices are completely foreign to me.

There are little things, too. I used to start the day at six o'clock in the morning, like most in the east. When I was in training in the Stuttgart office, I was shocked that nobody was there by seven. Then I found that western lawyers don't start their practice before eight, but often stay until eight or nine in the evening. These are things that become easy to get used to after a while, but for a westerner they probably sound ridiculous. You have to imagine a puzzle. Every day one recognizes where another piece should go. Beyond those minor everyday problems, fear for one's financial existence grows rapidly. The first euphoria is gone. Everywhere you go the discussion revolves around one major topic: do you still have work, how long will you have work, can you keep your work? Saxony is one of the five new states of East Germany that merged with West Germany. It is blessed with textile, wood and metal industries, maybe now outdated, but with tradition. Before the war it had the reputation of being the most modern and industrialized state of all Germany. It will take lots of money and patience to rebuild.

Many on both sides have been disappointed. We don't understand why our free day-care centres and health clinics have to be closed, why rents are five times as high as before. The old system paid everybody a minimum wage, whether the work was needed or not. An electric railroad still employed coal shovellers who were paid to do nothing.

Many organizations employed twice as many workers as they needed in order to hide unemployment, which would have looked bad internationally. Our products are totally outdated, many parts are probably not even usable anymore. Very high unemployment and resulting social unrest are inevitable.

I see many West German entrepreneurs coming here hoping to

invest heavily, but they find nothing but indifference and envy, greed and belligerence from the old 'Seilschaften' (the Communist old boy network). On the other hand, our law firm has started to give free seminars on Saturdays for those who want to start a business on their own. The initial sessions were packed. Around 3,000 people showed up for the first four weekend seminars.

Wolf von Holleben

East Germans have lived for four decades under abnormal circumstances, and most have developed a no-responsibility, no-future mentality. I noticed this during my visit to the studios in the east. Most of the East Germans are very friendly, but they wait to act until you tell them what to do and how to do it. The only light in the tunnel is that the young people are eager to drive a Golf or own a house and that's their only motivation. This might sound sad, but at least there is that initiative. One should think that since the reunification West and East Germans speak the same language. But after 40 years of separation, the words seem to mean different things to each. East Germans generally have a very different mind set, characterized by self-pity.

Anyone who ignores our responsibility for East Germany and looks only at the economic facts would say 'no, thank you' to reunification today. Of course, those who doubted that reunification was the right thing to do never believed in Germany as one country again. The problem, as a whole, cannot be looked at from a purely economic perspective. The reunification of Germany is a challenge, a political and economic situation no other nations have dealt with before and, unfortunately, there is no model to follow. I fear that if unemployment and pessimism on both sides spread any further, Chancellor Kohl will also bear the political responsibilities. Three years ago he was a hero; this year he is the bad guy to be blamed for everything. One of the key issues will be to solve the property questions very quickly within the former GDR. The Treuhandanstalt moves much too cautiously. As long as nobody knows whether to get the house, the land or the factory back which was lost years ago, you can't sell it and you won't waste even one can of paint on bringing it up-to-date again.

The investment situation in the former GDR can be compared to a barrel without a bottom: you pour and pour and you wonder why the barrel never fills up. The list of items that need to be funded is endless. First, there is the commitment we made to the Soviets to bring the Red Army home, pay for their transport and build homes for them in the Soviet Union. The German Federal Mail and Telephone Service will invest over 50 billion Deutsche Marks to make telecommunication possible. The environment is in a disastrous condition. It will take billions to clean up the mess. Houses have not been updated for over 40 years.

Chapter Twenty-five

Berlin Normannenstrasse

Everybody knew that the Stasi was ubiquitous. Just passing by the enormous grey building on East Berlin's Normannenstrasse gave most GDR citizens the shivers. Before the Wall fell, one knew that telephone conversations to the West were tapped, workplaces were bugged and that maybe some co-workers were being paid to observe one's political behaviour. Simply applying to travel to the west for a few weeks could result in harsh reproaches against one's children in school or in an order to move to a smaller apartment. It was also known that the Stasi headquarters held files on some people. One could only speculate on how many files there were, and on whom they were kept. Most people had barely an inkling on who the Stasi really encompassed and how it worked.

The anger of over 40 years was vented when on 15 January 15 1990 several hundred GDR citizens overran the People's Police who were guarding the Stasi headquarters. Many in the west who followed the events on TV thought that it appeared almost as through the scenes were taken out of a history book and that Bastille Day was being re-enacted.

There were graffiti on walls, kicked-in doors, files all over the place: the crowd had taken over at Normannenstrasse. These events were understandable for many. Hans Modrow, a turncoat who had been elected ministerpresident, had tried to appease an angry populace by appearing to get rid of the Stasi. In fact, he hoped to preserve the Stasi and its work for the current government by simply giving it a new name. Consequently, to many citizens force seemed to be the only possible way of demonstrating their disapproval of the continued operation of the secret security system. The uniformed East German People's Police made no effort to intervene.

After hours of appeals from opposition groups who had carried the silent revolution, the raided building became calm again. The angry crowd had left but had opened up what many later became to believe was a Pandora's box, the legacy of the Stasi.

An earnest Protestant clergyman from Rostock in East Germany, Hans Joachim Gauck, and a team of helpers became the heroes of the hour for many Stasi victims as they quietly insisted that Germans 'face the truth about the Stasi'. Others vehemently opposed the idea of opening up the files, fearing that more harm than good would come of it. Many of the files tell the truth, others are full of lies and denunciations designed to set people up for blackmail or prosecution. Some files are banal, others contain definite documentation of the party's spying and include the names of people engaged in the set-ups. Who will judge the files' veracity? More important, what will the effects be if files are made public?

Officials considered a number of options for dealing with the files, such as burning them and forgetting about the past, distributing them to their subjects, and keeping them locked away for several decades. Closely linked to the question of what to do with the files was the question of what to do with the information if they were opened. Should the Stasi be declared a criminal organization, all of whose members should be prosecuted, or should Germany issue a blanket amnesty?

For a brief time, an apparent tug-of-war over the files between the Soviet Union and the west lent urgency to the matter. A West German daily newspaper reported unconfirmed statements that Moscow would grant asylum to top Stasi officials, among them Markus Wolf, East Germany's former chief spy. Exactly two years after the Wall had fallen, following heated public discussion and debate in the Bundestag about what to do with the files, the German parliament in Bonn decided that the notorious archives of the Stasi would be made accessible to the victims of communism: police and the media, however, would have only limited access. The debate in the Bundestag had been dominated by East German legislators who told the members of the parliament about their own harrowing experiences with the Stasi.

The debate over the Stasi files was the most divisive issue since the merger of the two Germanies; indeed the pros and cons of releasing them are still argued by many even today. Did the opening of the files start a healing process for a reunited Germany, or did it just tear open old, deep wounds?

Before Pastor Gauck became the official custodian of the more than 6 million files, a number of documents had vanished, having been burnt or hauled away by Soviet trucks during the chaotic months between November 1989 and the spring of 1990. Even before the files were opened, allegations about their contents had destroyed the careers of numerous politicians; often the personal devastation was justifiable, but sometimes a great deal of pain was inflicted based on mere rumours. In 1990 some Stasi officers used rumour as a tool for revenge. Through their network, they spread to the press a rumour that Lothar de Maizière, the first elected prime minister of East Germany, had worked for the Stasi from 1981 to 1989. De Maizière felt compelled to leave the Kohl government until he could clear himself. After quitting his political post, he was able to prove that he had not worked for the Stasi. Manfred Stolpe, now ministerpresident of Brandenburg, was also accused of having had Stasi connections while working as a church leader and civil rights advocate in the east before the Wall fell. Stolpe survived the charges and has successfully continued his political career.

Today it is known that Stasi members keen on advancing their careers often falsely accused people of being collaborators, knowing they really weren't. Insecurity about distinguishing between rumour and truth has resulted in a lot of bitterness, particularly in the east. Stories such as that of Olympic bob-sledder Harald Czudaj, who publicly apologized before the 1992 Winter Olympics for spying on team-mates from 1988 to 1990, have created even more uncertainty in East Germany and have intensified the urge to confront the past.

Many of those who have seen their files are appalled by what they found in them: treachery levelled against them by friends, parents, spouses, brothers and sisters. The personal ordeals were overwhelming, but seldom hit the newspapers unless they involved well-known figures such as East German writer Vera Wollenberger, who was imprisoned and later exiled. She learned from her dossier that the main informant against her was her husband. Heinz Eggert, now interior minister in charge of law enforcement, read in his 2,500-page file that for years he had been drugged by the Stasi to 'disintegrate his personality'. Eggert recovered and continued his dissident work throughout the 1980s after he noticed the pills' influence on his personality and simply stopped taking them.

In addition to exposing shocking personal tragedies, the opening of the files led a number of Stasi members to co-operate with the West German external intelligence service Bundesnachrichtendienst (BND). These Stasi members confirmed the GDR's close ties with Middle Eastern secret services, particularly those of Syria, Yemen and Libya as well as with radical Palestine liberation groups. Moreover, these 'deserters' confirmed that a number of Red Army Faction terrorists—who were responsible for the assassinations of, among others, Jürgen Pontos, chairman of Dresdner Bank; Siegfried Buback, chief prosecutor; and Alfred Herrhausen, chief executive officer of Deutsche Bank—had not only sought and found support within the Stasi system, but had also been given new identities and hiding places in the former GDR.

The full scope of the Stasi operation might never be completely revealed. Gauck and his team are looking into the files searching for criminal conduct that can be prosecuted. Nobody wants a vendetta or a witch-hunt, but Stasi victims—especially those who were charged under false pretences, jailed and tortured—should have a chance to seek justice.

Moreover, Stasi members should be prohibited from holding any jobs in the judicial system, universities and the civil service.

At this point, many former East Germans are disillusioned about democracy. As time passes, trials for Honecker and the spy chief Mielke are not being held, since their actions were partially legal under GDR law and the reunited Germany could not—or would not—see a way to prosecute them. Nobody wants to be responsible for stirring up a political and legal hornets' nest, but sweeping the Stasi past under the carpet would be a slap in the face both of all of its victims and of justice.

What seems ironic today is that in the end, after 40 years of Stalinist horror enforced with an endless list of informers, the regime still collapsed and with it the technical structure of the Stasi. The unique combination of the Prussian obsession with accuracy with a Marxist single-mindedness overloaded the system with so much information that it did not even need much help to grind to a halt. The Stasi state in the end became a paradox of total control and total incapacity, bloated bureaucracy that collapsed under its own weight. The technical structure of the Moloch is gone. What still exists is a certain amount of mistrust and fear about the possible existence of a Stasi old boy network that is still functioning and undermining efforts to find the truth and make the reunited Germany a success. The opening of the Stasi files has proven to be painful, but probably no more so than the prolonged trauma of uncertainty intensified by continued allegations and denials would have been.

Elke Zimmer

We were among the hundreds of people who for several nights kept a vigil outside the Stasi headquarters in Berlin. Here the regime stored its files—records of who was being snooped on and by whom, who went to prison for political reasons, who received hush money, who were the secret service agents, and who was sent to Siberia. I used to avoid even walking by the building if I could.

Finally, on a Monday night we forced our way in. The building was empty; the Stasi had already fled. The next day, reports of our break-in dwelled on vandalism. I remember none of that. We did enter forcibly, shoulder to shoulder, but I saw no vandalism. There was only a table overturned here and there, some opened drawers. The walls were spray-painted in red, black and gold. What I remember most was the awful emptiness and the turbulence of my own feelings. But strangely, I felt no anger. I picked up several letters that were lying on the floor. I stared at one for a while. It gave a detailed description of an official ten-day junket to the USSR. The correspondent reported who had dinner and lunch with whom, as well as whole conversations among travellers who naïvely believed nobody else was listening. He noted that one man had stood too long in front of the monument of the czar, and had paid no attention to Lenin's bust. Ludicrous, absurd stuff! But far too sad for laughter.

And this was merely a hint of what the Stasi were up to—a maddeningly slight memento. It became obvious that most of the evidence had been already destroyed.

Most depressing was my sense of déjà vu. When Germans learned about Hitler's crimes, most couldn't believe it. I too felt disbelief now. I had lived for over 40 years in a society that was a perfect recreation of the Third Reich.

David Gill

Looking into the files, we increasingly get the idea that Honecker was very well-informed about the disastrous state the country was in: there were few goods, rotten services, poor wages and bad working conditions. The main sources of this kind of information were OIBEs, 'officers on special mission'. In the past few months, Gauck and his team have uncovered the identities of about 2,000 of those officers. But thousands in the field are still undiscovered, and many will probably remain so.

We have worked hard to find them, but they are well prepared in covering their tracks. They first infiltrated the citizens' groups that occupied the Stasi office after the bloodless revolution. Many of the citizens' groups agree today that they were hoodwinked into destroying some Stasi records, including those on the central computer in which all records in the system were filed alphabetically. That is one of the major problems in our task now. We only have 1,000 people, and we must go through the files page by page. After the fall of the Wall the Stasi also became very busy changing their skill from spying on people to shredding documents day and night. Therefore, some things we'll never know. We have interrogated Werner Grossmann, the last head of Hauptverwaltung für Aufklärung (Headquarters for Reconnaissance—HVA), who said proudly that we won't find anything that could endanger his former agents. He also insisted that none of the agents were passed on to the KGB, which seems highly unlikely, since the KGB helped to establish the Stasi. We know that the KGB has taken on some of the Stasi head people and also that it has a list of former Stasi agents and informers in West Germany. These people can all be intimidated into working for the KGB, particularly under the current unstable situation in Russia. What is not surprising is that the Stasi infiltrated the state committee under the communist-led administration of Modrow.

What is more surprising to most westerners is that under the authority of the East German Interior Minister, Peter Michael Diestel, a Christian Democrat, who was elected in 1990, the anti-Stasi campaign didn't make any headway. Diestel even proposed making spymaster Markus Wolf his adviser. After a public outcry, that idea was quickly dropped. Diestel ignored a list we provided of proven informers who were working in his office.

Many things went very wrong in the period between the fall of the Wall and reunification on 3 October of the following year. Documents and people vanished. As if that weren't frustrating enough, many have asked me why I'm active in the Gauck commission and if it isn't time to stop the chase. That is a western view I can't share. First, victims must have a chance to pursue justice. We have to identify the main villains, collect evidence of criminal conduct and bring charges against them. Second, top Stasi people need to be kept out of influential jobs. We now know of many OIBEs who hold posts in firms that have changed their legal form from 'people-owned businesses' to limited partnerships but otherwise work as they did in the past. They are starting to rekindle the old boy network involving the ex-Stasi members and the Party of Democratic Socialism, the successor to the SED, which is still flush with money and influence.

The files had to be opened in order to hunt for Stasi criminals and to help screen people seeking a political appointment.

We face a very difficult task. The government has given us a political mandate and support, but not everybody feels this is a job that has to be done. Apart from that, the sheer mass of work, the millions of files we have to go through with just 1,000 assistants, is overwhelming. Hans Joachim Gauck is the perfect person to deal with it. He is now 50 years old, very level-headed, and he doesn't want to start a witch-hunt; he just wants an opportunity to get a clear look into the past. Gauck, whose father was deported to Siberia by the Russians when he was a child, was himself a victim of the Stasi because he wouldn't kowtow. Already, he has got the nickname 'St Gauck and "the Dragon"', and a solid and honourable intention are asked of anybody examining those files.

It is relatively easy to read that phones were bugged or even that a close friend was an informer. It leaves a different, more horrible impression when you read through file after file after file, in which whole phone conversations, personal or otherwise, are transcribed. The details are so shocking. Also, everybody knew that some postcards or letters from friends in the west didn't reach the people they were addressed to. But when you open up a file and there are stacks of letters dated as far back as 1965, it's shocking. We have found children's paintings and letters with no political contents at all that were kept on file for decades. They were collected just to give the people in the GDR the feeling they were under control. We have many files that make clear what reasons people had for working with the Stasi. Some were as banal as blackmail for a drunken outburst against the regime or for an extramarital affair. Some techniques used to gain co-operation were more vicious, as when a youngster caught shoplifting was told that the case would be hushed up if he would report what was going on in his parents' house. We found many cases where medicine was denied patients unless they would snoop on neighbours. The whole scheme is perverse since victims and collaborators of the Stasi seemed to be in the same boat, just pulling the oars in different directions.

So far we have found files on 6 million people; that's a bit less than one-third the population of the GDR. Of these, roughly 2 to 3 million are files on informants. The rest are files on victims. Some files just list the peoples' names, with no other commentary. The files on victims usually describe people who were thought to be political dissidents, people uncomfortable with the regime who wanted change in any way. Many files are full of lies and attempts to insinuate a criminal behaviour into the dissidents' actions and are usually a dangerous mixture of fact and fiction.

These files came in especially handy for the SED at times when the GDR needed more hard currencies. Most of them were sorted by 'urgency', meaning those victims who could be arrested relatively easily were first on the list. When the regime needed money, old charges were brought up again, the prisons were filled with political prisoners, and West Germany was contacted about an exchange of humans for money. From the files we know that some of the people who were exchanged were not political prisoners but instead were spies sent into West Germany via the exchange.

We currently have a backlog consisting of 300,000 people who want to see their files and government offices checking the background of Eastern German officials and judges trying to get jobs in the reunified Germany. Individuals who are interested in their personal files must fill out an application form in which they are asked why they think they would be in the files. Because of our huge backlog we've had to prioritize. For example, someone who had to serve a five-year or longer prison term in the former GDR because of his political conduct is first in line and has preference in looking at his files before somebody who had just once been called to a police station.

We'll have work to do here for decades. Sensitive decisions have to be made about who can be a judge, who can be a teacher, policeman or politician. Those who want to see their files will have to be prepared to deal with personal scandals and disappointments.

Many will find that they didn't live with truth.

Ulrike Poppe

I just started to make the attempt to look into my files a few weeks ago. It was a decision I had wrestled with for some time. I thought it would be an emotional roller-coaster to go through my own file, and it is. About sixty full- and part-time Stasi agents had followed me and my husband to report on our activities. I was able to recognize some of the people, although they all have cover names in the dossiers. (Certain events involved only two or three people, and no one else could have known what I was doing and saying at the time.) Those whom I recognized I once considered close friends. What one reads in these files just shows how pervasive the system was. For example, the Stasi also tried to break up my marriage. As we learned from the files, one sergeant was set up to seduce me, but the plan was eventually abandoned because I didn't respond to his advances.

On the other hand, it is amazing to read what banalities the Stasi knew about me. For example they knew which foods I prefer to eat, when I typically take the children to nursery school, even the toothpaste I usually buy. Some of those pages are filled with such useless information and nonsense that if it weren't so sad and serious one would have to start laughing.

One of the informants who related information on us attempted suicide recently, and I feel deeply sorry for his inner turmoil. But I strongly believe this is a catharsis that the people who worked for the snooping system have to go through. The people who have advocated burning the files or putting them away for some years want us to throw away our past. We cannot do that. As awful as the Stasi experiences were, it is part of our past and we have to know who the bad guys were. The majority of the Stasi's former informers are free, and most of them are frustrated, with little money and feelings of revenge in their guts. We cannot allow these people to rock the democracy, which is still wearing baby shoes, with false allegations or dirty tricks. The technical structure of the Stasi apparatus seems to have gone, but we cannot be sure if there is not a second or even third layer left. We have to find them all—all of them.

Jorge Seidel

When the Ministerium für Staatssicherheit (Ministry for State Security—MfS) dissolved in 1990, I wanted to draw a big long line under that part of my life and start a new one. With the fall of the Wall, the GDR—in other words, my employer—ceased to exist. Yet we were working in the counter-espionage until February 1990.

When I worked for the Stasi, I was absolutely convinced of the political need for my work. I was also absolutely convinced of the evil of the western bloc countries. When I read American documents, I saw them as being tools of the devil. Today I'm not proud of it, but until the very end I was convinced that I was serving my country and protecting it. Gauck will go through my files and they will be interpreted one-sidedly. We'll be portrayed as bogeymen so that others can wash their hands of the whole period in history. I'm guilty of many things, but what I have done is neither totally wrong nor unique.

Like many, I came to the ministry via my service in the army. For political reasons, and because I was looking for adventure, I became part of counter-espionage. I'm proud to have served my country for 12 years, although today my work appears to have not been morally correct. I was schooled in English, and was prepared physically as well as mentally for the task of counter- espionage.

You knew that you were doing the right thing and that your work was justified when you encountered incidents such as my colleague Klaus Eichner's discovery of documents suggesting a first-strike plan against Gorbachev by some western powers. On the other hand, I'm ashamed of arrests I made of opponents of the regime during the time I was assigned to counter-revolutionary work. There were a series of arrests, imprisonment and trials of people who opposed the party. Although I was not responsible for the decision to arrest them, I was part of the outcome.

I'm happy and yet somewhat concerned about the fall of the Wall. East Germany was a kinder and fairer society than the west in my eyes. I don't gain anything from the reunification but punishment for my past, by being banned from any public job.

I don't think making the files available was the right move. There will be generalizations and very little room for understanding. That is the reason why we formed the Insider Committee for Re-examination. One part of me didn't want to be silent about my past. I want to talk about why things happened and what the consequences really are. We also don't want show trials or the blanket attacks we usually get from West Germans nowadays.

Wolfgang Schäuble

The Stasi files are packed with unspeakable dirt. Many careers of well-meaning and clean politicians have been destroyed. Bonn should have tightened its control over the files of the dreaded East German Stasi secret service much earlier in order to stop the stream of rumours and smearing of names. Originally, the Reunification Treaty included no law on the safeguarding of the files of the former state security service. Understandably, there was some opposition to handing over the Stasi files to the West German Federal Archives in Koblenz. Just hours before the treaty was signed we found a solution acceptable to both eastern and western delegations.

One must be very careful when comparing the crimes of the Third Reich and the Holocaust with those of the Stasi. I am a staunch opponent of socialism and a proponent of a united Germany, but I believe the Holocaust had different dimensions. The existence of the GDR and the Stasi developed from the rule of the Soviets in their occupied territory, after they placed the power in the hands of communists. At the end of Second World War, Germany capitulated and half of Europe was in ruins. At that point the Nuremberg trials took place under very different circumstances than would exist if there had been a trial after the peaceful revolution of 1989.

Apart from moral issues, there are legal obstacles to a prosecution of ex-Stasi members. We cannot prosecute the entire membership of the SED. In Germany we have the Partei des Demokratischen Sozialismus (Party of Democratic Socialism—PDS) which developed out of the SED in the Bundestag. In other words, we have to deal with the PDS politically, but not via criminal law.

On the other hand, there are people, citizens of the former GDR, who have not acted according to the law, and they should be prosecuted. In theory, that sounds all well and good, but the reality is different. If you take the case of Honecker, the expectations in the east and west were high that he would be prosecuted for his deeds. But these expectations were summarily crushed when it was announced that Honecker would be allowed to go to Moscow and then to Chile. I strongly believe that if we have a democracy that honours human dignity, we have to acknowledge that he is too old to stand trial. Admittedly it is hard to swallow, knowing what injustices have happened in the former GDR over the past 40 years, but for our constitutional state it is the only possibility. Ex-Ministerpresident Stoph of the former GDR was also released from his detention for investigation just a while ago. And now of course, the issue of whether he should be compensated arises, since he was detained without a legal reason. Well, those are the laws of a constitutional state. Understandably, the people who have suffered for so long under the regime are not only disappointed, but also doubt the justice of our system. But democracy and our constitutional state are worth so much that we cannot jeopardize them for a witch-hunt.

Chapter Twenty-six

Germany's Forgotten Trials

As the work of the secret police and the techniques they used became more and more apparent and the majority of former East Germans gasped at the numerous revelations of Stasi crimes, both east and west called for the trials of those responsible. Everybody knew the major players who were responsible for the existence of, and methods used in, the terrorist state: Honecker, Stoph, Mielke, Wolf, Schalck-Golodkowski, Wolfgang Vogel. In the minds of victims of the regime and most West Germans there was no question that the 'handlanger' (lackeys) should be made accountable.

Memories of the Nuremberg trials came back to the older generations, and many questioned whether Germans should try Germans.

Nevertheless, it came as a shock and a surprise when it was announced that Honecker, who was now 81 and who had been staying in a Soviet-run hospital for medical treatment, had been flown to Moscow on a Soviet airliner in the early spring of 1991. While Germany's Justice Minister Klaus Kinkel asked for his return to Berlin, news leaked that the German government had known about the plan for quite some time and had not tried very hard to prevent Honecker's flight. Critics even said that the Kohl government was relieved to see Honecker leave the country, because a show trial would now be unlikely. Resentment and bitterness spread among the citizens in both east and west. Was Honecker's flight the first sign that there would be no trials at all? Would those responsible for the sins of 40 years go unpunished?

Honecker, who had flown to Moscow under Gorbachev's rule, had been given the help that was expected among 'comrades'. The official explanation was that his condition had necessitated the shift from the German hospital to a better-equipped hospital in the Soviet Union. Honecker, who had manslaughter charges pending an extensive period of illness in Germany, had declared through an official in Moscow that he had no intention of returning to Germany. He had found a safe haven in the Chilean embassy in Moscow, a refuge protecting him from arrest in Germany.

Honecker had at least two good reasons to choose the Chilean embassy: his daughter is married to a communist in Santiago, and Honecker himself had protected over 4,000 Chilean leftists in the 1970s. Nevertheless, the Chilean government, after months of back-and-forth discussions, finally gave in to pressure from Chancellor Kohl's government and returned him to Berlin. Rather quietly, the charges against Honecker were dropped in January 1993 because of his age and illness. He went to Chile.

The majority of German people were not just disillusioned about a system of justice that freed the author of the tyranny of the GDR; they were also baffled by the obviously luxurious life Honecker enjoys in Chile. According to official sources, he lives on a pension of only $500 a month, which he earned before the war by working for 14 years as a roofer in Saarbrücken, a city in southwest Germany close to the French border. The Germans were also perplexed by the fact that nobody seemed to care or do anything about the billions of Deutsche Marks that Honecker and the party spirited away and accumulated in Swiss bank accounts over the years. This money, which Honecker now lives off, came from the sales of political prisoners to West Germany and other shady business transactions the party had initiated during its rule.

Meanwhile, as the German government came under public bombardment, it rushed to start the trial of Erich Mielke in early 1992. The former chief of the Stasi, 84 years old at the time, was expected to stand trial for embezzlement, wiretapping, election fraud and human rights abuses. The Berlin prosecution, anxious to produce results, deemed one case the obvious choice to be tried first: a murder case from 61 years before. Mielke, then a young communist and street fighter, was allegedly one of the gunmen who shot two Berlin policemen. A Nazi court had found him guilty and sentenced him to death together with other men involved, but he was able to flee to the Soviet Union. As much as the citizens of East and West Germany wanted to see Mielke tried, they had to agree with his defence lawyer, who argued that today's Germany could not rely on investigations by Nazis who were murderers themselves. The trial started with demonstrators present and a press eager to report it, but soon the proceedings came to strike most people almost as ancient history. For some two years the court convened every week for no longer than a half-hour because of Mielke's frailness; the trial could be stopped at any time if the judge concluded that the old Stasi boss was in no condition to stand trial.[1]

Certainly, nobody can speak of a witch-hunt for Stasi members or the

---

[1] Mielke was convicted of murder in the 1930s deaths of the police officers, and received a six-year sentence. He has requested freedom on grounds of failing health. His activities during the existence of the GDR were never an issue during the trials.

ones responsible for the horrors of the SED regime in Germany. The tendency seems more to put the past aside and let the old communists die in peace. Most politicians want to put the trials behind them; some have even called for a general amnesty for everyone involved.

The calls for justice are fading with every passing month since the Wall fell. The initial high expectations—that GDR citizens, to whom so much harm was done, might finally obtain some justice so that they can find their peace—have turned into a more modest goal that those soldiers who killed people fleeing at the border be sent to prison, along with those who initiated the shoot-to-kill orders.

Donald Koblitz

The former ruler of East Germany, Erich Honecker, sat for a few hours a week before a Berlin court, answering for his sins. But what was supposed to be the most sensational trial since the Nuremberg war crimes was a disappointment. Honecker, 80 and dying of cancer, was charged solely with ordering the use of deadly force on the inter-German border. His trial focused mainly on liver metastases. His real crime, presiding over a dictatorship that must have made Brezhnev proud, was left for others to judge. But the real sensation is soon to come if, as expected, Markus Wolf, East Germany's espionage chief for a third of a century, goes on trial for treason.

The Wolf trial will be an extraordinary event. He remains as true to his East German ideals as ever, but East Germany has been subsumed into West Germany, and his own state would now try him for his successes as a dutiful spymaster. For 35 years Wolf fought the west: he was lionized as Karla in John Le Carré's spy novels, and placed his agents in every major agency in the Federal Republic of Germany. His spies even ran West Germany's own counter-espionage for a while. One sat in the Chancellery Office next to Willy Brandt, until his discovery occasioned the latter's resignation in 1974. West Germany was so thoroughly penetrated for so long by Wolf that sharing intelligence information with the West Germans was for decades akin to making a strategic revelation to the east. When in 1979, *Der Spiegel* published the first photo of the phantom Markus Wolf, taken surreptitiously in Stockholm by the Swedish service, it created a sensation. Wolf's agents gave new meaning to the word 'mole'. By the time of his resignation in 1986 he had run

5,000 agents in the west, some for 30 years or more. They don't know how many are still there, or which master they might now be serving.

Wolf's life mirrors many of the pivotal events in 20th-century German history. His father was a Jewish doctor, a gifted playwright and an active communist party member who was driven from Germany by the Nazis and ultimately settled his family in Moscow. Markus was raised there in the highly refined world of expatriate intelligentsia, an idealist curiously aloof from the Stalinist terror. He was flown by the Soviets to Berlin in May 1945 with a group of German expatriots that included the future East German Defence Minister, Heinz Kessler. In 1946 Wolf reported on the Nuremberg trials for German radio. Then in 1951 his public life ceased and he began his extraordinary career as the most sophisticated, successful spymaster of the 20th century.

His forthcoming trial is not without its moral and legal ambiguities. There is no question that Wolf has more than a few lost souls on his conscience. His agents ripped through a generation of Bonn secretaries like an animated scythe in a horror movie, romancing one after another into treason, disgrace and even suicide. He is too refined and well-educated a man not to have recognized the brutality of the people's dictatorship in his land, whatever his fine ideals may once have been. There is no more thorough dictatorship than a German one.

But it is hard to escape the notion that Wolf is being tried for beating us at our own game, and the German Constitutional Court could conceivably bar his prosecution for that reason. Despite our DM30 billion intelligence budget and all those grey computers, blackbird planes and spy satellites that it bought, it was Wolf's people who often seemed to move West German politics like pieces on Karla's chessboard. We could be more comfortable if Wolf were being tried for espionage excesses at least formally forbidden to our own people, such as murder. But his crimes, bribery and espionage, are our crimes—only we are on the winning side. Nor should we forget that, driven by the Cold War, we in the west gave the Nazi's spymaster, Reinhard Gehlen, a man whose vest, as the Germans would say, was a lot more bespeckled than Wolf's, the job of building the West German spy network.

No one in East Germany will shed a tear for Markus Wolf. He

was, after all, deputy minister of the Stasi, the state security organ despised by East Germans—at least the bare majority not on its payroll.

The facts represent themselves differently in the case of Wolfgang Vogel. He and his wife were taken into custody this summer.[2] Vogel is still being held in Moabit prison for tax evasion and also on charges that he extorted real estate and large sums of money from clients for whom he tried to get permission to leave the country. The basic charge against Vogel is that he blackmailed 30 families, who wanted to leave East Germany, into selling their properties as a condition for leaving. The question here is, was he in cahoots with the Stasi to get those properties into the hands of the regime? None of us had any doubts whom Vogel represented all those years. He must have at least worked with the Stasi; he must have had a very close relationship with them. But for the west, it is rather late in the day to say that he is a 'bad' man because he worked for the Stasi. My own gut feeling is that the basic charges of blackmail are disgraceful. In the meantime, charges of very serious tax evasion have been added on. From what I understand, some East German lawyers including Vogel had tax-evading privileges. He has been treated more harshly because of the coincidental sequence of the trials. As many are angry that Honecker and some other comrades have skipped out of town, Vogel seems to be the scapegoat for earlier negligence. The Germans have been burned once, and they do not want to be embarrassed in a high-profile case. There is an element of vindictiveness in the Vogel case.

The issue of trials is extremely difficult to judge. The Germans have had opportunities twice now during the last 50 years, and they certainly screwed it up the first time. Nobody can doubt that the denazification was not well done. Not a single West German judge was ever convicted and imprisoned on the basis of Nazi crimes. Some of the same pressure that existed in Germany during the late 1940s and 1950s appears to exist today in East Germany. But as West Germany is covering the bill, the priorities are different. The trials aptly illustrate one of the dilemmas of the reunited Germany. The two Germanies did not merge in 1990, but East Germany acceded to West Germany to form an enlarged, but constitutionally—and even politically and socially—largely unchanged, Federal Republic of

---

[2] Vogel and his wife Helga were taken into custody on 18 July 1993 in Berlin.

Germany. But can the West Germans, not particularly well-known as humble missionaries, convert the east into their mirror-image while at the same time dismissing 40 years of East German history as an embarrassing diversion on the way to West German rectitude? If the westerners manage to evoke sympathy for even the likes of Honecker and Wolf, what treatment can the rest of the population expect? It is an irony worthy of note that the seeming abuses of the most hated people in the former East Germany should become a standard by which to measure the west's occupation of the east. What is sorely lacking is a differentiated treatment of East Germany before reunification that acknowledges the good and the evil and that places its former citizens in the political and social context of the times before judging them. Tiny East Germany was swallowed whole and little-mourned. There is nothing left but the indigestion.

Ludwig R. Rehlinger

Since the collapse of the Wall, Wolfgang Vogel has been arrested several times on various charges. Twice because of allegations that he was not a mere lawyer but a part and parcel of the secret police apparatus. It is totally clear that Dr Vogel had to be close to Honecker and the Stasi, otherwise he couldn't have had the power and privileges he enjoyed. We used him in his role as a middle man who made the exchanges possible. To what extent Dr Vogel was an instrument or member of the Stasi, I cannot tell. The recent charges of tax evasion and of perjury are legally difficult issues to prove. Dr Vogel received West German money from us for his services, which, according to GDR law, did not have to be taxed if it wasn't spent in the west. In the end, the charges against Dr Vogel deal with his role in the GDR. Was he, like Schalck-Golodkowski, an active member of the regime who helped to keep it alive with illegal methods?

Wolf von Holleben

Erich Honecker, who headed the system from the early 1970s until two years ago, did not find a place to live after his regime had collapsed. A Protestant minister was asked to give him and his wife a home. This minister has five or seven children, none of whom could receive higher education, because under the Honecker regime, children of ministers and other representatives of churches were excluded. Now Mrs Honecker, who served as a minister of education, and her husband shared a house with that family. This is only a little story from the sidelines, but it shows how difficult the situation in the GDR is, not only economically, but also emotionally.

Some people have been brainwashed. All have been cheated for several decades. I don't think those scars will ever heal.

I'm flabbergasted again and again by how people accepted the way the system treated them. The Third Reich was the precursor of the totalitarian system that was to come under Ulbricht and Honecker, who perfected the system of snooping and control. In each house, on every floor, there was someone who made it his responsibility to monitor his neighbours and their loyalty to the regime. It made no difference if somebody was a politician or played any other visible role within the system; they had sold their souls, either because they believed in what they were doing or because of opportunism.

Chapter Twenty-seven

Berlin, the Old and New Capital

Once Berlin was uttered in the same breath as the names of cities like London, Paris or New York. Before the Second World War it was not only the cultural and financial centre of Germany, but also the only metropolis Germany had. True and long-time Berliners never gave up on this period of time, when Berlin was the symbol of Prussia's 'Glamour and Glory'. With their well-known arrogance, impudence and humour, the people of Berlin have mastered more problems and crises than the citizens of probably any other German city.

Since the end of the war, both East and West Berlin developed a special status. Each lived off its 'mainland', supported by heavy subsidies. While West Berliners listened to complaints from West German taxpayers who did not quite understand why the island city had to be supported with high subsidies, easterners from Saxony and Thuringia were venting their anger about the privileges of East Berliners, who usually were the first to take advantage of the rare shipments of fruit from Cuba or other goods from other communist satellite states. Young West German males who wanted to avoid conscription in the army could find refuge in West Berlin as students at the university and were released from their duties when they stayed in the city for a prolonged time. Bonn had instigated such a regulation to reduce the number of young people leaving West Berlin and to prevent Berlin from becoming the retirement home of Germany. Both parts of the city, east and west, were also symbols of Cold War politics. East Berlin was skilfully turned into a showcase city of communist success, while West Berlin, following President John F. Kennedy's 1961 'Ich bin ein Berliner' speech at the newly erected Wall, had become a beacon of hope for democracy and the western world.

Berlin seems to be a city that grew by struggling. At a time when neither the city nor Prussia was flourishing economically, King Friedrich Wilhelm III, under the guidance of Wilhelm Humboldt, established the Humboldt University, where the unity of teaching and research developed the essential philosophy of modern universities. As Berlin increasingly attracted young intellectuals such as Kleist and Hegel the city became an

346

oasis of culture. Friedrich Wilhelm III, known for his unpretentiousness, supported cultural inspiration with a principle that is still at work in the city of Berlin today: he confronted failing politics and economic difficulties with spiritual strength. Another Hohenzollern king, Friedrich Wilhelm IV, aroused the anger of Berliners through his timidity and blind allegiance to the absolutist concepts of his forefathers. He failed to grasp a new mood among his subjects and Berlin became the focal point of the March revolution in 1848, which was put down by Prussian troops, but which nevertheless persuaded the king to grant a new constitution. At the behest of his brilliant minister Otto von Bismarck, Wilhelm I ascended to the thrown and made Berlin the capital of all Germany. During those so-called 'Gründerjahre' (founding years), Berlin lived through an economic and cultural renaissance, which was enhanced by the industrial revolution. In 1888 Wilhelm II came to power with great pomp and ceremony. His reign ended with Germany's humiliating defeat and destruction at the end of the First World War.

Once again, with not just Prussia but all of Germany lying in ashes and tormented by runaway inflation, revolution and civil war, Berlin developed into one of the cultural centres of Europe. Bertholt Brecht and Kurt Tucholsky became part of a kind of lost generation that previously had been known only in Paris and probably was best described in Christopher Isherwood's Berlin stories. During the early 1920s, Berlin also became a haven for some 300,000 Russian artists who had found a new home in the German capital—among them Andrey Bely, Ilya Ehrenburg and Aleksey Tolstoy. Roughly 10 per cent of Berlin's population consisted of Russians living in exile, leading some Berliners, tongue in cheek, to rename Charlottenburg 'Charlottengrad'.

The times were a mixture of glory and decay in Berlin. Culturally, Berlin held its head high, but politically the streets were dominated by the violence between the Spartacists (extremely radical socialists) and ultra-nationalist ex-army officers. By the 1930s, the collapse of the Weimar Republic ushered in the Third Reich and the marches organized by Hitler's propaganda machine headed by Joseph Goebbels. Berlin's Jews, who had contributed so much to the city's growth as a cultural and industrial centre had to flee to escape the aftermath of the 1938 Kristallnacht. During World War II, bombs destroyed most of Berlin. More than 76,000 bombs were dropped on the city, leaving an estimated 600,000 homes in ruins. The population, slashed by nearly one million during the war, struggled for food. 'Trümmerfrauen' (rubble women), working alongside returning men, cleared away ruins.

Berlin's fate was now in the hands of the Allies. They agreed to divide Germany into four zones of occupation and, though Berlin lay deep within the Soviet zone, to subject the city to four-power occupation as well. When wartime co-operation deteriorated into Cold War feuding, Berlin once again became the centre of the world's attention. Berlin lived through several crises, the airlift, the ultimatum of Khrushchev and, finally, barbed wires and the Wall. For most of the world, the Wall soon became an abstract political symbol representing the confrontation between totalitarianism and the hope for freedom and liberty. Not so in Berlin, where people on their daily shopping rounds could see the Wall very clearly and feel personally the hardship and tragedy, the pain and anguish it imposed. With typical ingenuity, many Berliners organized escape plans, and western student groups began helping their friends in the east to flee. Escape was only possible for a few, however; sometimes, attempts at flight ended in death at the Wall. To give encouragement to easterners, Berliner Axel Caesar Springer, founder of Germany's largest publishing house, intentionally built his corporate headquarters in West Berlin as high as possible so the people in the east could see the names of his well-known newspapers. Many like Springer never gave up the idea that their city would one day be undivided again.

Over the last seven decades, Berlin and its population showed a strength that characterizes its emotionally strong attitude. The famous *Berliner Luft* (the air of Berlin), which has been celebrated in a number of songs, is only one term that hints at the plain-speaking, plain-dealing atmosphere of the central European melting pot that is blessed with a touch of originality. For people living in Berlin and others with some historical ties to the city, there was never any question that Berlin would be named the German capital again after the country's reunification. For them, it had never ceased to be the capital; they believed there was an implied promise to the German people that had to be kept.

Others approached the issue of Berlin as a capital more pragmatically. For many, Berlin evoked bitter and awful historical memories of brown-uniformed Nazis marching in front of the Reichstag with clicking heels and raised arms. They wondered, would Germany project a wrong picture of the modern nation by reinstating Berlin as its capital? And then, of course, there was the cost. Bonn, which has been pampered as 'kind of a capital' over the last 40 years, has a brand new Bundestag building constructed at a cost of millions, and thousands of diplomats and politicians, with wives and children, who would have to be moved to Berlin—where living space is already scarce. These facts didn't seem to favour Berlin becoming the capital. But diplomacy and politics prevailed; in a very tight vote, the Bundestag in Bonn decided in June 1991 to make Berlin the capital. To end months of continued debates about whether Germany's government should move to Berlin, Helmut Kohl announced at the end of 1993 that the transfer would be completed by the year 2000. Nevertheless, many Berliners are unimpressed with Kohl's announcement and say that this move comes politically and economically too late for the city. Those who are sceptical about the move note the high cost of moving the government from Bonn to Berlin which could amount to up to $15 billion. Yet Berliners don't know what the fuss is all about.

Dieter Hildebrand, a comedian with *Berliner Schnauze* (Berlin big mouth) and best known for his wit on stage and screen, said in a serious moment, 'Berlin is for Germany what America used to be for Europe, and what the Wild west once was for America: a chance to make a new start'.

Eberhard Diepgen

Berlin has always been the capital of Germany. Now we must bring the government, the Bundestag and the president to Berlin as quickly as possible, as well as send signals to persuade the national and international management communities that Berlin will again be the capital of Germany. Because Berlin is the very crux of German unity, all the conflicts appear there first and strongest. The biggest and most obvious problem here in Berlin is the difference in income levels and standard of living in the two sides of the city. As long as the reconstruction of the eastern part of Berlin is uncompleted, salaries will be lower there. With the differences in lifestyle, the aggressions we have experienced in the population will not end. Conflict will be more visible here in Berlin than anywhere else in the reunited Germany. But once these initial 'birthing problems' are overcome, Berlin will be one of the most modern metropolitan areas in the nation. It will develop into a centre of service, science, economy and culture. What we struggle with in Berlin day by day are the reuniting pains of a city which has been separated into two parts for decades. In this sense Berlin is also a symbol for the growing pains of a United Europe.

Berlin has always been a link to the east—historically and culturally. There is no other city in which a majority of people can speak Russian, Czech or Polish. People in Berlin do not only speak these languages, but also understand the mentality of the eastern countries which, at some point, will be parts of a United Europe. Berlin in a United Europe will be a welcome link between east and west, a link to the countries behind the Oder-Neisse line.

349

Wolfgang Schäuble

There are a number of people abroad and in Germany who resent Berlin becoming the German capital again. I have a strong feeling, though, that nobody in France would question that Paris should be the nation's capital. I have the same attitude over the lengthy controversy about Berlin's role in Germany. There is no doubt that only Berlin can be the capital of a reunited Germany. The three Allies have granted the safety and security of the city's population for the last four decades, as Berlin was and is now again a beacon of hope. Berlin is a symbol of the West German commitment to the eastern part of the country to make true on promises made before 3 October 1990.

Walter Momper

The most urgent task facing the new and old capital, Berlin, is the reconstruction of the city's infrastructure. We need a bigger airport, new streets and new housing. Currently, Berlin has three airports, one in every corner of the city. The streets in the eastern part are not only old, damaged and inadequate, but they also don't have any links to the western part. There is very little housing for those pouring into the city since the reunification. The old subway and S-Bahn systems have not functioned since the Wall was built in 1961.

Apart from the missing infrastructure, many industries have survived in Berlin, because they were subsidized. With the reunification, Berlin is becoming more and more expensive every day. I foresee that many of these industries that have survived here will have to move to cheaper areas, which means unemployment, retraining and frustration for many. All those projects mentioned will take two to three decades to be realized. Nevertheless, I believe that moving Bonn to Berlin was the right decision. Although the costs involved are exorbitant, the government's move to Berlin is a symbolic gesture for the people living in the east. It is also a historical promise that we have to keep. It would be wrong to start reunification on a broken promise.

Part Seven

Rethinking Unification 1994

I try to be philosophical as the old lady who said that the best
thing about the future is that it only comes one day at a time.
Dean Acheson

Chapter Twenty-eight

Looking at the Changes

The dancing in the streets is over. Now, only occasionally do the joy of freedom and an innocent impatience for future developments overshadow the disappointed and shocked reactions to the aftermath of 40 years of SED dictatorship. In many respects the revolution that the Germans simply called 'Wende' (turn) carries on. Unlike the neighbouring eastern European states, East Germany and its population are being completely transformed. Economically, socially and politically, the old system is being replaced with West German standards. Many in the east welcome the changes, which bring with them new and unanticipated opportunities. Those who have difficulty adapting speak of colonialization and mourn the loss of East German institutions that had proven useful but were uprooted with the entire system. Westerners, in turn, resent those who look backwards since they have to dig deeply into their pockets to foot the bill for integrating East Germany into the nation.

As enthusiastic as westerners have been about investment and development opportunities in the east during the initial months after the reunification, many complain, often rightly, about bad or non-existent working habits, ill-educated and unmotivated workers, and a lack of understanding of a free market. West German leaders wrongly assumed that billions in public spending would spark private investments. Additionally, hopes that the privatization of old state-run companies would create a new set of East German entrepreneurs proved ill-founded. Today there are some home-grown successful entrepreneurs, particularly in the communications and environmental sectors, but they are still exceptions to the rule.

Nevertheless, as one thinks back it seems clear that at least parts of the GDR and its population have come a long way during the last three years. The Communist Party that monopolized power and terrorized people from 1945 until October 1989 has lost its influence. The colourless, boring and lying propaganda machinery of the party belongs to the past. The hopeless economic situation of the GDR and its environmental sins, the corruption within the party and its crimes are no longer taboo subjects; they are talked and written about regularly. People have planted trees, bushes, roses and other blooming flowers in the front yards of houses; they have laid new streets, opened stores and added some colour to the otherwise greyish street scene. And as they have made physical progress, people have gone forward in their efforts at democratization.

Still, the process is moving too slowly for most in the west and even for some in the east. Instead of a thriving economy and the democratic free-market utopia they had envisioned, there is unemployment, inflation and crime. The revolution against communism brought not only bananas and free speech, but also responsibility and the competition of the survival of the fittest. Some in the east enjoy it, most cannot handle it.

The expectations that were tied to the reunification of Germany were high in both east and west. Nobody expected the human-psychological components that would lay burdens even heavier than the economic one on the shoulders of both sides. People of two worlds, people with different attitudes, value systems and habits have been thrown together to rebuild what has been neglected since the Weimar Republic. West Germans thought initially that the recipe for success that worked so well after World War II could be applied to the east as well. They expected the *W*irtschaftswunder to revive the east in as little as two to three years after the reunification. Even Bonn, or better Berlin, has noticed that the consensus-based corporate capitalism that shaped Germany after World War II does not work anymore. It must be replaced in favour of more competition. In a speech in the autumn of 1993, Chancellor Kohl alluded to the spirit of the hardworking Germans who rebuilt the country after the war and berated contemporary Germans for having turned the country into a 'big recreational park' by insisting on longer vacations and shorter work days. The numbers emerging from Germany's current battle with the world's highest labour costs, low global demand and an overvalued currency are chilling. In the past 12 months, German industry has cut 739,000 jobs; the unemployment rate in the western part of the country has climbed to 7.4 per cent of the labour force, and in the eastern half to 15.2 per cent.

The high unemployment rates are read with apprehension by older Germans with poor memories of the Weimar Republic, where unemployment, turmoil and street fights between communists and brownshirts led to Hitler's succession. Munich's daily *Süddeutsche Zeitung* summarizes today's ample unemployment benefits that make the situation a far cry from Weimar: 'Parks then were packed with the card-playing, hungry and aggressive or apathetic unemployed; today, one kills time on vacation in Majorca'. Nevertheless, the persistent unemployment threatens the social stability and has strengthened extremist political parties on both the left and the right during the past months. Unfortunately, there is also the ugly presence in the population of relatively small groups who express their discontent with the new German reality by openly attacking and beating up resident foreigners and even young American tourists. Unemployed East German youngsters, apparently unfamiliar with the bloody face of communism, celebrate 'GDR Revival Parties' while opportunistic rightwing politicians in the west try to work their way into the German parliament by playing on voters' economic fears.

It seems only now to be dawning on the majority of Germans that unity was not accomplished on 3 October 1990, the day the former GDR officially ceased to exist, but that date only marked the beginning of a period during which a number of serious socio-economic problems would unfold. East Germany was not just added on to Germany. The two Germanies together make up a very different new Germany. Higher taxes, poverty, unemployment, tent cities and unknown faces and dialects have come to Germany with the reunification. Germans, who are so fond of introspection, ponder the new inequality that is visible in almost every larger city. Germans have never been good at associating with the weak; now it seems weakness is part of everyday life.

It was an uneven marriage proposal. Many former GDR citizens argue that their West German cousins were obliged to pay the price for the national identity because they had enjoyed all the benefits of western alignment for the last four decades while easterners had been suffering under Soviet-dominated communism. Average West Germans see the problem quite differently. While their counterparts in the east complain, some in the west ask why the East Germans have not been made to bear even greater sacrifices in order to join their western cousins. Easterners who had held their heads high during the revolution and had envisioned an improved but intact GDR even speak of annexation of the former GDR into West Germany. This assessment has become grist to the mill of everyone who bemoans the loss of distinctive and, as some in the east would argue, superior values.

The view that former values might be recaptured has also been a source of solace for those who believe that the reunited Germany is just a bigger Germany with the same economic prosperity, the same stability and order. But the European neighbours noticed it before the Germans noticed it themselves: Germany is different today from the summer of 1989. The new Germany must carefully nurture the new-found democratic culture in the former east, stabilize its own internal politics, and simultaneously confront a range of foreign policy tasks that Europe expects of the United Germany. Hopefully, Germany will not collapse before reaching its goal.

Ludwig A. Rehlinger

All politicians say today they didn't know about the economic and social situation in the former GDR. That is a barefaced lie. Anyone who wanted to know before the reunification that the process of bringing the two systems together would be expensive, arduous and lengthy could have known it from all the files existing on the GDR. There are shelves and shelves of information on how unproductively the GDR was run. We knew that companies in the GDR were not competitive by western standards. Totally new structures cannot be mapped out in a few years; it takes a generation or more. What was missing in the early months after the reunification was the honesty to admit that it would cost billions and billions to reunite. Kohl should have told the people that there would come a time when they would have to share. Now there is disappointment and social tension between the two sides.

Klaus Bölling

We greatly underestimated the differences in mentality between east and west. Don't misunderstand me, I don't think most people in the east turned out to be communists, but they are people with vastly different value systems. Another issue is that the real socialists created an economy that is in a shambles. Even with big money transfers the inequality of the standard of living between the east and the west will be with us for a long time. Our political, legal and economic systems are still very foreign to most people in the east. It is understandable that people from the group around the Neues Forum recently complained publicly that they wanted justice, but what they ended up with is a constitutional state. That the laws of the constitutional state replaced those of the SED is not widely acknowledged among those who are out of work in the east. People between 20 and 40 years of age, who had a certain social stability under the SED regime, are asked to be part of a free-market system now. For them it is a difficult transition and for many it is a tragic psychological shock. The cries for free speech, for a free market and for democracy are forgotten very quickly when people are unemployed. We in the west have to work very hard to ensure that these democratic values will become a natural part of the society in the east. We owe that to the historical debt that we carry on our shoulders.

Robert W. Becker

The people in the east had 45 years of different experiences, so that a different outlook should not be surprising. I worked in the US Congress for a while. I grew up on the east coast and then worked for Dick Cheney, who at the time was a congressman from Wyoming. When I went to Wyoming to talk to his constituents, I discovered that they had a very different idea of how to do things than I did, coming directly from Washington. We had hard times talking to and understanding each other initially.

Communication is difficult and hard to achieve. If you look at Germany now and add a kind of moral dimension to it, communication becomes even more difficult. It will take Germany a generation until the teenagers from both sides of Germany can communicate with each other. What is needed now in Germany is patience. The east will have a very subtle effect on the whole body of politics, on the economy and on Germany as a whole. The West Germans ask, 'Why should we change since we have a wonderful society?' The answer is, because you have absorbed 16 million people and with them a whole lot of problems, which are now part of the new Germany.

I foresee that Germany will have to restructure politically. It will be interesting to follow how a largely non-Judaeo-Christian east is merged with a nominally Judaeo-Christian west. Here in the east, only 15 per cent of the people identify with the church. Between 75 per cent to 80 per cent in the west say they get their morals and values from the church. The east is strong on less institutional, humanistic values that are based on a sense of social responsibility. The reunification of Germany brought a remix of politics, analogous to what happened in the United States in the 1970s when we had the so-called neo-liberals and neo-conservatives. Then the Democrats became protectionists and Republicans changed into free traders. When a remix like that happens, it is an exciting time because old structures are reformed and revamped.

Wolfgang Mischnick

Many people misinterpret the problems of the GDR today as economically or even politically related. They forget that money and investments are not the real factors involved in getting an economy rolling, but rather psychology. Most East Germans have trusted their government representatives—even though they hated doing so—to take care of such needs as housing, pensions, insurance and employment. Most easterners are not used to working independently without somebody looking over their shoulders. Our role should be that of advisers who simply provide information. I'm deeply upset about stories of West Germans going into the east with the attitude that East Germans are second-class citizens who know nothing about the modern world. We have to dispel the fear of the 'new' in the east.

East Germans on their side are going through phases of acknowledging reality, and despising it. First, it was believed that they desperately needed our help. Then, in the euphoria of reunification, hopes rose that the east could pull the economy together without western help. Today realism tells them that without financial and material assistance from West Germany and other western European nations they won't make it. Most citizens don't even understand yet that the economy they lived with for so long is not just weak; it is unable to survive under normal market conditions.

The same experience exists on other levels of everyday life. Many easterners have no idea what a democratic administration means, what it can do. Just a little while ago a young woman told me that she wouldn't even know where she was supposed to pay her taxes, or to whom. She is not an exception to the rule. With the reunification, Germany has acquired many new tasks and obligations. We have a larger population with a multitude of problems—economic and social problems—that we didn't have before. I'm convinced that most of the help has to come from West Germany. Any help which is given hesitantly from our side is unsocial.

Donald Koblitz

There is a new wave of introspection in Germany which follows the same pattern as German politics and economy. It is largely a process imposed on the east by the west. While East Germans are certainly better off in a united Germany, there is no doubt about who runs the country. As long as the distinction between Ossies and Wessies holds true, the people from the east will be subjugated people. Rarely are Wessies asked, 'What did you do to help East Germany in those dark days? Did those years of quiet complicity prolong the suffering?' Victors tend to be less introspective, and anyway those questions are not as compelling as those directed at the Ossies: 'Did you shoot to kill at the Wall? Did you betray your friends?' For me the problem boils down to the general helplessness of the German justice system to address the wrongs of the past. The rule of law imported by West Germans can only address the most obvious cases. If the system has trouble reconciling sensational crimes, like shootings at the Wall, with the obvious requirements of the rule of law, it is hopeless in trying to deal with the subtler, much more prevalent and ultimately more important crimes of complicity and betrayal.

I have the feeling that Germans are confronting their past in the east through random and episodic prosecutions of visible figures such as Vogel, Honecker and others. However, that kind of confrontation not only portrays the wrong picture, but also defiles the respectability of the rule of law. Whether Vogel or Manfred Stolpe (the Ministerpresident of Brandenburg), both of whom are caught up in the latest inquisition, are guilty or innocent, German reckoning with the past has settled on those available few whom we know because they were indispensable to us.

I believe that the disturbing right-wing resurgence in two state elections in Hamburg was more a protest against the shortcomings of the German state than a reversion to a brownshirt past. I'm not worried about extremist parties taking over. The only potential scenario that would worry me would be a red–green government, meaning a government coalition between the far left and the environmentally oriented groups. The response could very well be the rise of extremist political groups on the right. I have lived in different places in the world, but nowhere have I watched a people dealing more than the Germans with *Vergangenheitsbewältigung* (dealing with and understanding the past). Germans are very good at talking about their past and they are now entering the second phase, the phase arising from the split. Historical introspection can be a noble quality as long as it stays on track and focused.

Wolfgang Schäuble

Without large money transfers from the west, East Germany cannot be rebuilt. Because the restructuring of East Germany is a belated consequence of the Second World War, for which mainly Germany was responsible, the East German demand for West German support is more than justified. What makes the issue problematic is that West Germany was not prepared to swallow such a big fish. At the same time, East Germans lived under the illusion that the adaptation of their standard of living to ours would happen overnight. Even many West German politicians thought initially that the adaptation process would be short. What we are experiencing now is the disappointment of shattered illusions: frustration, combined with high unemployment and the difficulties of adapting to new standards, forms the soil in which radicalism can germinate. I don't overestimate the importance of headlines Germany made some months ago because of violence against foreigners, but those incidents are not insignificant. The people who clapped their hands when molotov cocktails were thrown into the apartments of foreigners are not neo-Nazis. They are confused people who are frightened about their future, people who cannot deal with the new complexity of their lives. Their normal thinking process is blocked. It is our task to overcome these blockages and present the reunification of Germany in a way that they do not experience as a financial or social burden, but as what it is: a lucky break in history.

Chapter Twenty-nine

Germany and Europe

Reunited Germany is not just an enlarged former FRG. Most European neighbours interpreted the reunification process, which started officially on 3 October 1990, as a dramatic restructuring not only of Germany, but also of Europe. Memories flowed back of the once privileged relationship between Berlin and Moscow, and many were reminded of Germany's past seesaw policies. Questions about the identity and the role of Germany arose not only internally, but also in the councils of other nations. How would Berlin/Bonn support the growing EC? Would NATO still be the security agency for Europe if the countries of central Europe joined the EC? So far there is only speculation, and Berlin/Bonn has not given clear answers. But two issues have been continuously stressed throughout the democratic parties of Germany: securing peace and achieving prosperity.

The immediate threat posed by the eastern superpower is gone. The reunited Germany kept its alliances with its western neighbours and signed treaties with its eastern neighbours. Furthermore, Germany continues to be part of NATO just as it continues to be 'a non-nuclear power and a continental middle power', according to guidelines of the German Defence Ministry published in November 1992. Ex-Foreign Minister Hans-Dietrich Genscher made it clear early on that a German reunification without membership of NATO would be unthinkable. He stressed that Germany's active role on European security issues, the maintenance of stable monetary and trade relations, and particularly the economic and political unification of the EC would be high priorities for the nation despite the obvious problems of reunification.

Nevertheless, in the first months after reunification some neighbours wondered whether a united Germany would not be too strong and pose a threat to the rest of Europe's stability, perhaps by developing into something far more unpredictable than the former West Germany. Others, observing the financial and political strains that accompany rebuilding East Germany, feared that Germany might turn inward, concentrating on internal affairs and shying away from a leadership role in western Europe.

These fears coincided with the collapse of the Soviet Union, which was replaced by the Commonwealth of Independent States, sending waves of immigrants from the east towards Germany. At the same time, civil war broke out in the former Yugoslavia and some old Soviet republics. As the rest of the EC and NATO started to struggle with the Yugoslavian issue, Germans sat on the sidelines, stalemated by the question of whether their constitution permitted sending troops to the potential Balkan front. Among certain groups within the population an anti-foreigner sentiment set in, which sent shock waves through Germany. Riots and violent attacks were exploited by opportunistic politicians, some of whom gained support at the ballot box during local elections in Hamburg. A general feeling of lost leadership, internal instability and a loss of focus on foreign affairs seemed to grow among the German public.

Some speak of a 'national option' (a form of isolationism) as a solution to the problem. But neither for safety nor for economic reasons would a national option work. No other European country its size is so dependent on export as Germany. Seventy per cent of German exports goes to the countries of the Europäischer Wirtschaftsraum (European Economic Market—EWR), and over 80 per cent goes into member countries of the OECD. Apart from these obvious reasons, the majority of the German population would agree that peace and prosperity are priorities whose attainment is possible only in co-operation with European neighbours and trading partners of the OECD. What many have feared—that Germany would leap into economic and political isolation after reunification and seek an exclusive position of power—has been far from true. Recession, unemployment, political turmoil and the loss of public faith in leaders have created an atmosphere in which the commitment to work hard for a united Europe is still very strong in Germany, even though the outlook for success has faded.

Germany's preoccupation with reunification is clearly diverting resources from the task of integrating western Europe. For the immediate future, Germany seems to be busy with itself. But as a senior planner in Germany's Defence Ministry recently summed it up, politicians and most of the public are aware that, 'Neither western Europe nor Germany is in any shape to respond to crises. Neither can afford to go it alone anymore. We cannot do separately what we can do together.'

Wolfgang Schäuble

Since the Wall fell and the military threat of the former Soviet Union disappeared, the world has become safer, but also more complex.

The risks are manifold and more difficult to control than in the former bipolar world of east-west conflict. Currently, we are not doing too well at co-ordinating or communicating goals for a new world order. I still haven't given up on George Bush's idea of a peaceful new and better world order, but we haven't even started working on it. The initial euphoria over the end of the Cold War took the focus off the turmoil in the Balkans. The world is not safer for anyone if Europe is in turmoil. That has been true for the last 500 years, including three times in the 20th century. We have maintained the goals of political and military integration, but unfortunately we must accept delays in accomplishing them. We are looking towards the US and its leadership in NATO to assist us. NATO comes to a standstill when there is no strong US leadership. It is in our best interest that American forces will still be stationed here in Germany. The United States has a critical role not only for NATO, but also for the stability of Europe.

Mark Whitehead

Europe has changed since the Wall fell. I see the European world in two windows. One encompasses the entire globe. The other is the European window, where I see unification of purpose. Currently Europe is going through an inexorable move towards more common solutions, though I think the idea of global uniformity will prove to be a myth. I call common European solutions, for example, such things as a stronger European court of justice. Germany will play a major role in the effort to achieve common solutions to problems affecting the entire EC. It will have much more of a unifying and westernizing role than in the past. Germany cannot afford to deal in isolation any longer. As one of the strongest powers in Europe, Germany has an obligation to see that issues of European foreign policy are pushed towards resolution, issues such as the need for peace-keeping forces, military contributions, the failure of Europe to respond to Bosnia. Germans don't want to admit to it yet, but their role is changing to that of at least a regional leader, a formulator of regional policies.

Donald Koblitz

I don't have a lot of sympathy for the Cold-War Berlin nostalgia that has been a trend here, particularly among the young. Since the Wall fell, portions of Europe have lived through a nightmare—countries like the former Yugoslavia—but its collapse also changed Germany from being one of three or four powers that were important to the United States to the most important. Germany is not ready for the role of being number two in the world. It would be scary if it were. Germany is properly cautious. Germans are truly socially engaged. They have a great concern about what is happening in their front yard. At the same time, Germans are very nervous about disintegration, particularly in Yugoslavia. This nervousness has handicapped them. Currently, they are more reactive than active. The question for Germany now is not simply, 'How can we help?' but 'How can we manage without being affected?' I believe there is a new generation of German politicians growing up who have not been part of the Second World War and cannot remember it. They will be much freer to take on a leadership role for Germany.

Robert W. Becker

Germany needs to get out of itself. The new role Germany has in Europe will not be found in the next three years but in the next 30 years. Germany is faced with a choice of playing an important role as a European leader, or sitting back and watching and being scared. Germany needs to take care of itself and not look over its shoulder at what others are doing. Germany has a role in Cambodia, in Mogadishu and Somalia. It has a role to play wherever else it is called upon peacefully. I think as Germany starts to solve its internal problems it will be able to deal with external ones. I would hope that the new Germany, which is growing together right now and is growing up in Europe, would say, 'All right, now we have a new set of principles, we have democratic principles, we have principles that are not aggressive, not hostile. We are ready to be co-operative in our very own way.' Only that will convince people that Germany is not a country where, when you scratch a German, you find the brown under the skin.

Selected Bibliography

Adenauer, Konrad. *Erinnerungen.* 4 vols. Stuttgart: Deutsche Verlags-Anstalt, 1967.

Akademie der Wissenschaften. *Wörterbuch zum sozialistischen Staat.* Berlin: Dietz Verlag, 1975.

Bahr, Egon. *Zum europäischen Frieden.* Berlin: Siedler, 1988.

Bailyn, Bernard. *The Great Republic.* Vols I + II. Lexington, Mass: D.C. Heath, 1977.

Barzel, Rainer. *Auf dem Drahtseil.* Munich: Droemer Knauer, 1978.

Berlin Economic Development Corporation. *Berlin.* Berlin: BEDC, 1991.

Beschloss, Michael. *The Crisis Years: Kennedy and Khrushchev, 1960-1963.* New York: Harper Collins, 1991.

Brinkschulte, Wolfgang. *Freikaufgewinnler.* Frankfurt, Ullstein, 1993.

Catudal, Honoré M. *Kennedy and the Berlin Crisis.* Berlin: Berlin Verlag, 1980.

Clay, Lucius D. *Entscheidung Deutschland.* Frankfurt: Fischer, 1950.

Clemens, Clay. 'Helmut Kohl's CDU and German Reunification'. *German Politics and Society,* 1991.

Deutsche Bundesbank. 'Auszüge aus Presseaktien'. Frankfurt: January to November 1991.

Diepgen, Eberhard. 'Perspektiven statt Illusionen'. *Deutschland Archiv,* March 1986.

Döllinger, Hans. 'Die Bundesrepublik in the Ära Adenauer'. München: Döllinger, 1966.

Eggers, Katja-Maria. 'Von einem, der auszog, den Markt zu erobern'. Hamburg: *ZeitMagazin,* August, 1990.

Finanz und Wirtschaft. 'Interview mit Birgit Breul—Ost-deutschland ist kein Closed Shop'. Zurich: F&W, April 1991.

Freitag, Michael. 'Kampfreserve der alten Kommunisten'. Frankfurt: *Frankfurter Allgemeine Magazin*, May 1991.

Gill, David and Ulrich Schröter. *Das Ministerium für Staatssichereheit*. Berlin: Rowohlt, 1991.
Glücksmann, Anslem. *Rechtskunde für Rechtsschaffende*. Leipzig: Edition Peters, 1987.
Griffith, William. *The Ostpolitik of the Federal Republic of Germany*. Cambridge, Mass: MIT Press, 1978.

Hafner, Katie. 'Reclaiming Family Property in Western Europe'. New York: *New York Times*, November, 1991.
Harbecke, Ulrich. *Abenteuer Deutschland*. Bergisch Gladbach: Gustav Lübbe Verlag, 1990.
Held, Joseph. *History of Eastern Europe in the Twentieth Century*. New York: Columbia University Press, 1991.
Heise, Joachim and Jürgen Hofmann. *Fragen an die Geschichte der DDR*. Berlin: Verlag Junge Welt, 1988.
Honecker Erich. *Reden und Aufsätze*. 12 vols. Berlin: Dietz, 1975–88.

International Society for Human Rights. *Political Imprisonment in the GDR*. Frankfurt: ISHR, 1987.
———. *Menschenrechte in der DDR und Berlin (Ost)*. Frankfurt: ISHR, 1988.
———. *Menschenrechte in der Welt*. München: Universitas, 1989/1990.
———. *Der Stasi Staat*. Spiegel Spezial. Frankfurt: ISHR, 1990–1. Hamburg: ISHR, 1990.

Kaase, Max and Wolfgang Gibowski. 'Deutschland im Übergang: Parteien und Wähler vor der Bundeswahl 1990'. *Aus Politik und Zeitgeschichte*, September 1990.
Knapp, Guido and Ekkehard Kuhn. *Die Deutsche Einheit*. Vienna: Straub, 1990.
Kohl, Helmut. 'A Ten-point Program for Overcoming the Divison of Germany and Europe'. Statements and Speeches, 19 December 1989. New York: German Information Centre.

Leonard, Wolfgang. *Die Revolution entlässt ihre Kinder*. Berlin: Ullstein, 1963.
———. *Das kurze Leben der DDR*. Stuttgart: Deutsche Verlags-Anstalt, 1990.

McAdams, James A. *Germany Divided.* Princeton: Princeton University
 Press, 1991.

Noelle-Neumann, Elisabeth. *Allensbacher Jahrbuch der Demoskopie,
 1977.* Vienna: Molden, 1977.

Noll, Hans. *Der Abschied—Journal meiner Ausreise aus der DDR.*
 Hamburg: Hoffmann und Campe, 1985.

Ploetz, Karl. *Auszug aus der Geschichte.* Würzburg: A.G. Ploetz Verlag,
 1960.

Preuss, Joachim. 'Ich führe ein unnützes Leben'. Hamburg: *Der Spiegel,*
 Number 42, 1993.

Rehlinger, Ludwig A. *Freikauf.* Berlin: Ullstein, 1993.

Ryshkow, N.I. *Über die Hauptrichtungen der wirtschaftlichen und
 sozialen Entwicklungen der UDSSR von 1986 bis 1990 und für den
 Zeitraum bis zum Jahr 2000.* Moscow: Verlag Progress, 1986.

Schmidt, Helmut. *Menschen und Mächte.* Berlin: Siedler, 1987.

Schmidthammer, Jens. *Rechtsanwalt Vogel.* Hamburg: Hoffmann und
 Campe, 1987.

Schneider, Peter. *The German Comedy.* New York: Farrar, Straus, and
 Giroux, 1991.

Scholze, Siegfried. *Zur Rolle der Frau in der Geschichte der DDR.*
 Leipzig: Verlag der Frau, 1987.

Schröder Münchmeyer Hengst & Co. *Deutschland ein Jahr danach.*
 Berlin: SMH, 1991.

Schwarz, Hans-Peter. *Geschichte der Bundesrepublik Deutschland: Die
 Ära Adenauer.* Stuttgart: Deutsche Verlags-Anstalt, 1981.

Siegmund, Bernd. *Vierzig Jahre und so weiter.* Görlitz: Graphische
 Werkstätten, 1988.

Smirnow, G.L. *Die Herausbildung der sozilalistischen Persönlichkeit.*
 Berlin: Dietz Verlag, 1975.

Sorensen, Theodor C. *Kennedy.* New York: Harper and Row, 1965.

Spiegel Spezial. *162 Tage Deutsche Geschichte.* Hamburg: *Der Spiegel,*
 1990.

———. *Das Profil der Deutschen—Was sie vereint, was sie trennt.*
 Hamburg, *Der Spiegel,* 1991.

Stern, Carola. *Ulbricht.* Cologne: Kiepenheuer und Witsch, 1964.

Swoboda, Jörg. *Die Revolution der Kerzen.* Wuppertal: Onckenverlag,
 1990.

Selected Bibliography

Turner, Henry A. *The Two Germanies since 1945*. New Haven: Yale University Press, 1987.

US Government Printing Office. *Public Papers of the President*. Washington, D.C.: GPO, 1963.

Veit, Valentin. *Geschichte der Deutschen*. München: Droemersche Verlagsanstalt, 1979.

Weber, Hermann. *Kleine Geschichte der DDR*. Cologne: Verlag Wissenschaft und Politik, 1980.
Weiland, Severin. *9 November—Das Jahr danach*. München: Heyne Verlag, 1990.
Weizsäcker, Richard von. *Von Deutschalnd aus*. München: Deutscher Taschenbuch Verlag, 1987.
Wolf, Markus. *Die Troika*. Berlin: Aufbau, 1989.

Zanetti, Benno. *Der Weg zur Deutschen Einheit*. München: Goldm: nn, 1991.

Index

The Wall Falls

An Oral History of the
Reunification of the Two Germanies

Manuscript edited by Colin Hutchens
Typography of Little Red Cloud
Cover design by Robert Jensen
Composed in 10 & 11/12 pt Times New Roman from the author's
    disk
Printed on Redwood high white acid free wove paper and bound by
    Redwood Books of Trowbridge, Wiltshire

Printed and bound in England